Frontiersman

ABNER BLACKBURN'S NARRATIVE

1

My parents weare born in bedford county Pensylvania
father was born in 1803 my mother in 1800
they had four children Matilda the oldest was born in 1822
Eliza the second in 1824   the third in 1827
Thomas the last 1829
father moved to Jefferson county Ohio in 1828. and purched mill
property a grist mill and saw mill and lived their four years
Caught the west fever. Sold out and moved to Richland county
Ohio. the neighbors come to bid us good by and said we weare
a going to the backwoods amongst the indians   1832
but the indians had left a short time before we arrived their
bought a new farm. and made verry comfortable home
1837 about this time some Mormon missionaries come along and held
several meetings in the settlement. and my parents joind their
Church. and shortly after Sold their posessions. and started
west to the north western part of missouri to Caldwell county
We wear going to the backwoods this time Sure enough. to ceath up
with the wildman. Started on our long journey to the far west
in the Spring of 1837 in company of a few of the same faith
passed through Ohio and indiana. then come to the plains

Abner Blackburn's narrative. Bancroft Library.

Frontiersman

ABNER BLACKBURN'S NARRATIVE

Edited by Will Bagley

University of Utah Press
Salt Lake City

∞ This symbol indicates books printed on paper that meets the mini-mum requirements of American National Standard for Information Services—Permanence of Paper for Printed Library Materials, ANSI A39.38-1984.

Library of Congress Cataloging-in-Publication Data

Blackburn, Abner. 1827–1904.
    Frontiersman : Abner Blackburn's narrative / edited by Will
Bagley.
        p. cm. — (University of Utah publications in the American
West : v. 30)
    Includes bibliographical references and index.
    ISBN 0-87480-401-9 (alk. paper)
    1. Blackburn, Abner, 1827–1904.   2. Pioneers—West (U.S.)—
Biography.   3. Frontier and pioneer life—West (U.S.)   I. Bagley,
Will, 1950– . II. Title.   III. Series.
F592.B57   1992
978'.02'092–dc20
[B]   92-53603
                                                                               CIP

To Jan, my wife
and to the memory of two great Westerners
Abner Blackburn and Dale Lowell Morgan

Contents

Contents

Preface

I find the more I find out, the more I need to find out.
—Dale L. Morgan

By 1889, retired farmer, seafarer, and aging pioneer Abner Levi Blackburn (1827–1904) began to write an account of his youthful wanderings across the North American continent. Deaf, in failing health, and surviving on eight dollars per month from his Mexican War pension, Blackburn determined to abandon the hard work that had been his lot for fifty years. He set about writing his memoirs, an exciting and colorful chronicle of the conquest of the American West.

I first encountered Blackburn's narrative in January 1989 while reading Dale L. Morgan's *The Humboldt: High Road of the West*. Morgan's effective use of material from Blackburn's memoirs immediately sent me searching for the complete work. I was surprised to find that the narrative had never been published. The cryptic entry in Morgan's bibliography led me to Special Collections at the University of Utah's Marriott Library, where I found the Mary Ream typescript that Morgan used in writing *The Humboldt*. I had no idea that I was about to start on a fantastic quest.

Searching for Abner Blackburn's place in history has been both an education and an adventure. Following this frontiersman across the untamed West was immensely challenging and deeply rewarding. His sprawling narrative covered the period from the mid-1830s to 1851 and described key events in the history of the frontier. I can understand how a tenderfoot must have felt following a veteran mountain man across the plains: I was continually astounded at his experience, knowledge, and savvy. When I was skeptical of Blackburn's outlandish tales and suspected exaggeration, I often learned that he was in fact telling— and sometimes understating—the unvarnished truth.

Blackburn reworked his memoirs until as late as 1902. Upon his death, his daughter, scandalized by the story's rough edges, hid the manuscript in a trunk. In about 1933, Blackburn's granddaughter, Blanche Blackburn Corby, made a typescript of the narrative. This work is based on the Corby typescript, corrected against a positive copy of a microfilm of a negative photostat taken of the holographic manuscript in 1942. Both the typescript and photostat are now in the Robert A. Allen collection at the Nevada Historical Society. The original manuscript—which historical tabloid editor Herbert Hamlin discovered and acquired from the Blackburn family in 1942—has vanished.

In editing Blackburn's life story, my purpose has been to amplify and support his singular tale. I have divided the narrative into ten chapters, each with an introduction providing an overview of the times, peoples, and places in Blackburn's story. These prologues make extensive use of parallel accounts and original sources; most of the longer quotations represent unpublished firsthand accounts or selections from western sources that are extremely difficult to access. To avoid overburdening the narrative's flow, longer parallel accounts are included in four documentary appendixes. I provide much detail about the lives of many obscure pioneers and trappers, whose connection with Blackburn might at first seem marginal, because I believe their exceptional stories deserve telling and shed much light on his life and times. The Afterword sketches the last half-century of Blackburn's life, while the Epilogue describes the fate of his manuscript, which raised considerable interest among historians in the 1940s before it tragically disappeared down a strange and crooked path. A bibliographical essay describes the main sources used to document the narrative.

The 1990s have seen a renewed interest in the glories of nineteenth-century prose, and I have tried to let the times and people speak for themselves, which they do most eloquently. This approach seeks to give a general reader a deeper understanding of the history the narrative describes and provide serious students of the American West with easier access to important source materials. I feel the depth and complexity of Blackburn's story justify my decision to follow the example of my favorite historians and provide ample supporting information. No one is forced to read footnotes (this is an invitation to skip them entirely), but their absence leaves the curious and the suspicious to their own devices.

In addition to Abner Blackburn, this book has a second hero, historian Dale Lowell Morgan. The debt I owe to Morgan cannot be understated. On 3 June 1942 Morgan sent Robert Allen of the Nevada Highway Department five single-spaced pages of annotations to the

Blackburn narrative. A month later, he sent corrections and additional information. The annotations are now in the Robert A. Allen Collection of the Nevada Historical Society, while the corrections are in the Dale L. Morgan Collection (cited hereafter as DLMC) at the Bancroft Library. These notes provided a detailed and invaluable research plan for the Mormon portions of the narrative. Material drawn from the Morgan annotations is not cited directly, but is obliquely credited with phrasing such as "Dale Morgan noted."

EDITING PRACTICES

The narrative's holographic manuscript was untitled. It had two cover sheets with a "Real Irish Linen" art-nouveau trademark design measuring approximately 3.5 inches by 6.25 inches in the center of the page. The paper measured about 8 inches by 10 inches and may have been bound at the top by two pairs of small rings. It consisted of about 162 pages and was divided into two volumes. "Volume No. 1" (as labeled on the cover sheet in Blackburn's handwriting) consisted of Blackburn's personal memoirs, while "No. 2" was "Lou Devon's Narritive." The cover sheet to Volume One had an engraving of Jim Bridger covering the bottom of the trademark. (The picture led the Nevada Historical Society to classify a duplicate photostat of the narrative as "Jim Bridger's Diary," a document that would certainly match Blackburn's for historical interest.) Volume One had pages numbered 1 to 44; a line was drawn across the middle of page 44 to indicate the break for Volume Two. Devon's narrative was numbered from pages 1 to 31. Volume One started again at page 10 and ran 87 more pages, including later insertions on separate sheets. The continuation of Volume One started with the sentence, "continued from Page 11 of the first book," suggesting that a much shorter draft of the memoirs originally preceded Devon's story. The numbering scheme in this section ran from 10 to 32; the next few pages were numbered 33/53, 34/54 and then ran from 55 to 71, where they started at page 1 and ran to page 18, the conclusion of the manuscript. It is likely that the two volumes were written at separate times, and the Devon narrative is probably a survivor of an earlier draft.

A perplexing problem is that a second handwriting began abruptly on page 7 and ran through the middle of page 17, where Blackburn's handwriting picked up again in mid-paragraph. On page 21 the handwriting changed in mid-sentence, "picket our camp and doubled the guard." The second hand ran to page 25 and Blackburn's handwriting (which can be identified by a signed 1894 holographic letter in the Utah State Historical Society) continued for the rest of the document.

No notation or other evidence associated with the photostat explains why these fourteen pages were composed in a second handwriting.

Creating a typescript of Blackburn's memoirs is difficult because so much is lost in the transition from handwriting to type. Blackburn's hand was bold and clear, consistently following a sharp, straight line, and compensated for grammatical and syntactical errors that jump out from a typewritten or typeset page.

To keep the spirit of the original manuscript intact and create a readable narrative for a modern audience, I have tried to be consistent and edit according to a simple, logical standard, but English itself is not consistent, simple, or logical. To preserve the flavor of the manuscript, as much of the original spelling and punctuation has been maintained as possible. I have added or modified punctuation, divided paragraphs for readability, and capitalized the first word of all sentences, personal pronouns, and formal nouns, such as American, Saint, and Indian, which Blackburn capitalized inconsistently. Direct quotations appear in quotation marks. Repeated words (such as "and and") were cut where they were obviously in error. Where a word is open to questionable interpretation (such as whether Brigham Young "hellowed" or "bellowed"), the most obvious (or colorful) alternative is used. Appendixes A and B provide verbatim transcriptions of Blackburn's letters for those who would prefer a more literal approach. Except where noted, quoted material follows the punctuation and spelling used in the source.

Although much of the original spelling is preserved, where a word is puzzling or can be fixed with a minimum of tinkering, editorial corrections are inserted in brackets: [ ]. I have kept Blackburn's spelling of place names and Native American tribes, but provide correct spellings in brackets on the first occurrence where they could be difficult to interpret. All other editorial changes are contained in brackets.

Where appropriate, *there* has been substituted for the possessive *their*; *been* for *ben*; *knew* for *new*; *were* for *wear*, *werre*, and *weare*; *heard* for *herd*; *too* for *to*; *off* for *of*; *one* for *on*; *like* for *lik*; *made* for *mad*; *make* for *mak*; *some* for *som*; *come* for *com*; *see* for *se*; *business* for *buisness*.

These changes have been made to support Blackburn's fantastic storytelling, which brings the West to life. Above all, I have tried to let Abner Blackburn's voice speak clearly.

Acknowledgments

This work would not have been possible without the help of many historians, archivists, librarians, friends, and relatives. I am very grateful to Amy Gallagher Hoffman of Sacramento, Blackburn's great-grandniece, who supplied me with a copy of the manuscript and countless insights into the Blackburn family. Amy and her husband Russ—a companion on an exploration of the Hastings Cutoff across the Salt Desert—have guided my search for Abner Blackburn. Cyril Grohs of Las Vegas, the widower of Blackburn's granddaughter, spent a most entertaining morning describing family legends to me. Amy Blackburn, apparently Abner Blackburn's sole surviving descendent, shared family heirlooms and, with the heirs of Herbert Hamlin, Lynn and Lee Fairchild, granted permission to publish the Blackburn narrative. Eugene Bell provided Nettie West's Blackburn family photo album. Don Blackburn turned up important deeds and personal insights. Elias Hicks Blackburn biographers Voyle and Lillian Munson gave me a wealth of family data and pointers to critical information.

I am indebted to the Walker and Hamlin families who assisted me in my search for the manuscript, including Margaret Hamlin Walker, Stephen Walker, Margaret Walker Paetz, Jack and Edith Walker, and their son Steve.

A work such as this one requires the resources of a great research library, in this case the Marriott Library at the University of Utah. Walter Jones and the entire staff of Special Collections have shown me the utmost consideration.

The staff of the Utah State Historical Society, especially Gary Topping and Jay M. Haymond, guided me through their collection. David Whitaker of the Harold B. Lee Library at Brigham Young University provided access to manuscripts. The personnel at the LDS

Historical Department, especially Michael Landon, Steve Sorenson, Ron Watt, Pauline Musig, Larry Draper, Linda Haslam, Nancy Hurtado, Scott Christensen, Chad Orton, Brad Jensen, Bill Slaughter, JoAnn Bitton, and Kim Farr, have shown tireless courtesy and patience through innumerable lunch-hour forays into their remarkable library and manuscript collection. (Material cited from this collection is courtesy of the Church Archives of the Church of Jesus Christ of Latter-day Saints and is used by permission.) Jeff Johnson and Val Wilson of the Utah State Archives have located source manuscripts and records. Eric Moody of the Nevada Historical Society gave my initial research a tremendous boost when he tracked down Blackburn materials in the Robert A. Allen Collection. John T. Furlong of the Missouri Historical Society supplied information on the American Fur Company. Gary F. Kurutz of the California State Library helped in locating significant source documents.

National Park Service employees Lyndel Meikle, Paul Hedren, and Thomas Thiessen have provided great help in my search to identify Lou Devon, as has anthropologist Jeffery R. Hanson. Virginia Petch of the Hudson's Bay Company Archives at the Provincial Archives of Manitoba provided invaluable assistance in searching the records of the Honorable Company. The Minnesota Historical Society provided microfilms of the Gilbert L. Wilson Papers, a wonderful ethnological survey of the Mandan and Hidatsa tribes. The Provincial Archives of British Columbia supplied me with a copy of the Fort Vancouver journal of Thomas Lowe. Oskar Moe, Sam Skelly, and Herbert Beckwith of the J. Porter Shaw Library at the National Maritime Museum in San Francisco assisted me in a survey of their collection. The Bancroft Library provided photographs of critical pages of the best surviving copy of the Blackburn narrative. The entire staff, especially Bonnie Hardwick, deserves many thanks.

Arda M. Haenszel of the San Bernardino County Museum Association helped me sort out the history of old San Bernardino and graciously spent an unforgettable day identifying valley historic sites and the trails in Cajon Pass. Jim Hofer of the San Bernardino County Archives located trial records, deeds, and tax records. Mary L. Lewis provided broad personal knowledge and an extensive collection of San Bernardino family records. Chris Shovey, Nick Cataldo, Dean Painter, and Thelma Press turned up much information about Blackburn's last days.

Howard Freed assisted me in a vain search of the Sons of Utah Pioneers collection at Lagoon Amusement Park for an 1845 portrait of Blackburn. Edith Menna of the Daughters of Utah Pioneers helped me survey the society's museum.

I am especially grateful to the Evans Biography Trust, which awarded *Frontiersman: Abner Blackburn's Narrative* the 1991 Evans Manuscript Award. F. Ross Peterson and Shannon Hoskins have won my lasting thanks.

Peter DeLafosse, Michael Kelsey, Michael Landon, Dorothy Pendleton, and Lynn Thorsen proofread the manuscript and provided much historical and literary help.

Special thanks go to historians Leonard Arrington, Ronald Barney, Don Buck, Robert Carter, Everett Cooley, Fred R. Gowans, Arda Haenszel, Michael Landon, Ben Lofgren, Edward Leo Lyman, Brigham Madsen, Floyd O'Neil, Kenneth N. Owens, Charles Peterson, Charles E. Rankin, Harold Rapp, W. L. Rusho, Jack Shapiro, Roy Tea, Greg Thompson, Jack Tykal, and Harold Schindler, who have reviewed parts of the manuscript and contributed valuable comments and insights. I am especially indebted to David L. Bigler, who repeatedly and carefully reviewed successive drafts and has been a perceptive critic and constant inspiration.

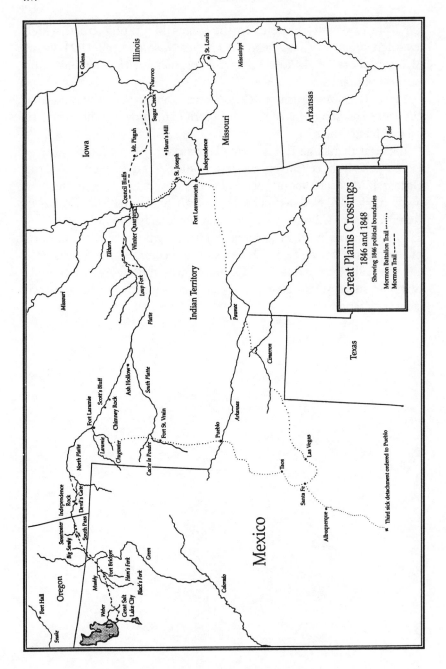

Great Plains Crossings
1846 and 1848
Showing 1846 political boundaries
Mormon Battalion Trail ·······
Mormon Trail - - - - -

* Third sick detachment ordered to Pueblo

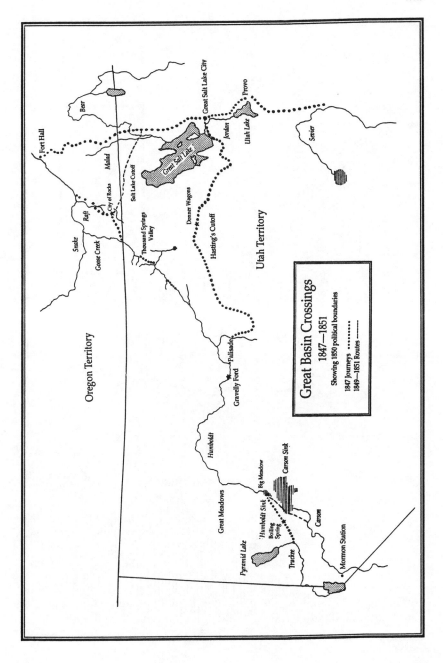

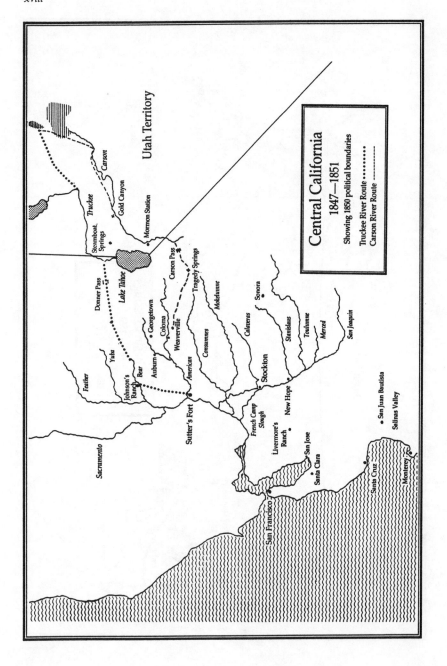

Central California
1847—1851
Showing 1850 political boundaries

Truckee River Route ●●●●●●●●
Carson River Route --------

Utah Territory

Carson

Truckee

Gold Canyon

Steamboat Springs

Mormon Station

Donner Pass

Lake Tahoe

Carson Pass

Tragedy Springs

Yuba

Georgetown

Coloma

Weaverville

Consumnes

Mokelumne

Calaveras

Sonora

Feather

Johnson's Ranch

Bear

Auburn

American

Stanislaus

Tuolumne

Merced

San Joaquin

Sutter's Fort

French Camp Slough

Stockton

New Hope

Sacramento

Livermore's Ranch

San Jose

Santa Clara

San Francisco

San Juan Bautista

Salinas Valley

Santa Cruz

Monterey

Abner Blackburn ca. 1867. Eugene Bell/Marriott Library.

*Lucinda Blackburn with daughters Ella Lucinda and Arnetta Matilda, ca. 1867.
"Nettie," the younger daughter, would suppress her father's manuscript for more
than forty years. Eugene Bell/Marriott Library.*

Abner Blackburn's sons (left to right) Charles, John Franklin, and William Byron, ca. 1867. Eugene Bell/Marriott Library.

Hester Rose Blackburn, Abner Blackburn's mother, ca. 1870. Eugene Bell/Marriott Library.

*John Franklin Blackburn and bride Suvonia Madella (Della) Blackburn, 3 July
1887. Eugene Bell/Marriott Library.*

Abner Blackburn, ca. 1880. Feldheym Library.

Lucinda Harris Blackburn, ca. 1880. Feldheym Library.

Emily Bartholomew Blackburn Hawley, ca. 1890. Married to Thomas Blackburn, "the Molly Pritchard of the Klamath River," she achieved limited fame in the 1890s for her role in the 1851 Indian fight that resulted in the death of Anthony Blackburn. Amy Gallagher Hoffman.

Lucinda Blackburn, ca. 1890. Amy Gallagher Hoffman.

Abner Blackburn, ca. 1890. Amy Gallagher Hoffman.

Abner Blackburn, 24 July 1897. This detail from George Anderson's "The Veteran Pioneers of 1847" shows Blackburn standing to the left of the flag. LDS Archives.

John Pope Bainbridge, ca. 1885. Abner Blackburn probably returned to Great Salt Lake City in 1850 to help John and Eliza Bainbridge to cross the Great Basin. Amy Gallagher Hoffman.

Eliza Blackburn Bainbridge with her twin granddaughters, ca. 1905. Family tradition says that John and Eliza had an infant kidnaped by Indians while crossing the plains. Amy Gallgher Hoffman.

Introduction

On 17 April 1894, at the age of 67, retired farmer Abner Blackburn wrote from his home in San Bernardino, California, to a Utah relative, composing the letter in the elegant and old-fashioned handwriting that masked his varied spelling and general disregard for punctuation. The letter contained family information and a summary of his life and current activities. There is no better introduction to Blackburn's remarkable story.

> If their is anny more information [you need] please let me know and i will freely inform you to the best of my ability—for i am glad to corespond with a persons that can think further than yesterday. I feel intrested in Utah for all my young days werre spent in Mormonism from Jackson County to far west and Nauvo to Salt Lak. I have ben in the employ of Joseph Smith and Brigham Young and have went through most all the early exciting times of the Mormon Church
>
> I am not an acomplished scholar but have abandoned hard work and ocupy myself in other ways more beneficial to old age. I have been writting a byography of my Adventures in an early day containing an acount of transacions in the Mormon church from 1836 to 1851. Also an acount of the mexican war which i was in and indian wars of whitch i have had a sad experience in—with seven trips across the plains through hostile indian bands and in the mines of california in her palmiest days. Have travled the Pacific Ocean from [the] Bering Straits to Valporazo the South Sea islands and sowed my wild oats [I] have settled down in this semi tropic clime to lay my bones to rest and have ben wrighting up an acount of my past miss-

1

deeds containing about thirty thousand words.

When it is convenient i would like to make [a] visit to Utah for i am acuainted with nearly all the first settlers. It is over forty two years since i left their.

I wish you would please wright me some information concerning Jehu and Elias and their familyes. I would have written long ago but when i left Utah they cut us all off from the church. I suppose they dropt me too. I suppose uncle Jonathan Rachel and Aunt Beckey are dead and gone. Their is no way for me to hear only from Utah

Give my regards to Elias and his and Jehues familyes. Hoping these lines will not be to tedious i remain your Nephew

Abner Blackburn[1]

The untitled memoir that is the heart of this work, the narrative of Abner Levi Blackburn, is the "acount of my past missdeeds"—or a later draft of it—to which Blackburn referred in this letter. It is a remarkable text. Blackburn's adventures traversed the continent, and his droll stories portrayed the opening of the American West in the 1840s. The narrative defies a simple summary: it described the fur trade; steamboating on the upper Missouri and Mississippi rivers; slavery in Louisiana; the early days of Mormonism in Missouri and Illinois; the bitter evacuation of Nauvoo in 1846; teamstering for Brigham Young across Iowa; the march of the Mormon Battalion; hunts for buffalo, bear, deer, elk, rabbit, eagle, duck, goose, and frog; the first days of the Mormon pioneers in the Salt Lake Valley; the Donner party; California in the fall of 1847; Utah's notorious Salt Desert; five key years of the western emigration; the gold rush; Forts Leavenworth, Pueblo, Laramie, Bridger, and Hall, and Sutter's Fort; the Fort Utah War; the founding of the first permanent white settlements in Colorado and Nevada; and the first documented discovery of precious metals in Gold Canyon, site of the Comstock. Blackburn toured the California mines in 1849 and used snatches of folk songs and large doses of his own crude but powerful verse to illuminate his story. On his way, he met contemporaries both famous and obscure, including prophets, slaves, private soldiers and generals, jack-tars and commodores, trappers, traders, scouts, promoters, pioneers, prospectors, speculators, counterfeiters, attorneys, governors, and horse thieves.

The narrative paints a complex portrait of Native Americans.

[1.] Elias Hicks Blackburn Papers, Utah State Historical Society.

Blackburn's attitudes were in many ways typical of his times, but given his bitter personal experience, the narrative is remarkably sympathetic. From childhood, Indians had fascinated Blackburn. The narrative tells of encounters with tribes as diverse as the Blackfeet, Shoshoni, Crow, Bannock, Sioux, Omaha, Ponca, Ute, Pawnee, Arapaho, Navajo, Goshiute, Paiute, unnamed California Indians, and, most provocatively, the Mandan.

Blackburn's story repeatedly describes otherwise obscure or undocumented events and challenges conventionally held historical dogmas. For example, although Blackburn was one of the few participants to leave an eyewitness account of the early white settlement of Nevada, some historians have chosen to ignore his story completely rather than address the questions it raises. Nonetheless, several exhausting searches for source material have consistently located accounts that authenticate Blackburn's version of events. The most telling example is the "Narritive of Lou Devon," Blackburn's recounting of a story told around a campfire in the summer of 1847. Not only is this tale of a young French Canadian's life with the Mandan tribe a spellbinding yarn, it is the only detailed account of the tribe from 1839 to the establishment of the Like-a-Fishhook village in 1844. It challenges the accepted view that the few Mandans who survived the smallpox epidemic all settled in present-day North Dakota; and while much of Devon's story is wildly improbable and highly unorthodox, it appears to be precisely accurate in details such as Mandan names and the sailing dates of ships trading for and with the Hudson's Bay Company. Finally, the only known Mandan sources describing these years place the tribe exactly where Blackburn said they were: roaming the headwaters of the Missouri and Yellowstone rivers.

The narrative is one of the best sources describing the corps of frontiersmen, many of them southerners, who played a vital role in the Mormon church as it moved westward. While New Englanders dominated the church's spiritual and temporal leadership, this band of "hard cases" provided the muscle and grit required to open a new country. Men such as Orrin Porter Rockwell, Ephraim Hanks, Howard Egan, Thomas S. Williams, John D. Lee, James Brown, and John Brown—all of whom Blackburn knew—were arguably essential to the success of Mormonism in the West. More peripheral figures, including Sam Brannan, Lewis B. Myers, "Old Rube" Herring, James Waters, and John Brown, Sr., were drawn to the church for the social protection it offered their often-illegal schemes. While the Mormon church ultimately had no room for men like Blackburn, they provided an essential ingredient in its survival.

The memoir profoundly challenges the stereotype of a monolithic

nineteenth-century Mormon church, exclusively composed of devout
and obedient pioneers. Blackburn's graphic account illustrates that
apostasy, dissent, and internal conflict are as old as the religion itself,
and the turbulent and varied host that made up the Mormon emigration was anything but a homogeneous band of sheep. Blackburn presents a skeptical but balanced view of Mormon society: while he
admired Brigham Young's leadership, he clearly resented his autocracy.

Blackburn and his narrative are very much products of his times,
the period when Jacksonian democracy exploded into Manifest Destiny.
The cauldron of the young republic produced both the Mormon religion and the western expansion—and Blackburn's life was inextricably
intertwined with both movements. His family "caught the west fever"
and his earliest memories were of continually moving closer to the edge
of civilization, "to catch up with the wildman." Blackburn experienced
it all: mob violence on the frontier, the fur trade in decline, the golden
age of steamboats, the conquests of the Mexican War, the flood tide of
the overland emigration, the stark madness of gold rush, and the glory
days and fall of the American Indian. In many ways he was the pioneer
incarnate. If his prejudices occasionally offend, they are remarkably
enlightened when compared to the prevailing attitudes of his times.

Although on its face the narrative is an artless and wonderful tale,
beneath its simple surface it has significance and meaning that reach
into the heart of now-legendary events. The dynamics of the western
movement, the hard edges of religious and cultural conflict, and the
struggle of a raw individualist against a communitarian ethic all give
depth and power to Blackburn's story.

The memoirs are an extraordinary frontier reminiscence, but represent a unique document in Mormon history. In 1943, Dale L. Morgan
wrote, "In my opinion, [the Blackburn narrative] cannot be published
too soon. I myself have copies of something like 600 Mormon journals,
autobiographies, life sketches, interviews, etc., running from a page to
7 volumes, but none has the elan and the humor of Abner's story. It [is]
just what Mormon literature needs by way of antidote to all the righteous solemnity."[2] In 1951, Morgan wrote that the Blackburn narrative
"is positively my favorite among all the journals I have, and nothing too
good can be said about it, whether for its value as source material or for
its readability."[3] Shortly before his death, he called Blackburn's reminis-

---

[2] Dale Morgan to Charles Camp, 13 September 1943, Dale L. Morgan Papers,
Bancroft Library.
[3] Dale Morgan to Charles Kelly, 22 February 1951, Charles Kelly Collection,
Utah State Historical Society.

cences a "jewel beyond price. . . . Blackburn brings to the Mormon literary and historical record an element that has been sadly lacking in it." After quoting two sections, Morgan asked, "Will anyone gainsay me? This is not merely history; it is literature of a high order. As far as the discovery of Mormonism is concerned, the best may be yet to come, as the buried folk literature slowly emerges into view."[4]

One of the most striking characteristics of the narrative is its perspective, which was neither that of zealot nor embittered apostate. Blackburn's personal view best matches that of the modern "Jack Mormon," a person with ties to the culture but with no belief in the doctrines of the Mormon church. This viewpoint gave him a singular perspective. After participating in the early struggles of the religion, he came to have serious doubts, and although ultimately he was unable to accept the spiritual and temporal claims of the Mormon church, his involvement gave him an insider's sympathy for and understanding of the Mormon experience. This outlook enabled him to comment on the history he had experienced with a singular objectivity, humor, and skepticism, but without the typical zealot sanctimoniousness or apostate bitterness.

Almost alone among Mormon chroniclers, Blackburn mixed a skeptical viewpoint with dry wit. Like the creators of the best western folk humor, which writers like Samuel Clemens and Bret Harte raised to a fine art, Blackburn used understatement extensively. He is positively brilliant in following a funny story with a pointed and insightful observation.

The narrative is so detailed that it answers several perplexing historical questions: Why did the Mormons bury their dead in a well at Haun's Mill? What were the Mandan Indians doing between 1839 and 1844? What happened on the first Mormon overland expedition to northern California with the mercurial Sam Brannan? When was the first permanent white settlement established in Nevada—and who first discovered gold in the Silver State? In addition to solving—or rekindling—these obscure but vexing controversies, Blackburn tells a wonderful story. His narrative evokes a voice that is dry, salty, and western. It has a remarkably oral quality—reading Blackburn is much like listening to him. Blackburn's tale evokes a campfire on the high desert and an old mountaineer recollecting the seizing and settling of the American West.

There is some question about when Blackburn wrote the existing version of the memoirs. He was at work on them in March 1889, and

---

[4] Dale Morgan, "Literature in the History of the Church," 31.

he had probably completed a draft much like the existing narrative in 1894, since the thirty-thousand-word length to which Blackburn refers in his 17 April 1894 letter very closely matches the current length of the manuscript.

Blanche Blackburn Corby told Herb Hamlin on 2 December 1941 that she never met her grandfather, but "my father told me of the years that they were together and things about grandpa that are not mentioned in his memoirs. One sad thing is that his wife made him burn up his first reminiscences because she thought he would get into trouble with the Mormons. Then he sat down and wrote them all over again, leaving out a lot of his cuss [w]ords and homely expressions that trappers and guides used in his day."[5] Hamlin claimed that since the first draft named the Destroying Angels allegedly killed by Blackburn, Lucinda Blackburn was afraid that the Mormon church would seek vengeance, even in the 1890s.

Internal evidence indicates that the surviving photostat of the narrative may indeed be a later draft composed or copied from an earlier version sometime between 1894 and 1902. The evidence—which is ambiguous at best—suggests that Blackburn recopied some sections and used portions of earlier drafts to create the surviving text. He probably tinkered with the manuscript until a few years before his death. The one internal date in the manuscript states that "55" years had passed since 1847, while a ballot or sample ballot dating from 1900 is folded over the top of page 58 of Volume One of the manuscript photostat.

As Dale L. Morgan noted, "Abner's narrative is amazingly accurate for a reminiscent account." In most cases, this claim would argue that the narrative was based on a journal, with the best evidence its usually precise dating. In the tangled story of the manuscript's discovery, it is often referred to as a diary or journal (which it is not), but only this circumstantial evidence indicates that such a journal ever existed. A more likely explanation for Blackburn's accuracy is that he possessed a remarkable memory, apparently a family trait.[6]

Blackburn's narrative is the self-portrait of a young man drawn from the perspective of old age. The first five pages of the manuscript are an adventuresome description of his childhood, while the rest of the

---

[5.] Blanche Blackburn Corby Testimony, Robert A. Allen Papers, Nevada Historical Society.

[6.] Blackburn's sister Eliza Jane "was said to have had a remarkable memory, and could relate many interesting tales of early life in the east, as well as early days of California and the wagon train trek from Illinois. But, alas, these tales never got told to anyone who put them down in black and white for her posterity." Gallagher, "Bainbridge Family History," 64.

memoir covers the years from 1845 to 1851. When he left home in 1845 to work on steamboats on the great inland rivers, Blackburn was lanky, rawboned, and eighteen years old, five feet ten inches tall, and dark complected. By his own account, he "was a good sort of a clown," easygoing and always ready for a good time. "I was fond of excitement and adventure," he wrote, "always wishing to go west." The narrative is the story of this wish coming true.

ONE

To Catch Up with the Wildman

A bner Levi Blackburn, the third child and first son of Anthony and Hester Rose Blackburn, was born 13 January 1827 in Bedford County, Pennsylvania. The Blackburns were Irish Quakers who arrived in America in 1736. They were a remarkably close-knit family: Anthony's father, Thomas M. Blackburn, and his mother, Elizabeth Bowen, were second half-cousins, while the intermarriages between Bowens, Roses, Blackburns, Harrises, and Oylers defy simple analysis.

Following his father's death in 1828, Anthony Blackburn moved his family to Smithfield Township, Ohio, and purchased a gristmill and sawmill. Like hundreds of thousands of other Americans, the Blackburns had "caught the west fever" and were swept up in the tide of migration. By a descendant's calculation, this westering would take Anthony Blackburn 3,441 miles, "all by primitive oxen drawn wagons, and most of it in hostile Indian country."[1]

In 1832, Anthony and Hester sold their property in Smithfield Township and moved to Richland County, Ohio. In May 1836, the Blackburn family's westward course united with the Church of Jesus Christ of Latter-day Saints, who called themselves the Saints and were popularly known as Mormons.[2] The visionary Joseph Smith founded

---

[1] Gallagher, "Bainbridge Family History," 150. The mileage figure is approximately accurate.

[2] At its founding, on 6 April 1830, the religion was named the Church of Christ by revelation. On 3 May 1834, the name was changed to The Church of Latter Day Saints. In 1838, revelation finally established the name as The Church of Jesus Christ of Latter-day Saints (abbreviated as LDS), the official title of the Utah branch of the church today. As early as August 1831 the term *Saints* was used in one of Joseph Smith's revelations. *Mormon* (or *Mormonite*) was originally a term of derision, but "members are no longer offended by it." See Allen, *The Story of the Latter-day Saints*, 47.

the church in 1830, amid the religious turmoil of western New York state's "burnt-over district" and soon established its headquarters in Kirtland, Ohio. Anthony's widowed mother, Elizabeth, converted to Mormonism as early as 1833, and many of Anthony's nine living brothers and sisters moved to Ohio. Anthony, born in 1803, was the oldest of ten children. His youngest brother, Elias Hicks Blackburn, was nine months younger than Anthony's son Abner. After his father's death, Anthony Blackburn assumed the role of patriarch for the extended family.

On 9 July 1836, Anthony Blackburn sold "one hundred acres more or less" in Richland County for thirteen hundred dollars.[3] In April 1837, the family moved to Missouri, following the Mormon migration to their new Zion on the edge of the western frontier. He left his mother and her family behind in Ohio. Anthony Blackburn, who would demonstrate an uncanny ability to be in the wrong place at the wrong time, moved his family to a farm on Shoal Creek in Caldwell County.[4]

By the summer of 1838, relations between the Mormons and earlier settlers deteriorated to the point of open warfare.[5] The Mormons had already been driven from Jackson County, the site (according to Mormon beliefs) of the Garden of Eden and their new Zion, and they were forced into neighboring Clay and Caldwell counties. The church had moderated its opposition to slavery, but many Missourians resented the Yankee and Canadian origins of the majority of Mormon settlers, found their religious beliefs and economic practices abhorrent, and feared their potential political power. The Mormons, who thought of themselves as loyal Americans with the right to enjoy their constitutional liberties of free speech, religion, and assembly, were also millennialists who believed that the end of the world was nigh, and that soon they would "literally tread upon the ashes of the wicked after they are destroyed from off the face of the earth."[6]

The church itself was undergoing a period of great internal conflict, and the loyalty of leading members was called into question. On 17 June, Mormon leader Sidney Rigdon delivered his fiery "Salt Sermon," which called for the suppression of dissent within the church and resulted in the immediate expulsion of founding members John Whitmer and Oliver Cowdery, among others. To handle this internal conflict, the Mormons or-

---

[3] Richland County, Ohio, Deed, Anthony Blackburn to Daniel Shiveley. Copy provided by Don Blackburn.

[4] Shoal Creek "takes a meandering course, though in the main flowing east, and finally empties into the Grand River." Roberts, The Missouri Persecutions, 233.

[5] LeSueur, The 1838 Mormon War in Missouri.

[6] Messenger and Advocate 1 (January 1835): 58, quoted in LeSueur, Mormon War, 18.

ganized the Sons of Dan, a secret paramilitary organization also called the Brothers of Gideon, the Daughters of Zion, the Destroying Angels, and, most popularly, the Danites. After routing the Mormon dissenters, the Sons of Dan turned their attention to external threats. Their leader, Sampson Avard, vowed that "the riches of the Gentiles shall be consecrated to my people, the house of Israel; and thus you will waste away the Gentiles by robbing and plundering them of their property."[7] Rumors of the Danite plans inflamed the passions of the Missourians.

Following more loose talk of blood and war from Rigdon at a Fourth of July celebration at Far West, hostilities broke out in Daviess County on election day, 6 August, when an intoxicated mob tried to stop Mormons from voting in the hamlet of Gallatin. The two sides fought the resulting brawl with whips, clubs, rocks, and knives. By September, Governor Lilburn Boggs had called out the militia and vigilantes organized to deal with the perceived Mormon threat.

In early October 1838, Mormons looted Gallatin and sent scouting and raiding parties into Daviess and Clinton counties. The situation deteriorated throughout the month. On 25 October, a battle was fought at Crooked River that resulted in the death of Mormon Apostle David Patten. Two days later, Governor Boggs issued his infamous "Exterminating Order," stating that the "Mormons must be treated as enemies and *must be exterminated* or driven from the state, if necessary, for the public good."[8]

These events played havoc on the quiet communities along Shoal Creek. Joseph Smith warned Jacob Haun to have the settlers move to the Mormon capital at Far West, but Haun watered down Smith's directive when he delivered it to his neighbors. On 28 October, Anthony Blackburn, Jacob Myers, and David Evans negotiated a peace agreement with the Missouri militia; but at four o'clock on 30 October, a second militia group launched the bloody assault on the settlers known as the Haun's Mill Massacre.

The Missourians, mistaken by the Mormons for their own forces, achieved complete surprise. David Evans, captain of the Mormons' impromptu militia, unsuccessfully called for quarter and then ordered his men into a poorly fortified log blacksmith shop. The Missourians shot through the cracks between the unchinked logs at nearly point-blank range until Evans ordered his panicked force to retreat. "Capt. Evans was somewhat excited, and, as he afterwards related, ran all the way to Mud Creek with his gun loaded, not having fired it during the fight."[9]

---

7. Roberts, *History of the Church*, 3:180. Information on the founding of the Sons of Dan is drawn from Schindler, *Orrin Porter Rockwell*, 34-65.

8. Roberts, *History of the Church*, 3:175.

9. *The History of Caldwell County*, quoted in the Journal History, 30 October 1838, 22.

Seventeen Mormon men and boys were slaughtered and a like number wounded. That night, "the groans and shrieks of the wounded made the night hideous and horrible beyond description. The women were sobbing in the greatest anguish of spirit; the children were crying loudly with fear and grief at the loss of fathers and brothers; the dogs howled over their dead masters, and the cattle were terrified with the scent of the blood of the murdered."[10]

Far West was already under siege and Smith, shaken by news of the massacre, surrendered on 31 October to avoid a bloodbath. Seven Mormon leaders were court-martialed the next day and narrowly escaped execution when General Alexander Doniphan refused to obey orders to shoot them. Smith was tried at a preliminary hearing in November and was held in Missouri jails until his escape to Illinois the next spring.

Blackburn related that his parents objected to several "verry seditious" Mormon doctrines, and in particular, one declaring that "the Lamanites or Indians would march through the land, slay all the gentiles [non-Mormons] and the Saints would follow after and geather all the spoil." Mormon apostates Nathan Marsh and John Sapp signed contemporary statements that reflect the perceptions of the Missourians and confirm Blackburn's statement. Marsh swore that "it is a very common source of rejoicing among all classes [of Mormons] that the time had arrived when all the wicked should be destroyed from the face of the earth, and that the Indians should be the principal means by which this object should be accomplished."[11] Smith and Rigdon denied Marsh's charges, saying, "We have never had any communication with the Indians on any subject; and we, and all the Mormon church, as we believe, entertain the same feelings and fears towards the Indians that are entertained by other citizens of this state."[12] This disingenuous statement sidestepped the complexities of the role of the American Indian in Mormon millennial beliefs and did little to calm the fears of the Missouri gentiles, especially with Mormon firebrands like Parley P. Pratt inflaming the frontier. Pratt cited the page in the Book of Mormon that set

> the time for the overthrow of our government and all other gentile governments of the American continent, [and] the ways and means of this utter destruction are clearly foretold, namely,

---

[10] Assistant Church Historian Andrew Jenson, writing in 1888, quoted in the Journal History, 30 October 1838.

[11] LeSueur, *The 1838 Mormon War in Missouri*, 71.

[12] Ibid., 84.

the remnant of Jacob will go through among the Gentiles and tear them to pieces, like the lion among the flock of sheep. Their hand will be lifted up upon their adversaries, and all their enemies shall be cut off. This destruction includes the utter overthrow, and desolation of all our Cities, Forts, and Strong Holds—an entire annihilation of our race, except such as embrace the Covenant, and are numbered with Israel.[13]

Ironically, despite the Mormon's hard experience in Missouri, this issue raised its head again during Blackburn's days in San Bernardino.

Disenchanted with Mormonism, Anthony Blackburn moved his family to Carlinville, Illinois, where they were reunited with the family matriarch, Elizabeth Bowen Blackburn, and most of her children. Anthony purchased a large block of land in May 1839, while his mother bought eighty acres in December.[14]

Blackburn gave a colorful account of his parent's reconversion to Mormonism. On 24 November 1844 Anthony Blackburn was ordained a high priest, a high-ranking office in the LDS Melchizedek priesthood.[15] The family conveyed their Macoupin county land to James Polly Brown of Nauvoo on 1 December 1843, probably trading the farm for a lot in the "Kimball subdivision" in the city of Nauvoo, the site of their home in the Mormon colony.

The Blackburns were again caught up in a turbulent phase of Mormon history. Illinois generously welcomed the Mormon refugees from Missouri and the church purchased eighteen thousand dollars worth of land surrounding the village of Commerce from speculator Isaac Galland. (Galland also traded eighty thousand dollars worth of land in Iowa's Half-Breed Tract, to which he held no title, for Mormon property in Missouri.) Smith named the new city Nauvoo, which he said was a Hebrew word meaning beautiful place of rest, and the Mormons began a third gathering. Late in 1840, the state of Illinois granted Smith and the Saints a city charter of sweeping powers. In February 1841, the Prophet (and now mayor) formed the Nauvoo Legion, a city militia, and assumed the rank of lieutenant general, the first officer to claim that rank since George Washington resigned his commission. The legion eventually consisted of three thousand men, the largest military force in the country other than the United States Army.

The Mormon capital soon became the largest city in Illinois, home

13. Crawley, *The Essential Parley P. Pratt*, 24.
14. Macoupin County, Illinois, Deeds.
15. Gallagher, "Bainbridge Family History," 147.

to as many as twenty thousand people, and the church began building a temple on a bluff overlooking the Mississippi River. The growing political and economic power of the Mormons again threatened their neighbors, and Smith added an explosive factor when he secretly introduced the doctrine of the new and everlasting covenant and the plurality of wives—polygamy. Rumors of the practice divided the Mormon community and fueled anti-Mormon sentiment. When Joseph Smith attempted to add the wife of his First Counselor, William Law, to his circle of wives, Law and other dissidents began publication of the *Nauvoo Expositor* to expose polygamy. As mayor, Smith ordered the destruction of the press. The order led to his arrest and imprisonment in Carthage jail, where a mob martyred him on 27 June 1844.

Joseph Smith did not clearly designate a single successor, and a scramble for power followed his death. Blackburn listed "William Smith, the prophets brother, Sidney Rigdon, Lyman White, Strang, and Emmet" as contenders for Joseph's mantle. William Smith claimed leadership of the church but was excommunicated in 1845. He eventually maintained that Joseph Smith III had inherited his father's office and had made a bid to tend it until his nephew reached maturity, but he was not taken seriously by most Mormons because of his erratic past.

Sidney Rigdon arrived in Nauvoo on 3 August 1844 to press his claim that while no one could succeed Joseph, he had been consecrated as "a spokesman to Joseph." He periodically had been the second man in the Mormon church, and the often-revived and usually discounted "Spaulding theory" credited him with plagiarizing an earlier manuscript to create the Book of Mormon. Rigdon posed the most serious challenge to Brigham Young's leadership, but the Quorum of the Twelve Apostles rejected his claim. He created a rival religion named the Church of Christ and made himself President of the Kingdom and the Church. Rigdon's religion ran out of steam by 1847, and he wound up packing shingles in Pittsburgh.

In August 1844, James Jesse Strang produced a letter purportedly from Joseph Smith that named the unknown Strang as his successor. Strang was immediately excommunicated, but he gathered a considerable following and eventually established himself as the polygamous King of Beaver Island in Lake Michigan. A disgruntled follower shot Strang in 1856.

Lyman Wight and James Emmett were not candidates for leadership, but attempted to carry out the plans Joseph Smith had formulated prior to his death. Wight, an apostle, apostatized and led a company of Saints working in the lumber industry in Wisconsin to Texas, where he died in 1858, "an intoxicated no-good," according to his fellow dissenter, George Miller.

In 1844, Smith commanded James Emmett and several families to plant crops on the Missouri for an already envisioned emigration. In September 1844, Emmett led a company of about twenty-five families on a strange odyssey up the Iowa River to a camp in modern Marshall County, "150 miles west of the settlements." After nearly starving, part of the company journeyed to the mouth of the Vermillion River in the Dakota country. (Blackburn may have encountered this party in 1845 on his steamboat voyage up the Missouri.) On orders from the Twelve, they joined the main Mormon emigration at Council Bluffs in 1846. Emmett was sent with Bishop George Miller and 150 wagons to winter on the Niobrara River in present-day Nebraska, but they were recalled in 1847, when the church determined to take the Platte River route to the mountains. Miller became "greatly disgusted at the bad composition and folly" of Brigham Young's revelation organizing and directing the emigration, and he left for Texas in July 1847.[16] Following their apostasy, "fellowship was withdrawn" from Miller and Emmett on 9 November 1847. Emmett emigrated to California in 1849, traveling with Jefferson Hunt's party, and died there in 1854 or 1855.[17]

Joseph Smith sealed his legacy with his blood, but left the future of his fledgling church an open question.

THE NARRATIVE

My parents were born in Bedford County, Pensylvania. Father was born in 1803 [and] my mother in 1800.[18] They had four children. Matilda, the oldest, was born in 1822. Eliza, the second, in 1824, and the third, Abner, in 1827.[19] Thomas the last [in] 1829.

Father moved to Jefferson County, Ohio, in 1828 and purch[as]ed mill property, a grist mill and saw mill, and lived there four years. Cautt the west fever. Sold out and moved to Richland County, Ohio. The neighbors come to bid us good by and said we were agoing to the backwoods amongst the Indians.

---

16. Bennett, *The Mormons at the Missouri*, 150–59.

17. Morgan, "The Reminiscences of James Holt," 164.

18. Anthony Blackburn was born 3 January 1803. His father, Thomas, was born in 1781 and died in 1828. His mother, Elizabeth Bowen, was born 8 May 1783 in York, Pennsylvania, and died in Provo, Utah, in June 1854. Hester Rose Blackburn was born 15 July 1800, married Anthony on 25 April 1821, and died 17 September 1876 in San Bernardino, California.

19. On the photostatic manuscript copy in the Nevada Historical Society, "Abner" appears to have been written over a previous erasure.

1832

But the Indians had left a short time before we arrived there. [We] bought a new farm and made [a] verry comfortable home.[20]

1837

About this time some Mormon misionaries come along and held several meetings in the settlement. And my parents joind their church and shortly after sold their posessions and started west to the north western part of Missouri to Caldwell County.[21] We were going to the backwoods this time sure enough to ceath [catch] up with the wildman.

Started on our long journey to the far west in the spring of 1837 in company of a few of the same faith. Passed through Ohio and Indiana [and] then come to the plains or pararies of Illinois. This country was nearly in its primitive condition [with] no settlements [except] only on the margin[s] of streams of water or timber. It was verryely a wild appearing country at this time. The few inhabitants lived on game, hog, and hominey. They dressed on what [they] made on com[m]on looms and the skins of wild beasts. They were verry friendly and obligeing.

Come to the Illinois River and to the Miss[iss]ippi, the great Father of Watters. Crost at Hanabal [Hannibal] into the state of Missouri. This is a slave state and settled up a little faster on that account. After travel[ing] several days the population became more scatterd [with] more pararies and fewer people, but the game was more plentyful. Deer, bear, turkeys, wild hogs, and bees and snakes galore and no whiteman in sight for a whole day or more.

Crost the Grand River and numerous other streams. This is a prairie country with timber on the streams of watter. This is the backwoods with out a dought.

Come to a beautiful place called Shoal Creek and began to look around for a suitable place to settle on. [We] had the whole country to select from. The land was rich and wild game [was] in abundance [with] wild strawberies and other kinds of wild fruit. [There were] fish

---

[20.] Don Blackburn, a distant cousin of Abner Blackburn, places the location of this farm to the south of modern Mansfield, Ohio. No buildings remain on the land.

[21.] Anthony Blackburn reported that he was "baptized in Richland County, state of Ohio, by Harvey Green, May 1836. Started to Missouri April 19, 1837. Ordained a deacon by Elder David Evans April 18, 1838." Holbrook, High Priests Minutes, LDS Archives. Abner Blackburn also dated his involvement in the Mormon Church from 1836. See Appendix A.

in the streams and bees in the forest with all kinds [of] nuts in the woods. This was truely a paridise on earth.

We had a beautiful place for a home. My parents were verry industrious and they, with the childrens help, soon had plenty of the neccesaries of life. By and by other setlers come in to the neighborhood and we had schools for the children. The grist mill was sixty miles off. A Mr Haun built a grist mill and saw mill in the settlement.[22] The soil was verry productive. I suppose it had not been under cultivation before or since the day of creation.

The Mormons taught some verry seditious doctrine [and] my parents objected to it verry much. Their leaders said the Lamanites or Indians would march through the land, slay all the gentiles and the Saints would follow after and geather all the spoil. About this time the Danites were organised, a secrete society to rob the Missourians or gentiles as they called them. The slave holders of Missouri would not submit to have such doctrine taught in their midst and trouble began to brew between the two partyes. The concequence was war.[23]

The Missourians tried to keep the Mormons from voting at the election, which started hostilities. The town of Far West was about twenty five miles from where we lived, which was the head quarters of the Mormons. There was frequent encounters between the two partyes and considerable blood shed. The governer called out the melitia or state troops to settle the quarrel. The Missourians threatened to burn the mills and all the houses of the Saints. All the men turned out to save the mill from being burned. There was some 25 or 30 men guarding the mills.[24]

[22.] In partnership with Ellis Eames, Jacob Haun had just finished the gristmill on Shoal Creek when it entered history as the site of a brutal massacre. Haun came to Missouri from Green Bay, Wisconsin, and was wounded in the fight that bears his name. The Reorganized Church of Jesus Christ of Latter Day Saints (RLDS) owns the site, located eight miles south of modern Breckenridge, Missouri. Nothing remains of the mill or settlement.

[23.] The 1837 *Gazetteer of the State of Missouri*, 93–94, called the Mormons "a tribe of locusts" and complained of "the impertinent and mischevious influence of the Mormons with the slaves of the country. Their threatened association with neighbouring tribes of Indians was a serious subject of alarm."

[24.] The Journal History contains an account of the Haun's Mill Massacre by "Ellis Eamut," actually Ellis Eames. On 28 October, "The mob . . . sent word to us that they wished to meet a committee of our people and have an understanding. . . . We immediately sent a committee who met them at the house of Mr. Myers, and after a short interview and explaining to them the object we had in view and that we desired to live in peace and they separated. Both parties seemed satisfied and manifested a kind spirit. The committee on the part of the . . . brethren were David Evans, Jacob Myers, and Anthony Blackburn."

[It was] in the fall, late, I have forgotten the date. One afternoon two hundred Misourians charged out of the woods and comenced fireing on the mill guard. The party at the mill returned the fire for some time from some shops and out houses, but the odds was against them. The mob shot down about twenty of our party and gave no quarter. A few escaped to the woods.

Mr Eames escaped the massacre and came to our house about dark and said the Missourians were a going to kill all the Mormons on Shoal Creek that night.[25] Every one grabbed their clothes and ran for safety to the woods. The mob satiated their thirst for blood [and] retierd from their glut of gore.

My father was sick with fever and ague, but went to the mill to assist in burning the dead and caring for the wounded. The ground was frosen so they could not dig graves and they put eighteen dead bodies in a well.[26] They did not know but the mob would return and kill them allso. Our house was full of wounded and dessolate famlies.

The Mormons surrendered to the state troops at Far West. They took the leaders of the Mormon church prisoners and had a long and tedious trial and acquitted them.[27]

The Mormons were ordered to leave the state in a short time. The slave owners would not allow such doctrine to be taught in their state.

---

[25] Here, Blackburn began an odd practice that continues throughout the narrative: almost every person named would later live in San Bernardino. Ellis Eames (later Ames) was born 19 January 1809 in Mentor, Ohio. He played fiddle for dances in the Nauvoo Temple and started west with Brigham Young's 1847 company, but turned back after spitting blood. Eames was the first mayor of Provo, Utah. He emigrated to San Bernardino about 1852, where he worked as a grocer, served as county attorney during 1856–57, and joined the RLDS church. Eames died 12 October 1882. He is quoted in the Journal History for 30 October 1838: "[On the night of the massacre,] I went about two miles [from the mill] and then returned with Mr. Blackburn about ten o'clock at night. I went amongst my friends who had been shot, and those who had been wounded. I assisted all I could and administered to their necessities, and early in the morning a few of us got together and interred the dead in a hole which had been dug for a well, and then we went and hid in the hazel bush, expecting the mob would be there to massacre the remaining."

[26] Blackburn is the first source to explain why the Mormons buried their dead in the well—or more exactly, a hole dug for a well. Beginning on 17 October, eighteen inches of snow had fallen in thirty-six hours and the weather had been extremely cold for much of the previous two weeks. See LeSueur, *The 1838 Mormon War in Missouri*, 116–17.

[27] Judge Austin King held a preliminary hearing on 13 November, but Joseph Smith was never actually tried or acquitted on the charges of "murder, treason, burglary, arson, larceny, theft, and stealing" that a grand jury brought against him. With the connivance of the Missouri authorities, Smith escaped to Illinois after five months in jail.

My parents were disgusted with Mormonism and removed to Illinois and left the Saints.[28]

The Mormons emegrated to Hancock County, Illinois, to a place they called Nauvo[o] at the head of the lower rappids of the Miss[iss]ippi River. We went to work and made another good home with everry convenience for comfort and engoyment. We were here about six years when some Mormon preachers come along preaching new doctrine. They said they had repented and acknowleged doing wrong in Miss[o]uri and other places. They did not teach the same principles.

The New Jerusalem was to come down from he[a]ven and all the holy prophets would come back to earth. They had seen some [of] them and talked with them. The angel Gabriel was to toot his horn and have a good time generly.

And we disposed of our posessions and moved to Nauvo[o] and took a place amongst the Saints once more. After we had arrived and settled down, the leaders would call every day for donations, tithes, and taxes. My brother and I were nearly grown. They would call on us nearly every day to work on the Temple or other church buildings. To work for nothing and board ones self is verry trying on [the] cons[ti]tution. Mine was not equal to the ocasion, so I joined the Nauvo[o] Legion under Joseph Smith, the Mormon prophet, and served under him until he and his brother Hiram [Hyrum] were assasinated at Carthage jail 27 of June 1844, which broke the Mormons up in business for a time.

There were several candidates for leadership of the Church. There was William Smith, the prophets brother, Sidney Rigdon, Lyman White, Strang, and Emmet. Brigham Young was on the mission at that time, but as soon as he returned they gave the reighen[s] to him and he ran the buissness for all it was worth.[29]

[28.] Anthony Blackburn reported to Joseph Holbrook that he "Left Missouri for Illinois Feb. 2, 1839 Moved into Nauvoo April 12 1844. Ordained high Priest under the hands of President George Miller Nov. 1844." See Holbrook, High Priests Minutes, LDS Archives. The Blackburns moved to Carlinville in Macoupin County and purchased $400 worth of land from Henry and Sarah Hall on 4 May 1839. See Macoupin County, Illinois, Deeds.

[29.] Gallagher, "Bainbridge Family History," 154, wrote, "Family tradition has it that Brigham Young . . . was enamored of Eliza Jane Blackburn, and wanted to take her as one of his wives in Nauvoo, Illinois, but was prevented from doing so by her brother, Anthony [sic] Abner Blackburn." It is unlikely that the teenage Blackburn could have prevented the powerful Young from doing anything. Eliza married John Bainbridge in 1844.

Two

Always Wishing to
Go West

At eighteen, Abner Blackburn struck out on his own. He pursued the chosen career of young men coming of age on the Mississippi River, steamboating, and became involved in the last days of the American fur trade.

While steamboating was entering its golden age, the fur trade was in decline. The two enterprises had been linked since 1829, when the steamboat *W. D. Duncan* began a regular packet trade to Fort Leavenworth on the Missouri. It commenced in earnest in 1831, when Pierre Chouteau, Jr., and Kenneth McKenzie, traders for the American Fur Company, built "a small steamboat for the trade of the Upper Missouri"—the *Yellowstone*. Due to low water that year, the *Yellowstone* only reached Fort Tecumseh, now Pierre, South Dakota; but in 1832, she made the mouth of her namesake river. The *Assiniboine* joined the trade in 1833, and these boats supplied the American Fur Company's trading posts and carried furs and buffalo hides south.

By the time of Blackburn's Missouri River voyage in 1845, the era of the beaver trapper was over. Due to the dwindling beaver population—and to the invention of the silk hat and the passing of beaver hats from fashion—much of the trade had turned to other pelts and buffalo hides. Still, the headwaters of the Missouri were truly wild country. On the *General Brooke*, Blackburn saw tribes of Plains Indians—by his own account, Pottawatomies, Omahas, Poncas, and Sioux—in their glory days.[1] These peoples had survived or escaped several devastating epi-

---

[1.] The *General Brooke* is the only steamboat known to have ascended the Missouri in 1845. Captain Joseph Sire's 1845 journal describing the voyage is in the Missouri Historical Society. While the broad outline of the journey described by Blackburn is discernible, Sire's log contained no references to the details in Blackburn's story. Sire's journal recounted a voyage plagued by cantankerous machinery and bad weather in which the crew was almost continually cutting wood.

demics and were learning white ways from trade with the fur-trade posts, but still preserved their culture and traditions of war and the hunt. Blackburn saw them hunting buffalo on the river and witnessed his first Indian fight, significantly a battle between tribes. He probably saw the ruins of the Mandan villages and and may have feasted with their cousins, the Hidatsas.[2]

Blackburn saw the lower Mississippi as a deckhand on the *Louisiana,* and he got a firsthand view of slavery. Like many northerners, he hated what he saw and the experience certainly contributed to his support of Lincoln in the 1860 election and his participation in the Union League during the Civil War.

After a short experience of working in Illinois lead mines, Blackburn returned to Nauvoo. The Mormons were rushing to complete their temple before abandoning the colony to begin their quest for a new home in the West. Brigham Young ordered the evacuation of Nauvoo in the dead of winter, on 4 February 1846. Blackburn helped ferry the first wagons across the Mississippi, but by the twenty-seventh the river froze, allowing later emigrants to cross on the ice. This exodus would be one of the most bitter and trying events in Mormon history. Blackburn served in Allen Stout's company of guards until 23 February, when he was seriously wounded in the first of several gun accidents described in the narrative.

Dale L. Morgan noted, "There are various Mormon accounts of Blackburn's being shot on Sugar Creek—in fact, his name turns up for the first time here in the Mormon annals. The manuscript History of Brigham Young says . . . 'Several guns were discharged in and around the camp. During the council [of the Quorum of the Twelve Apostles and captains of hundreds] Benjamin Stewart came up to the tent fire of the guards, caught up a large pistol and discharged it across the fire; it contained three small rifle balls which entered the left thigh of Abner Blackburn, son of Anthony Blackburn, two balls passed out the opposite side and one hit the bone and passed down remaining in the leg.'" Hosea Stout wrote in his journal:

> While the council was in session intelligence was brought in that a man by the name of Abner Blackburn had been shot by accident. I afterwards learned that a man by the name of Benj[n] Stewart had shot him. He took up a pistol which lay near by

---

[2] Joseph Sire noted on 29 June 1845, "We are soon at the village of the Gros Ventres—We lose a good three hours in giving them a feast." The Gros Ventres of the Prairie, or Hidatsas, had absorbed some remnants of the Mandan Nation following the smallpox epidemic of 1837.

and was loaded and pointing it at the unfortunate man who was shot the man told him that the pistol was loaded and not to shoot him but Stewart Seemed to not know what he said not even as much as to understand what was said but fired direct at Blackburn and the ball passed into his thigh and severely wounded him but I think not dangerously. The man who was shot belongs to my brother Allen J. Stout's company and it took place in front of his tent and across the fire. When my brother discovered what was done he kicked Stewart out of camp for it was a palpable violation of orders for any man to even handle another's arms much less to fire one. After the council was over I called out all the guard and gave them a severe reprimand for their disobedience of orders & want of discipline and their practice of firing guns in camp which had been so often forbid.[3]

After recovering at his parent's home in Nauvoo, Blackburn rejoined the emigrant company as a teamster. He described the trek across Iowa with characteristic humor and perception. Following a droll encounter with the Mormon leader, Blackburn noted: "Brigham was ever on the watch. Nothing mist his observation." Young's constant attention to detail was a key factor in the success of the Mormon emigration. Still, the emigration was behind schedule and the church was broke: it appeared that it would take a miracle—like Abraham's ram in the thicket—to raise the capital required to cross the plains successfully.

The Narrative

About this time I began to weaken on the whole outfitt and thought the Saints were no better than the gentiles were. Concequently I quit and went steamboating. Hierd out on the steamer *Osprey*, next on the *War Eagle*,[4] [and] changed on to another boat bound up the Missouri River to take suplies to the trading posts at the head of navigation.[5]

---

[3] Brooks, *Hosea Stout*, 1:126. Stout was the captain of the police and a distant relative of Blackburn's future brother-in-law, William Stout.

[4] The *Osprey* engaged in the Indian trade on the upper Mississippi. The *War Eagle* engaged in the lead trade between St. Louis and Galena, Illinois, and was "perhaps the swiftest boat to navigate the Upper Mississippi before 1850." Under Daniel Smith Harris, she set a record for the trip in 1845, covering the four-hundred-mile distance in forty-three hours and forty-five minutes. See Hunter, *Steamboats on the Western Rivers*, 25; and Petersen, *Steamboating on the Upper Mississippi*, 108, 240, 260, 264.

[5] Blackburn's handwriting temporarily ended at this point.

At St. Louis I shipped on another boat going up the Missouri River, that muddy, rappid, and crooked stream, which appeared full of snags and bars. It was [as] difficult in those days to navigate in low water as at present. It was a dangerous stream to all appearance, the water continually rolling and boiling like water in a cauldron. We bent our way through snags and bars on dark nights and tied to the bank until morning. The river was very low at this time of the year. At last we arrived at Council Bluffs, unloaded and the boat returned to St. Louis. Leaving the boat here, I hired to some trappers to go up the river when the watters raised. We were going up with some supplies for the Indian traders on the head waters of the Missouri River and return with furrs.[6] We were hired by Sar Pee & Charbomene, old trappers.[7]

As soon as the water raised we put every thing aboard a small steamer and started up the river. We were outside of all civilization, nothing but nature and wild savages. First was Pottowattomes [and] next Omahaus & Panquans [Poncas]. Next the Sioux and so on. One tribe was nearly like another. They all wanted to trade for something when we stopped on the bank. They kept the traders busy passing out supplies such as amunition, blankets, calico, knives, and beads. All would finish with fire water and a grand old time.

One morning we saw a great number of buffalo crossing the river ahead of the boat. The current being so swift that they would land nearly a mile below the place on which they started.[8] The Indians were on the bank waiting for them to land. The buffalo were nearly exausted when they came out of the water and the Indians riding up close would send their arrows into them up to the feathers. They killed all they wanted in less time than it takes to write it. Unlike the whites, who killed for sport, they never killed more than they needed.

Some days before we came to the mouth of the Yellowstone we witnessed an Indian battle. It was in a large bend of the river. A band of Siou[x]s hemmed in another tribe of Indians. All appeared mounted and fought in a circle. Some shot arrows from under their horses necks while others fought with blunderbuses or bell muzzled guns which made a great noise. But as near as we could see there was very little ex-

---

6. The American Fur Company supply ship for 1845 was the *General Brooke*.

7. Peter A. Sarpy was the American Fur Company agent at Bellevue, Nebraska. Pierre Chouteau, Jr., was a partner in the American Fur Company and outfitted the 1845 supply ship *General Brooke*. Blackburn also used "Charbomene" as the name of a Mormon Battalion guide, clearly referring to Jean Baptiste Charbonneau, but in August 1845, Charbonneau was at Bent's Fort.

8. On 26 June 1845, Joseph Sire noted, "Left at daybreak—we stop before breakfast a little below Heart River to kill a buffalo who is crossing and at the same time I have some wood cut."

ecution, only a few dead horses and some wounded warriors. The wounded were not so badly injured as to prevent their escape to the rear of the fight.

The Siou[x]s being more numerous drove their adversaries before them. The squaws and pappooses took to their canoes. The beaten warriors ran to the river and jumped in, horses and all, and crossed to an island in the river for safety.

We tied our boat at the island to take on wood and took a look at the poor wretches while they were running for their lives. The Siou[x]s shot arrows into their backs, wounding a great number. We gave them what assistance we could but two of them died.[9]

It is strange but true, that the wounds of the Indians are generally on their backs, which does not speak well of their courage.

After laying in a fair supply of wood, we took the beaten Indians on board and landed them a few miles up the river and kept on up the torturous stream, landing at various places, delivering supplies for the trading posts of the American Fur Company. We had a good view of all the Indians and saw many tribes that frequented the stations to barter their pelts. Of all the wild countries I had ever seen this took the lead.

Two of our crew deserted our boat to go with the Indians and we never saw anything more of them. We did not need their help very much as we intended returning down the river before long.

We were nearing our destination and within a few days would return laden with a few bows and arrows and some other notions to show our folks when we arrived home. We were nearly [ready] to return. An Indian cheif wanted the Captain to take him down the [river to] St. Louis and fetch him back next trip and he would give him big heap pelts. The Captain did not like to take him and contrived some way to scare the old chief off. After fixing up we put on a full head of steam. The old Chief came on board and stood close to the boiler. Everything being in readiness the Captain told the Engineer to blow off steam. The old chief stood it for a second or two when he ran for the gang plank and out into the woods. That was the last we saw of him.

Then we steamed out into the stream, turned around, and we

---

9. Although Sire did not mention this fight, at the beginning of the return voyage, on 5 July, he noted, "we meet several Krees and Santins. we have a good deal of trouble preventing them from taking several Ricaras whom we have on board." On 11 July, "Meet a war party of Yankton whom we take on aboard and set on land below the river at Bazille. They are going to war with the Pawnees."

were on our homeward trip, taking in all the traders had on hand which made a full and valuable cargo. The river was high and running with the swift current. [We] were soon landed in a few days in St. Louis.[10]

After we rested up and had a blowout we shipped on the steamer *Louis[i]ana* and ran on the lower Mississippi, the Arkansas, and Red River.[11] I liked the change and seeing the sights, but it was very laborious work being a common deck hand. I never will forget the negro slaves that were shipped on the steamer *Louisiana* below St. Louis. There was about twenty of them and six of them were women. Their master was taking them to a Louisiana sugar plantation.

They would cry and sing all kinds of Negro melodies: Miss Lucy Long; Mary Blaine; Uncle Ned or anything to drown their sorrow.[12] The women were taken from their children and some of them made a most pitiful lamentation. Some boatmen were so touched with the sight they turned their heads away and cried for pity. Their master took it as a matter of business and was as mean to them as though they were a drove of hogs.

I liked work but this suited me too well. We made a trip to Cincinatti, drew our pay, and quit. My chum and I concluded to go to the lead mines of Galena.[13] Took passage on the steamer *St. Croix* and started and came to the mouth of the Ohio, fell in company with another steamer, the *Fortune*, and a race was the usual result.[14] Both boats [were] about the same size [and] began to crowd on steam. We crowded the fires with pitch, tar, and resin; run the weight to the end of the safety valve and fastened it down, kept up the race for several hours, and gave up the race to the *Fortune* of Louisville.

We came along up the Mississippi until we were a short distance below the mouth of the Missouri where our boat struck on a snag. We

---

[10.] The *General Brooke* departed from St. Louis shortly before noon on 22 May 1845, reached Fort Union on 2 July, and returned to St. Louis on 18 July with five hundred packs of buffalo robes, setting a new record of fifty-seven days for the round-trip. See *The Niles Register*, 2 August 1845, 339–40. The steamboat burned in the great St. Louis fire of 1849.

[11.] The *Louisiana* exploded while embarking from New Orleans in 1849, killing between one hundred and two hundred passengers.

[12.] Stephen Foster published "Uncle Ned" in 1848. "Mary Blaine" may be a version of the South Carolina slave reel "Miss Mary Jane."

[13.] Development of lead mines in northeastern Illinois began as early as 1690. In 1847, $8,676,647.39 worth of ore was taken from the mines, which can be compared to the estimated total worth of $300,000.00 for the 1848 fur trade at St. Louis.

[14.] The *St. Croix*, whose captain was Hiram Bersie, conducted excursions for the passenger trade and was engaged in the Galena lead trade for six years. The *Fortune* sank a keelboat loaded with eighteen hundred pigs of lead at the mouth of Fever River in July 1846.

backed off onto a sand bar and sank. There was a lot of old country emigrants on board who kept up more jabbering than all the geese. The crew went ashore in boats. One old lady gathered all her traps except her water bucket who exclaimed; "Hans! Hans! Git de vatter pucket! De vatter pucket!" And her husband replies; "Got in himmel! Vat you vants mit de pucket? You no gits vatter enough already?"

We lost part of our outfit and went on another boat. At last we arrived at Galena and went back into the mines where we found a job of work at sixteen dollars per month. After finishing the work, we jumped a claim, cleaned out an old shaft, and ran a drift about twenty feet.[15] We worked here until the latter part of August. At that time our mine caved in and broke my partners leg, George Squires, a most faithfull and honest fellow. This unfortunate accident broke us up in business and we sold out mine and outfit.

My partner went to his home in Cincinatti and I went home to my parents in Na[u]voo.

September 1845

About this time there was great preperation for the Saints to leave Na[u]voo. With the Saints it appeared to be a case of compulsion. I was fond of excitement and adventure, always wishing to go west, so I joined to help at anything. They gave the job of sand papering the floors of the Endowment rooms and other sacred apartments of the Temple to me.

They were in a great hurry to pass the faithful through and receive their Endowments and blessings before they left for the land of Zion.[16] After nearly all had passed through, they hunted up the common help. Some were loading, others were packing up boxes of goods. I was assisting to ferry across the river.

They hunted up all the young bloods to give them their endowments, myself being about the last one on the docket and told me to come along. I said I had to help finish it off and knew all about it. The man I worked with had been through the sacred apartments the day

---

[15.] A shaft is a vertical or inclined opening made for mining ore, while a drift is a mine passageway driven along the course of a vein of ore.

[16.] Completion of the temple held equal priority with preparation for the emigration. The Mormons believed the temple ceremony was necessary for "full salvation" and the uniting of families for eternity. Brigham Young promised "a rich endowment in the Temple of the Lord, and the obtaining of promises and deliverances, and glories for yourself and your children and your dead." Five thousand persons received their endowments before the church leadership departed in February.

before and I thought the endowments did not improve him very much. So the Elders of Israel hunted some other worthies.[17]

I joined Brigham Youngs company as a guard. They were in great fear of a mob and crossed over the river and established a winter camp on Sugar Creek in the State of Iowa.[18] The main body of the people could not start before spring.

Here I met with a severe accident. There was a young gawky fellow fooling with one of those old Flint-Lock horse pistols. It was loaded with three rifle balls. At the discharge of the pistol two of the balls passed through my thigh and one struck the bone, glanced down and is there now. They expected me to pass in my check. Brigham and Kimball were there and prayed me out of danger.[19] My parents came after and took me home and by good nursing came out as good as new in about six weeks.

When my recovery was perfected I returned to camp on guard as usual. Spring had come, the grass began to start and it was time to go. Brigham gave me charge of one of his teams to drive. The motive power was oxen; some of which had to be trained to work.

I trained the cattle round a day or two before we started on our higeria; loaded up with live stock and their effects.[20] They belonged some place in the company and I called them jay birds. Well, we started and such a time I had with that team of raw unbroken wild steers. I was in the road part of the time and that was when I was crossing it.

---

[17] Despite Blackburn's skepticism, posthumous rights were performed for him in the Salt Lake Temple, on 3 October 1951. An ordinance sealing him to his parents, incorrectly listing his grandparents, Thomas and Elizabeth Blackburn, was later performed in the Provo Temple.

[18] Sugar Creek was located six miles west of Nauvoo.

[19] The Archives Division, Church Historical Department, the Church of Jesus Christ of Latter-day Saints, Salt Lake City, Utah (hereafter cited as LDS Archives), has a contemporary account of the affair called "Abner Blackburn's Misfortune (Shot)." In the handwriting of LDS historian Franklin D. Richards and headed "Camp of Israel Febr 23 A.D. 1846," it reads: "Monday Morning About ten in O.C. After taking some refreshment we were standing round the fire, when of A sudden a young man by the name of Benjamin Stewart took a pistol into his [hand] and discharged it acrost the fire and Lodged the contents [in] the thigh of Abner Blackburn, Son, Anthony Blackburn. The pistol was loaded with three Small rifle Balls. Two passed threw his leg and [one] struck the bone, and passed down towards the nea. Doctors Brady and Sprague were sent for and much Credit is [due] to them for their attentiveness and also to sister Middleton, and others." The doctors were probably Samuel L. Sprague, who in 1848 would be the first doctor to settle in Utah, and Lindsay Anderson Brady, an 1850 Utah pioneer who participated in the evacuation of Nauvoo. Sister Middleton could be Mary Butler Middleton, an 1850 Utah pioneer, Rachael Middleton, a resident of Ogden in 1870, or Betsy Middleton. The Nauvoo Temple records list all three women.

[20] At this point, Blackburn's handwriting began again in mid-paragraph.

My waggon ran against brother Brighams amidships and tore off the whole stern end, but arrived in camp after a fassion. The next day [we] had a few more mishaps. One of the jays wanted some flowers on the side of the road [so] I started [to] pull them and the oxen geed off the road and upset the waggon and its load in the mud, the Lords annointed and all. The boss come along and began to scold me for carelessness. I handed the whip to him and told him I was working for acomodation and there was no glory in it. "Never mind," sayes he. "Try and do better."

There was much talk about poligamy. Some knew it trew and others did not know wheather to believe it or not. My cureosity was sattisfied. Being right amongst it was very convincing, but kept mum on the subject.[21]

The roads were bad when we did have them. Generaly we had no roads [and] had to bridge two or three streams a day. Come to a very steep place and slid down all right. In going up I thought the cattle went easy, but the waggon toung unhiched and dropped. I did not notice it until the top was reached. Brigham was sitting on top of the bank watching every move. He bellowed out, "Where is your waggon?" I looked back and there was the waggon at the bottom of the hill. He gave me such a look that [it] cured me of carelessness. Brigham was ever on the watch. Nothing mist his observation.

Prophets, Priests, Apostles, and the Lords anointed all eat togeather with the vulgar. There was but a step between the sublime and the rediculous. Mush and milk for dinner and but little better for supper or breakfast. All set around on waggon toungs or ox yokes eating their allowence. Made a halt at a place they called Mt Pisga[h] and some of the Saints stopt here to put in crops and garden to acomodate those that were comeing after.[22]

[21.] Blackburn's comment reveals the conflict generated by polygamy within the church. Rumored to have been practiced as early as 1831, Joseph Smith formalized the doctrine of the plurality of wives in a secret revelation in 1843. It was publicly announced in Great Salt Lake City in 1852. Since the practice was secret in 1846, some Saints refused to believe it was doctrine. Blackburn's policy of keeping "mum" on the subject reflected the nineteenth-century Mormon motto: "Mind your own business."

[22.] Mount Pisgah, located near present-day Talmadge, became a supply center and assembly point for the Mormon migration across Iowa.

THREE

Good-bye Vain World

Mormon leaders had long been searching for a way to persuade the United States government to fund their western migration, beginning with Joseph Smith's petition to Congress in March 1844 requesting an army commission and authority to raise 100,000 volunteers to police the borders of the West from Texas to Oregon. Late in 1845, Brigham Young asked for federal contracts to build a string of forts along the Oregon Trail. On 20 January 1846, Young and the Council of Twelve Apostles named Jesse C. Little of New Hampshire as president of the Eastern States Mission, instructing him, "If our government shall offer any facilities for emigrating to the western coast, embrace those facilities."[1] Events played into the Mormons' hands when Congress declared war on Mexico in May.

Preaching in Philadelphia, Little had the good luck to interest Thomas L. Kane, son of the former attorney general of Pennsylvania, in the Mormon cause. Kane provided introductions to members of the Polk administration, supplementing a letter that Little carried from the governor of New Hampshire.[2] After a frustrating ten days of lobbying in Washington, Little drafted a carefully worded letter that he sent directly to the president, stressing Mormon patriotism but delivering a veiled threat to resort to foreign—meaning British—assistance. Polk met with Little for three hours the next day and immediately authorized the enlistment of five hundred Mormons, to "attach them to our country, & prevent them from taking part against us" and "to conciliate them and prevent them from assuming a hostile attitude towards the U.S. after their arrival in California."[3]

[1] Bigler, *Azariah Smith*, 4.
[2] Roberts, *The Mormon Battalion*, 6–7.
[3] Quaife, *The Diary of James K. Polk*, 1:444, 446.

President James Knox Polk, who had sworn to serve a single term, envisioned a United States one million square miles larger than the nation he had governed in 1845. Polk saw the Mormons as a useful tool of his policy of expansion, but he intended that the Mormons should make their own way to California and be enlisted "on their arrival in that country." Bureaucratic bungling in the War Department sent vaguely worded orders to General Stephen Watts Kearny that resulted in the battalion's enlistment in Iowa on terms remarkably favorable to the Mormons.

Mormon plans to send an advance party of five hundred men to the Rocky Mountains in 1846 had bogged down in mud, suffering, and poverty during the crossing of Iowa. When Captain James Allen of the First Dragoons arrived in the Mormon camp at Council Bluffs on 30 June, common church members did not greet him with anything approaching enthusiasm: some suspected he was a spy sent by the Missourians. Many were positively affronted that the government would seek their aid, and without the support of Brigham Young it is unlikely that Allen could have enlisted the 292 men required by his orders to secure his promotion to lieutenant colonel. "I do not suppose," said James Brown in 1855, "there is an individual in the Battalion, who, had he been left to his own thoughts and feelings, independent of counsel, would have enlisted."[4] Young, however, saw things very much in the light that Allen presented in a circular issued on 26 June at Mt. Pisgah: "Thus it is offered to the Mormon people now—this year—an opportunity of sending a portion of their young and intelligent men, to the ultimate destination of their whole people, and entirely at the expense of the United States."[5] In addition, Young secured permission from Allen to settle on Indian lands, on the west bank of the Missouri, and appropriated much of the battalion clothing allowance and pay to support the emigration.

On 16 July 1846 Colonel Allen mustered the 526 men who had enlisted in the Mormon Battalion of Iowa Volunteers and led more than 600 men, women, and children on the first leg of their journey. They marched away to the tune of "The Girl I Left Behind Me" and camped the first night at "a trading post on the Missouri River kept by some Frenchmen"—including Blackburn's old employer, Peter A. Sarpy.[6]

[4.] Tyler, *A Concise History of the Mormon Battalion*, 357.
[5.] Bieber, "Cooke's Journal," 24.
[6.] Gudde, *Bigler's Chronicle*, 19.

At Fort Leavenworth the battalion was equipped with muskets, cartridge boxes, bayonets and scabbards, knapsacks, canteens, cups, clothing, haversacks, blankets, and twenty-four rounds of ammunition. It was, as Albert Smith observed, "a hevy load for a Mule."[7] As the men crowded around the arsenal to collect their weapons, Colonel Allen said, "Stand back, boys; don't be in a hurry to get your muskets; you will want to throw the d——d things away before you get to California."[8]

Allen, whose "good-natured, humorous" ways had gained him considerable popularity with his troops, was delayed at Fort Leavenworth where he fell ill and died of "congestive fever" on 23 August.[9] Henry Bigler darkly suggested that he had been poisoned for his friendship with the Mormons.[10] The markedly unpopular Lieutenant Andrew Jackson Smith replaced Allen. The battalion's Mormon captains outranked Smith, but he claimed and held command as the most senior regular army officer.

Leaving Fort Leavenworth, the battalion's line of march followed the Santa Fe Trail with slight variations, basically tracing the path of General Kearny's Army of the West, which had left Leavenworth on 6 July. From the Arkansas River, the battalion took the Cimarron Cutoff instead of the trail's "mountain branch" through Bent's Fort, which Kearny had used. After crossing modern Kansas, Colorado, and Oklahoma, the battalion trail reunited with the mountain branch near present-day Watrous, New Mexico. The leading companies arrived in Santa Fe on 9 October.

Informed of Allen's death, Kearny, already on the march to California, sent Captain Philip St. George Cooke to take command of the battalion as a lieutenant colonel. If ever a soldier had a thankless task, it was Cooke's assignment on 2 October to march eleven hundred miles to California, pioneering a wagon road across an unmapped wilderness with virtually no supplies, while leading an untrained militia—a nightmare for any professional officer. Cooke would later write that the battalion was

> enlisted too much by families; some were too old,—some feeble, and some too young; it was embarrassed by too many women;

[7.] Bigler, *Azariah Smith*, 14.

[8.] Tyler, *A Concise History of the Mormon Battalion*, 136.

[9.] Brigham Young called Allen "a friend to the uttermost." Young stated that "he was thrown upon a sickbed where I then believed, and do now, he was nursed, taken care of, and doctored to the silent tomb." See *Journal of Discourses*, 10:106.

[10.] Bigler, *Azariah Smith*, 21.

it was undisciplined; it was too much worn by travelling on foot, and marching from Nauvoo, Illinois; their clothing was very scant;—there was no money to pay them,—or clothing to issue; their mules were utterly broken down; the Quartermaster department was without funds, and its credit bad; and mules were scarce.[11]

Cooke graciously omitted a specific reference to the complaining and backbiting that were endemic in the battalion, but in his journal he noted that "there is a wonderful amount of stolidity, ignorance, negligence, and obstinacy which I have to contend against."[12]

The battalion was divided three times, creating what is collectively called the "sick detachment." At the crossing of the Arkansas, Lieutenant Smith dispatched Captain Nelson Higgins and a guard of ten men to winter at the trapper settlement at Fort Pueblo with the sick and many of the women and children. The process continued in Santa Fe when Cooke sent Captain James Brown north to Pueblo with eighty-nine men and eighteen laundresses, taking all but four or five of the battalion's women. Finally, after a march of twenty-two days down the Rio Grande, as Cooke entered unknown territory with few rations and worn-out stock, he ordered fifty-five men—including Abner Blackburn—to return to Santa Fe under Lieutenant William Wesley Willis, Sr.

Low morale, bad weather, and half-rations plagued Willis's command after he accidentally left the best part of his small allocation of rations behind in the supply wagons. The annals of the sick detachment are a litany of complaints. Joseph Skeen made a substantial case against Willis in his reminiscences, reporting that

> we started for santefee and hardly a one of us could walk. we pushed the wagons threw the sand the same as we did going down. . . . We buried three of the soldiers before we came to santefee which died for want of care and ware used more like niggers by our lutenant then white folks. when a brother would Die he would say he was glad of it, he was out of the road. he would threaten to cut their Damned throats and scalp them and to cut them to pieces if they would not keep up when they ware not able to scarcely to walk. the wagon got stucke in a mud hole one day. their was 6 or 8 men in it that could not walk. the lutenent orde[re]d me to get in and throw

---

11. Cooke, *The Conquest of New Mexico and California*, 91.
12. Bieber, "Cooke's Journal," 84.

them out in the mud. i told him i would not do it. he would get Drunk whenever he could get it and then he would curse the sick men because they were not able to walk and keep up. so we were used by him who should of been our friend and our brother. when he had an oportunity to get us something to eat he would not let us have it but would get Drunk with the money that was given to him to buy us wood.[13]

we came to Santefee the 1 day of December . . . [Willis] was Drunk and would not provide us any thing for us to eat[14] brother wilson went to the quartermaster and told him our situation and he gave him A sack of flower so we got something to eat . . .

this was the way that lutenent willis used this companey of sick men when he had it in his power to get every thing that would make them comfortable and he would not. he loved liquor better than he Did his brethren. the last man that was left in a town the name of tows [Taos] the lutenent would not let eny person stay to take care of him and the Spaniards murdered him and took his clothes. he was the name of [William] coleman. i was in the foremost crowd we came to perbelow the 21 of December and found Captain Brown with his company in good quarters and hale and harty.[15]

After backtracking to Santa Fe, Colonel Price ordered the detachment to Pueblo and issued them ten mules and pack saddles. "With this outfit we had to perform a journey of about three hundred miles, over the mountains, and in the winter," remembered Willis. "Packing was new business to us, and at first we were quite awkward." After five days, occasionally leaving sick men behind, they reached Arroyo Hondo, where Willis left "quite a number of sick with Mr. Turley." After three days of trudging through snowbanks, they crossed the summit of the Sangre de Cristo Range. "To our inexpressible joy, we saw the valley of the Arkansas below, where the ground was bare." They had "good weather and pleasant travelling" to their winter quarters at Fort Pueblo.[16]

James A. Scott, who would die on 5 February 1847 in Pueblo of "winter fever and liver complaint,"[17] left a contemporary description of

---

[13.] Willis claimed, "I had fuel and everything to buy, and spent $66.00 of my own private money before reaching Santa Fe." Tyler, *Concise History*, 192.

[14.] The narrative indicates that Blackburn supplied the wine Willis used to get drunk.

[15.] Joseph Skeen, Reminiscences and Diary, LDS Archives.

[16.] Tyler, *A Concise History of the Mormon Battalion*, 192.

[17.] Ibid., 196.

the adventures of the Willis party in a letter written on Christmas Day 1846:

> I have arrived safe & sound at the Mormon settlement which is on the head waters of the Arkansas within a quarter [mile] of Fort Purbelow, tho on the opposite side of the river which is the boundary between New Mexico and Indian Territory. Purbelow is on the American side.
>
> On the 19th we left S. Fe with 60 days provisions. Our road lay along the Rio Del Norte. we followed it 22 Days making a distance 250 miles. Near 150 miles below Santa Fe we left the main road & followed Kearny's trail. then commenced hard times living on 8 oz of Flour & 10 of meat per day & pushing waggons over sand hills & having to carry our guns and kampsacks. This was rough fare. *Sure.* After 22 days march, it was found necessary to send the sick & feeble & a sufficient guard back to Purbelow and there let them recruit until spring & then proceed to California. I was detached as one of the guard we reached Santa Fe on our return on the 1st of Dec . . . we left our waggons at S. Fe & took pack mules to cross the mountains upon which the snow was from 12 to 18 inches in depth. we reached here on the 21st & found Capt Brown's Company, which left Santa Fe on 18 Oct, composed of the [illegible] sick & weakly, [now] well & hearty. Immediately on our arriving here we set to make some houses. we have several on hand though none finished.
>
> The Fort is on the American side of the Arkansas river. The Mormon town or settlement is on the opposite side in the newly acquired territory of New Mexico.[18]

George Frederick Ruxton, a British Army officer and keen observer of the American West, passed through Pueblo early in 1847. Before his tragic death in 1848 at age twenty-seven, Ruxton wrote a wonderful fictionalized history, *Life in the Far West,* and a series of sketches. Ruxton provided an intriguing and colorful picture of the Pueblo winter quarters.

> In a wide and well-timbered bottom of the Arkansas, the Mormons had erected a street of log shanties, in which to pass the inclement winter. These were built of rough logs of cottonwood, laid one above the other, the interstices filled with mud,

---

18. Mormon Battalion Letters, LDS Archives.

and rendered impervious to wind or wet. At one end of the row of shanties was built the 'church' or temple—a long building of huge logs, in which prayer-meetings and holdings-forth took place. The band wintering on the Arkansas were a far better class than the generality of Mormons, and comprised many wealthy and respectable farmers from the western states, most of whom were accustomed to the life of woodmen, and were good hunters. Thus they were enabled to support their families upon the produce of their rifles, frequently sallying out to the nearest point of the mountains with a waggon, which they would bring back loaded with buffalo, deer, and elk meat, thereby saving the necessity of killing any of their stock of cattle, of which but few remained.[19]

Francis Parkman described the trapper settlement at Pueblo as "a wretched species of fort, of the most primitive construction, being nothing more than a large square inclosure, surrounded by a wall of mud, miserably cracked and dilapidated." Parkman wrote that the Mormons he encountered there in 1846 were "blind and desperate fanatics."[20]

The day before arriving at Pueblo, James Scott noted in his diary, "This morning after travelling 3 miles we came to a small creek named Green Horn upon which is a settlement made by an American named Brown."[21] Blackburn wrote that Pueblo was "a paridise for hunters with all kinds of game in abun[dan]ce. There [were] several old trappers living here, [including] James Watters, Liew Mires, John Brown, Rube Herron, Kit Carson." While Christopher Carson is the only one of these men to have won enduring fame, they were all well-known mountain men in their time. Three of them, James Waters, John Brown, Sr., and Valentine Johnson Herring, would later be Blackburn's neighbors in San Bernardino.

James Wesley Waters was born in Brainard's Bridge in upstate New York on 30 January 1813. He came to the Rocky Mountains about 1834 and worked with the Sublettes, Thomas "Broken-Hand" Fitzpatrick, Jim Bridger, and Kit Carson on the headwaters of the Missouri, Columbia, and Arkansas rivers. In 1842, he helped found the fort at El Pueblo. Waters was shot in a three-day battle with Indians (some sources say Apaches) on the Rio Las Animas (or the Purgatoire River) and barely escaped with his companions, Bill Williams and Dick Woot-

19. Ruxton, *Life in the Far West*, 204.
20. Parkman, *The Oregon Trail*, 356, 361.
21. James Allen Scott, Diary, LDS Archives.

ton. Waters is said to have cut the bullet out of his side by himself with a butcher knife.[22]

Waters left Colorado with Jim Beckwourth on a California trading venture and arrived in San Bernardino in December 1844.[23] On this "extraordinary trading expedition," Waters collected abalone shells off the coast of Lower California and "packed them on mules back to the Rockies and traded them to the Indians for furs and buffalo robes. He took these to St. Louis, where he bought supplies and goods, which he carted back to Colorado to trade with the Indians."[24] He and Beckwourth may have run briefly a hotel in Santa Fe, but Waters appeared in John Brown's account book late in 1846, in time to meet Blackburn at Fort Pueblo.[25] Waters killed Ed Tharp in a duel at Pueblo on 2 February 1848; some say Waters shot Tharp in the back, others that the fight was over a woman named Nicolasa, while still others state that the fight was over Waters's wife, Candelaria Sena.[26]

John Brown, Sr. (not to be confused with the John Brown who was among the first Mormons to enter Salt Lake Valley), was born 22 December 1817 in Worcester, Massachusetts. In his teens he rafted down the Mississippi River, was shipwrecked on the coast of Texas, and joined Sam Houston's forces in the Battle of San Jacinto. After working for two years at Fort Leavenworth, he wintered on the headwaters of the Arkansas and in the spring accompanied John Swanock and other Delaware Indians and mountain men on a risky expedition into Blackfeet country. His son wrote that Brown worked for fourteen years as both a free trapper and for the Hudson's Bay Company. Mountain men such as Calvin Jones, Tim Goodale, and Bill New nicknamed him "Prophet" because of his alleged prescience, and Brown would later write an eccentric spiritualist autobiography, *The Mediumistic Experiences of John Brown, Medium of the Rockies.*

---

[22] Brown, *History of San Bernardino*, 1:676. Wootton, who called Waters "Walters," wrote: "The ball had entered the left side just above the hip, but strangely enough, its course had in some way been deflected, so that it passed just under the skin half way round the body and came out on the right side nearly opposite where it entered. We dressed the wound as best we could and made our way back to Fort Bent, where Walters finally recovered, although he was never much inclined to venture into any portion of the Indian country where he did not know that he would be perfectly safe, after that." See Conrad, *Uncle Dick Wootton*, 129.

[23] Beattie, *Heritage of the Valley*, 115.

[24] Hafen, "Mountain Men Who Came to California," 24; and Camp, *James Clyman, Frontiersman*, 324–25.

[25] Woodward, "Jim Waters," 10.

[26] Hafen, *The Mountain Men*, 3:306–8. Louis Tharp reported to the *Jefferson Inquirer* that the fight was over a "trifling difficulty," and that his brother was "off his guard when shot." A woman named Nicolasa was credited with causing the fight. See LeCompte, *Pueblo, Hardscrabble, Greenhorn*, 73, 205, 314; and Woodward, "Jim Waters," 9.

In 1845, Brown opened a store on Greenhorn Creek that sold axes, hoes, thread, buttons, trousers, hats, shirts, cloth, lead, ribbon, powder, percussion caps, candles, moccasins, beans, corn and flour, and rented traps.[27] He built a log cabin and planted wheat and corn, digging a rifle pit in the middle of the field to use in case of Indian attack.

On 1 May 1845, Brown married Louisa Sandoval, who had convinced the authorities that she had been abandoned by her previous husband, Jim Beckwourth, who was in California with Jim Waters. (Tom Autobees, a Colorado old-timer, remembered that Brown had already killed a Frenchman in a duel over a Mexican girl named Nicolasa—the same woman sometimes blamed for starting the fatal duel between Jim Waters and Ed Tharp.) Louisa had a daughter by Beckwourth whom Brown raised as his own child. Their son, John Brown, Jr., who would lead the singing at Blackburn's funeral, was born 3 October 1847 at Greenhorn Creek.[28]

"Old Rube" Herron was Valentine Johnson Herring, born 26 March 1779 in Surrey County, North Carolina.[29] George Frederick Ruxton met Herring at Pueblo and left a vivid description of him in 1846:

> Dressed from head to foot in buckskin, his face, neck, and hands appeared to be of the same leathery texture, so nearly did they assimilate in colour to the materials of his dress. He was at least six feet two or three in his mocassins, straight-limbed and wiry, with long arms ending in hands of tremendous grasp, and a quantity of straight black hair hanging on his shoulders. His features, which were undeniably good, wore an expression of comical gravity, never relaxing into a smile, which a broad good-humored mouth could have grinned from ear to ear.[30]

Herring had already been in the mountains at least sixteen years. He had been part of John Gantt's 1831 trapping expedition to the Rocky Mountains, and in 1833 he accompanied William Sublette to the upper Missouri. In 1835 Herring was working out of Fort Hall, which he

---

[27.] Woodward, "Jim Waters," 10.

[28.] L. Burr Beldon, "John Brown," *Mountain Men*, 7:45.

[29.] The 1869 John Brown, Jr., diary provides a contemporary source which indicates that "Old Rube" was truly old: "Valentine Johnson Herring was born in Surrey County, North Carolina, March 26th 1779; died . . . at his residence west of Roubidoux [near Riverside] on September 30th 1869."

[30.] Ruxton, *Life in the Far West*, 79. Ruxton described Herring near present-day Soda Springs, Idaho, "making medicine" against Indians who had stolen his horses and traps. The name *Herring* is carved on Name Rock, an Oregon Trail landmark in western Wyoming.

helped Nathaniel Wyeth build. During the winter of 1841–42 he was in charge of Fort Lancaster.

Like Waters and Brown, Herring was linked to the Mexican woman Nicolasa, and one author suggested she was the Maria he would later take to California.[31] Herring fought a duel over Nicolasa with Henry Beer in the winter of 1841–42: Beer wagered his life on Herring's reputation as a poor shot, but lost the bet. Rube and Nicolasa settled down, "quarreling incessantly," at Hardscrabble, a farming settlement near Pueblo.

Ruxton described Herring's hot and cold involvement with the Mormon church at Fort Pueblo in the winter of 1846:

> A mountaineer, Rube Herring . . . became a convert to the Mormon creed, and held forth its wonderful doctrines to such of the incredulous trappers as he could induce to listen to him. Old Rube stood nearly six feet in height, and was spare and bony in make. He had picked up a most extraordinary cloth coat among the Mormons, which had belonged to some one his equal in stature. . . . A slouching felt-hat covered his head, from which long black hair escaped, hanging in flakes over his lantern-jaws. His pantaloons of buckskin were shrunk with wet, and reached midway between his knees and ankles, and his huge feet were encased in moccasins of buffalo-cow skin.

Ruxton wrote that Herring "was never without the book of Mormon in his hand, and his sonorous voice might be heard, at all hours of the day or night, reading passages from its wonderful pages." Rube had his motives:

> [Herring] let out one day that he was to be hired as guide by this party of Mormons to the Great Salt Lake; but their destination changed and a wonderful change came over his mind. He was, as usual, book of Mormon in hand, when brother [James] Brown announced the change in plans [the sick detachment chose to go north to the Platte rather than across the Rockies to Salt Lake]; at which the book was cast into the Arkansas and Rube exclaimed—"Cuss your darned Mummum and Thummum! thar's not one among you knows a fat cow from poor bull and you may go to h— for me." And turning away, old

---

31. LeCompte, "Valentine Johnson ('Rube') Herring," *Mountain Men*, 9:206.

Rube spat out a quid of tobacco and his Mormonism together.[32]

The apostasy Ruxton reported was short-lived, since Herring was active in the church in San Bernardino until his excommunication in April
1855. Brown, Waters, Herring, Alexis Godey, and others left Colorado in
June 1849 and were in Salt Lake City on 4 July 1849. On 15 September,
they reached Sutter's Fort. They variously tried their hands at mining and
hostelry, but by 1852 Brown and Herring were living in San Bernardino,
where Waters would join them. (Their later lives and continuing connection with Abner Blackburn are related here in the Afterword.)

Arnold Stevens described life at the Mormon fort in a letter to his
wife:

> We are here about 140 of us, of which about eighty-five
> men and twenty women under command of Capt. Brown,
> camped here on the 6th November and in about one or two
> weeks we all got moved into our cabins. I am now dressing
> dear skins. I and my partner have dressed fifteen and can have
> all we can do; they are worth about two dollars a piece.
>
> I traded my horse on my way to this place for a good mule.
> Our horses, mules and cattle live here and keep fat without
> feeding. It seldom rains here. There has been about two inches
> of snow twice, but no rain. We are in about twenty miles from
> the mountains that are covered with about nine feet of snow.
> They raise some corn here, but have to water their land for a
> crop, by taking the water out of the river in ditches. The corn
> is of an inferior quality and is the only thing cultivated here.
> There are men living here that have lived in California for six
> or eight years and have been almost in all parts of it and about
> Bear River and Salt Lake, they say it is a fine country and it
> rains in some parts, that it produces good crops, that it is
> mountainous and abounds with bear, elk, deer, antelope, etc,
> and its waters abounds with fish, geese, Indian Ducks, etc.,
> that the climate is mild. We are about three hundred miles
> from Fort Laramie and about the same distance from Grand [illeg-
> ible]. I had a talk with Captain Brown this evening. He thought
> it likely we would be paid off in the spring and discharged with
> provisions to last to the Bluffs, or to California.[33]

[32.] Ruxton, *Life in the Far West*, 206–7.
[33.] Mormon Battalion Letters, LDS Archives.

Brown was partially right: the men of the sick detachment would remain in the service until their one-year enlistments expired on 16 July 1847; some would return to Iowa, but most would continue to the Salt Lake Valley in "Upper California," while Captain Brown and Abner Blackburn would reach Monterey on the shores of the Pacific Ocean.

THE NARRATIVE

Arrived at Council Bluffs. Here Coronel Allen, a goverment officer, was enlisting volunteers for the Mexican War. Brighams folks did not want me to enlist for I had been with them as chief cook and bottle washer, or as a necessary evil. They forgave me the hard words I said on the cattle and thought I was a good sort of a clown. I told them I was going and all the kings oxen could not hold me. There was five hundred enlisted in this place. [They were] called [the] Mormon Battalion and started to Ft Leavenworth to fit out for the war. There were no provisions [at] the Bluffs and we had to beat our way partly to the fort of several days journey.[34] [We had] no cooking utensils or conven[ien]cies.

The soldiers made dough and wrapt [it] around [a] stick and held it over the fire to bake. The farmers along the rout[e] thought we were a rough sett. Chickens, ducks, pigs, and all kind of vegetables suffered without price. Some of those fellows would steal anny thing. One set of theives carried [off] several bee hives while the o[w]ners were at dinner. One soldier drove off a cow and milked her to the fort and then sold her for whiskey. [We] arrived at the fort [and] made all preperation to goe.[35]

We had to be sworn into the service.[36] The officer read the military law to us. It was death to desert and death for several other offences. There was a company of Misourians heard the law read. They said if the Mexicans did not get them the military law would sure. That was too much of a gammet for them to run. So they threw up the sponge and went home.[37]

[We] drew our arms and acouterments and bounty money [and]

---

34. The battalion left Council Bluffs on 21 July 1846. They followed the east side of the Missouri River and crossed the river to encamp on the west side of Fort Leavenworth by the evening of 1 August.

35. Dale Morgan noted, "The detail that Blackburn gives about the Battalion march is to be found in no other narrative I have seen, and I have been inexpressibly delighted with it. I have no doubt it is all true."

36. Blackburn was enrolled as a private in the Mormon Battalion of Iowa Volunteers, Company C.

37. The Second Missouri Mounted Volunteers was being mustered at Fort Leavenworth, but no account has been found that describes a Missouri company returning home, rather than face military discipline.

layd in a suply of clothing and other neccessaries for the trip across the wide plains to Mexico and Montuzumas Halls.[38] Started the 10 of August 1846.

> The eagle screamed and took his flight,
> Over lofty mountains in the West.
> On the Pacific shore he will alight,
> And on her crags will find a nest.

Coronel Allen our commander was taken sick and stayed at the fort and died shortly after. Cornel Smith took command of us and led us through to Santefe [Santa Fe].[39]

It was hard on us carrying our knapsacks and accouterments. By and by we hierd teams to haul our luggage.

Come to the Pawnee Fork of the Arkansas River.[40] The Comanche Indians had attackted several trains of waggons here lately [so we] kept a sharp lookout. [We] picket[ed] our camp and doubled the guard.[41] Slept on our arms but were not molested.

We then came to the Arkansas River and were very much disapointed as we expected to see a large stream of water with steamboats running on it as they passed through a thickly timbered country.[42] But instead we were compelled to dig in the bed for water. There being a scarcity of wood, we burned buffalo chips for fuel.

Well good-bye vain world, this looks like a new lay-out. This change made us forget what little we did know and we went on like lambs to the slaughter. We kept up the river two or three days until we came to a place to leave the river, wher[e] the buffalo were very plentiful and crossed over a dessert of forty miles onto the Cimerone [Cimar-

---

[38] "On the 3rd of August, companies A, B, and C drew their arms, which consisted of U.S. flint-lock muskets, with a few cap-lock yaugers for sharpshooting and hunting purposes." Tyler, *A Concise History of the Mormon Battalion*, 136.

[39] Allen died on 23 August. Lieutenant Andrew Jackson Smith commanded the march to Santa Fe, beginning on 31 August. Many of the men regarded Smith as "our Tyrant." He fought for the Union in the Civil War at Chickasaw Bluffs, Vicksburg, and Mobile, and rose to the rank of brevet major general.

[40] On 8 September, the battalion reached the Pawnee River and camped in what is now Larned, Kansas.

[41] Alternate handwriting begins at this point.

[42] The battalion reached the Arkansas five to six miles north of modern Kinsley, Kansas. They followed the north side of the dry river for seventy to seventy-five miles, crossing at present-day Ingalls, Kansas, where the Cimarron Cutoff left the Arkansas River.

ron] river.[43] We started in the evening.[44] Our water did not hold out long and a great many suffered for want of it. We drank out of buffalo wallows that was thick with mud.[45] The Cimerone was a dry bed of sand into which we dug for water, which tasted like powder.

The antelope were very numerous; dozens of herds in one sight. We then began to climb the wide base of the Rocky Mountains. The air was different and all felt good and our rations felt better. Here we left the buffalo and the hostile Indians and began to come into the Mexican settlements.

Camped one afternoon about three oclock. Presently there rode up several Spainiards. Amongst them was a Spanish Hidalgo and his daughter with their rich caprisoned horses and their jingeling uniform. The Sinuretta lit off her horse like a nightengale. The whole camp was there in a minute. Their gaudy dress and drapery attracted all eyes. The dress of the Sinuretta is hard to describe, all the colors of the rainbow with ribbons and jewelry to match. She was the Rodope [?] of the great American plains. We gave them presents and made them welcome to our camp and also to martial music as a greeting.

The damsel was struck with our drummer boy, Jesse Earle, and his violin.[46] He played "The Girl I Left Behind Me." She could not contain herself and with her companaros started a dance and made the dance fit the tune.

[43.] After crossing the Arkansas, the battalion rested on 16 September, and Lieutenant Smith dispatched ten men and many of the women and children accompanying the battalion to Fort Pueblo. Early the next morning, the battalion buried Alva Phelps and started on the Cimarron Cutoff, which entailed a waterless fifty-mile crossing between the Arkansas and the head of the Cimarron River.

[44.] The battalion did not begin any of its Cimarron Cutoff marches in the evening, but on 19 September, "Started at 4 o'clock this morning in order to get the start of some Missouri Volunteers, who were encamped here." See Golder, *Journal of Henry Standage*, 166.

[45.] Henry Standage's diary entry for 17 September confirmed Blackburn's account: "I drank some water today that the Buffaloes had wallowed in and could not be compared to anything else but Buffalo urine, as a great portion of it was of the same, yet we were glad to get this. Saw many buffaloes today and many wounded by the Battalion. Some killed. Camp'd without water in this desert and not a blade of grass for our mules." Ibid., 165–66.

[46.] Jesse Earl was a musician in Company E. Earl was in Utah by the spring of 1849, when he may have been involved with Blackburn in a scrape with Mormon authorities. He settled for a time in the San Francisco Bay area. On 8 January 1857, Ellen Pratt McGary reported, "Jesse Earl is up there [north of San Francisco] teaching dancing school, they have very fine times." Earl returned to Utah that year, where he spied on Johnston's army.

She was beautiful, graceful, and slender,
Her saddle was spangled with gold.
Whose gleam her eyes dark splender,
Outshown a thousand fold!

Upon the drum she took a seat,
Her image made the fifer smile.
She showed her pretty ivory feet,
And slender ankles all the while.

She took a fancy to our drummer boy. The attachment was mutual; but his admiration cooled off somewhat when she appropriated his handkerchief and pocket-knife. After taking the whole camp in they made their departure for their beaut[i]ful hacienda.

After this the camp was as dead as a last years pancake. We began to have a view of Mexican civilization. They had not gained but little over the Aztecs and Toltecs. Their implements of agriculture were the rudest kind of structure, as old as Damascus. We came to the Moro and Los Vagos and by the appearance of things it carried us back to the time of Moses and the Cannonites.[47] [The inhabitants were] a most miserable set of poor, half clothed wretches, covered with vermin, who cared for nothing except a few meals and a Fandango to kill time. The rich were very rich and the poor very poor and worthless.

Oct. 9, 1846

Arrived in Santa Fe.[48] Colonel Donophen saluted us with one hundred guns, which was not given to Colonel Price, our enemy, who arrived the next day.[49]

[47.] On 3 October, fifty men from each company were picked to make a forced march to Santa Fe. The battalion crossed the Mora River near Watrous on 4 October and camped at Las Vegas, New Mexico, on the fifth. Blackburn's 9 October arrival date indicates that he was with the vanguard; men straggled into Santa Fe until the thirteenth.

[48.] Already more than 235 years old, Santa Fe was the center of Spanish civilization and government in the Southwest. As the capital of New Mexico, it remains the oldest continuous seat of government in the United States. Located at the junction of the Chihuahua Trail from Mexico, the Santa Fe Trail from Missouri, and the Spanish Trail from California, it had a population of about three thousand in 1846.

[49.] Colonel Alexander W. Doniphan had refused to carry out what he termed the "cold blooded murder" of Joseph Smith following the Prophet's court-martial in 1838. In October 1846, Doniphan commanded American troops in New Mexico. Congressman Sterling Price, commander of the Second Regiment of Missouri Mounted Volunteers which shared much of the Santa Fe Trail with the battalion, had won the undying hatred of the Mormons for his role in the 1838 war. Price commanded Confederate forces in Missouri during the Civil War.

We recruited, drew our pay and had a grand old time in the Montezuma town. There was new kinds of knicknacks; Penoche, torti[ll]as, chile colorow.[50] We had been kept on [a] close diet on the plains and had eaten all the new things without asking questions or asking the name of the comestable. There was a mess of us boys strolling up an alley. We saw some Mexican women cooking in a kind of restaurant and went to buy something to eat.

On the end of a board was something which looked good to eat. One of our crowd began to eat it, who soon found it to be very stringy. The Mexican women looked wild at him and putting her hands to her stomach exclaimed; "Corambo Americano!" The fellow tried to throw it up and caught hold of the end and pulled it out like a snake. We supposed it to be some kind of rat poison as there were plenty of rats around.[51] We were a little careful about eating their amunition afterwards.

There was 88 sick soldiers sent to the Pueblo on the Arkansas River at the foot of Pikes Peak in charge of Cap Brown to Winters [Quarters].[52] Corolnel Phillip St George Cook took command of our force to lead us to Callifornia.[53] The Pilots were Pauline Weaver, Leroux, and Charbomene.[54]

[50.] Penuche (also *penuchi* or *panocha*) is a fudgelike candy. Chile colorado is beef in a hot red sauce.

[51.] Blackburn's handwriting resumes and continues to the end of the manuscript.

[52.] James Brown was born 30 September 1801 in North Carolina, converted to the Mormon church in June 1839, and served a mission in Mississippi before joining the battalion. George Ruxton saw Brown preach in Pueblo in the winter of 1846–47: "The preacher was one Brown—called, by reason of his commanding a company of Mormon volunteers, 'Cap'en Brown'—a hard featured, black-coated man of five-and-forty, correctly got up in his black continuations, and white handkerchief around his neck, a costume seldom seen at the foot of the Rocky Mountains." At Pueblo, John Steele noted: "Sunday, 3rd of January, 1847, there has been told this day that Captain Brown is something above all the men that is here in priestly authority and he has told us often that we do not know who he is, he is so high. We all feel the hands of tyrants." Domestic strife dogged Brown during his stay at Pueblo: one of his wives, Mary McCree Black Brown, would complain to her brother-in-law, Curtis Black, that "the treatment which I have received from Mr. Brown fully sho[w]es to me his inability to bring me and my husband that is dead [George Black] into an Exalted Stetion which is the greatest Blessing. . . . I have to stand and here the insults of an unfeeling Man." Mormon Battalion Letters, LDS Archives.

[53.] Colonel Philip St. George Cooke took command of the Mormon Battalion on 13 October. Born 13 June 1809 near Leesburg, Virginia, he attended West Point and spent almost twenty years on the frontier before assuming command of the battalion. In 1857, Cooke commanded the cavalry in Johnston's army during the Utah War. Cooke's son, John, and his son-in-law, J. E. B. Stuart, fought for the South during the Civil War, but Cooke remained loyal to the Union. He wrote the army manual on cavalry tactics and retired in 1873 after forty-six years of service, dying in Detroit on 20 March 1895.

[54.] The guides were Pauline (or Powell) Weaver, Jean Baptiste Charbonneau, and Antoine Leroux. Weaver began trapping the Gila and Colorado rivers in 1830

Had a good rest and started for California by way of the Hele [Gila] and Collorado River. In a few days come to the Rio Grand[e] River. Passed through the town Albukirke [Albuquerque] and down this river.[55] The Rio Grande Valley is furtile and thickly settled [with] watter di[t]ches runing whear needed for irigation and numerous towns and villeges. Their merchandize comes principaly from Chuchuahua [Chihuahua] or St. Louis on the Miss[iss]ippi. Horses, cattle, sheep, and goats are raised in large quantities. They raise the sweetest onions here. One can eat them like apples.

The Navahoe [Navajo] Indians are the inhabitants greatest dread. They decend on them like the wolf on the fold and drive off herds of stock, slay and capture.[56]

We bought our vegetables with pins, needles, buttons, and other trinkets. The Mexicans were short of all such things. We sold for a high price and bought for a low price.

Our meat was poor sheep and goats [that] had been running to-geather so long there was hardly anny difference in their looks. When they were drest one could hold it over the fire with a stick. We could eat them as fast as the quartermaster could issue them out.

We traveled down the Rio Grand[e] River about ten days. Here the valley began to narrow. [We] come in to the sand hills and we had to tie ropes to the waggons and string on soldiers to pull them over the hills.

---

and would later live in the San Bernardino area near Blackburn. Half Cherokee, he was an expert on the Apache Indians and served for years as a U.S. Army scout. He died in Arizona on 21 June 1867. Charbonneau was the son of Toussaint Charbonneau and Sacajawea of the Lewis and Clark expedition. He was educated in St. Louis by William Clark and in Europe by the Duke of Wurttemberg. Charbonneau settled in California and died in 1866, on his way to Montana. Cooke called him an "active and useful" man. Leroux was a French-Canadian who became a Mexican citizen in Taos. He later served on the New Mexican Territorial Organization Convention and as a guide for western military surveys by Sitgreaves in 1851, Gunnison in 1853, and Whipple in 1854. The battalion had other guides: Cooke reported on 2 November, "Of all the guides sent to me by the general [Kearny], only Leroux joined me this afternoon: the others have come up tonight more or less drunk."

[55.] Founded in 1706, Albuquerque was named after the Duque de Alburquerque, Viceroy of Mexico. By 1790 the town had 5,959 residents and had eclipsed Santa Fe as a commercial center.

[56.] Colonel Price assigned three companies to guard against Navajo depredations, but Cooke noted in his journal that Major Benjamin Edmonson's command was even more disorganized than his own and that "the Navajo, it is to be feared, will escape lightly this season." On 26 October, he noted that all the "effective males" at the village of Valencia had gone after the Indians, who had stolen 6,600 sheep and killed two shepherds.

A great manny soldiers were taken sick for some cause.[57] For Chichuahua we started. The hills were deep with sand. Our comerads took sick and died along the Rio Grand[e]. There was 55 sick sent back to the Pueblo in charge of Lieutenant Willis.[58] I was one of the number.

The 10th of November we started on our loansome trip and not a well man in the lot fit for service. There was two teams loaded with sick and provisions. The mules were worn out with service. The men that were able had to push the waggons up hill [f]or hours at a time. The second day two soldiers died. At night we scraped a hole in the sand close to the river, wrapped them in their blankets [and] put them in the hole. Stript off some cottonwood bark and fitted it a around them and covered up the grave. The next day another died and [we] served him the same way.[59]

After this the weather turned cool and all felt better, but [we] were on half rations. The Mexicans wanted our pins, buttons, and needles and drove some good bargains for something to eat. The Mexicans were organizing a secret rebellion. Our officer got wind of it and we were warned to be on our guard. The inhabitants began to be shi of us and did not [want] to trade, but we demanded what we wanted.

One evening [we] campt close to a village and were awful dry for something to drink that was stronger than watter.[60] Saw an old Padra come out of [a] kind of cellar with a large bottle of the needfull. Three of us went up to him and told him that we [were] dry and had not taken a sniff since we left Santa Fe. He says, "Nither nither notengo Augedente no tengo veno no no tengo."[61] We pushed him up against the door of the cellar. He fumbled around in his pockets and raked [up] an old rusty key and gave it to a servant who unlocked the door and we followed him in.

The man took us back to the further end of the dungeon and lit a tapor and shew us how to draw the good out of the cask with a hollow reed. You suck it full [and] hold it over a vessel and let it run out, then

[57.] No source explains exactly what made the sick detachment sick. On 23 October, Cooke noted in his journal: "All my servants, too, are sick, and many of the men. . . . An influenza is prevailing." Three days later, he wrote that he was "still sick of a cold, which is very prevalent." He also noted an outbreak of measles, but it seems likely that the sick detachment was ill with an intestinal disease, such as *giardia*, brought on by unsanitary camp conditions.

[58.] William Wesley Willis, Sr., was born in Swaneetown, Illinois, on 16 August 1811. Willis would later be the mayor of Cedar City, Utah, and a member of the Iron County Brigade of the Nauvoo Legion. He died 8 April 1872 in Beaver, Utah.

[59.] John Green and James Hampton died on the night of 11 November. Elijah Norman Freeman and Richard Carter died on 19 November.

[60.] This village was probably Isleta or Los Lunas, New Mexico.

[61.] This roughly translates, "I don't have any liquor, I don't have any wine, no, no, I don't have any."

suck again and so on. As soon as he learnt us the gamet he left us in our glory. We took our time. It was slow work. We filled up to the Plimsol mark before we suspected anny thing [was] wrong.[62] Started back in the dark for the door. Groped arround and found it locked. Well, the old devil had us in a trap [so we] went back to the cask to die hap[p]y. Took another bait of wine. Then scratched our heads in a deep studdy [on] how to get out. Hunted for a soft place in the adoby wall and with our bayonets dug out. In a short time [we] slip[p]ed out and sneaked into camp as though nothing happend. The boys had been hunting for us for an hour. They went to the village and enquired for us, but the Mexicans had not seen us.

After [that] things quieted down. After dark we took the boys back [and] crawled through the adoby wall and with canteens and kettles [we] cleaned the old sinners cellar dry.

The next morning our officer noticed something unusual with the boys. We made it all right with him by giving him a canteen of Nectar for the gods, or sangre christe.

The next d[ay] came to Albuekirke. From thence to Sante Fe and recruited a few days and started [on] the first of December to the Pueble [Pueblo] wheare the other detachment was orderd. We went by way of Taos, eighty miles north of Sante Fe along the back bone of the Rocky Mountain. There was no waggon road. We were furnished [with] a few pack animals and we had to pack the ballance on our backs in the beginning of winter and with one blanket apeice and snow several inches deep. Travled over the snow and tried to sleep on it at night. We sufferd with the cold. We managed to get in deserted Mexican houses at night, but they were stocked with gray backs or body lice. So there was no rest until our journeys end.

Come to Taos, a Mexican town.[63] Here they raise the famous wheat, the finest in the world.[64] An Englishman has several mills here and a large Distillery. He was killed in the Mexican rebellion a short

---

62. Plimsoll marks were lines on a ship's hull showing the level to which it could be legally loaded, and were named after Samuel Plimsoll (1824–1898), who proposed the Shipping Act of 1876, the British legislation that regulated the loading of merchant vessels.

63. Hernando de Alvarado discovered the Pueblo Indian village at Taos in 1540, and the first Spanish church was built in 1617. In 1680, Taos was the center of a successful Indian revolt that temporarily drove the Spanish from New Mexico. In Taos, on 19 January 1847, Thomas Ortiz and Daniel Archuleta led an attack that killed American Governor Charles Bent.

64. The sick detachment brought to the Salt Lake Valley "the variety of wheat known as 'taos,' which, mixed with the club-head, became for many years the staple wheat sown in Utah fields." Roberts, *The Mormon Battalion*, 63.

time afterwards.[65] Here we lef[t] two sick soldiers and they were killed also.[66]

Concluded to rest a day or two for we were complet[ely] tired out. We had been on short rations for several days and eat a turkey buzard for dinner. I went to some Mexican houses a short distance off. Went over to buy something to eat. There [were] ten or a dozen men and women standing around. An old slut ran out with three or four pups and [they] tried to grab my heels. I turned around and steck my bayonet in her side and she ran back in the house.

Then I tried my Spanish lingo on them and asked for what I wanted. They one and all bursted out laughing. I laught too. I thought I had made a mistake and tried it again, with no more success than before and they laught louder and longer than at first. I thought there was something wrong with my Spanish and leaned on my musket and began to get mad through to the bone. And felt like cleaning out the whole bastard band of them and gave up trying my Spanish [on] the degenerate wretches and motioned to the woman of the house with my hand for something to eat. She noded with her head and went back in the house whear the dogs were and brought out a kind of dirty pot with some goat meat mixed with some other villian[ou]s compound. She set it down and gave me a horned spoon with both ends open. Put my hand over one end and left the other open to run out in my mouth and soon scoupt enough to sattisfy my craving appetite. Come to some dark grounds in the bottom of the dish when my gastric juices failed me. The mixture warmed me down in my boots. Next asked for some bread, but she was attracted by some nice braid I had on my coat collar. Made a bargain. She had a dangerous looking knife to cut the brade with and commenced cutting close to my ears. I took off my coat [for I] was afraid she would make a mis lick on my jugler vein. She took off the braid and stuck it away and would not let the others see it.

[I] went in after the bread and there was a women turning some thin batter on a hot slab of rock on a slant of about twenty degrees. The

---

[65.] Rebels attacked Simeon Turley's mill and distillery at Arroyo Hondo, twelve miles north of Taos, on 21 January 1847. Turley fought for two days and lost six men before being burned out. Turley escaped, but he was betrayed by an old friend and shot. John Albert carried the word of the fight to Fort Pueblo, "which threw the fierce mountaineers into a perfect frenzy." Two other men escaped and alerted American forces in Santa Fe. Turley was a Kentuckian but had "one or two Englishmen" with him at the time of the attack; Blackburn probably confused him with Theodore Turley, an English San Bernardino pioneer.

[66.] No battalion men are known to have been killed in the Taos Rebellion. However, one of the men left at the mill, William Coleman, later died of exposure, although Joseph Skeen reported "the Spaniards murdered him and took his clothes."

batter would run off at the lower end into a vessel. She had a hot fire under the slab. She would pour the batter on with a kind of dipper. After it ran off there was left a thin seale, thin as paper. This layer was taken off and another pourd on. After she worked a half hour she had a roll one half inch thick. Then it was rolled up and cut in strips to suit. I do not know what the batter was made of. It looked like goats milk [and] flour or any good thing that was handy.

One of my messmates come onto the scene of action and he asked the question that I did and the Mexicans had another harty laugh and I joined with them and laught too and that suited them. My messmate was mad as a hornet. Sais he, "Have you turned traitor too and turned in with those darned hounds to laugh at me?" I explained to him that we had been speaking vulgar language. So that sattisfied him. We then joined with the Mexicans and had a jolly laugh. We both concluded to let some others do the talking in the future and let our Spanish rest awhile. So we left the Mexican house after haveing a good jolly time. I felt sorry for the Pups. I think I eat their dinner up.

A few days more on the snow and we crost the mountains and decended out of the cold into the valley of the Arkansas. Built a fire and burnt our underclothes with the vermine. In two days more [we] arived at the Pueblo, our winters quarters.[67] This place is a great rendevouse for trappers, trader[s], mountaineers and Indians, Mexicans, and Americans, the lofty Pikes Peak in view and crowned with perpetual snow. [It was] a paridise for hunters with all kinds of game in abun[dan]ce. There [were] several old trappers living here, [including] James Watters, Liew Mires, John Brown, Rube Herron, Kit Carson, and several others.[68]

[67.] John Steele, like James Scott, stated that Willis's detachment arrived at Pueblo on December 21. See John Steele, "Extracts," 14.

[68.] Historian LeRoy R. Hafen identified mountain man Lewis B. Myers as the model for La Bonte, hero of Ruxton's *Life in the Far West*. Like Blackburn, Myers was a native of Bedford County, Pennsylvania, born on 26 October 1812. Myers guided the advance party of the sick detachment to its rendezvous with Brigham Young at Fort Laramie. Myers "joined in with" the Mormons and was the first to explore Utah Valley. In 1848, Myers settled briefly in what would become Ogden, Utah. He was one of the first men to reach California in 1849, where he set up a canvas restaurant in El Dorado County and opened a store. Myers eventually bought the Chimney Rock ranch, where he lived until his death in 1893.

Christopher Carson was born 24 December 1809 in Kentucky and grew up on the frontier. At sixteen, he escaped an apprenticeship and ran away to New Mexico. Carson trapped throughout the Rocky Mountains and first achieved fame as a scout for John C. Frémont. He married into a New Mexican family, settled in Taos, and converted to Catholicism. Carson and Navy Lieutenant Edward Beale left California with government dispatches on 25 February 1847, arriving in Taos sometime in mid-April. His party encountered George Ruxton on 6 May, at the mouth of the Purgatoire River. It is unlikely that Carson met Blackburn in Pueblo.

This place was surrounded with wild Indian tribes, the Utas, Arappihoes, Aricahoes, Crows, Syoux, Chamanches, Pawnees, and others. There was about twenty American familys and about one hundred and fifty soldiers wintering here. Which made it appear home like.[69]

Wild Indians on the war path was [a] com[m]on sight going to fight their neighbors. Some time in the winter a war party of Arrappahoes campt. On their way to fight the Utas, [they were] tall, fine appearin[g] wariors armed and equipt for the fray, drest in fighting custom and painted to look like old Nick. They said they were agoing to mash the Utas. In about two weeks they come sneaking back. They had found more Utas than they wanted and had lost most of their wariers.

We put the winter in here in fine stile [with] all the game we wanted. With a dance ocasionly with the seneretoes. There was no nice floors to dance on but we made the gravel fly.[70]

There was here the notorious Tom Williams who made his brag that he had stolen [everything] from a hen on her [roost] to a steamboat engine. He crost the mountain to Taos and stole a band of horses and sold them to the emegrants.[71]

---

[69]. The Mormons who wintered at Fort Pueblo included a group of southern converts known as the "Mississippi Saints," who had emigrated in 1846 from Monroe County via Independence, Missouri. When they reached Chimney Rock on 6 July, east-bound trappers informed them that there were no Mormons on the road ahead. The company turned south to winter on the headwaters of the Arkansas.

[70]. At Council Bluffs on 18 July, Brigham Young met with the departing battalion officers and counseled, "Let the officers regulate all the dances. If you come home and can say the officers have managed all the dancing, etc., it will all be right; to dance with the world cannot be admitted." Golder, *Journal of Henry Standage*, 129. Ruxton commented on the Mormon dances: "Dancing and preaching go hand in hand in Mormon doctrine, and the 'temple' was generally cleared for a hop two or three times a week, a couple of fiddlers doing the duty of orchestra." After an introductory sermon by Captain James Brown, whom Ruxton said preached on polygamy, "Brother Dowdle" [Porter Dowdle, president of the Mississippi Saints] admonished the Saints "that dancing was solemn like, to be done with the proper devotion, and not with laughing and talking, of which he hoped to hear little or none; that joy was to be in their hearts, and not on their lips; that they danced for the glory of the Lord, and not for their own amusement, as did the Gentiles." See Ruxton, *Life in the Far West*, 204–5.

[71]. Thomas Stephen Williams, 2d Sergeant in Company D, was born on 2 January 1826 in Tennessee. Dale Morgan noted: "This horse stealing episode doubtless occurred early in 1847. It appears that some of the mountain men who wintered at Pueblo this winter, notably Tom Goodale, made off with a lot of Mormon horses (some of these very horses?). In the spring, Williams and a dozen others followed them, but before catching up with them, ran into Brigham Young's company. Although the combined Mormon company caught up with Goodale at Fort Bridger, Young would not let Williams start any trouble, but instead sent him back to guide the rest of the Battalion. [Mormon promoter] Sam Brannan went with him." Blackburn would engage in a trading expedition in the fall of 1847 with Williams, who later became a prominent lawyer and merchant in Salt Lake City.

[With] the mountaineers, Mexicans, Americans, and soldiers, Indians, trappers, [and] explorers it was an interesting scenery all the time. Spring come at last. The soldiers were ordered to California by way of the South Pass of the Rocky Mountain.

FOUR

A Home in the
Far West

The sick detachment spent a bitter winter at Fort Pueblo, haunted
by at least six deaths and racked by contention with its inept
and quarreling commanders. One remarkable characteristic of
Blackburn's battalion memoir is its good humor and positive tone;
many battalion journals and reminiscences are litanies of complaint.
For example, Joseph Skeen did not enjoy his winter in "Purbelow":

> We remained at Purbelow from the 21 of december till the 24
> of May and many things hapened while we lay at perbelow that
> is too mean to mention . . . [A soldier] Dare not open his
> mouth not even to ask for his rashens which the officers would
> steel from us. they would take every thing off the soldiers that
> they could and then curce them be cause they could not get
> more. thare is captain [Brown—crossed out] as big a raskel as
> ever graced the soil of purbelow. he took some of the cattle that
> belonged to the government and put his own brand on them
> and many things he done that the Devil is A shamed of. he left
> a stink behind him when he left purbelow. lutenent willis goes
> hand and hand with [Captain James] brown in every thing that
> he does.[1]

Brown would have disagreed with Skeen's contention that Willis
was an obedient subordinate, because when he compiled a short his-

---

[1] Joseph Skeen, Diary, LDS Archives. Skeen's friend George Deliverance Wilson
got in trouble for writing a poem critical of the officers, in which he said it was the
ambition of "Old Blaso" to be an "Ass wiper in eternity." See George Deliverance Wilson, Journal, Utah State Historical Society, 18. John Steele reported that W. W. Willis
called the poem "a perfect masterpiece."

tory of the detachment for LDS church historian George A. Smith in 1859, he wrote that Willis "had his orders from Colonel Price to report to me at Pueblo, but refused to do so, and went on his own hook."[2]

The sick detachment had orders to proceed to California in the spring, though technically Upper California at that time included almost everything west and south of present-day Wyoming.[3] In late spring, James Brown dispatched seventeen men, including Lewis B. Myers, to Fort Laramie. On 24 May 1847 Brown led the remaining Mormons, including many of the Mississippi Saints, north to the Platte River road to rendezvous with Brigham Young.

In Nebraska, the lead wagons of the Camp of Israel left the Elkhorn River on 17 April, consisting of "148 persons, 72 wagons, 93 horses, 52 mules, 66 oxen, 19 cows, 17 dogs and an unspecified number of chickens."[4] Under the command of Brigham Young, the company was the vanguard of an immense wagon and handcart emigration that would continue even after the completion of the transcontinental railroad in 1869. Highly organized and tightly disciplined, the Mormon trains were notably more efficient and successful than their non-Mormon (or "gentile") counterparts. The emigration was deliberately staged, so that the first pioneers who arrived in the Salt Lake Valley could put in a crop for those following in the larger emigration of 1848.

Brigham Young had made up his mind to settle in the Great Basin, and on 6 June he wrote to Samuel Brannan, "The camp will not go to the west coast or to your place at present; we have not the means."[5] He kept his options open as to the particular place, listening to descriptions of the valleys of Utah from veteran trappers Moses "Black" Harris and Jim Bridger.

While camped on the Green River, the pioneers encountered the remarkable Elder Samuel Brannan, who had led a group of Saints around Cape Horn in the ship *Brooklyn* to the village of Yerba Buena in

---

[2] Journal History, 29 July 1847. John Steele noted that, on 17 January, "Captain Brown made quite a speech to us on parade. He soft-soaped as much as he was able." The captain speculated on his future. "'I shall be a Colonel then and I will help the poor with the pay that I shall get. . . .' I think he is very much troubled with the big head." John Steele, Journal, LDS Archives.

[3] John Steele noted: "April 9th. This time the officers returned from Santa Fe bringing us word that there was no one there that had power to discharge us or to give us any orders to leave until Colonel Cairney returns from California . . . the boys are getting themselves drunk as fools." Ibid.

[4] Morgan, *The Great Salt Lake*, 189.

[5] In the Journal History, Andrew Jenson noted that this letter was never sent. Several historians have assumed that it was, but Brannan wrote a letter from Fort Hall, on 18 June 1847, which said nothing about hearing from Young. See *The Millennial Star*, 15 October 1847.

1846.[6] Horace Whitney's journal described the encounter:

> During this afternoon we were all much surprised by the unex-
> pected arrival of Elder Samuel Brannan who was at the head of
> the company of the brethren that went round by sea last year
> from New York city to California—He was accompanied by 3
> men, 2 of whom had come thro' with him from the latter coun-
> try—with 1 of them I was well acquainted. This man is
> [Charles C.] Smith & is I believe some distant relation of our
> prophet Joseph. He left Nauvoo (where I made his acquain-
> tance) some 2 years since for Oregon. One of the other 2 men
> was one of the individuals seen with Mr. Bridger the other
> day—the other man I did not know. Elder Brannan gives a very
> favorable account of climate, soil, etc. of California & appears
> quite anxious that we should immediately go there to take pos-
> session of the country before it becomes occupied by others.
> He had left Yerba Buena April 13th—This place is situated on
> the bay of San Francisco & from all accounts bids fair to be-
> come in time a flourishing city. He brought a number of news
> papers with him which he distributed among the "Twelve"—
> among these was a file of his own entitled the "California Star"
> 12 all in number. Mr Smith informed us that in Oregon they
> had 2 seasons, rust & dry.[7]

Brannan brought the first news of the fate of the Donner party and
reported that the main body of the battalion was quartered at Pueblo de
los Angeles, "quite destitute as to clothing and shoes" and "their animals
nearly all worn out."[8] Brannan, who had established a farming colony at
New Hope in the Central Valley, had his heart set on leading the Mormons to California. On 3 July, Brigham Young noted that the Mormon
colony at New Hope had "150 acres of wheat growing, besides potatoes,
etc., etc., expecting us to help eat it, but our destination is the Great
Basin, or Salt Lake for the present at least, to examine the country."[9]

On the Fourth of July, the rear guard of the pioneer company met
thirteen of the "Battalion boys" under Thomas S. Williams, hot on the
trail of horse thieves. Brigham Young personally led the Hosannahs.
The Council of the Twelve almost immediately decided that "in as

6. Hansen, "Voyage of the *Brooklyn*."
7. Horace Kimball Whitney, Journal, LDS Archives.
8. Thomas Bullock, Journals, LDS Archives.
9. Journal History, 3 July 1847.

much as they have neither received their discharge nor their full pay,
Bro. Brannan should tender his services as pilot to conduct them to
California."[10] The next day Brannan, Sergeant Williams, "and a few others" set out from Fort Bridger "to travel east towards the South pass to
meet the sick detachment of the Mormon Battalion."[11]

Abner Blackburn was marching with the Pueblo party—a substantial wagon train in its own right—as they followed the pioneer vanguard. Blackburn gave a colorful description of the trapper's trail from
Pueblo to Fort Laramie and what he called "the California road"—more
popularly known at the time as the Oregon Trail. The sick detachment
crossed the South Platte on 5 June, and six days later at Pole Creek, they
met the remarkable preacher Apostle Amasa Lyman. Lyman—whose
party had lost the trail and subsisted on pelican and antelope—carried
letters from families at Winter Quarters, counsel from Brigham Young,
and "news of the travels and probable destination of the Church."[12]

The detachment, after a march dogged by rain and hailstorms,
camped at Fort Laramie on 16 June, twelve days behind Brigham
Young's pioneers. Following the south bank of the North Platte, the
company traversed the "dreary Black Hills" (actually the Laramie Range
of central Wyoming) and, on 29 June, ferried the North Platte River
near present Casper, Wyoming.[13] On the twelfth the detachment
crossed the Sweetwater, where they found "an old Indian squaw about
120 years of age left by her tribe to die."[14] Blackburn described Independence Rock and Devil's Gate, famous landmarks on the Sweetwater.
Next, the party began the long ascent of the backbone of the continent,
crossing the continental divide at South Pass. The battalion's enlistment
expired on 16 July, and on the Big Sandy River, "at daylight there was a
salute of small arms in honor of our enlistment and more especially the
finishing of our one year's service to Uncle Sam, and to let every one of
Uncle Sam's officers know we were our own men once more. We still
kept up our organization, and respected the command as usual, and
was rather better than some had been before."[15]

---

[10] Roberts, *History of the Church*, 3:204.

[11] Jenson, "Day by Day," *Salt Lake Tribune*, 9 July 1947.

[12] Tyler, *A Concise History of the Mormon Battalion*, 198.

[13] Thomas Grover forwarded a letter to Brigham Young with Lyman and Brown,
noting, "We have just finished ferrying Capt. Brown and company consisting of 19
wagons, four extra loads, three dollars per trip, and also 150 men and women." Morgan, "Mormon Ferry on the North Platte," 156, noted the adherence of the Mormon
ferry to "a long-established American practice, of soaking the government twice as
much as a private individual for services rendered."

[14] Steele, "Extracts," 16.

[15] Ibid.

The Mormon leaders had pondered the problem of securing the detachment's discharge from the army. On 8 July, they sent a letter from Fort Bridger to Apostle Lyman with their solution:

> We understand that the troops have not provisions sufficient to go to the western coast, and their time of enlistment will expire about the time they get to our place; they will draw their pay until duly discharged, if they continue to obey council; and there is no officer short of California, who is authorized to discharge them; therefore, when you come up with us, Capt. Brown can quarter his troops in our beautiful city, which we are about to build, either on parole, detached service, or some other important business, and we can have a good visit with them, while Capt. Brown with an escort of 15 or 20 mounted men and Elder Brannan for pilot, may gallop over to the headquarters, get his pay, rations and discharge and learn the geography of the country. If Captain Brown approves these suggestions and will signify the same to Brother Brannan, so that he [Brannan] can discharge his men and remain in camp; otherwise he is anxious to go on his way.[16]

After crossing Green River, the detachment proceeded to Fort Bridger. Horace Whitney, traveling with Brigham Young's party, was not impressed by the fort: "This is not a regular fort as I at first supposed but consists of 2 log houses where the inhabitants live & also do their trading. Adjacent to these and about a mile back is a number of lodges made of skins—these belong to the Snake Indians."[17] Captain Brown had gone ahead of the main party with several men. John Steele described their encounter with Jim Bridger: "Captain Brown invited me to go ahead with him to Fort Bridger. We found the old mountaineer and in conversation he told us we could not live in Salt Lake valley for it froze every month in the year and [he] would give us a thousand dollars for the first ear of corn raised-there, but if we would give him $1000 he would take us to the G-d-d best valley ever was. I spoke to Captain Brown if it was a G-d-d valley we did not want to go there."[18]

[16.] Journal History, 8 July 1847. This same letter ended, "Brother Brannan wishes to borrow fifty dollars in money from some one, and we say unto those who are able, lend it to him." Brannan probably wanted to pay off Charles Smith (and possibly Isaac Goodwin), who returned to Sutter's Fort without entering the Salt Lake Valley. Battalion veteran Robert Bliss noted, on 24 August in northern California, that they had reports from men who "have seen two men who went with Bro. Brannan to relieve the church." See Alter, "The Journal of Robert S. Bliss," 118.

[17.] Horace Whitney, Journal, LDS Archives.

[18.] Steele, "Extracts," 17.

From Fort Bridger, the trail made a difficult crossing of the Wasatch Mountains through Echo, East, and Emigration canyons. On 29 July, the sick detachment marched into the Salt Lake Valley to a considerable welcome. An official history reported that the "Battalion company were caught in a storm in Emigration Canon and the water rose up to their wagon beds. They had designed to proceed to the bay of San Francisco, but, many of their wagons being broken and their teams failing, they were under the necessity of waiting for further orders."[19]

On 28 July, the pioneers had unanimously voted to "locate in this valley for the present, and lay out a city at this place."[20] The Mormons immediately began building their new Zion, digging irrigation canals and plowing fields. On the evening of the detachment's arrival, "a general meeting of the camps was held," and Brigham Young preached that "the brethren of the Battalion had been the means of saving the Saints from destruction."[21] The meeting opened with hosannahs and closed with a request that the battalion build a "Bowery" from poles and boughs to provide a meeting place on the site of the temple block. Some of the men were sent to locate timber in the canyons feeding into the valley. On 1 August, at an afternoon meeting in the newly built Bowery, battalion members joined Sam Brannan in advocating that the Mormons build adobe (rather than log) houses in their new home.

On 3 August, "Orson Pratt and H. G. Sherwood surveyed a base line and commenced to survey the Temple Block." By the eleventh, the survey had run fifteen blocks north and south and nine blocks east and west.[22]

---

[19]. Knecht, *History of Brigham Young*, 5–6. Since the Council of Twelve had already determined on 8 July not to send most of the detachment to California, they appear to have seized upon the flood as a justification for their commonsense decision. Rather than remain "waiting for orders," many battalion men returned to Winter Quarters to join their families.

[20]. Egan, *Pioneering the West*, 111.

[21]. Howard Egan wrote that Young preached that the government "made a demand for five hundred men, that they might have women and children suffer, and, if we had not complied with the requisition, they would have treated us like enemies and the next move would have been to have let Missouri and the adjoining states loose on us, and wipe us from the face of the earth. This is what they have in contemplation, and your going into the army has saved the lives of thousands of people."

[22]. Knecht, *History of Brigham Young*, 7, 8. Blackburn's obituary in the San Bernardino *Times-Index* reported that "when Pioneer Fred T. Perris laid out the city of Salt Lake Mr. Blackburn carried the chain for that eminent surveyor." Perris was a prominent surveyor and railroad engineer in San Bernardino, but he did not arrive in the United States until 1853. Perris was an associate of Elder Sherwood, who would be elected San Bernardino County surveyor in 1852, and the obituaries may preserve a mangled remembrance of Blackburn's participation in the initial survey of Great Salt Lake City, though Blackburn did not mention it in his memoirs.

On Saturday, 7 August, the pioneers dammed City Creek and, in the evening, performed baptisms. The next day, despite considerable rain, "the ordinance of baptism was recommended and all who felt disposed were invited to come forward and receive the ordinance, which they did in great numbers."[23] Abner Blackburn was baptized by Tarleton Lewis, a veteran of the Haun's Mill Massacre and the father of Samuel Lewis, who would accompany Blackburn on his return to Utah that fall. Apostle Wilford Woodruff, who became president of the Mormon church in 1887, confirmed Blackburn.[24]

On 9 August, Brigham Young dispatched Brown to Monterey to get the battalion's pay and carry messages and mail to the Mormons in California. Brown took with him the muster rolls for the detachment.[25]

Dale Morgan noted, "There is some uncertainty about the number of men who went with Brown to California." Young's manuscript history recorded, "A number of men were sent on various expeditions—Samuel Brannan and J. S. Fowler to San Francisco; Jesse C. Little, Jos. Matthews, James [John] Brown, and J. Buchanan to go with them to Bear River and explore the [Cache] valley; Ebenezer Hanks, Thomas Williams, and Edward Dalton to Fort Hall for provisions for the Battalion men; James Brown, Jesse S. Brown, Wm. Squires, William Gribble, Lysander Woodworth, Gilbert Hunt, and ——— Blackburn to California to get discharges for the Battalion men."[26]

Historian Edward Tullidge, using an account derived from James Brown's son Jesse, wrote, "The company that left the valley for San Francisco consisted of Captain Brown and nine others—namely, 'Sam' Brannan, Gilbert Hunt, John Fowler, Abner Blackburn, William Gribble, Lisander [sic] Woodworth, Henry Frank, and Jesse S. Brown.[27] Norton Jacob recorded that Brown, Brannan, "and eight of the brethren" started the trip.[28] Howard Egan's diary reported, "Captain Brown, Samuel Brannan, William H. Squires and some others started this morning on pack horses for California."[29]

---

23. Egan, *Pioneering the West*, 116.

24. "Records of Members 1836–1970," LDS Archives. This ledger also lists baptisms or rebaptisms of Samuel Brannan, J. S. Fowler, Lysander Woodworth, and James and Jesse Brown.

25. These muster rolls, which include two Abner Blackburn signatures, are preserved in the LDS Archives. For a James Brown letter written shortly before his departure for California, see Appendix C.

26. Knecht, *History of Brigham Young*, 7.

27. Tullidge, *Histories of Utah*, 4. Note that Tullidge's list of "nine others" consists of only eight names.

28. Jacob, *Norton Jacob*, 77.

29. Egan, *Pioneering the West*, 119.

Blackburn stated that Brown "selected five soldiers and I was one of them. Brannan and two others went with us," for a total—counting Brown—of nine men. Blackburn appears to have miscounted the number of soldiers, since Hunt, Woodworth, Gribble, Jesse Brown, Blackburn, and Squires were all battalion soldiers. John S. Fowler was the husband of Jerusha Fowler, a *Brooklyn* pilgrim who had taken the couple's four children around Cape Horn; one child died on the journey. Henry Frank's widow unsuccessfully applied for a pension based on service in the battalion, but he does not appear in any Mormon records of the emigration or of the battalion and his inclusion in the party is almost certainly a mistake. The confirmed members of the party are James Brown, Sam Brannan, John S. Fowler, William Gribble, William H. Squires, Gilbert Hunt, Jesse Brown, Lysander Woodworth, and Abner Blackburn.

Leaving the Salt Lake Valley on 9 August, the party arrived at Fort Hall, a Hudson's Bay Company trading post, about 16 August.[30] They purchased supplies from Chief Trader Richard Grant, a famous patron of overland emigrants. Robert Bliss, traveling with battalion veterans from California, noted on 14 October 1847, "Arrived at Fort Hall visited Capt Grant of the Establishment. . . . Grant read his remarks on our people who had passed him this fall, as recorded in his Journal; He says they were gentlement payed for all they got of him & he heard no Oath or vulgar expression from any of them but he could not say so in regard to Other people who had passed him this season; He is a Gentleman of Inteligence & Observation."[31] Dale Morgan noted, "If this journal is ever turned up, in the archives of the Hudson's Bay Company or elsewhere, we may derive a few more details about this expedition to California."[32]

Grant provided the Mormons with a French-Canadian guide—one more insult to Samuel Brannan, who had been designated as pilot for the trip. Brannan and Brown, as Blackburn noted, "could not agree on

---

[30.] Dale Morgan noted, "At this season it was about seven days' travel from Salt Lake Valley to Fort Hall."

[31.] Alter, "The Journal of Robert S. Bliss," 125. Former Hudson's Bay Company officer John McLoughlin received a less complimentary report about the Mormons. McLoughlin wrote from Oregon on 10 October 1847 to Nathaniel Wyeth: "It is said that the Mormons have begun a settlement in the Vicinity of Bear River on a Rich tract of Country and I understand that they are Disagreeable Neighbors." Sampson, *John McLoughlin*, 58–59.

[32.] Despite the reference to Grant's journal in the Bliss diary, the Hudson's Bay Company Archives in the Provincial Archives of Manitoba has no record of such a document. It may survive in private hands. Archivist Virginia Petch states, "Unfortunately, few documents relating to the Hudson's Bay Company post of Fort Hall have survived" in the HBC Archives. Correspondence with editor, 9 December 1991.

any subject." From Fort Hall, the party descended the Snake River to American Falls and turned south at the Raft River, where the Oregon and California trails diverged. In the Goose Creek Mountains, the company encountered Commodore Robert F. Stockton and his entourage, "orderd to Washington to settle the quarrel between Kerney, Frémont and Stockton," a quarrel that historian H. H. Bancroft called "a comedy of errors." As senior officer of the Pacific Fleet, Stockton had assumed military command in California and appointed Frémont governor in January 1847. When General Kearny arrived in California, carrying official orders to assume military command and establish a civil government, Frémont refused to submit to his superior's orders. Kearny ordered Frémont home, and their pack trains (which maintained separate camps) had come east on the Humboldt trail some weeks before Brown's party came down it. Frémont was eventually court-martialed, convicted, and pardoned, and then resigned from the army.

Stockton's men had encountered hostile Indians, and the commodore was wounded in the leg, but recovered enough by the time he reached the plains to kill forty-five buffalo.[33] H. H. Bancroft and biographers Dale Morgan and Charles Kelly identified "the old trapper" who guided Stockton as Caleb Greenwood, the first to lead a wagon party to California and certainly the "oldest trapper in the mountains" at an age of over four-score years.

In Thousand Springs Valley, the party had its first encounter with hostile Indians—the first of many for Blackburn. To break up the monotony of the trip, Captain Brown asked the party's guide to relate his life story to the company. Lou Devon proceeded to tell a long tale that provides a unique picture of the American Indian.

THE NARRATIVE

20 OF APRIL 1847

Started for Ft. Larime to strike the California road.[34] Crost over to the South Platt [and] pased the old St. Vrain Station.[35] From thence to

---

[33.] For a colorful account of the fight, see Anonymous, *A Sketch of the Life of Com. Robert F. Stockton*, 161.

[34.] Blackburn's 20 April date for the departure of the sick detachment from Pueblo is incorrect. Joseph Skeen, James Brown, John Steele, and Daniel Tyler all gave the date as 24 May.

[35.] Established by Bent, St. Vrain and Company in 1838 and named after Ceran St. Vrain, Fort St. Vrain was located on the South Platte River near modern Johnstown, Colorado.

the Cash Lapood and on to Ft. Larime.[36] Here we fell in company with
Brigham Youngs Pioneers going to lookout a place for the Saints to
make a Home in the far west and we journeyed on with them.[37] Passed
through the Black Hills [and] crost the North Platt. And come to the
Sweet Watter River [and] camped at Independence Rock, a huge mass
of granite which covers several acers of ground with hundreds of names
marked on its huge sides. A short distance above here is the Devils
Gate. Once upon a time the river cut through this mountain and cleft a
chasm several hundred feet deep. It looked as though one could step
across on top. If there was anny difference in width, the bottom was the
widest. Some of our party were afraid to goe through the gate for fear
the[y] might land in the bad place.

We went arround the gate, over a ridge and come in[to] a most
beautyful valley carpeted with green grass and herds of buffalow [and]
a few Elk and some Deer grazing on its rich meadows. The Sweetwatter
River rippeled along in its course from the lofty sumit of Fremonts
Peaks [in] the Rocky Mountains. There was a low mountain running
paralel with the river. The mountain was granite and not a particle of
vegetation growing on it and not a dust of earth on it. The like I never
seen before. They must have run short of material when it was con-
tracted for. All the companyes lay over to rest a few days in this lovely
place [with] the hunters after game and sight seers on the mountains.
Continued our journey up this stream with a gradual asscent untill we
reached the summit or the South Pass.[38]

There was a coupple of young folks in the company spooning and
licking each other ever since we started on the road. The whole company were tired of it and they were persuaded to marry now and have
done with it and not wait until their journeys end. The next evening we
had a wedding and a reg[u]lar minister to unite them and after come
the supper with the best the plains could furnish. Then came the dance

---

36. The Cache la Poudre River (noted by John Steele as "Cashley Pond, named by
some Frenchmen that hid some powder") enters the South Platte at present-day Gree-
ley, Colorado. From here the detachment cut north to the Chugwater River, which it
followed to its confluence with the Laramie. There were three posts called Fort
Laramie. On 31 May 1834, William Sublette and William Marshall Anderson established Fort William. In 1841, an adobe fort replaced the stockade and served as an
outpost of the American Fur Company. It was renamed Fort John for John Sarpy, but
most emigrants called it Fort Laramie, the name officially adopted for the military
post that was established in 1849.

37. Since Blackburn was with the sick detachment, he could not have met Brigham Young's company.

38. A party east-bound from the Columbia River under Robert Stuart discovered
South Pass in October 1812. Jedediah Smith rediscovered the pass in 1824. Its gradual ascent of the continental divide made overland wagon travel possible.

or howe down. The banjo and the violin made us forget the hardships of the plains.[39]

The next day was the Holy Sabbath. Some were in the shade reading novels [and] another the bible, some mending clothes, others shoeing cattle and a number in a tent playing the violin. By and by a runner come around to notify the company that our minister was a going [to] observe the sabbath and preach a sermon. All hands quit work and the fiddle stopt playing. They went into [a] tent to play cards. A few took their guns and went hunting and a few heard the sermon.[40] Such is life on the plains.

This is a beautiful country with a most invigorating climate [and] good feed for the tired animals and nearly all kinds of wild game. Finally we arrived at the pass. Here the watters divide. We will follow down the Pacific slope from here on. Campt at the Pacific Springs. The next stream was the Little Sandy. Crost it and camped on Big Sandy River. Next day come to the Green River, the prettyest stream in the west. It rises in the Wind River Mountains and is the longest branch of the Collorado River.

Next day campt on Hams Fork, then to Blacks Fork [and] from the[re] to Ft. Bridger. Old Jim Bridger and his trappers gave us a hearty welcome to our company. He is the oldest trapper in the mountains and can tell some wonderful stories.[41] Crost over to a stream called Mudy [Muddy Creek] and from thence to Bear River and campd. Crosed to Echo Canion, that celebrated place whear every noise makes an echo. The boys made all the noise they could going through. It was truely wonderful.

[39.] Martha Jane Sargent Sharp, widow of battalion casualty Norman Sharp, married Harley Mowery on 4 July 1847, on the trail with the sick detachment to the Salt Lake Valley. See Carter, *Our Pioneer Heritage*, 4:442. In 1847, however, 4 July was a Sunday.

[40.] John Steele described one of Amasa Lyman's sermons: "Sunday 13th [June]. This day had Elder Amas E. to preach. He said to leave off our card playing and profain swearing and return to God, and a great many other things. He said we were not as bad as he expected to find us. Captain B . . n then got up and made an acknowledgement and said that he had just played one game and how he had kept public worship and preaching twice a week." On 20 June, Steele wrote, "Amas E. Lyman preached and said he had watched us and to leave off our folly and be men of God." John Steele, Journal, LDS Archives.

[41.] James Bridger is said to have been born on 17 March 1804 in Richmond, Virginia, and was orphaned by age thirteen. He left for the Rocky Mountains in 1822 with the first Ashley-Henry trapping expedition. He became "the most celebrated trapper of the Rocky mts" and is credited with the discovery of the Great Salt Lake by a white man. Three men accompanied Bridger when he met the Mormons near Green River, on 28 June 1847. One man was sent back to Fort Bridger, perhaps to carry word of the emigrants, and on 30 June, guided Sam Brannan and two companions into the Mormon camp. At forty-two, "Old Gabe" was certainly not the oldest trapper in the mountains. Bridger came into conflict with the Mormons and abandoned the fort in 1853. After a successful career as a guide, Bridger died in Westport, Missouri, on 17 July 1881. The Blackburn manuscript had a picture of Bridger on its cover.

Camped on Weaver [Weber] River.[42] Here we layed by to work the road ahead of us over the mountains to Salt Lak[e] Valley. The next camp [was] Emegrant [Emigration] Canion. The dust was deep and black [and] all hands looked like negros. Stayed here one day to finish the road ahead.

Three of us soldiers undertook to climb a high mountain in sight of the camp to take a view of the surrounding country. [We] went up until nearly exausted and kept going until the top was reached. We would not have undertaken the job if we [had] known the dificulties to be surmounted. Passed the timber line far enough [and] landed on the sumit [of] the highest peak in sight. [It was] the grandest view that ever mortal beheld. The air was clear and perfect for a good view—the Great Salt Lake glittering under the suns rays, range after range of mountains in every direction, the great desert to the west and Utah Lake to the south east and the mountains beyond. A more sublime view was seldom seen from a mountain top.

There were some verry large granite bolders on top which would weigh several tons. We dug and pried them loose. Started them down the mountain. They sped through the air. Some split to peices and some held togeather and crashed down the mountain until they reached the timber line. They would strike the fir trees nearly to the top and goe right through them and start other rocks and make an awful avlanch. The grouse and wild animals scatterd in all directions. Rolling rocks paid us for the feterge of climbing up.

Brigham Young went ahead of us one day to examine the place the Lord shew him in a vision and sur[e] enough he found the identical land marks in his dream. They had all the wind work done before we come to the place. The 24 of July 1847 is the day they celebrate of their arivle in the valley of the Great Salt Lake.[43]

The Saints laid out plans for the city and the Temple of the Lord and commenced clearing the ground for cultivation, makeing di[t]ches for irigation and plowing up the ground to put in such vegetables that would ripen before frost. They had a buetifel location for a city here, [with] the ice cold watter coming out of canion and spreading over the fertile plains whitch appeard to be rich to the view. Brigham and his council were buisey laying plans for the future greatness of the city.

[42.] Muddy Creek feeds into Bear River, which winds as far north as Soda Springs, Idaho, before turning south to empty into the north end of the Great Salt Lake. The Weber takes a much more direct course through a steep canyon in the Wasatch Mountains to enter the lake at modern Ogden.

[43.] Blackburn provided the correct date of his arrival in the valley—29 July 1847—in his affidavit in the 1897 "The Book of Pioneers," now preserved at the Utah State Historical Society.

Some Utah Indians come into camp with some Shoshone prisioners and were loitering about camp when two prisoners mounted two horses and put out to the South towards Utah Lake. As soon as they were missed, some Utah wariers mounted their horses and started in persuit of them. In about three hours they returned with their scalps.[44]

The crikets or a kind of locust were verry plenty[ful]. Some of the bushes were loaded down with them. The squaws were geathering them for food. They would hold a basket under a bush and shake them off into the basket, then scorch them over a fire [and] then sac[k] them up for future consumption.

Samuel Brannan arrived here from California to induce Brigham to continue on his journey to the Pacific coast but failed to move him further. He had stuck his stakes here and was a going to stay.

Our Captain Brown was ordered to California on buissness for the government. He selected five soldiers and I was one of them. Brannan and two others went with us. We started the ninth of August 1847 and went by way of Ft. Hall on Snake River in the Brittish possessions.[45] We layed in our suplyes for the trip. Captain Grant commanded the fort and was [a] verry obligeing Britton.[46] He furnished us every thing necessary and also a guide, a French Canadian, a verry interesting companion for the trip. He had a beautyful Indian squaw for a wife, one of the best looking woman in the mountain[s].

[44.] The Indian Skirmish occurred on 31 July.

[45.] Nathaniel Wyeth built Fort Hall, near present-day Pocatello, Idaho, in 1834, and sold it to the Hudson's Bay Company in 1837. The company owned the fort, but after the 1846 Anglo-American treaty settling the Oregon question, it was not in English territory.

[46.] Captain Richard Grant, born 20 January 1794 of French and Scottish descent, joined the North West Company about 1815 and the Hudson's Bay Company in 1821. Hudson's Bay Company Governor George Simpson commented on Grant in his 1832 *Character Book*: "Writes a tolerable hand but deficient in Education. Can manage the affairs of a small Trading Post very well, but does not speak Indian. Is active and bustling, but not Steady, would Drink if not under constraint, speaks at random and is scampishly inclined." Beginning in 1841, Grant directed the company's Snake Country operations and was chief trader at Fort Hall for ten critical years. Popular with overland travelers, Grant encouraged emigration to California. According to one forty-niner, "The Captain himself is a most remarkable looking man. He is 6 ft., 2 or 3 inches, high, & made in proportion, with a handsome figure. His face is perfectly English, fat, round, chubby, & red. His hair is now getting in the sere & yellow leaf & his whiskers are also turning grey." Not all emigrants enjoyed their stay at Fort Hall; Chester Ingersoll, traveling a week ahead of the Brown party, wrote, "We left Fort Hall or the shaving shop on the 9th of August. It is the worst place for emigrants that we have seen,—they are almost destitute of honesty or human feelings." Grant took early retirement in 1851, due to rheumatoid arthritis, and he pioneered ranching in the Bitterroot Valley. He died at Walla Walla, Washington, on 21 June 1862.

When we started she come out to shake hand[s] with her husband and bid him good by. She saluted all of us. We will hear more of her further on. There were a great many Indians at this place trading, Blackfeet, Shoshones, Crows, Bannocks, Mandans, and other tribes.

Started down [the] Snake or Lewis river. Camped at the Great Falls.[47] The canion below the falls has an echo that is verry strange. Our guide had an Indian legend to relate about those falls.[48] A few miles further [we] come to the forks of the road [with] the right leading for Oregon [and] the left to California. We took the left. In a few miles further past the City of Rocks, a mountain of rocks in every conceiveable form representing castels, fortresses, temples, spires, and [a] few resembled Cleopatras needles.[49] And nothing to inhabit them but owles and bats with out molestation.

At Goose Creek [we] met Comodore Stockton and suite, Captain Gelespie, Peterson, and J. Parker Norris with fifty two marenes with them to keep them from harm.[50] They were orderd to Washington to settle the quarrel between Kerney, Fremont, and Stockton. They said the Trucky [Truckee] Indians attackted them at night killing some of their horses and wounding some of their men. Stockton was wounded in his [k]nee with an arrow. They cautioned us to be on our guard all the time. Our pilot said he knew dem ingen and he could slip us true.

The scenery was little varried for a few days [with] rolling hills and sage brush and mountains ever in sight [and] a few wild naked savages with no fig leaves to cover them.[51] They would come close up to us and gaup. They were fat this time of the year. There were plenty of crickets

---

[47.] The American Falls, now dammed, "tumbled spectacularly" from the lava canyon of the Snake River. See Stewart, *The California Trail*, 136.

[48.] Vardis Fisher recorded an Indian legend about nearby Shoshone Falls, in which a "slender wild girl . . . dived in a long swift arc" from the falls following the death of her "deep-chested Shoshoni buck." Devon's story was undoubtedly cut from the same cloth.

[49.] Widely noted and called Silent City of Rocks, Rock City, Pyramid Circle, City of Castles, or simply Castles in emigrant journals, this series of granite formations is located near present-day Almo, Idaho.

[50.] Commodore Robert Field Stockton began his naval career before the War of 1812. In 1846, he assumed command of the Pacific squadron and served as military governor of California until General Kearny replaced him in January 1847. J. Parker Norris was Stockton's secretary. Marine Lieutenant Archibald H. Gillespie served in the California Battalion as Frémont's adjutant, was wounded in the battles of San Pascual and San Gabriel, and provoked a revolt in Los Angeles. William H. Peterson was an assistant to General Kearny. Bancroft wrote that Stockton's company "is said to have numbered forty-nine, 'a heterogeneous collection of all nations almost, and professions and pursuits.'"

[51.] The party crossed modern Thousand Springs Valley, still a remote area with some of the best-preserved sections of the overland trail.

and other stuff to eat. Our guide sayes in the spring they are so poor the skin on thier bellies sticks to their backs.

One morning [we] started on the road [but] did not goe far before one of our men mist his canteen. He had left [it] at the watter. He started back after it. We waited for him awhile and two of our men went back to see what was the matter. They come to the top of the hill and seen [him] running his horse through and the Indians after him and shooting arrows and yelling. The horse fell dead pierced with arrows [and] our boys ran to help him. He was shot in the shoulder. The Indians ran off when they were discovered. [We] took the man on to the company, washed and dressed his wound, sucked the poison out and he felt better. Made a short days travel and stayed close togeather after that. It would not doe to seperate in this savage Indian country.

Come to the head watters of the Ogden or Maryes River.[52] We travled down this stream until we were tired of it. The scenery is not verry strikeing unles one is desirous to be struck. It appeared like some fervent heat had taken the life out of it. Brannan and Cap Brown could not agree on anny subject. Brannan thought he knew it all and Brown thought he knew his share of it. They felt snuffy at each other and kept apart.

Over took a company of emegrants. They had trouble with the Indians. They ran off a lot of their cattle. The emegrants persued them and recovered all except two which the Indians killed to eat.[53]

[52.] Peter Skene Ogden originally named this the Unknown River, but trappers and emigrants called it Ogden River and Mary's River. Frémont renamed the river in honor of German scientist and explorer Alexander Humboldt, who never laid eyes on it.

[53.] The 1847 California emigration consisted of about ninety wagons, less than half the 1846 total, since "few cared to come to California on account of the Mexican War." Charles Hopper, "an old mountaineer," led about one hundred men, women, and children down the Humboldt, including young William A. Trubody, who would recall the trip in 1927 for Charles Camp. James Findla, with the Hopper party, remembered, "At one place on the Humboldt River, the Indians had placed large stones in the road, and we caught them engaged in that business with the design of impending [sic] the trains that came along." This party crossed the Sierra via the Truckee River and arrived in detachments at Johnson's Ranch in California between 3–9 October. Chester Ingersoll was with a party of twenty wagons that met Stockton's escort on 19 August on the road to "Hot Spring valley" (present Thousand Spring Valley), only a few days ahead of Brown. "On the dead waters of Marey's river," Ingersoll encountered Indians he called the "Shawshawnees. They have no horses, and are almost naked. This tribe will steal and kill your cattle—they will come as friends, but you must treat them as enemies, and keep them out of your camp. We treated them as friends until they stole 4 oxen, 1 cow and one horse; we followed them 20 miles into the mountain and found one ox killed, the others we could not find. After that we shot at every Indian we saw—this soon cleared the way, so that we did not see any Indians for 200 miles." Ingersoll's company arrived at Johnson's Ranch on 20 October. See McMurtrie, *Overland to California*, 37–39; Mattes, *Platte River Road Narratives*, 100, 110; and Stewart, *The California Trail*, 185–89.

Our pilots name was Lou Devon. We allwais called him Lou. He told a long story about his adventures in the Rocky Mountains and the head watters of the Misouri River and how his uncle was killed. And he was taken prisoner [and] lived with them. [How he] joined the tribe and his marriage and [how] his wife [was] taken prisoner. His persuit after her and [her] rescue [made] a verry interesting narretive. Captain Brown become verry intrested in his story and wanted [him] to relate it to the whole company at the camp fire of evnings. The narretive runs as follows.

FIVE

Lou Devon's Narrative

Of all the puzzles in the Blackburn narrative, none approaches Lou Devon's Indian romance in complexity. This play within a play is problematic: it is inserted in the manuscript, apparently as an afterthought, so that it disrupts the flow of Blackburn's personal narrative, but a close examination shows that the surviving manuscript has been carefully reconstructed to include the story. Although Devon tells the tale in the first person, the voice is unmistakably Blackburn's. Its distance from its source makes analysis doubly complex: this is another man's story remembered some fifty years after the telling, and some of the details, such as specific dates and the identification of Mandan enemies, are certainly open to question. All the problems associated with such distant reminiscences are found in the narrative, compounded by the fact that it is a secondhand retelling. Still, the yarn is told with such energy, detail, and immediacy that it has the ring of truth.

The "narritive" makes a remarkable claim: Devon declares that in the early 1840s he lived with a band of Mandan who left their native country to join the Shoshoni tribe in the Rocky Mountains. This assertion poses a complex historical problem: it completely defies the traditional view that the handful of Mandans who survived the smallpox epidemic of 1837 were absorbed by their neighbors, the Hidatsas, in a small village on the upper Missouri to become virtually extinct by the mid-twentieth century.

It is possible that other sources, such as press accounts from the 1880s and 1890s, may have influenced Blackburn's telling of the tale. Blackburn seems to have used much more license in recounting Devon's life than in his own memoir, which included no long suspenseful chase scenes and no love stories. The heroine, Leaping Faun, is the only female character of any substance in the entire manuscript. It is even possible that Blackburn purposely altered the original story told around a campfire in 1847 to create a fictionalized version that included the colorful Mandans, but he never mentioned such dramatic events as the 1837 smallpox epidemic or the tribe's near extinction. Though Devon's story contradicts the accepted view of Mandan history, it contains so many descriptions of specific Mandan cultural traditions that it is hard to imagine it could be about any other tribe. Strikingly, it agrees in detail with the surviving Mandan "winter counts"—almost the only Mandan sources describing the tribe's "undocumented years" from 1839 to 1843.[1] It also gives striking insights into the character of the storyteller—Abner Blackburn.

The Devon narrative reflects Blackburn's fascination with Indians, which began in childhood and encompassed the golden age of the buffalo Indian. Blackburn met the village and Plains Indians of the upper Missouri on his 1845 steamboat adventure, was personally involved in some of the first contacts between whites and the tribes of the Great Basin, participated in the decimation of the California tribes, and experienced great personal loss during "Indian wars in which I have had sad experience." If Lou Devon's tale is removed from the narrative, Blackburn's memoir takes a typical nineteenth-century white view of the American Indian. While he never specifically claimed to have killed an Indian, his narrative—which grows more bitter toward them as it rushes to its climax—contains evidence that he killed more than one during his life on "the plains." Family tradition states that he once used an axe to kill a drunken Indian who threatened his wife.[2] In his personal narrative, he was always intrigued, occasionally bemused, and sometimes kind to these people. In Devon's tale, Blackburn unconsciously wrestled with the most terrible problems and ethical dilemmas in American history. This conflict gives the Devon story, apparently a simple and romantic folktale, the significance and complexity of classic literature.

The dramatic fulcrum of the narrative hinges on Devon's acceptance of Indian ways: "I gave up trying to escape, for this was the best place after all." Despite eventually determining that "I had seen enough of savage life," the storyteller voices a sentiment that echoes through

---

[1] Meyer, *The Village Indians,* 98–99, referred to "the otherwise undocumented years from 1838 to 1845," but stated that the tribe, "few as they were," divided into three groups.

[2] Blackburn's granddaughter-in-law wrote: "Abner Blackburn, while cutting wood, heard his wife, Lucinda, scream. Ran with his axe and found a drunk Indian attacking his wife with a knife in the chicken house. He split the Indian[']s head open with the axe." Ruth Towle Blackburn Papers. The entry ends, "This is on record in San Bernardino somewhere," but no other record of this story is known to exist.

American history: that the Indian is right—the white man is a menace, a destructive force whose wanton ways carry the seeds of his own inevitable destruction.

To further complicate historical analysis, the clear influence of two American literary genres, the captivity narrative and the dime novel, color Blackburn's retelling of Devon's tale. Hundreds of captivity narratives survive, with the oldest examples predating Captain John Smith's encounter with Pocahontas. Several narratives record a white captive's conversion to Indian ways—an event more common in practice than in the literature. These narratives have influenced writers like Cooper, Hawthorne, Thoreau, and Melville. With its lively pursuits and hairbreadth escapes, Blackburn's retelling of Devon's story is even more closely related stylistically to "penny dreadful" novels. Beadle and Adams's first "dollar book for a dime" was a "white Indian" story, *Malaeska, or the Indian Wife of the White Hunter*, published in 1860. In the same year, *Seth Jones; or the Captives of the Frontier* appeared and eventually sold 300,000 copies.[3] The captivity theme lost popularity by the 1880s, but it still maintains a hold on the American psyche, as demonstrated by its reappearance in movies such as *A Man Called Horse* (with its striking similarities to Devon's story) and *Dances With Wolves*.

A summary of accepted facts about the Mandans shows one aspect of the narrative's historical problems: the Mandans were well-known and long-established friends of the whites, and the massacre of Devon's trapping party would be a unique and uncharacteristic event; whites had lived with the tribe for long periods from as early as the 1770s, and in the historical record the Mandans held no white captives; the pattern of intertribal warfare described in the narrative—especially with the Crow, their traditional allies—violates known tribal relationships; and no record survives of a Mandan party joining the Shoshoni, or even being at Fort Hall. Finally, although whites repeatedly observed Mandan ceremonies, no explicit record of white participation in any of the various Plains Indian sun-dance rituals is known to exist.

The vagaries of the historical record is one explanation of the narrative's problems. Each of the alleged facts about the Mandans can be argued to tedium, in large part because this indictment assumes that a detailed and accurate interpretation of Mandan history exists for the period described in the narrative. F. A. Chardon's journal gives an almost day-by-day account of the bands around Fort Clark from 1834 until 6 May 1839, but the activities of the tribe from 1839 to 1845 are a matter of speculation. Historians have tended to regard Chardon's extraordinary ac-

---

3. Levernier, *The Indians and Their Captives*, 189–91.

count as comprehensive, but Chardon made no such claim. The accepted "facts" about Mandan history are so removed from primary sources—the Mandans themselves—that they in no way preclude the possibility that the narrative presents a broadly accurate picture of one band's life after the smallpox disaster of 1837—a conclusion born out a by a close look at ethnological surveys conducted in the early twentieth century.

When French trappers first encountered the Mandans and the Hidatsas in the early eighteenth century, the tribes had about twelve thousand members.[4] According to the earliest accounts, they were village Indians who were successful farmers, traders, and buffalo hunters living in heavily fortified towns on the upper Missouri between the Knife and Heart rivers and near present-day Bismarck, North Dakota. Their agricultural surpluses helped the Mandans develop extensive trading contacts that they later used to become key middlemen in the trade in guns and horses.[5] The tribe suffered from a devastating smallpox epidemic in 1781, which was but one incident in a grim cycle.[6] The Lewis and Clark expedition spent the winter of 1804–5 at Fort Mandan and described five villages, including those of the Hidatsas, where they found their guide, the Shoshoni captive Sacajawea. (The Mandans, Hidatsas, and Arikaras, closely related in blood and culture, are now collectively called the Three Affiliated Tribes.) In 1832, artist George Catlin visited the tribe and later wrote several volumes on Mandan life, colored by his belief that the tribe was descended from lost Welshmen. Karl Bodmer created a stunning artistic heritage when he accompanied Alexander Philip Maximilian, Prince of Wied-Neuwied, to the Mandan lands in 1833–34, while Maximilian recorded detailed observations of Mandan life, culture, and language.[7] Tragically, the eloquent portraits of Catlin and Bodmer were pictures of a doomed people: in 1837 smallpox again swept through the Mandan villages, reducing the already decimated population of 1,600 in June to about 150 by year's end. "What a bande of RASCALS has been used up," Chardon commented, "it has destroyed the seven eights of the Mandans and one half of the Rees [Arikara] Nations."[8] The devastation was so great that George Catlin believed them to be extinct.[9]

---

[4] Lehmer, *Selected Writings*, 88.

[5] Ewers, *Indian Life on the Upper Missouri*, 14–33.

[6] Trimble, "Epidemiology on the Northern Plains," i, states that "a minimum of fifteen major epidemics took place on the Plains between 1520 and 1840."

[7] Porter, "Marvelous Figures, Astonished Travelers," 36–52.

[8] Abel, *Chardon's Journal*, 137, 138.

[9] Catlin thought that the Arikara enslaved the survivors of the epidemic, and that they were later slain by the Sioux. He noted, however, "There is no doubt whatever

Conventional history states that the tribe merged with the rest of the Three Affiliated Tribes and settled at Like-a-Fishhook village about 1844, preserving ways that ethnologists George F. Will, Robert H. Lowie, and Gilbert L. Wilson recorded early in the twentieth century. No secondary source reflects Blackburn's claim that part of the tribe hunted buffalo on the Montana plains and fought the Sioux, Blackfeet, and Crow on the headwaters of the Missouri and Yellowstone rivers, though it is confirmed in the ethnological reports. Thus, the Devon story would seem at best a dim and hopelessly confused recollection or, at worst, pure fiction, yet two long-ignored sources—the "winter counts" of Butterfly and Foolish Woman—confirm the story in one important detail, its location.

On 11 July 1929, Mandan survivor Foolish Woman (a male) gave anthropologist Martha Beckwith a "Mandan Winter Count" that provides support for Devon's tale. For 1839, Foolish Woman stated, "In the spring they crossed to the south side of the river, the band split up, and part camped where they had crossed and the other half went up the Yellowstone and made camp about Rosebud creek, in the gumbo tree timber." Assuming that Beckwith accurately interpreted the reference to Rosebud Creek, and the reference matches the stream of the same name in present-day Montana, this places part of the tribe in the exact area described in Devon's story.[10]

In 1913 and 1918, Gilbert Wilson recorded the Hidatsa Goodbird's interpretation of Butterfly's Mandan winter count. It is a more ambiguous version that has the tribe winter in 1839 "at Prairie Dog timber. Some Hidatsas and Mandans went to visit some other Indians at Rose River. Small Ankle was one of these visitors. . . . The men who had gone visiting returned in the spring about the time the ice breaks on the Missouri." In 1918, Goodbird's mother, Buffalo-Bird Woman, commented on Butterfly's chronology. For the year 1839, she told Wilson

that a few straggling Mandans who fled to the Minatarrees, or in other directions, are still existing." Catlin, *O-kee-pa*, 90. Traditional estimates of Mandan survivors are probably low.

[10.] Beckwith, *Mandan and Hidatsa Tales*, 309–10. It is difficult to assess the reliability of Beckwith's interpretation of Foolish Woman's geography. For 1838, Foolish Woman stated that "the winter camp was down in old Cold Harbor where there is a creek known by the Indians as Mussel Shell Creek." While it is tempting to identify this with the modern Musselshell River in Montana, archaeologist Thomas D. Thiessen points out that a town named Coleharbor is located near modern Garrison Dam, and anthropologist Jeffery R. Hanson agrees that the 1838 site was in the traditional Mandan lands. Correspondence with editor. Foolish Woman's reference to the Yellowstone River and Buffalo-Bird Woman's commentary on Butterfly's winter count support the identification of the location of the Rosebud camp.

that her father "Small-ankle's family and others of their camp remained two winters in the Crow country, in the mountains. They were about thirty teepees in all; and they returned to Five Villages the second spring, there rejoining the rest of the tribe." Buffalo-Bird Woman admitted, "Of these two winters I do not know much; I was not born until the third year after the smallpox year [about 1840]."

Buffalo-Bird Woman also gave some cryptic "historical notes" to Wilson that implicate the Mandans in a captive episode: "A man named No Rain was struck on the head by a soldier with a pistol. No Rain was a Crow Chief who had a captive white woman whom he did not want to give up. Hence the quarrel with the soldier." Goodbird and his mother told Wilson about events in the early 1860s that place the Mandan and Hidatsa tribes in the area described in Devon's narrative. "Buffaloes were getting scarce in the vicinity of old Fort Berthold and the whole village had gone up the Missouri to hunt and winter on the Yellowstone," where Goodbird was born "at a place between the Yellowstone and Missouri Rivers."[11]

No plains tribe fits the events in Devon's story better than the Mandans. Blackburn gave a detailed depiction of the Okeepa (or Okipa), the rituals that other tribes eventually adapted into the many and varied sun dances. While far from exact, Blackburn's descriptions are accurate enough to suggest that either he retained a vivid memory of Devon's story or was influenced by early accounts such as Catlin's (which is unlikely) or by stories in the press about the sun dance and the ghost-dance movement. One telling possibility is that Blackburn read a March 1889 article in *Harper's Weekly*. George Louis Curtis had paid a visit to the Fort Berthold reservation and viewed the crumbling ruins of Like-a-Fishhook village. Curtis noted that the "bloody tortures of the Nahpike, or sacred dance of the Gros-Ventres," and the "annual religious ceremonies of the Mandans," (which he said lasted for four days and commemorated "their legend of the Deluge,") had been "suppressed by government order." Curtis called the participants "votaries" of the "sun god" and much other nonsense but made one observation

---

[11] Gilbert L. Wilson Papers, "Hidatsa-Mandan Reports—Fort Berthold Reservation, 1911–1918," Minnesota Historical Society. For two versions of the Butterfly Winter Count and Buffalo-Bird Woman's commentary, see vol. 13, 2:1114–15 and vol. 22, 4:890, 922 (these references list the microfilm roll and frame number). In 1913, Wilson noted that he did not have time to verify the winter count "from Butterfly's own lips. It is probable that it would be worth while going into it with Butterfly in some detail." Butterfly died before Wilson could discuss the count with him. For the 1860s hunt, see vol. 13, 2:955. For Butterfly's account of the Yellowstone hunt, see vol. 14, 3:170–261. For No Rain's story, see vol. 13, 2:1124, and an alternate version, vol. 22, 4:900.

about the Hidatsas that indicates his article may have affected Abner Blackburn's telling of Devon's narrative: "Woe betide the youth who weakened or whose physical courage fainted under the terrible ordeal! No longer a brave, he was henceforth condemned to wear the costume and share the menial duties of the squaw." Such loss of status was not associated with failure to endure the tortures of the Okeepa, but Devon's narrative contains a very similar statement.[12]

The Okeepa dramatized Mandan origin myths and was an initiation ceremony for young warriors, a rite of passage "the chiefs and other dignitaries of the tribe [witnessed] that they might decide whom to appoint to lead a war party, or to place in important posts, in time of war." It was held in conjunction with the bull dance, "to the strict performance of which they attributed the coming of the buffaloes to supply them with food during the ensuing year." Participants fasted for four days, enduring a series of preparatory rituals before engaging in two important ceremonies. In the first, the *pohk-hong*, they were suspended from the roof of the medicine lodge by thongs inserted through the muscles of the back or chest. In the second, the *Eeh-ke-náh-ka Na-pick*, or "the last race," buffalo skulls and other weights were hung from the skin of the legs and arms of the initiates, who raced around an altar, dragging weights while the rest of the tribe "raised their voices to the highest key, to drown out the cries of the poor fellows thus suffering by the violence of their tortures." To produce honorable scars, "the flesh must be *broken out*, leaving a scar an inch or more in length."[13] In this way, the young warriors acquired *hopini*, power.

Everything in Blackburn's description of the Okeepa could have been based on sources other than Lou Devon, but his description of an eagle hunt points to much less well known Mandan eagle-trapping rites. There is little resemblance between Devon's eagle hunt and the highly structured Mandan rituals, which prescribed how to build lodges, fireplaces, and trapping pits; how to prepare meals, bedding, fires, pipes, snares, and bait; how to burn incense and make offerings to the eagles; how to conduct ceremonial weeping and wailing; and finally, how to "put the eagles to sleep." Still, the fact that Devon described both the Okeepa and an eagle hunt confirms Blackburn's identification of Devon's captors as the Mandan nation.

While the evidence supporting the Mandan elements of Devon's narrative is ambiguous, Lou Devon's historical identity is a complete mystery. Blackburn's manuscript is enigmatic about the trapper's real name:

---

12. Curtis, "The Last Lodges of the Mandan," 246.
13. Catlin, *O-kee-pa*, 47, 66–67.

he spelled it as both Devon and Duvon, and in some occurrences the name is first spelled one way and then modified. The problem is compounded because internal evidence indicates that Devon was not the man's actual name. In the manuscript, Blackburn wrote, "Our pilots name was" and then erased the original name and the following sentence, which can still be deciphered: "I have forgotten his other names—no difference." He may have replaced this text with an alias, or "dit name": Lou Devon.[14] In the sentence, "We alwais called him Lou," Lou is written over an erased name that appears to begin with an F (or possibly a J) and end with K. Based on spacing and what survives of the erasures, the manuscript originally read, "Our pilot's name was Francois. I have forgotten his other names—no difference. We alwais called him Frank." (Of course, if the manuscript actually read Jacques and "we alwais called him Jack," Devon could be identified with virtually every French-Canadian trapper on the American frontier.) It is impossible to puzzle out what Blackburn was up to. Perhaps Frank was the alias, and Lou Devon is the closest phonetic rendition Blackburn could give when he later recalled the trapper's name. Blackburn's failure to remember the trapper's name further strains his credibility and complicates any attempt to identify a historical Louis Devon.

Nonetheless, Blackburn painted a detailed picture of Lou Devon. The narrative says he was born in Montreal in 1822. His parents moved to Sault Ste. Marie in 1830, where they died of smallpox in 1832. Devon's western adventure began when his uncle, a Hudson's Bay Company trapper, took him west about 1833. They "went on the mountains" for "about five years," where they "trapt on the Red River, [the] Columbia, and the head watters of the Missouri," bringing the date up to about 1838. Devon's life with the Mandans covered three to five years. About 1842, Richard Grant, chief trader at Fort Hall in the Snake Country, persuaded Devon to go "into his service of the Hudson Bay Company and nothing would do but I must engage with him"—an interesting use of words, since *engagé* is the French word used to describe the "servants" of the HBC, and a direct statement that Devon was an employee of the Columbia District and not a free trapper. Blackburn implied that Grant gave Devon quarters in the fort and employed him as an express man, carrying messages throughout the vast Columbia District, which included modern Oregon, Washington, Idaho, Montana, and western Canada. About 1845 or 1846, "[Grant] sent two of us

---

[14.] This evaluation is based on an examination of photostats of the manuscript at the Nevada Historical Society and Bancroft Library. The original manuscript, which would supply additional clues, is now lost.

to the mouth of the Columbia River to Fort Vancouver, a long distance. We changed horses at everry post and travled verry fast. Went safe [and] delivered the dispatches. The agent [Dr. John McLoughlin or James Douglas] then sent us down the coast to California to Monterey with more orders and letters." Devon returned to Fort Hall via Sutter's Fort (where "Captain Suiter fitted us out") and the Truckee River. After guiding the Brown-Brannan party to California in the fall of 1847, the Hudson's Bay Company agent at San Francisco, James Alexander Forbes, sent Devon to Fort Vancouver. Devon must have parted ways with the Honorable Company in the summer of 1849, since he had come to California from Fort Hall "on pack animals" two weeks before Blackburn encountered him on the Yuba River about the middle of September.

Given this level of detail, it would seem to be an easy task to place Lou Devon in history. It simply requires locating him in the Hudson's Bay Company records of the Columbia District and matching the name in California gold rush accounts. Unfortunately, the record is vague.

Almost no documentary sources for Fort Hall in the 1840s survive. While Mormon Robert S. Bliss's diary described hearing Richard Grant read his journal's description of the Brown party, and Grant certainly made the requisite semi-annual post reports to his superior, John McLoughlin, neither of these primary sources is known to exist. The single most detailed contemporary account of the post is a series of Richard Grant letters written between 1844 and 1851 to Sir George Simpson, the chief officer of Hudson's Bay Company in North America. These colorful, literate documents describe the fur trade, the overland emigration, and Fort Hall and are filled with references to Jim Bridger, Louis Vasquez, Peg-Leg Smith, John Sutter, Lansford Hastings, and "my Mormon friends," but they contain no clues to the identity of Lou Devon. Grant's comments on the emigration are remarkable: he called the Americans "animals," and wrote, "So far I have kept good friends or rather on good terms with them all but I assure you they are a rough and uncouth set, it requires all my Yankeeship and knowing them and their ways of days past."[15] The content of these letters explains why the documents that might positively identify Lou Devon have vanished. Grant's Fort Hall journals, semi-annual reports, and correspondence to Dr. John McLoughlin would not long survive in the possession of the "White Eagle" and Father of Oregon, especially after the doctor left the

---

15. Richard Grant to Sir George Simpson, 2 January 1846, D.5/16 fo. 23–25, Hudson's Bay Company Archives, Provincial Archives of Manitoba (hereafter cited as HBC Archives). For other Grant letters, see D.5/13 fo. 289–92; D.5/20 fo. 713d; D.5/24 fo. 226–29; and D.5/27 fo. 335–37.

Honorable Company's service and became an American citizen.

The cryptic ledgers of the Columbia District, particularly the "List of Servants," contain detailed financial records and much information about the men in the Snake Country, listing their capacity, years of service, pay, length of contract, and sometimes their date of discharge, age, and national origin, but they paint an incomplete picture of life at Fort Hall. The Grant-Simpson letters point out the deficiencies of these accounts. For example, in August 1845, Grant "succeeded in collecting together a party of free Trappers and Engaged Servants, in number twenty six, to hunt the Queaterra Country," but the Snake Country 1846 Outfit listed only twenty-five men, some of whom were stationed at Fort Boise, while a number of others must have been employed in other tasks. Remarkably, twelve of the servants were "Kanakas,"— Hawaiians. Clearly, Grant was dependent on free trappers for much of the Queaterra contingent, in addition to "such hands as I had in the Snake Country." Although the narrative clearly identified Lou Devon as an engaged servant, if he was actually a free trapper, determining his identity with any certainty goes from the problematic to the impossible.

The Company whittled away Grant's command: in 1846, six men had "Half Wages transferred to Fort Vancouver Depot," and in 1848, the accounts list only eighteen men in the Snake Country. The 1847 Outfit, which presumably should list Lou Devon, contains no men named Louis, Francois, and no more likely candidates than one Jean Baptiste Silvestre, an old hand with fourteen years service. Of the twenty-one men at Fort Hall in 1847, twelve were Hawaiians.[16]

So, who was Lou Devon? The 1842 to 1848 Columbia District and Snake Country account books include information on six likely candidates: Narcisse Raymond, Grant's right-hand man, "a very trusty young man"; Louis Francois Dauney, who would settle with his Indian wife and two children near Raymond in the Walla Walla Valley in the 1850s; Louis Daunt (Ledoux), an *engagé* from Montreal; and Louis Dubeau, 21, an express man and "comer and goer" in the Snake Country from Montreal who had two years of service in 1843. A close examination of the record positively disqualifies most of these men, while the case for Daunt is too circumstantial to present seriously. This leaves only two possibilities who cannot be ruled out with some certainty: Francois Proulx and Louis Aimé Daunais.

[16.] For the Snake Country records, see B.223/g/7 fo. 10d for 1842 Outfit; B.223/d/169 fo. 20–22 for 1846; B/223/d/176 for 1847; and B.223/d/184 fo. 3–18 for 1848. Note that the company's fiscal year ran from May to May, so the 1846 Outfit covered May 1846 to May 1847.

If the Brown company actually called their guide Frank, Francois Proulx may be Lou Devon. Proulx appeared in the 1846 accounts of the Snake Country Outfit, and had four years service. The Columbia District "List of Servants" described Proulx as a deserter from Fort Vancouver in 1849, and either he or Charles Proulx (another 1849 deserter) was probably the man who guided the Regiment of the Mounted Rifleman down the Columbia in October of 1849. Some circumstantial evidence supports Proulx's identification as Lou Devon: a cluster of Proulx family members still lives near Sault Ste. Marie, and the 1860 census listed a Frank Proul at Nevada City, California, but gave his age as 29 and his birthplace as Pennsylvania. Proulx, however, was married on 2 January 1847 at Fort Vancouver and listed in the Columbia District 1850 Outfit.[17]

Louis Aimé Daunais was born about 1824 in Canada. The "Statement of Servants" for the Columbia Department listed him in the 1846 Snake Country Outfit with three years of service as a "middleman." Daunais was one of six men (along with Francois Proulx) whose "Half Wages [were] transferred to Fort Vancouver Depot" that same year. The 1847 Outfit listed him at Fort Vancouver (in present-day Oregon) as a middleman. Daunais deserted the Honorable Company at Fort Vancouver on 1 March 1849.[18]

An entry in Fort Vancouver clerk Thomas Lowe's 1845 journal, however, casts some doubt on Daunais's case. On 19 August, Lowe reported:

> An examination took place this afternoon of Louis Dubeau and Louis Daunais two Canadians who attempted to desert last night. Mr. Douglas awarded the sentence of flogging and imprisonment to Dubeau, who had not only deserted from the Brigade while going up [to the Snake Country], for which no punishment had been inflicted two of his comerades having become security for him . . . , but he yesterday left his work in the Mill Plain, came down here clandestinely, and endeavored

---

[17.] Munnick. *Catholic Church Records, Vancouver,* 78, M42, and B.223/d/187 and B.223/d/195, HBC Archives.

[18.] B.223/d/176, fo. 3d & 4 and B.223/d/187, fo, 12, HBC Archives. Other men named Daunais appear in fur trade records: the York Factory 1849 accounts listed a Jean-Baptiste Daunais, while Oliver Daunais, born in 1836, "worked in the United States, Red River, and the United States again before he came to Silver Islet in the 1870s. He then branched out for himself in trading and prospecting [and married] the daughter of the Chief at Lake Nipigon. His mining successes brought his existence to the attention of his first wife. . . . His fame as the Silver King was limited in time [and] he died in 1916." Arthur, *Thunder Bay District 1821–1892,* 161.

to persuade Daunais to accompany him to the Willamette. He therefore received 13 lashes at the gun and was afterwards put in prison. Daunais had likewise deserted from the Brigade, for which offense he was liberated in the same manner as Dubeau, having found sureties. He was pardoned at this time, as nothing could be proved against him except his intention at one time to desert last night with Dubeau, but he had thought better of it before starting, and was quietly returning from the beach to his own house again when taken into custody by some of the Gentlemen.[19]

Given this swamp of contradiction and ambiguity, is there any reason for historians to take Lou Devon's narrative seriously? Probably not. Yet, despite significant problems it also offers intriguing possibilities.

Devon's narrative is not history—it is legend. Like all good legends, in addition to its rollicking adventures and hairbreadth escapes, it touches deep wells of meaning. It contradicts the common nineteenth-century view (which often used the Mandans as a case study) that the Indians were a "vanishing breed." Finally, the narrative of Louis Devon is what it is: a splendid and moving myth of survival, adventure, and love.

THE NARRATIVE

I was born in Montreal in the year 1822.

My parents moved to Salt St Maryes [Sault Ste. Marie] when I was eight years old. They both died with the small pox three years afterwards and my uncle took me to his home in the neighborhood. He joined the Hudson Bay Company. [He] went trapping and took me along with him.

Trapt on the Red River, [the] Columbia, and the head watters of the Missouri and other streams. For about five years a small party of us went on the mountains and [then] we were attackted by a savage band

---

19. Thomas Lowe, "Private Journal," Provincial Archives of British Columbia, 22. This Louis Daunais hardly seems to match Blackburn's description of Lou Devon, but Lowe may have confused Louis Aimé Daunais with the similarly named Louis Francois Dauney. Given Lowe's position as clerk of the Honorable Company, this seems unlikely. Still, this may actually refer to Louis Dauney (also spelled Dauny, Donee, and even Davis), who had the children of his Walla Walla Indian wife baptized at Fort Vancouver in 1846 and 1849.

of Indians.[20] They killed my uncle and three others of our party and took me prisoner and took me along with them.[21]

We traveled south several days and come to their village. It was the Mandan nation of Indians. They kept close watch over me for some time and set me to carrying wood, for it was cold weather. I worked with some squaws and boys. I had not much clothing. The Indians had nearly stript me clean and [I] slept with the dogs to keep warm. Helpt the squaws in all kinds of drudgery, tanning buffalow robes and deer skins and other chores.

I made up my mind when warm weather come to escape from captivity. I got manny a beating from my captors dureing the winter. They began to treat me better after [a] while and tak[e] me out to hunt and to carry in the game for them. I could beat them hunting and they had a better opinion of me. They learnt I could beet them at anny thing [and] they wanted me to join their tribe, and [I] could speak their toung verry well. [I] now began to get used to their ways and learned them manny new things. Went hunting with [th]em. They gave me back my gun [that] they took from me when captured, but they kept a very close watch over me yet. I killed a brown bear that come verry near catching one of the braves and they thought I was a mighty brave. They treated me much better.

We had a feast of bear, horse, and dog meat.[22] The spring had come. The grass was good and everry thing was nice. A friendly tribe, the Crows, a cheif and a few braves, come to smoke the pipe of peace. This time [we] had a big feast. Killed two of the Crows horses and some

---

[20.] Several anthropologists have cited the Mandans' reputation for never having harmed a white man as reason to doubt Devon's claim that Mandans killed his hunting party. Chardon, however, records a dramatic change of heart following the smallpox epidemic in the summer of 1837. "An Old fellow who has lost the whole of his family to the number of 14, harangued to day, that it was time to begin to Kill the Whites, as it was them that brought the small pox in the Country. . . . A Mandan cheif came early this Morning and appeared to be very angry—telling me that I had better clear out, with all the Whites, that if we did not they would exterminate us all." Abel, *Chardon's Journal*, 127.

[21.] A tempting possibility is that Devon was related to trapper Jean Baptiste Dufond (also Defond and Defont) who appears in the American Fur Company account books from 1834 to 1838. Dufond was listed for 1836–1839 as a "pilot, patron, trader" in the Chouteau-Maffitt Collection; could this be the uncle Devon said was killed on the upper Missouri about 1839? Chardon noted that Dufond's death was reported to him in 1836, but upon investigation, concluded that it was an Indian, and not Dufond, who was killed. See Abel, *Chardon's Journal*, 56, 307.

[22.] Jeffery Hanson observed, "The Mandans and Hidatsas only recently turned to eating horse and dog, and this was due to a shortage of usual meat sources. . . . I am not sure that the Mandan or the Crow would eat their horses if game was as plentiful as the narrative implies." Correspondence with editor, 10 January 1992.

of our dogs and two large Elks. Made all ready. Put up a high pole in the center of the ring and hung war trophies and scalps on it. They were going to make me and four young bucks wariers.[23] They slit our backs and breasts with knives and passed thongs through under the skin and tied old buffalow heads to us and tied each one to the center pole and [we were to] dance arround the pole until the skin tore loose. And the show commenced. The[y] were dressed in all the paint and feathers. [They] beat the drum and [played] a kind of fife, yelled and danced, and a perfect hell turned loose and other ceremonies going on at the same time.[24]

The blood [was] streaming down our breasts and backs while we were dancing arround the pole. I knew it was going to be hard on me and began to look arround for something to cut loose with. Saw a flint arrow head close by and picked it up on the sly and when there was a chance, [I] would saw on the skin a little at a time. By and by one head dropt off. That encouraged me. I jumpt and yelled and ran against the pole and another dropt off. The wariers gave a hoop. The one on my back I thought would kill me and [I] gave the skin a scrape when no one was looking. Gave a hoop [and] ran against the pole. [Went] arround a few jumps more [and] tore loose and I was a brave. They put me in the sweat house to cure up. Two young bucks fainted and lay down. They were cut loose and were called squaw men. The other two tore loose on the square.[25]

After we healed up, [we] had a war dance. Painted up to look [like] Devils and went [to] hunt the Blackfeet. They were our enemyes at this time.[26] They had stole some horses that fall before from us and we were a going to get even on them. Went into their country and sneaked ar-

---

[23.] The initiation of whites into a sacred tribal ceremony like the Okeepa has a long tradition in popular literature and movies, but not a single such event survives in the documentary record.

[24.] For George Catlin's eyewitness account of the ceremony, see *O-kee-pa*, 66–67.

[25.] Blackburn's version should be compared to the 1889 account of George Curtis. Referring to "the bloody tortures of the Nahpike, or sacred dance of the Gros-Ventres," Curtis wrote that "appalling feasts for several days were succeeded by the sickening tortures of the dancers. The sun god beamed fiercely upon his votaries as they swayed to and fro to the shrill music of eagle bones, the monotonous beat of the drum, and the hoarse chanting of the medicine-men. At length outraged nature yielded to the strain. The buffalo skull, suspended on skewers thrust into the pierced muscles of the dancer, was torn loose by his movements, or the lariat which in like manner secured him to the cotton-wood severed the flesh of breast or shoulders into which it had been inserted." Curtis, "Last of the Mandan Lodges," 246.

[26.] Writing about war parties, Maximilian observed, "The Mandans and Manitaries make excursions as far as the Rocky Mountains, against their enemies, the Blackfeet." Maximilian, *Travels in the Interior*, 389.

round for a while and found them too strong for us. Stole five horses and come back without anny scalps. The tribe were disipointed because we brought no trophies of victory, but the horses suited them verry well.

In about two weeks warriers, squaws, dogs, and all went south on a buffalow hunt. We found some Crow Indians there and run them off. Killed all the buffalow we wanted and dried the meat and saved some of their skins. Went over to another place to fish. There was plenty of good [fish] in this river, but it is verry [dangerous, with] rappids, steep banks, and falls.

I was fishing and setting on a large rock. Was thinking about makeing my escape from the Indians, for I had not given up [watching for] a good chance to get away. Looking up the rappids of the stream, I saw some Indian girls picking berries that hung out over the stream. Heard a cry [and] looked again. The bush had broken and one fell in the watter. She had cau[gh]t hold of a stick of wood but the rappids drew her down over the falls and she disappeard beneath the foam. She rose shortly, holding on to the piece of wood. She went arround in the whirl pool. By this time I had come to her resque and threw her a long grape vine so she could reach it. When she come around to it, she cau[gh]t the vine and [I] pulled her out. She was so weak she could not stand for some time.

The other young squaws ran screaming to camp. She belonged to our cheif. He was her uncle, Sutek Sacote, or Lame Cougar in English.[27] He told me to tak[e] her for she was mine for saveing her. And [I] did not care about takeing [her] at this time and concluded to wait a while. Her name in Indian was Sinute Kota, in English [she] was the Leaping Faun.[28] This Indian girl would never leave me afterwards, [but] only for a short time, when she would return and sit by my side. When I went hunting she appeard lost. When I returned she would come to me and combe my hair with her long fingers. I could not help it. In time I could not do without her, for she had me. And I was gone on the Leaping Faun and I gave up trying to escape, for this was the best place after all.

Our warriers wanted eagle feathers verry bad to decorate their heads when they have their war dance and they wanted me to kill some eagles

---

[27.] Curtis gave *shu^n-ta^n-shka* (long tail) as Mandan for Mountain Lion, while Maximilian translated "Panther, *schunta-haschka*; literally, the long tail." Curtis, *The North American Indian*, 5:171; Thwaites, *Early Western Travels*, 24:248.

[28.] Maximilian translated "leap" as *ska-sch* and *kohta* (*o* full; *ta* short) as "father"; "uncle" uses the same word. Ibid., 238, 241. Blackburn enclosed most of these names and their translations in parentheses, which have been omitted throughout.

for them, for they could not do it themselves.[29] Kota told me where to
find the eagle nest up the river in a verry rough place in some ragged
over hanging cliffs of rocks.[30] She did not know wheather we could
climb to the nest or not. She offerd to goe with me and show the place.

The next morning we started with two young Indians. Went up the
river, arround the falls and rappids, verry rough [going]. Come up to
the cliffs of verry high over hanging rock and tried to find a place to
climb but could not.

We had provided a long buffalow rope made of the hide and
brought along two deer skins to throw over our heads in case we were
attacted by the eagles. We went arround the cliff of rock and gained the
top and rolled some large rocks down over the bluff and that started
the eagles out. There was two of them. One flew on top of a stunted
pine tree that grew out of a crevice in the cliffe. I took good aim and
killed it and the eagle fell a short distance and lodged on a limb. We
lost sight of the other eagle. I wanted the two young boys to goe down
and get the one I had shot, but could not coax them to goe. They were
afraid of the other eagle.

The Leaping Faun sayes, "I goe," but I would not let her goe down
that awful chasm of over hanging rock. We stuck our knives in our
belts and [took the] two extra deer skins to throw over our heads in
case we were attackted by the other eagle.

Fixt a loop in the rope. Threw it over a sharp cragg and I decended
first and dangled in the air and found a projection in the face of the cliff.
Kota next decended to the narrow ledge. I gave the rope a flip. It come

---

[29.] Devon's direct method of procuring eagle feathers and Blackburn's statement
that the Mandans "could not do it themselves" may reflect the cultural disorganiza-
tion afflicting this Mandan band following the epidemic of 1837. Devon's actions are
a total desecration of sacred rituals, but the Hidatsa Wolf Chief's account of an eagle
hunt in the 1860s indicated that even participants were confused about exactly how
the rituals were to be observed. "We young boys were a little reckless, and not
knowing all the proper eagle-hunting ceremonies, did not do everything in the accepted way. . . . We Hidatsa were particular about things pertaining to the god, but
young men were apt to be a little irreverent. . . . We did not know how to observe
all the eagle hunt ceremonies and did not try to do so." Wilson, "Hidatsa Eagle
Trapping," 142–226.

[30.] Eagle trapping began when the leaves turned and ended "when ice began to
form along the edges of small creeks. . . . Usually three to eight weeks were spent
trapping." See "Ben Benson's Narrative of Closing Rites," in Bowers, *Mandan Social
and Ceremonial Organization*, 252. Wolf Chief gave Gilbert Wilson specific dates:
"When I was old enough to observe such things I found that eagles flew southward
about October 4th, 5th, and 6th. We saw them pass for about three days; and they
came on these dates more than on any other." Wilson, vol. 16, 3:593. Bowers, ibid.,
208, stated that "the Mandan claimed [eagle] trapping rights to all the rough lands
between the Little and Big Missouri rivers as far west as Powder River in Montana."

loose from above and [I] fastened it to another sharp rock and decended about thirty feet to another narrow shelf in the face of the cliff. Kota slipt down the rope to whear I was. Gave the rope another flip. It come loose and we were on a narrow ledge close to the eagles nest.

We clome along the ledge to the nest. There was two eggs in it. Heard a whir in the air and the old bird was on us. We threw our skins over our heads, but the eagle knocked them off. She was all over both of us at once. She grabbed Kota by the sholder and nearly knocked her off the ledge. I told her to keep between me and the rock. I knocked the old bird down over the cliffe several times and she would come back with greater vengence. She would scream as only an eagle can.

She come down on my back with her bill and claws. She fastened one of her claws in my shirt. I grabed her by the leg and struck my knife in her boddie several times and killed her. Then went to the nest and secured the eggs, but could not carry them down without breaking them. Cut a hole in the eagles breast and put the eggs inside. We were badly scra[t]ched and torn and covered with blood and dirt.

And then went for the other eagle I had shot. Looked for a place to decend to the tree. Clome along the narrow place and found a place to climb down. Went up after the bird. It in its death struggle had clutched a limb and I had to break off the limb to get it loose. Clome down and started [back] with our eagles. Called out to the young Indians on top of the cliffe to goe back the way they come. We managed by our rope to decend some verry difficult places. Found the Indian boys at the bottom and made them carry our load to the village.

The Indians used everry thing about the eagles—claws, bill, feathers, and the medicine man took the eggs. After takeing all the charms out, they eat the eagles and had the good of them. The tribe wanted to make me cheif, but I refused and told [them] I was too young and did not know their ways yet.

The summer whiled away. We hunted and trapped on several streams. The Blackfeet come in to our country and we drove them off.

The cheif come to me one day while my faithful Indian girl was by my side. He looked at me and then at the girl. Then held up his two fingers that was to say she was mine. Shortly afterwards we had a feast and were united in true Indian stile. Set up a lodge of our own, me and the Leaping Faun. And had to give up making my escape for the present, but intended to await for a good chance.

Stayed with the tribe and learnt them a great manny new things. The Crows brok[e] the treaty and come around on the sly and stole some horses from us. We went after them, but could not catch them, but [we] stole four squaws and two boys and made a stand off. The

Crows sent word to us that they wanted peace. The two tribes met and had a great palaver. [They] smoked the pipe of peace and reterned the stolen property and promised by every thing, good and bad, never to go to war again, all to be broken [at] the first good oportunity.

The Indians told me some wonderful tales about the land of the evil one. They said a long, long time agoe there lived in that land a verry large tribe of verry wicked Indians. They made war on all their neighbors, took them prisoner, and eat them up. The Great Spirit sent large savage beasts and mighty birds to devour them [and] so the beasts and birds eat up the whole tribe of wicked Indians. The beasts and birds stayed there, but no Indians goe near the place. The great beasts live in the ground and throw to a great hi[gh]th hot water and red hot stones. The great birds could carry off buffalow to their nests and eat them.

I had heard from the mountaineers of that wonderful place on the head watters of the Yellowstone River, but the Indians had it pictured out as a fearful place.[31] Of course, I did not believe their yarns about the place. I wanted them to goe with me to the edge of the bad land and I would goe alone the ballance of the trip, but no, they were afraid of the great birds that would carry them off and I had to give up my trip to the land of the evil one. It was only a few days travel from our village to the place.[32]

The next expedition was down the Missouri River to a trading station of the American Fur Company to barter off furs, pelts, robes, or anny thing we could sell. Took the squaws, dogs, and all. While here, we saw a steamboat comeing up the river to the station and that was a grand sight to most of the tribe. They thought the boat a puffing was some live thing and were afraid to goe near it for a long time.[33]

After takeing in all the sights we commenced trading. Bought guns, blankets, amunition, paint, and red hankerchiefs and various other notions. The squaws bought all the flashy calico beads, needles, paint, and numer[ou]s other tricks. The Indians wanted fire water, but the agent told them they could not have it until they went a days travel towards their home and then he would send out all they could drink on a pack horse.[34]

[31.] Blackburn referred, of course, to modern Yellowstone Park.

[32.] Yellowstone Park is almost five hundred miles from the traditional Mandan homelands in North Dakota, but it is a relatively short distance from the "Crow Country" where some of the Hidatsa and Mandan bands may have wintered in 1839.

[33.] The Mandans would have had at least five years of experience with steamboats.

[34.] Although trading liquor with the Indians was illegal, the practice was universal during the years of the fur trade.

The Indians lost no time in starting. Went about fifteen miles and camped. All eyes were turned to look for the pack horse with whiskey. About three oclock, men a horseback [came] leading the pack horse with three kegs of liquor. They told the cheif to divide it equaly with the tribe. The squaws hid away all the arms and knives, for they knew what was comeing.

And [they] were readdy to take a nip themselves. Every mothers son was there. The cheif had an old tin cup and took the first dip and kept passing it out until he got top heavy and then gave the cup to me to distribute to the needful. Gave the squaws their allowence and blood was on the moon. They all had some old scores to settle. [There was] such fighting and pulling hair [that] pandimonium was nothing. The dogs left camp and thought Old Nick was comeing.

The Indians yelled and hooped themselves hoarse. On Earth was not its like. It took a day to sober up. Heard the Sioux were after us. We lit out towards our own country in a hurry.

We made a war dance to show off our new purch[as]es at the trading post and were ready to goe on the war path again. Did not know which to attack first and we joined the Blackfeet against the Sioux. Were gone about six weeks. Found the Sioux and fought them. A few were killed on each side and a great many wounded with arrows and manny horses were shot, for they met the brunt of the battle. The Indians fought in circles on horse back and would lean over the side and shoot over and under their horses necks. Made a great noise and little execution. Tired out [of] fighting and both partyes turned to stealing. We took four prisoners and some horses. It did not pay to fight the Sioux. They were too strong for us [and we] returned to our own country.

I was sorely wounded in the shoulder with an arrow. My dark eyed spouse was glad to see me come back alive. She dressed my wounds and cooked my meals and was all the friend I had on earth, the Leaping Faun.

The next trip was to the head watters of the Missouri River. Trapt and hunted. Returned in about two months and had good success in our expedition. I led them to a place I knew long before. There was a surprise for me when I come back. There come to our lodge a nice half breed little girl a month old. I fussed around and did not know what to do with myself. And [I] knew such things were liable to happen and concluded I was a man of family and settled down to home life.

One day the little one was lying in its strait basket all strapt up. My dark eyed pardner wanted me to name the little one before I went on another trip. She was sleeping so nice in the basket and she looks so much like her mother I will call it the Sleeping Faun and pretty soon the whole village sang out, the Sleeping Faun!

The next performance was a grand sun dance.[35] [We] painted up with war stripes, feathers, and the usu[a]l mode of such opperations and had a high time. Took in a few young wariers in the usual way [with] dancing, yelling, and music and sham fighting. It lasted three days and I was tired of such devilish nonsence.[36]

We come in from a hunt one day. Did not kill anny game, but brought back in several snakes and hedge hog or porcupine. There was something on the fire in a black dish. I tasted it and it cut and stung my toung. Spit it out but the taste was there. It was the most villianous concoction that ever was brewed by mortal savage. It was prepared by our medicine man and if it did not cure, it would kill and no one would be blamed. I [had] seen him in the woods geathering black ants and putting them in a kind of sack. I suppose he geathered all the vile and venemous insects he could find. I h[eard][37] the trappers discribe how they operate on their sick patients. [It] is past beleif and I shall not discribe the performance.

We next went away to the south west on a grand buffalow hunt. They were plenty and fat. [It was] the best of all the hunts. Killed, cut, and dried, feasted, and fattened. Heard the Sioux were not far off. Come back with loads of choice meat, dried toung, and all kind[s] of good pieces. The day before we come back, [we] heard the Crows had com[e] into our country and carried off some prisoners and some horses.[38] Made all haste to get home, but too late. They had left three days before we arrived and had taken my mate, Sinute Kota or the Leaping Faun, and several horses. She was gone, the light and the life of all I had on earth and was a captive amongst savages. I sank to the ground, over powerd with greif and sorrow, and thought of throwing myself in the river, but I would not give her up and thought of giveing chase and was affraid they would kill her. The Indians said they would bring her back. I could not trust them for fear she would come to harm.

No sleep for me at night and [I] gave our child to [a] good squaw to nurse and set myself to planning her rescue and wanted to start

---

[35.] "Sun dance" was a term applied to a variety of Plains Indian ceremonies long after the Mandans had practically vanished. Blackburn's use of this term supports the belief that he had seen later accounts of these ceremonies.

[36.] Catlin and most authorities agree that the Okeepa and its associated ceremonies lasted four days.

[37.] Hole in manuscript, also obscuring following [It].

[38.] This and the previous horse-stealing incident contradict the well-known and long-established friendship that existed between the Mandan and the Hidatsa and Crow tribes. Devon, however, noted that the Crow—a tribe at one time part of the Hidatsa nation—were a "friendly tribe," and this conflict is consistent with the tumultuous intertribal relationships common between Plains Indians.

soon. I knew of some trappers in three or four days journey. They were friends of mine and [I] would goe to the[m] for assistance and have them goe with me into the Crow nation a trapping, whe[re] I could find her and fetch her away. I asked the cheif and he approved my plan and fitted [me] out with two good horses and [I] asked the cheif to see that the little one did not suffer. He said he would feed and keep it warm and the great spirit would wa[t]ch the Sleeping Faun.

The next morning I bid good[bye] to the tribe and in three days come to the trappers camp. One of the trappers knew my uncle well and [I] was soon on good terms with them and related all my adventures since my uncles death. They were ready and willing to goe with me and assist all [they] could. They took up traps and tricks and made ready to goe with me and felt interested in my case.

We started and in four days come near the place she might be kept. Selected a good place to camp and trap. Put every thing in running order. [Found] some few Indians and look[ed] arround. Our leader made some enquiries whear their villages were and how far off. There was three camps with in a few miles. The trappers said they would do the trapping and I could do the trading, which would give me a chance to spy out what was wanted. Next morning started with a lot of notions that the Indians would want. Found one village and commenced bart[er]ing and trafficking for some beaver pelts and other skins. Visited all the lodges, but could not see my lost mate. Went back to camp disheartend. Next day went to a village a little further off and commenced trading. I could speak their toung a little and thought I would do some talking and find out that way more than [by] looking. Could not see her in this place.

I seen the old cheif that had been to our village several times smokeing the pipe of peace and feasting on our horses and dogs. I felt like shutting his wind off. It was time to talk. I spoke of the Blackfeet tribe. They sayed, "Bad Indian, they kill us, got scalp heap." I changed to the Mandan tribe. They did not like them either. "We steal horses from Mandan, fight them, take squaws [and] kill them." Then told what wars [they fought] and how all the other tribes were. I then asked weather they killed the squaws. One Indian says, "Mandan squaw down river," and motioned with his hand and mouth over a ridge as though it was not far off. I listened to everry word he said and motion he made. This was important news. They had taken manny prisoners at various times and this one may be the one I was after. Well, I will see what is to be found. Wound up my traffic soon and returned to camp with [a] lighter heart. If she was not the one I wanted, I would hunt the mountains through.

Told the trappers and they were delighted with my success. Went next morning to the other village and disguised myself so she would not know me if I found her. Went into the village. Opend out and commenced trading and kept a sharp look out for a long time and traded with them until I was tired out. Bundled up my things and went arround the lodges looking for my lost mate. Went in nearly all of them and was afraid she was not hear. Went into another large lodge and there sat three squaws on some mats, working porcupine quills into some leggings, and Cinute Kota, or the Leaping Faun, was one of them. My heart stopt beating and [I] could not move [and] dare not speak. She looked up and ga[z]ed at me. I put my finger across my mouth and shook my head and she knew me. The work fell from her hands. There we were [but] durst not speak. I commenced to trade with the other squaws to throw off suspicion. They could not understand me and pointed to my mate and [I] made a trade for the leggings. I bought several little things. We talked between trades [about] how to escape and set the time and place to meet. I was free with my goods. The Indians crowded arround thick. Wound up my traffic and returned to the trappers camp over joyed at my luck and sattisfied with my days work.

Told the trappers of my success and they were delighted with my success and wished [me] all the good luck there is, but they thought they had better leave two days before I did, for the Indians might suspect them of having something to do with it. The trapping was not verry good here and we made arrangements accordingly. Two days before our appointed time my friends pulled up stakes and started for the head of the Green River country. They said they knew a place that was good for them.

With two good ponies and a good outfit, I lay in the brush and hills. My mate and me had planned to meet [on] the seventh night at moon rise at a lone tree below the camp about a half mile and I would be there with the horses ready. I lay arround in the hills out of sight until the time was up and started to get there at moon rise. Come to the appointed [place] a little earley and waited. By and by the moon rose. Kept on waiting. The minutes seamed hours. Began to get verry impatient and thought there was something [wrong] and went up the trail to meet her but stopt. She might come another way and I would miss her. Went back to the tree. Sat down awhile and heard something pattering in the distance. Strained my eyes looking along the trail and saw something moveing.

It was her and [I] ran to meet her. Cau[gh]t her in my arms, placed her in the saddle, and we lit out and defied the whole Crow nation to ceath [catch] us. We found the great trail leading north towards our country and travled about sixty miles before sun rise.

Come to a river. It was deep and rappid and carried us down, but our ponies swam and reached the opisite bank after being carried down a long distance. Went a mile further and stopt to feed and rest. We wanted [to] give our horses a chance, for on them we depended [for] our escape. We stopt whear we could look back a long distance on the trail to see if we were persued by the Indians. By and by we saw three wariers comeing on our trail. Their horses appeard fagged out.

They come to the river and looked at it. One started in but backed out. Went up the river a short way and turned their horses on some good feed. Built a fire and cooked something to eat. After [a] while they come down to the trail and took another look at our tracks and started back on the trail. We were all sadled and ready for flight if they had crost the river. We felt relieved there was nothing to fear now except roveing bands of Indians.

My wife now felt safe and related her adventure[s] with a strange band of Shianeese Indians in the last four days.[39] [She told of] her sale, captivity, and escape, and the cause of her being late to meet me at the lone tree.

This is her narritive. About four days before our agreement to meet at the lone tree at mo[o]n rise there come into the camp seven friendly Shianeese Indians. The men that captured me brought me out to show me to the strange band. I could understand some of their talk and found out I was to be traded off to the strange Indians. They looked at me and appeared pleased and said, "Good squaw, heap work." Went back in the lodge and [I] thought by their actions they were agoing to sell me and take me off from my child and husband for ever. I made up my mind to escape or die in the attempt. I would not be taken far away and I could not tell what to do. After [a] while they come in, took me by the arm, and led me out. [They] placed me on a horse and deliverd me to the strange Indians and started. They took a southern course. I took notice of everything—the mountains, trees, and land, for back I was bound to come.

Went about ten miles and camped. They set me to work at chores. One of them treated me well. His name was Souchet, or Porcupine. He would call me good and give me presents and something to eat. I took every thing in a good humor to throw off suspicion. They did not think I would leave them. Next day went a little east of south until noon and stopt. The Indians went out to hunt buffalow. They were plenty and fat.

[39.] Although this would seem to be a reference to the Cheyenne Indians, it may refer to the Saones, one of the bands of the Sioux tribe who often traded with the Mandans.

I brought in a large stick of wood [and] put it on the fire and out crawled a rattle snake. Cut off its head and put it on the fire to roast. The Indians are verry fond of roasted snakes. The Indian that treated me so well come back first and when he saw the snak[e] on the fire, he laught all over and was in a verry good humor and gave [me] more presents. Some red paint, a hankercheif, and a bunch of porcupine quills with a dressed deer skin to work them in a shirt. After the snak[e] was cooked in the hot ashes until done, he took it out, gave me a large slice, and eat the rest himself.

I asked him how far it was to their village and he held up four fingers. That meant four days travel. The other Indians come back a little before sun down loaded with good fat meat. They threw every thing down and told me to do the rest of the work. I staked out their horses and picked out a gentle horse for my own use. Carried wood for the night. When the Indians were rested, they commenced roasting meat and holding [it] over the fire on sticks. I put a large piece in the ashes for myself to eat, for I had made up my mind to goe no further with them. They kept on eating meat until they could put no more in their mouths. It was now dark and the Indians rol[l]ed themselves in their robes and went to sleep.

I took out my peace of meat, slipt out, mounted my horse, and took the back track. They would not wak[e] up for a long time, being tired and full of meat. I went off verry quiet for a while and then put [the] whip to my horse until I had a good start. Then slact up for fear my horse would [not] hold out. The moon would give light so I could see my way. There was no trouble to follow the trail up the stream, through a canion, and over the divide onto the next stream and follow up that to the place I started from. I would stop and listen and let my horse rest and eat grass, but could [see] nothing.

Once I felt scared at a great running behind me and left the trail. Went into the brush and listend. It was some buffalow I had started up. Kept going on the trail until [al]most daylight and come near the place I was sold to the Indians. Turned my horse loose and put out for the hills and brush. Concealed my tracks all I could and hid myself so I could wa[t]ch the trail. Waited a long time [but I] could see nothing and found a better place to hide.

Looked again and saw two Indians comeing on my track verry fast and a looking down at the path for tracks. They come to my horse, jumped off theirs, and hob[b]led them and started looking for my tracks. They followed them a ways and lost them, but got my course and went to the hills and rocks. They knew I was there and found my track again, but soon lost it and hunted without tracks. Hunted the hollows and rocks. They come verry close to me once. My heart beat against my side and thought they might hear it beat, but they missed me [by] a verry little. They passed on and hunted other places and went out of my sight and [I] did not see them for a long time. When they come back after their horses, they mounted them and rode towards the village whear they bought me, thinking I would come back there. Saw nothing more of them.

Being verry thirsty, [I] went over the hill and found some watter. Come across some berrys. Went a little further and started a sage hen from her nest and found ten eggs to eat with the berries and had enough to last me one day and night until the apointed time to meet at the lone tree.

I spent the time in the hills and brush picking berries and kept a good wa[t]ch for being seen. The night was cold, but I had a way to make a fire down in a hollow whear the fire was out of sight.

I think I was mistaken in the distance to the lone tree. It was a little further than I expected. Spent the next day on the wa[t]ch, anciously waiting for the night to come. As evening drew near, I went as near the edge of the brush as I could and come in sight of two Indians on horses. They seen me and gave chaise. I ran back in the thick brush with all my might and took a circle around and started for the lone tree. Being dark, I eluded their persuit. The distance was further than I expected which made me a little late, but oh how glad I was to see you and the horses to take us away.

This ends Cinute Kotas naritive of her escape from the Shianeese Indians.

After the Indians turned back, we started and rested often to give the horses a chance to recruit and thought it was safer to travel at night to avoid the roving bands of Indians. I knew the road [and] had been over it before.

The second night about nine oclock our horses smelt something, stuck up their ears, and stopt. Soon some dogs come a running out and barking and heard some jabbering. Whirld our horses arround and took the back track for a while and then made a circle around the camp through the roughest kind [of] country, [across] rocks, brush, and thorns and nearly tore the clothes from us. My mate was held up by thornes. I went back and cut her loose. Her horse went [out] from under her [and] she was cau[gh]t by a bush of thorns. Come around and found the trail. Rushed a head to make up for lost time.

In the morning we looked at the tracks and my mate said they were Sioux. All the Indians tribes know the others tracks by the make of their mockisons. The tracks were going in the oposite way from ours and in four days we arrived at our village. Every one come running out with a hoop. Sinute Kota had come back to us. I took the child and placed it in its mothers arms. The Doe and Faun.

There was general rejoicing in the village. We concluded to leave more force to protect our camp from attack in the future. Put in the winter here.

We thought of moveing over the mountains on the head watters of the Clombia [Columbia] River and get away from the maurauding bands of Indians and live with the peacable Shoshoneese [Shoshoni] or Snake tribe, so about ten of us went over the mountains to the head of the Columbia River. Trapped a while and had verry good luck and found a good country to goe to with our tribe. The Shoshoneese were willing for us to come into their country.[40] Return[ed] by the head of Green River and the Wind River mountains and found good hunting and trapping on that rout[e] and were loaded with pelts and furs, beaver, otter, mink, and started home to our village.

On our way over the mountain [we] stopt to hunt. Wounded a large Elk. We followed him up the mountain and come onto a she bear with two cubs. The Indians wounded one of the cubs. It set up [a] cry and the old bear come back with a vengence [and] ran the Indians up the trees. I shot her but that did not stop her the least bit. I ran up a tree and she after me. Clome out on a long limb. The bear followed close up. The limb broke off. The bear and me come to the ground to-geather. I ran for the tree and started up. The bear cau[gh]t my leggings and ripped them off with my mockassin. She followed as fast as I could clime. Clome out on another limb. The bear clome up and [I] thought my time had come. Pulled out my knife and struck for her nose. That is the tender part of a bear. She backed [off] a little and come again and [I] struck one of her eyes out. The next time, struck her in the nose. She thought I was her ma[t]ch and she made a miss lick and went to the ground and started after her cubbs.

I slipt down the tree [and] put a load in my gun. Followed her up and shot her in the back bone and killed her. The Indians come down. We followed the cubs and killed them and we had bear meat instead of elk.

---

[40] Anthropologists believe that the Mandans traded through Crow intermediaries with western tribes at the Shoshoni Rendezvous, but trade contacts may have been more direct. For example, Sergeant Ordway of the Lewis and Clark expedition found steel axe heads that the expedition had traded to the Hidatsa during the previous winter used as gambling stakes among tribes west of the Rockies. See Ewers, *Indian Life on the Upper Missouri*, 17, 32. However, no known record exists of a Mandan migration to Shoshoni lands in modern Idaho.

Returned to our village. They were glad to have us back again. After resting a while we took all our effects and the tribe moved over the mountain to the place we had selected in the Shoshonee nation and we liked it better than the place we left.

In a month or two, went [with] all hands down to Ft Hall to trade off pelts and furs and lay in a suply of what we wanted. Captain Grant and me had some talk about going into his service of the Hudson Bay Company and nothing would do but I must engage with him and told him I could not leave the tribe verry well with my wife. He said he could fix that verry easey with the cheif. We both went to the Cheif and made him some presents. Gave him a gun, two blankets, and fire watter and told what we wanted. He did not like to have me goe but come to an agreement. The tribe begged me to stay with them. The cheif said, "We will see them on the great river. The white man will wa[t]ch the Leaping Faun." The Indians set up a great howl when we left camp. I had seen enough of savage life and wanted a change and I left the tribe with all I had.

The agent gave me a house to live in with my little family and provided all things necessary for house keeping. My mate not being accostomed to such things, I learnt her the use of things which pleased her verry much.

Capt Grant sent me to the head of the Colombia River with letters and orders to some trappers an[d] so forth. It was the same men that went with me after my wife in the Crow nation. They were glad to see me again and learn of my success in regaining my lost mate.

When I returned to the fort, I noticed a strange woman at the house. A Canadian woman had dressed my wife in French stile and it was a surprise to me. Our little one was rigged in a new fassion from top to tow and I did not know for a while wheather I belonged there or not. This good Canadian lady had shown my mate all the uses of things generaly in the house keeping art.

The agent next sent two of us to the mouth of the Columbia River to Fort Vancouver, a long distance. We changed horses at everry post and travled verry fast. Went safe [and] delivered the dispatches.[41]

The agent then sent us down the coast to California to Monterey with more orders and letters.[42] From there [we went] to Suiters Fort on

[41.] The itinerary described at the end of Devon's narrative has an eerie plausibility. Thomas Lowe, "Private Journal," reported on 25 January 1845, "An express arrived from the Snake Country, bringing letters from Mr. Grant."

[42] Devon might have traveled on one of the Hudson's Bay Company barks, the *Cowlitz*, *Columbia*, and *Vancouver*, which traded between the Columbia River and San

the American River.[43] Captain Suiter fitted us out to return to Fort Hall and we crost the Siere Nevada mountains down the Trucky River and crost the desert and up the long Maryes river to Fort Hall.[44]

My Indian wife was glad to see me return home. The Sleeping Faun had grown much and was a smart and lively little half breed. Rested a few days and was then sent north to the Saskasawan [Saskatchewan] River a long way off and was gone about six weeks.[45] Cap Grant paid me good wages and I could speak nearly [all] the Indian toungs in the mountains. I rested a week and was ordered to Spokan [Spokane] and the Lewis Fort and returned again.[46]

This is the end of our Pilots Narritive of Louis Devon.[47]

Francisco Bay in 1845 and 1846. All foreign ships had to get clearance from the Mexican government at Monterey before landing at any other California port. These ships' logs are in the HBC Archives, but they do not include passenger lists for the years in question.

[43.] Until 1843, Hudson's Bay Company parties under Francis Ermatinger trapped and traded in central California. John Sutter remembered, "They entered the valley in the fall, trapped during the winter and left in the spring with their skins. . . . When their tents were pitched the scene had the permanent look of a large tent city." Sutter complained to the Mexican government, which "assessed a heavy export duty against these furs, and soon my trappers were the sole fur-seekers in the Valley." See *New Helvetia Diary*, x, and Dillon, *Siskiyou Trail*, 266, 361. John McLoughlin had every reason to dispatch a messenger to visit New Helvetia: Sutter had owed the Hudson's Bay Company $3,400 since at least 1842, a debt that he would finally settle for $4,000 in early 1849. See Dillon, *Fool's Gold*, 129–30.

[44.] On 31 July 1845, John Sutter wrote American consul Thomas Larkin that "in a few days," William O. (*Le Gros*) Fallon "with two other men are going to the U.S. via Fort Hall." Hammond, *The Larkin Papers*, 3:291.

[45.] The Rocky Mountain House and Fort Edmonton were among the Hudson's Bay Company posts on the Saskatchewan River in 1847.

[46.] The Hudson's Bay Company closed the Spokane House in 1826, transferring its goods to Fort Colville on the Columbia River. In 1847, Elkanah Walker ran an Indian mission at Tshimakain, near what is now modern Spokane. Fort Lewis at the mouth of the Judith River in central Montana was named in 1846. It was christened Fort Benton after the American politician Thomas Benton on Christmas Day, 1850, but it appeared as Fort Benton in the ledgers of P. Chouteau, Jr., and Company as early as 1848.

[47.] Brigham Madsen, historian of the Shoshoni tribe, wrote of Lou Devon's narrative: "This story is so full of believable detail, one is encouraged to take it as truth. . . . Devon's interaction with the Sioux, Blackfeet, and Shoshoni would be possible." Correspondence with editor, May 1990.

Six

The Biggest Torn Fool
Errant Ever Known

Following the evenings spent around the campfire listening to Lou Devon's tale, the Brown party continued its ride down the Humboldt River, with tensions mounting between Brown and Brannan. Blackburn chronicled their travels from "the dry, parched up deaserts of the interior of the continent," across the "sumit of the great ridge" of the Sierra Nevada, and through the valleys of California to a camp where he could hear "the mighty surf breaking on the Pacific shore." Finally, with a remnant of the original party, he made an arduous return trip to Utah. In the 1940s, this part of Blackburn's story generated considerable excitement among western historians. The quarrel between Brown and Brannan had long been known in general terms, but only Blackburn recorded the details of this singular argument, which nearly ended in gunplay, and he gave the only account of an 1847 crossing of Utah's Salt Desert by a participant.[1] Blackburn also painted an engaging portrait of California before the storm, only four months before the discovery of gold.

From Fort Hall to the Humboldt Sink, Blackburn described the classic route of the California Trail; the company then crossed the Sierra by Donner Pass. On subsequent journeys, Blackburn traveled over many of the important variations and cutoffs of the California road, so an examination of the origins and topography of this important emigrant trail is in order.

The Bartleson-Bidwell party made the first attempt to cross the

---

[1.] Besides Brown's company, only mountain man Miles Goodyear and a party of five or six men crossed the desert that year, driving a large herd of horses from California in June. See Kelly, *Miles Goodyear*, 66. Edward Tullidge published the only parallel account of the return to Utah, which is derived from Jesse S. Brown. This account is quoted in Appendix C.

plains to California in 1841, but was forced to abandon its wagons after crossing the mountains and deserts of Utah. In 1843, mountain man Joseph Reddeford Walker guided an emigrant party to California through the southern pass that Walker had discovered in 1833, but the company left their wagons in Owens Valley. In the next year, Caleb Greenwood interpreted information provided by Chief Truckee and helped pioneer the first wagon road across the Sierra for the Stephens-Murphy-Townsend party, but winter snows forced this company to abandon their wagons in the mountains and retrieve them in the spring. Early in 1845 Greenwood made for Fort Hall and persuaded about fifty wagons to follow him to California, and these wagons made the first single-season crossing of the trail. The enterprising adventurer and promoter Lansford Hastings led a remarkably lucky pack-train party across the mountains in the late fall.

Hastings would be a central figure in the 1846 emigration that is primarily remembered for the disastrous fate of the Donner-Reed party. Hastings, who hoped to play the role in California that Sam Houston had played in Texas, needed Americans as his supporting cast, and he went eastward in the spring to recruit them. He traveled with a pack train that included mountain men James Clyman, James Hudspeth, and the indefatigable Caleb Greenwood. Hastings persuaded Clyman to leave the established trail near present-day Elko, Nevada, to explore a route that Frémont had probably described to him the previous winter. On paper the route looked to be very much a shortcut, going in an approximately direct line between Fort Bridger and the Humboldt, instead of following the Oregon-California Trail's long detour north to Fort Hall. The realities of the rugged country of Utah's Wasatch Mountains and the "fearful long drive" across the waterless wastes of the Salt Desert did not intrude on Hastings's fantasies even after he saw the country traveling east on horseback. Clyman was astounded that anyone would propose taking wagons across the route that came to be known as the Hastings Cutoff.

Hastings went as far east as Independence Rock and persuaded several emigrant companies to meet him at Fort Bridger, though the "great bulk" of the California migration that year chose the Fort Hall route—many after listening to warnings from Greenwood and Clyman about Hastings's proposed cutoff.[2] The followers of Hastings can be divided into four major groups: the Bryant-Russell party, a mule pack train consisting of nine Kentuckians and three scouts, guided by James Hudspeth; the Harlan-Young party, a company of about forty wagons and two hundred people that left Fort Bridger with Hastings as guide on 20

---

[2] Kelly, *Old Greenwood*, 206, and Camp, *James Clyman, Frontiersman*, 225.

July; the Lienhard-Hoppe party—which included mapmaker T. H. Jefferson—of about twenty wagons, and following closely behind Hastings; and finally, the Donner-Reed party, which left Fort Bridger on 31 July, consisting of eighty-seven people—with a disproportionate number of women, children, and old men—in twenty-three wagons. The Donners would always lag far behind the rest of the Hastings followers.

The progress of the Donner-Reed party through the maze of the Wasatch Mountains and across the eighty-three-mile dry stretch that included the unearthly Salt Desert, their wanderings around the Ruby Mountains, and their tedious journey down the Humboldt have been chronicled in detail, as has their final fate near the crest of the Sierra Nevada. Blackburn would stand guard at the Donner camp in the Sierra, and on the return trip he would use one of their abandoned wagons to fuel a fire on the Salt Desert.

The trail followed by Brown's men was a mere scratch on the surface of an unrelenting wilderness. The land that now makes up northern Nevada was volcanic in origin, traversed by ragged granite ridges, an irregular north-south washboard of mountains and valleys. The name that John C. Frémont gave the country—the Great Basin—derived from the fact that the scant rainwater that fell between the "rain shadow" of the towering Sierra Nevada and the Rockies did not drain to the sea but was trapped in an interior drainage system that created salt lakes and flat alkali playas, or "sinks," the remnants of ancient lakes such as Bonneville and Lahontan. A much more appropriate name for the country is basin and range, since it consists of a series of mountains running north and south and intervening valleys. The Humboldt River slashed across these ranges like an axe cutting across the ridges of a washboard, creating a virtual highway for overland travel. Its scant grass and dwindling, bitter waters disgusted many travelers, who called it the "Humbug"; nonetheless, the river was, as its chronicler Dale Morgan dubbed it, the "highroad of the West."

From Fort Hall, the Brown party followed the Oregon Trail down the Snake River Canyon to the mouth of Raft River, where the California Trail turned south. The road crossed the Goose Creek Mountains and descended into modern Thousand Springs Valley (generally called "Hot Springs Valley" in emigrant journals). Crossing the rim of the valley brought the trail to the Humboldt River drainage. From near present-day Wells to Lovelock, Nevada, it simply followed the meandering river as it cut west through the mountains, gradually bending southward. The Humboldt, in contrast to all common sense and emigrant experience, diminished rather than grew in its course—and by most overlanders' standards, the Humboldt did not even merit the name of river at its largest place. At present-day Rye Patch Reservoir, the emigrants stopped to recruit at Great Meadows (which would be renamed Lassen Meadows in 1848, when rancher Peter Lassen opened another long "cutoff" that went northwest from Great Meadows along much of the Applegate route to southern Oregon). In 1847, the trail continued on to the Big Meadow at Humboldt Lake—now Lovelock, Nevada—and the alkali flat where the river flowed into the sands of the Humboldt Sink. Next came an arduous, dry *jornada*, the crossing of the Forty-Mile Desert to the Truckee River. Here they found grass and water, but the narrow river canyon demanded continual fording as the trail began the long climb up the Elephant's Backbone—the one-hundred-mile wide, four-hundred-mile-long slab of elevated granite that made up the western rim of the Great Basin, the Sierra Nevada.

The geographic immensity of the mountains, with their extreme elevation and tortured slope-and-canyon topology, were a final torment to overlanders worn down by months of traveling. Blackburn noted that his party could scarcely credit that men had taken wagons through these mountains. The challenge of the Sierra was no empty threat, as Blackburn discovered while camping at Donner Lake.

Anyone who has crossed northern Nevada can appreciate the accuracy of Blackburn's description of the Great Basin country, but modern travelers can only imagine what the trip must have been like on horseback with bands of desperately poor and unhappy natives thrown in for added interest. Blackburn—like many overlanders—first encountered hostile Indians on this part of the journey. Despite the popular image of mounted tribes attacking wagon trains on the central plains, most buffalo Indians ignored the initial emigrant trains in the 1840s, while the destitute tribes of the Great Basin, their fragile life-support systems already seriously disrupted by the relatively light migrations that preceded the gold rush, proved to be an elusive but life-threatening menace to the trail-worn overlanders.

The emigrants universally called the tribes "Diggers," an epithet referring to their practices of gathering roots and insects for food and of living in crude dugout shelters. "They are miserably poor, armed only with bows and arrows, or clubs," Frémont noted in 1843. "Roots, seeds, and grasses, every vegetable that affords any nourishment, and every living animal thing, insect or worm, they eat. Nearly approaching to the lower animal creation, their sole employment is to obtain food; and they are constantly occupied in a struggle to support existence."[3] Frémont's judgments were models of charity compared to the opinions of later travelers.

[3.] Nevins, *John Charles Frémont*, 230.

The Diggers were actually several tribal and language groups. The Goshiutes were part of the Shoshoni Nation, cousins of the Snakes and Bannocks, and ranged from the Raft River to the middle course of the Humboldt, in the approximate location of present-day Winnemucca, Nevada. The Northern Paiutes inhabited the even more desolate lands of modern central Nevada and called themselves after their primary food sources, taking names such as the Cattail Eaters, Trout Eaters, Sucker Eaters, or Ground-Squirrel Eaters. Finally, the Washoe Indians lived in the Sierra Nevada and in the areas that would become Carson City and Reno, though these were by no means fixed boundaries. Horseless, with no weapons more powerful than crude bows and arrows, and subsisting on a diet that revolted the emigrants, these tribes avoided frontal confrontations with whites, preferring to raid stock at night, and thus further enraging emigrant sensibilities. A preferred tactic was to fill the animals with arrows, which reduced the overlanders' food supply and transportation to carrion. Inevitably, the emigrants responded with frustrated rage and violence. Men and their families already exhausted from a thousand-mile journey and still facing the fearsome Sierra Nevada were in no position to consider that their stock had destroyed the grasses and reeds that formed the basis of the Indians' food supply.

Relations between the races did not get off to a good start. Peter Skene Ogden had Indian problems on his initial exploration of the region in 1828–29, and Joseph Reddeford Walker killed thirty-nine "hostile savages" on the Humboldt in 1833. Relations had not improved by 1847. The primitive tribes were pitted against the pioneers of the industrial revolution. As Thomas Hunt observed, "The scale had been tipped away from the Indian forever by the weight of that first wagon wheel."

A Paiute woman, Sarah Winnemucca Hopkins, provided the only account of the impact of the white migration on the Indians of the Great Basin from the Native Americans' point of view. In memoirs published in 1883, Hopkins, who was born about 1844 and claimed to be the granddaughter of Chief Truckee and the daughter of Winnemucca, wrote that the whites "came like a lion, yes, like a roaring lion, and have continued so ever since."[4] By Hopkins's account, Northern Paiute legends led Truckee initially to welcome the whites, whom he mistook for long-lost brothers. Her father, however, was more pessimistic: "I fear we will suffer greatly by their coming to our country; they come for no good to us, although my father said they were our brothers, but they do not seem to think we are like them." Winnemucca described a dream

---

[4.] Winnemucca and Truckee were contemporaries, which has cast doubt on Hopkins's genealogy.

he had for three nights running: "I looked North and South and East and West, and saw nothing but dust, and I heard a great weeping. I saw women crying, and I also saw my men shot down by the white people. They were killing my people with something that made a great noise like thunder and lightning, and I saw the blood streaming from the mouths of my men that lay all around me. I saw it as if it was real. Oh, my dear children! You may think it is only a dream,—nevertheless, I feel that it will come to pass."[5]

Winnemucca's prophetic dream was much more accurate than Truckee's legends.

"We took in California with all eyes open for the grand sight," begins Blackburn's description of California in 1847. His tour covered Johnson's Ranch, Sutter's Fort, New Hope, Livermore's Ranch, Monterey, and San Francisco, an impressive array of northern California historical sites. He painted a vivid and romantic picture of Old California on the eve of the gold rush. Bancroft estimated that the non-Indian population in 1848 was only fourteen thousand, and the interior valleys were almost unsettled.[6] Anyone who has wondered what California was like before modern civilization altered the landscape will envy Blackburn's experience and appreciate his colorful portrait of the unspoiled land.

Blackburn visited the missions San José, Santa Clara, San Juan Bautista, and Dolores. Dolores and Santa Clara were among the earliest missions, established in 1776 and 1777 under the direction of Fr. Junipero Serra. Father Fermin Lasuen founded San José and San Juan Bautista in the summer of 1797. The missions' golden age was long since past when Blackburn saw them in 1847, and they were rapidly sliding into ruin. The Mexican government had secularized the missions in 1833, in theory to extend private landownership and to encourage the formation of pueblos under the authority of the civil government. In practical application, secularization spelled the end of the mission system and disaster for the native population.

Brown caught up with Governor Richard Mason on the trail from Monterey to San Francisco, and they hit it off very well. The governor was on his way to a grand ball and the two men enjoyed a brandy-fueled binge. Upon his return to Utah, Brown claimed that Mason had given him extensive rights regarding government property, which Brown did not hesitate to exploit. From the viewpoint of the Mormon church, the trip was a spectacular success. John Smith, the Mormon

---

[5] Hopkins, *Life among the Piutes*, 5, 14. Hopkins's book shows the influence of her Victorian editor, Mrs. Horace Mann.

[6] Bancroft, *History of California*, 5:524, 643.

leader in the Salt Lake Valley, reported, "Captain James Brown returned from California about the middle of November; bringing about five thousand dollars, mostly in gold."[7] This was all the cash money in the valley for both 1847 and 1848, and allowed the Mormons to buy out the only existing real-estate claim in the entire Great Basin.

Captain Brown experienced considerable trouble in recruiting the return party, which consisted of three members of the original company—Blackburn, Jesse Brown, and Lysander Woodworth—and one new member, battalion veteran Samuel Lewis. The arduous return made the outbound journey seem like a pleasure trip by comparison, taking more than twice as long under substantially more difficult weather conditions. The small party proved to be much more prone to Indian attack, and Blackburn probably engaged in his first fatal encounter with Native Americans. Accidents with their recalcitrant pack animals caused them to lose much of their limited supply of food. The Hastings Cutoff's false promise of a shortcut home (and possibly directions written by Hastings himself) brought the men to one of the most imposing physical barriers in the West, the salt flats of the Great Salt Lake Desert.

THE NARRATIVE

(continued from page 11 of the first book)

Kept down this long river. The mountains looked like they had been burnt with some great heat. The rocks would ring like crockery ware, with no timber in sight, only willows on the river. The alkily covered the plains.

Come to the long sink of the river. It had run so long through salt and the alkily the watter was [so] brackish and stinking [we] could hardly drink it. Made coffe[e] with it and [it] was no better. Filled the canteens with it and started a cross a forty five mile desert, deep with sand.[8] Half way across, come to a very large sulphur spring boiling hot.[9] Next, come to the Trucky [Truckee] River about

---

[7] Journal History, 6 March 1848.

[8] This desert is usually called the Forty Mile Desert.

[9] Overland emigrants called this site Boiling Springs. It became the Hot Springs station on the Central Pacific Railroad and later a resort named Brady's Hot Springs. It can be seen three-tenths of a mile above the geothermal onion-drying plant that diverts the spring's water at the Hot Springs–Nightingale exit on Interstate 80. Robert Bliss described the springs on 12 September 1847: "the Hot springs we passed are a Great Curiosity they Boil in one place so as to throw the water some 3 or 4 ft high & steam & smoke over a large place; there are holes where hot air bursts out over probably an acre of Ground with a continual noise making it dangerous to travel among them." Alter, "The Journal of Robert S. Bliss," 121.

sunddown.[10] The animals [were] nearly worn out. This [is] a fine large rushing stream of cold watter from the Siere [Sierra] Nevada mountains. This is the place Stockton was attackted by the Indians. Our guide picked a [camping] place back on open ground. [We] kept a good guard and were not molested.

Started up the Trucky Canion and crost the river twenty seven times in twenty five miles.[11] The watter was swift and large bolders [lay] in the bed of the stream, [which] made it verry difficult to cross. Some Indians come to look at us and gaup. Passed through the canion into a wide meadow.

One morning Cap Brown wanted [to] travel on several miles before breakfast. Brannan said he would eat breakfast first. Brown sayes the horses would goe anny how for they belonged to the goverment and were in his care. They both went for the horses and a fight commenced. They pounded each other with fists and clubs until they were sepperated. They both ran for their guns. We parted them again. Started on and left Branan with his own horse. After we stopt, Branan went past. We thought the savages would get him certain. He met some soldiers comeing back from California and prevailed [upon] some of them to accompany him to the coast.[12]

We come to the Donner camp whear the most of them perrished the winter before. They had trim[m]ed the pines of their limbs for fuel. Their camp was in a thick forrest of pines not far from Donner Lake. The snow was verry deep. We found bones and sculls scatterd

---

[10.] The Truckee River drains modern Lake Tahoe and flows into Pyramid Lake in Nevada. William Baldridge gave this account of its naming in the 26 October 1876 issue of the *San José Pioneer*: "In 1845 James M. Harbin and a few others were on their way to California and on arriving at the sink of the Humboldt they met with an Indian and employed him to pilot them across the desert. While en route Harbin noticed a resemblance in him to a Frenchman he had previously known, and therefore bestowed the name of the Frenchman (Truckee) on the Indian, and on arriving at the river (Truckee) they were greatly elated at their good fortune, and named it Truckee river." A Northern Paiute, Chief Truckee served with Frémont in the conquest of California and died in Lyon County, Nevada, in 1860.

[11.] Numerous emigrant journals complain about the many crossings of the Truckee; Nicholas Carriger remembered that in 1846 he crossed the river thirty-eight times. Mormon Battalion veteran Henry Bigler wrote that Sam Brannan reported that the "very deep and rapid" river required twenty-seven crossings.

[12.] The fight took place on the morning of 5 September. Battalion journals state that the quarrel took place on the morning they met Brannan, 6 September, but after reaching San Francisco, Brannan wrote, "the next day after I left [Brown], I met part of the Battalion, about 200 men, on their way to Salt Lake." See the Journal History, 18 September 1847. Brannan arrived at Sutter's Fort, on 10 September, "in the evening with one Man from the Mountains," a "Mr [John S.] White [a] Shoemaker." See Sutter, *New Helvetia Diary*, 77.

about. It was a most horrible sight. They had mashed the bones to get the marrow.

Some wild Indians come in[to] our camp in the evening to take observations, the wildest looking savages we had seen. They had never seen a white man before according to their actions. By and by their leader said, "Wedy, wedy, hoddy-hoddy," and dissipeard in the dark forrest.[13]

I stood guard in the latter part of the night and thought of all the ghosts and hobgoblins I could think of or ever heard of. Besides the sculls, bones, and the dark forrest, it was a most dismal place.[14]

Day come and drove all the specters away. Next morning crossed over the sumit of the great ridge. The road was verry rough [with] rocks [and] trees fallen across the road. Camped early [and] went to hunt, several of us. Shot squirrels, some grouse, [and] wounded a deer, but lost it. Started looking for camp and come right onto a bear. He started to run [and] we shot and wounded him. He ran into a thicket of brush and we after[wards] met the bear open mouthed comeing at us. One of the boys shot him in the mouth and that checket him a moment, [but] he started for us again. Our guide shot him in the head and finished the sport. We had meat enough, but come verry near paying dear for it.

The next day [we] passed through heavy forest and [took a] rough road down verry steep places. One place was a quarter of a mile decent. The waggons that proceded us were rough locked and [had] young pine trees tied behind the waggons and then slid down to the bottom.[15] Camped in a grove of pines, the tallest we had seen. They looked to be three hundred feet high.

One day more through the tall forrest and come to Jonsons [Johnson's] Ranch, the first house in Callifornia, situated on Bear River. Jon-

---

[13.] These were probably Washoe Indians.

[14.] General Kearny's east-bound escort passed the Donner camp on 22 June. "The General called a halt and detailed five men to bury the deserted bodies. . . . This place now goes by the name of Cannibal Camp. . . . After we had buried the bones of the dead, which were sawed and broken to pieces for the marrow, we set fire to the cabin. . . . One mile above here there is another cabin and more dead bodies, but the General did not order them buried." J. Cecil Alter, "The Journal of Nathaniel V. Jones," 19. Robert Bliss saw the camp on 5 September 1847, and wrote, "To see the Bodys of our fillow beings Laying without Burial & their Bones bleaching in the Sun Beams is truly Shocking to my feelings." Alter, "The Journal of Robert S. Bliss," 120.

[15.] Blackburn described the descent into Steep Hollow, where two years later overlander John Banks noted that "the number of trees at the bottom might remind one of a wood yard." Scamehorn, *The Buckeye Rovers*, 90. This passage brought travelers into Bear Valley.

ston had married one of survivors of the Donor party.[16] And we are now in the beautyful valley of the Sacramento. Next morning started for Suiters Fort on the Sacramento River at the mouth of the American River.

We took in California with all eyes open for the grand sight. It is indeed a strange land and a great change in scenery from the dry, parched up deaserts of the interior of the continent. Changed our weary tierd out horses with Cap Suiter for fresh ones. Suiter paid every attention to our wants, the accomodating Swede.[17] We rested several days here.[18] Mr. Suiter raises large fields of wheat [and] has manny white men and Indians employed in his business.

Next started for Monterey, the capitol of California, to transact some business with Govener Mason.[19] In two days brought us to the Mormon Slough whear Stockton now stands. Here we found a Mormon colony established by Samuel Brannan to raise wheat for the Mormon emegration.[20] Cros[sed] the San Joukin [Joaquin] on tuly boats. Pulled them out on the bank to dry so others could cross and

---

[16.] Located three miles east of modern Wheatland, Johnson's Ranch was the easternmost settlement in northern California in 1847 and the staging point for the Donner-Reed party rescue. American sailor William Johnson settled on the site of the Gutierrez Rancho in 1845. In June 1847, Johnson married Mary Murphey, a Donner-Reed party survivor, but after several months she found him to be a "drunken sot," left him, and had the marriage annulled.

[17.] John Augustus Sutter, born Johann August Suter in the German province of Baden in 1803, became a Swiss citizen. He arrived in California in 1839, via Oregon, Hawaii, and Alaska. Armed with little more than charm, he pioneered the Central Valley of California and purchased the last Russian interests in California, all on credit. Gold was discovered in the foothills of the Sierra in 1848 during construction of a sawmill for Sutter. In the ensuing hysteria, Sutter's empire disintegrated in a fog of alcoholism and mismanagement.

[18.] The *New Helvetia Diary* recorded the arrival of "Capt. Brown of the Mormon Battalion" on 12 September 1847 and his departure the next day: "Capt. Brown, Mr. fowler & C[ompan]y left for Monterey after having purchased 6 horses of Mr. Kyburz."

[19.] General Kearny appointed Colonel Richard B. Mason as military governor of California. In April 1847, John C. Frémont had challenged Mason to a duel. Mason selected double-barreled shotguns as the weapons, and Kearny ordered Frémont to proceed no further in the matter. Mason returned to St. Louis in 1849 and died shortly thereafter of cholera.

[20.] Late in 1846, Samuel Brannan sent twenty Mormons under Blackburn's future brother-in-law, William Stout, to establish a farming colony. New Hope was located on the north bank of the Stanislaus River, a mile and a half above its junction with the San Joaquin. After the colonists built a log house and planted and fenced eighty acres, Stout claimed the farm and advised the colonists to select other land. Brannan removed Stout, but the colony was flooded, its crops failed, and the colonists wives "began to take in washing from the sailors" to support themselves. Brannan disbanded New Hope in October 1847, and "the land, the oxen, the crop, the houses, tools, and lounch [sic], all went into Brannan's hands, and the Company that did the work never got anything for their labor." See Glover, *The Mormons in California*, 21.

swam the horses acrost. Then crost the wide plains of the Joquin valley. On this plain were manny bands of wild horses and elk.

Crost the Coast Range to Livermores ranch. The ground was covered with cattle and horses. Mr Livermore is an Englishman and come here many years ago.[21] Come down out of the mountain[s] to Mission St. Joe, [a] strange building with an antiqated appearence.[22] They are a going to ruin gradualy.

The next place we come to was Santa Clara Mission.[23] Every thing was so different, strange houses and people and the guaud[i]ly dressed Spaniards mounted on their horses with lassoes in hand. It is their sole occupation to keep their riding rig[g]ing in order. They could not surprise us [as] we were acustombed to surprises.

Went over another lovely plain coverd with cattle and few horses and the hilles coverd with wild oats. Camped at the place Gilroy is now. In the evening, the Spanyards took a fancy to one of our horses and they ran a band of their own through ours and in the mixture took the horse they wanted, a verry sly way of stealing. One of us was afoot until we reached Mission of San Juan.[24]

Here we bought a half bronco horse. He looked real mean. Dragged him up to a post, put blinds over his eyes, put on the saddle, [and] sinch it up tight. The animal [is] qu[i]vering in every joint and stands braced ready for action. Put on the spurs and tie down your hat. Mount quietly on the saddle, put a strap arround the horse [and] over your knees to keep from going up. Reach over between the ears, raise the blinds, sink in the spurs, and the show is open. This is the most excit-

---

[21.] William Livermore became a naturalized Mexican citizen in 1844 after twenty years in California. An Englishman born in 1799, he established himself in what came to be called Livermore Valley. About 1846 he purchased the Canada de los Vaqueros, the ranch Blackburn saw and "a well-known station" on the route from Monterey to Sacramento.

[22.] San José de Guadelupe, located fifteen miles northeast of modern San Jose, was occupied by renters and squatters in 1847. Santa Clara and San José were under the administration of Fr. José María del Real, who persuaded Governor Mason to send troops to deal with the Americans. Governor Mason noted that emigrants, "to the exclusion of the priest," had not left "even one room at his disposal." Englehardt, *The Missions*, 4:584. A section of the original mission's monastery wing has been restored.

[23.] Mason's 11 July orders, which sent Captain Henry Naglee to deal with the Americans at Mission Santa Clara de Asis, warned, "I am told you are going into a bad neighborhood; it will therefore be necessary that you keep up a good discipline and a close watch on your horses, lest they be stolen." Ibid., 4:584–86. The mission grounds are now the University of Santa Clara, a Jesuit college established in 1851.

[24.] San Juan Bautista is located four miles south of Highway 101 in the Salinas Valley. The plaza of the old town is one of the few places to preserve the atmosphere and look of early California.

ing performences a new beginer can find. He is not apt to continue in the business verry long and will find an easyer way of sailing. San Juan is the finest mission we have seen, situated in a beautiful valley.

The busards [were] sitting around and cleaning up the offall of the slau[gh]terd cattle and [it] is against the rules to kill them. There was copper cannon lying arround as though there had been war hear lately. Crost over a low mountain and come into Salenos [Salinas] Valley and in sight of the Bay of Monterey. We come into a raveine right onto a lot of condors or large vultures devowering a fresh carcass. They flew up and darkend the air with their wings. They were certently the largest bird of flight in America and we called them condors. Camped on the Salenas River and heard the mighty surf breaking on the Pacific shore.

In the morning arrived at Monterey. There was six men of war lying in the bay at anchor. As soon as we found quarters we went down to the beach and went out by invitation of an officer of the ships and took in all the sights to be seen on a man of war. We interested the sailors in our outlandish mountain gear and out fitt.[25] It was new to them.

Governer Mason had started to San Francisco the day before and we mist him.[26] He was moveing the seat of goverment to yerbuena [Yerba Buena] or San Francisco so we started to o[v]ertake and overhall him at San Juan mission, but the payrolls of the army were at Monterey.[27] He told two of us, Lysander Woodworth and my self, to return after them.[28] We had orders to change horses when we come to Monterey. We had

---

[25.] After his arrival in the Salt Lake Valley, John Steele noted, "Our men that looked natural enough when they left Council Bluffs, now look like mountaineers, sun burned and weather beaten, mostly dressed in buckskin with fringes and porcupine quills, moccasins, Spanish saddles and spurs, Spanish bridles and jinglers at them, and long beards, so that if I looked in the glass for the young man who left the Bluffs a year ago, I would not have known myself." Steele, "Extracts," 17.

[26.] Governor Mason reported, on 7 October 1847: "While on my way up to San Francisco, I was overtaken by Captain Brown of the Mormon battalion, who had arrived from Fort Hall, where he had left his detachment of the battalion to come to California to report to me in person. He brought a muster-roll of his detachment, with a power of attorney from all its members to draw their pay; and as the battalion itself had been discharged on the 16th of July, Paymaster Rich paid to Captain Brown the money due to the [Pueblo] detachment up to that date, according to the rank they bore upon the muster rolls, upon which the Battalion had been mustered out of the service. Captain Brown started immediately for Fort Hall, at which place and in the valley of the Bear River he said the whole Mormon emigration intended to pass the winter." Mason either misinterpreted Brown's information or was intentionally misled. See Bancroft, *History of California*, 5:494.

[27.] Lieutenant Washington Bartlett changed the name of the village on Yerba Buena Cove to San Francisco in January 1847.

[28.] Lysander Woodworth was born 3 February 1828 at Ashtabula, Ohio, and was a private in Company A of the battalion. Woodworth was six feet tall and died on 26 March 1898 in San Francisco.

been riding hard to overtak[e] him and this made it double. Received the Pay rolles and returned to camp all most exausted. Lay down [and] had a good sleep.

The California horses are of Arabian stock and have wonderful endurence, with powerful nerve and muscle and if propperly treated can surpass anny others in hard service. We never thought of shoeing them. Their hooves are as hard as mountain goats feet.

Nex[t] two days come to Santa Clara mission. Campt with some emegrants from Illinois. They intended to settle here. They told some horrible tales [of] how they sufferd on the plains. They lost half of their stock and winterd on Bear River. Started in the spring and were ambushed on Ogden River by the Indians and lost three of their men and more of their cattle. Their provisions gave out and [they] had to cash [cache] a great manny things. One man cashed thirteen rifels he was taking to Callifornia to sell. They told us whear the cash was and discribed [the] place so when we returned we could find it. They had bought some land of a Spanish Don and were putting up som[e] shanties.[29]

[With] the beautiful bay of Sir Francis Drake in plain sight, we traveled along its shore all day. It would not take a prophet to tell there would be a large comercial city here some time in the near future. Next, come to Mission Dolores with[in] four miles of Yerbuena.[30] There were a few familys of Mormons liveing here. They had come arround the Horn in the ship Brooklin with Brannan. They had a hard story to tell against him.[31] We come to our journeys end at San Francisco. This is a small town with a few adobe and frame houses along the beach [and] some few canon scatterd arround. [There was] no wharf [and] the ships boats slid up on the beach.

[29.] No published record exists of any overland party wintering on Bear River (in modern Wyoming, Utah, and Idaho) before 1847. While it is tempting to believe that Blackburn's tale refers to an otherwise unknown company, the papers of Henry M. Naglee list the "squatters" with whom he dealt at Santa Clara in the dispute with Father Real in July 1847. These men included Stephen C. Young and Thomas West, who played prominent roles in the 1846 emigration. The *New Helvetia Diary* stated that, on 28 May 1847, "the Settlers from Bear Valley [are] nearly all here and gone"; these may have included some of the emigrants Blackburn met at Santa Clara. Blackburn may have misinterpreted their account of wintering on Bear River in California as a reference to Bear River in the Rocky Mountains.

[30.] San Francisco de Asis was founded on 29 June 1776. The surviving church was begun in 1782 and dedicated in 1791. In continuous use, it remains one of the best preserved of all the mission chapels. It can still be seen on Dolores Street between Sixteenth and Seventeenth streets.

[31.] One of the residents of the Mission Dolores was young James Skinner, who told the following "hard story" about Brannan in memoirs written in 1915: "the men

Lying out at anchor were a few ships of war and some whalers. Our pilot went to see an agent of the Hudson Bay Company on some business and this agent wanted him to goe north on a vessel to Fort Vancouver on the Collumbia River and return to Ft Hall in the Spring. He was verry much disipointed when he returned, for he expected to return with us to his Fauns. She would have to stay alone at Ft Hall this winter. He sat down and had a good cry. He wrote a letter to Capt. Grant and told him to explain it to her.

The next day the vessel sailed.[32] He was a real good fellow and we were sorry to see him goe. When he bid us good by, he cried like a baby and wanted us to stop at Ft Hall and see his wife. The poor fellow. We did not goe that way, but sent his letter direct by some trappers.

We lost another of our messmates, William Squires, a general good companion and favorite of all the company.[33] He concluded to stay here with a dashing young widdow who lost her husband while comeing around the Horn and that come near breaking up the company, but we promised to return acording to agreement. Our Boss thought [it] best to return soon or the dark eyed sinueretos would capture his whole outfitt. There was great inducements to stay in this beautiful land.

My friends and fellow Pionee[rs],
Who have met here this day,
In remembrence of former years,
When we came here to stay.

chorus:
We are glad we[']re in this tropic land,
To meet and greet this little band,
            the Early Pioneers.

---

of our company [from the *Brooklyn*] was called to go up the Sacramento River to load the ship with Redwood, Hides and Tallow. . . . While they were gone their Families were to draw rations from the stock that was brought with them from home. But what they got was something scandelous! Not enough to hardly keep life in their bodies, not but what there was plenty for all. But the (Big Fish) bug . . . got it [all], as they most allways will—and still do. The President of the Co., [was] Sam Branning. Him and his family lived high at the expense of the poor and needy, the widows and orphans, what he dident need, [he] sold which laid the foundation for [the] wealth that he afterwards accumulated." Joseph Skinner, Autobiography, LDS Archives, 5–6.

[32.] In 1847, the Hudson's Bay Company agent in San Francisco was British Vice-Consul James A. Forbes. The ship may have been the *Janet*, Captain David Dring, which left San Francisco 5 October 1847.

[33.] William Squires mustered out of Company C of the battalion a corporal. Squires had a "Saddler and Stamping business" at Sutter's Fort in 1848. There were two *Brooklyn* widows whose husbands died on the voyage: Prudence Clark Aldrich, forty-three, and Jerusha Ensign, fifty-six. Squires ran a tavern near Sacramento and died of cholera late in 1850.

EARLY DAYES IN CALIFORNIA

We loved this country at first sight,
When first our flag was raised,
And saw the ocean in its might,
Bathed in her angry waves.

Over 55 years have come and past,
Since that eventful time.
Can see the stars and stripes at last,
Wave over this tropic clime.

Such balmy winds blew over the plains,
With sun sets gorgeous sight,
And cattle on a thousand hills,
It was lovely day and night.

The noble elk here stalked the plains,
It was astonishing to see,
Never molested and so tame,
With wild horses to be seen.

Jolly times we had then,
The natives good and kind.
To change a horse with one of them,
Until another ranch you find.

There was no fences there to climb,
We roamed at our sweet will.
To take a bullock was no crime,
And manny a one was killed.

And lay upon the ground at night,
It was softer then than now.
The insects [g]nawed until daylight,
Some times a grizley grould.

At every door a horse did stand,
His owner a basking around,
Ready to coral his broncho bands,
When ever a trade was found.

Chele colorow beside every door,
And dogs to great you there.

The houses had no us[e]less floors,
We were as welcome as the air.

The caty dids sang us to sleep,
With the coyotes dismal howl.
A sentinal we did not keep,
And snakes a crawling round.

The lizards twined around our necks,
And slumberd safe and sound.
We scraped the rocks from round our beds,
With the broncoes staked around.

With tooly boats to cross the streams,
And naut to bar the way.
While fishes in the rivers team,
In this land we[']re bound to stay.

Stories in books were filled,
The half it was not told.
With oats on top of all the hills,
And mountains seamed with gold.

To New Helvetia we were bound
The best place in this land.[34]
The gold then it was not found,
It was buried in the sand.

It slumbered quiet under ground,
And did not know its power,
And sho[o]k the world around and around,
From that eventful hour.

We started an empire in the West,
From the war with Mexico.
Our brothers from the East come next,
To this Opphir whose sands were gold.[35]

[34.] New Helvetia was John Sutter's name for all the lands in his central California empire.

[35.] Ophir, a favorite allusion of the gold-rush era, was a biblical land renowned for its gold.

Took a boat ride with some marines out to some islands and had a jolly time. Finished our business, drew our pay, and were discharged from the service.

Started for Suiters Fort. Went about fifteen miles and campt after dark, when Cap Brown mist his saddel bags with about five thousand dollars in Spanish doubloons.[36] He sen[t] two of us back. We found the treasure back about three miles. The govener and he had been takeing too much of the needful and he had brought a bottle of auguedente along with him to keep level.

In three days come to the San Joquin River. There was a large bend in the river [in] the shape of a horse shoe. In it was a band of elk. One of our boys [was] a rash kind of a fellow [and] struck out to lasso one of them. He gave chaise, having the inside track, and soon had one by the horns before they could get out of the bend. He held on and soon horse and elk got tangled up in the lasso. One of our men ran to him and shot the elk with a pistol. The horse was badly hooked. The elk was fat and we had a good feast on elk.

Crost the Juaquin on the same tule boats and stopt at Tommy Tompkins place at New Hope or Mormon Slough.[37] They were all sick with fever.

In two more days arrived at Cap Suiters.[38] This is the most important place in all this country. There was a great many Indians and trappers, soldiers, emegrants, and others. Here we fitted out for Salt Lake Valley to winter and from there to the states. Layed in suplies for the trip. Had two

---

[36.] Blackburn's $5,000 figure matches the amount that Patriarch John Smith reported to Brigham Young on 6 March 1848. Edward Tullidge gave the amount as ten thousand dollars, and Charles Kelly calculated that the total battalion pay could not have been much over $3,000. "Tullidge has vaguely said that Brown bought out Goodyear 'with his own proportion and accumulations while in the service and in probable business gains on his recent trip,' but the former sum could not have amounted to much, while if he made thousands of dollars in the two days between the time he reached the coast and the time he turned back to Salt Lake Valley with the Battalion funds, he was a financier whose talents deserved more scope than was afforded by the desert valleys of Utah." Morgan, *A History of Ogden*, 19.

[37.] Thomas King Tompkins was born 15 August 1817 in Lincolnshire, England. A *Brooklyn* pioneer, Tompkins was at Sutter's Fort in 1847–48 and then briefly traveled to Salt Lake Valley. In 1852, following a Mormon mission to the Society Islands, Tompkins settled in San Bernardino. He left in the exodus of 1858, "but not being quite satisfied with the entire workings of the Mormon faith there," he moved to San Francisco. He returned to San Bernardino in 1862 and died there on 14 January 1885.

[38.] According to the *New Helvetia Diary*, the party arrived at the fort on 4 October, "with an express for [sic] receive the Mail from the Emigrants." On the next day, "Saml Lewis left with Capt. Brown."

pack horses load[ed] with seed wheat, double sacked for Brigham Young.

I thought that it was a venture, for it was apt to get scatterd. There was five of us all told: Cap Brown, Samuel Lewis, Lysander Woodworth, Jesse Brown, and myself.[39] We started the 5 of October 1847 on the biggest torn fool erant that ever is known. A whole band of half broke animals to pack and drive through a rough mountain country and hostile Indians tribes. If we had a leader, we would of followed him to Hades. My consience smote me, but would not back out at this stage of the game. With our pot gutted horses we packed and unpacked a dozen times a day and then [had to] herd them at night. In this camp there came verry near being a mutiny and nothing but fair promises and extra pay kept us from it. We were like the woman with the steamboat engine: she admired its ambition but not its jughment.

In two days more began to climb the Sierea Nevada mountain and [it was] verry tedious work keeping the animals in the rough road. Half way up it began to rain mixt with snow and looked dark ahead of us. Found a good camp and dried out by the fire. The next morning was bright and clear and [we] gained the summit of the moutain. Campt at the Doner place. Went down the Trucky River and camped in the Big Meadows.[40]

Nex[t] camp was in the Trucky Canion. In the morning at daybreak [we] heard a nois[e]. Jum[p]t up and looked across the river and the Indians were starting to cross. We fired over their heads and they ran back. Three held them off while two packed up the horses and got ready to start. The Indians were crossing above when we started. Our boss lost his hat and all lost their breakfast. Went as fast as we could goe, about fifteen miles, to the place whear the road leaves the river and starts on the desert. Here we had to stop for breakfast and lay in watter for the desert. Made all hast[e] and just as we finished eating, we saw the savages comeing on the run. We slung our packs and sad[d]les on and put out on the desert. Traveld fast for a while until the deep sand stoped our progress. If the Indians had followed us, they would have cau[gh]t us about half way across. Come to the boiling sulpher spring. The horses were verry tired and away in the night we made supper. The

---

[39.] The son of Tarleton Lewis, Samuel Lewis, was born 27 October 1829 in Simpson County, Kentucky. Lewis was a private in Company C and was discharged with most of the battalion in Los Angeles. Lewis settled in southern Utah, where he worked as a stonemason. In 1897, Lewis was living in the polygamist Mormon colony at Colonia Juárez in Chihuahua, Mexico. He died in Thatcher, Arizona, on 31 August 1911.

Jesse Sowel Brown, son of James Brown's wife, Martha Stephens, was born 29 March 1829 in Lexington, North Carolina, and was a private in Company C. He helped his father pioneer Ogden, Utah.

[40.] Blackburn's Big Meadows is now the site of Reno, Nevada.

boss was missing. Went out to look for him and found him praying: "Oh Lord, save us from those red Devils." We broke in on his devotions [and] cried out "Supper!" and had a good laugh on him the rest of the trip.

Crost over the desert to the sink of Maries River or Stinking Watter. Here we hunted for a cash of thirteen rifels made by a man from Missouri. We had a discription of the place, but could not find them. A good thing for us [as] we had our hands full without them.

Kept on up the river and saw wild naked savages by the hundred. In the fall of the year they are all fat. We camped out on the open ground away from the brush. One morning after starting, one of the packs come loose and the horse began to bellow like a mad cow. The frying pan, coffe[e] pot, and all flew in the air. The bronco whirled around and around and stept on Cap. Browns sword and broke it off close to the hilt. He had put it on the pack horse because it hurt his hips to carry it. The sword was useless for we were not likely to come in close quarters with the Indians. Tore a hole in the flour sack and made a fog of flour dust. The boss sayes, "Who put that pack on?" The boys said I did and he began [to] dam[n] and berate me in old stile. I told [him] I could pack as good as he could pray. The boys began to laugh and that settled him.

We geatherd up the remains as well as we could. The flour was a great loss and [we] went a little short on bread. Had one sack left. Started again and nothing but the everlasting greece wood and stinking alkly to look at. Come to an Indian camp. They apeard friendly and [we] traded for some fish. After eating, two of our men turned sick. We thought of poison and gave them some brandy and that releived them somewhat. One felt paines in his stomach and wanted another drink, but we all knew him for an old toper. We whatched him for a while. He got no worse and [we] saved that drink for a future occasion.

Another camp was close [to] the river. The brush was full of Indians. Moved back a ways [and] baricaded the camp with rocks and saddles. They would come to the edge of the brush and look at us and [they] had long bows and arrows. All hands stood guard. In the morning [we] found two horses shot with arrows. Pulled the arrows out. One was not hurt much [but] the other died.

Went on until noon onto a plain of good grass and all except one took a good sleep. We were nearly worn out for the want of sleep [with] only five of us and every other night half a night on guard.

Come to the Pallisades [as] it is called now.[41] A mile or two

---

[41.] Palisade, on the Central Pacific line at the western end of Emigrant Canyon, was the northern terminus of the narrow-gauge Eureka & Palisade Railroad. The name also referred to the canyon between Gravelly Ford and the Hastings Cutoff's

above is whear [the] Hastings cut off road turns off from the main road.[42] We thought we would try the cutoff road, whitch goes to the south of Salt Lake.[43] The road was verry hard to find being not traveld much. The grass had grown over it in places. We found it by directions of an emegrant.

Started on it. Went up a long canion allmost perpendiclur on the sides and camped whear the whole stream come out under the mountain.[44] One night while [we] were getting away from the Indians one of our men lost his hat. He made one out of ropes, rags, and grass. On earth was not its like. It looked like a buzard. We told him if he would charge on the Indians they would run on sight of his hat. It was as good as a reinforcement of fifty men. The boys joked him so that he made a new one, but it was more ghostly than the first one.

Past through the canion. A few Indians [came] in sight and would run off on sight. Come right onto one. He was fishing with a long stick forked and had barbes on the end. He had a lot of fish. We traded for them.

There was sage bushes pulled up and about everry ten yards was a bush with the roots sticking up. We supposed it was something about catching rabbits and let it go at that. Our course was south along a mountain to the east of us until we saw a low pass and the road turned east through the pass.[45] There was timber on this mountain, some low pines and juniper. There was a high fence made of brush and small pines. Well, this bothered us again: who made the fence? It looked like it was made for deer and we let it goe at that. The company that come through here could not have made it for the fence ran clear over the mountain.

---

junction with the California Trail. Blackburn is incorrect in placing this junction at Palisade, which is to the west of the actual location.

[42.] Promoted by Lansford W. Hastings in what Bancroft termed "a worthless book called an *Emigrant's Guide*," this cutoff across Utah's Salt Desert contributed to the demise of the Donner-Reed party in 1846. Hastings, a lawyer born in Ohio in 1819, crossed the Oregon Trail in 1842 led a party to California in 1843. He returned to the United States via Mexico and published his guide to recruit emigrants. After leading the emigration to California in 1846, Hastings acted as a Mormon agent in California, became a judge, and served in the 1849 California constitutional convention. In the 1860s, he endorsed the secessionist cause in the West. Hastings died in route to Brazil about 1870, promoting a refugee Confederate empire.

[43.] The following description of Blackburn's route on the Hastings Cutoff is based on information provided by trail historians Don Buck, Ben E. Lofgren, David L. Bigler, and Roy Tea.

[44.] Blackburn described the canyon of the South Fork of the Humboldt River. The camping place was near the confluence of the South Fork and Tenmile Creek or Huntington Creek.

[45.] The company crossed modern Harrison Pass. Captain Brown was very likely following instructions that Lansford Hastings gave to Sam Brannan early in 1847. See Appendix C.

Three deer jum[p]t up and crost the road ahead of the horses and our best hunter grabbed his gun and sayes, "Le[t']s have some venesen for supper," and started arround a hill to get a shot and we lost sight of him. Went on a little distance and waited an hour or more and he did not return. Two of our men went to look for him. They hunted all over, but could not find him. Went on to the first good camp an stopt. Sent two men to look. They scoured the country good, but without success. We were in a fix and so was he.

Brown sayes, "The Indians have taken him and that is the last." We all thought the same for there was plenty around here. We sat arround the camp fire wondering what to do. "Look at that fire on top of that hill," says one. "I['l]l bet thats him."

"Le[t']s goe to it," says another. And off [the] two started to the fire and took an hour to reach the place. They approached cau[tiou]sly for fear of a trap and found him roasting venesen. He said he was going to live while [he] did live and he built the fire so we could see it, for he was lost and could not find the road. Well, we come out of that lucky.

Come to a beautiful valley. The road turned north here along the mountain and springs every few rods ran out into the plain. This we called Thousand Spring Valley.[46]

Went about twelve miles along the mountain and campt. We had been on short rations some time. Killed some ducks and hares to help out the meal. The next morning lo[o]ked stormy. Hunted up the road. The grass had grown over it. [We] hunted an hour or more and found it whear it left the grass and turned east onto the desert. We followed it about three miles and lost the road in a blinding snow storm.

Stopt, unpacked, turned the animals loose except two, and rol[l]ed up in blankets. The storm pas[s]ed off shortly and [we] began to look for our animals [but] could not find them. Went again and found them on a spring branch on good feed. Packed up, wen[t] back to camp, and thawed and dried out. Started again. The snow soon went off [and we] found the road.

We shot more rabbits and hares. They went well with our boiled wheat. There was an awful goneness in our stomacks all the time. One of our messmates had an appitite that would discount a shark. He would take the hare skins and scor[t]ch the fur off over the fire and then ro[a]st them to a turn. He sayed they went splendid.

Capt. Brown said, "I do not care what you eat so [long as] you do not taccle our saddles and boots." All hands were cross when we come

---

[46.] Blackburn referred to the western side of the Ruby Valley, called by some emigrants the "Valley of Fifty Springs," and not to the modern Thousand Springs Valley, which sits astride the California Trail that the Brown party had crossed in August.

into camp. Our boss was a jolly old chap. He would tell some out-landish story and put all in a good humor.

We next crost a salt plain.[47] The ground grass and the bushes were stiff with salt. One could smell it in the air. We were affraid to look be-hind for fear of being turned into a pillar of salt like Lots wife. I am sure we were no better than she was.

We expected to come to the Ninty Three Mile Desert anny time.[48] Next morning [we] fill[ed] the canteens full of watter [and] cut some sage wood for the horses to eat. They will eat it when there is no grass to eat. Struck out and about noon began to be thirsty and drank spareingly and come to a large spring of good water. We were not on it [yet].[49]

Campt and prepared in earnest this time. Went on top of a high hill and could see far ahead on the dry bed of the old lake. The Salt Lake coverd a vast extent on the southern side of the lake at one time in the past and this is called the great dessert. Made preperation this time and no mistake.

Killed two crains. Layed in more wood [and] cooked an extra lot of wheat. Capt. Brown said he would cook it himself so as to have one good mess on the desert. He commenced to dance around and sing a dilly.

> Pretty Betty Martin,
> Tip toe fine.
> She could not get a man,
> To suit her mind.
> Some were too coarse,
> And some too fine.
> She could not get a man to suit her kind.

---

[47] The party followed the wagon road north until it turned east across Indepen-dence Valley, which contains a large alkali flat between Spruce Mountain Ridge and the Pequop Mountains. James Clyman noted, on 25 May 1846, that he went "across another dry clay plain covered with shrubs of a very dwarfish character." Camp, *James Clyman, Frontiersman,* 215.

[48] In 1846, mapmaker T. H. Jefferson measured the distance of the "fearful long drive" across this desert from Hope Wells, near present-day Iosepa, to "Bonark Springs," present-day Donner Springs at Pilot Peak, at eighty-three miles, a figure that "checks out exactly" against the United States Geological Survey orthophotoquad map of the Great Salt Lake Desert. See Spedden, "Who Was T. H. Jefferson?" 3, 7. Jef-ferson also noted that a good well at Dell (now Redlum) Spring "would reduce the drive to 70 miles." See Korns, *West from Fort Bridger,* 182–83. The desert is also known as the Seventy-Five Mile Desert and the Salt Desert.

[49] The party crossed Jasper Pass into Goshute Valley, turning northeast to cross the Toano Range near Silver Zone Pass. They then rounded the foot of Pilot Peak into Utah and probably camped at Donner Springs on the edge of the Salt Flats. The party then followed the clearly visible wagon road across the desert to Skull Valley and the Great Salt Lake country.

At the last word, he kicked out his foot and spilt all in the fire and cooked another.

In the morning the north wind was blowing cold. Started on the smooth bed of the ancient lake. Nothing but baked mud [with] no shells or sign of marine life. We supposed the watter had receded to the north. There appeard a mirage away to the north, but we could not tel[l] whether it was watter or not.

The [lake] bed we were traveling on appeard level and extend[ed] to the south as far as the eye could reach. It appeard like a few inches rise in the lake would send the watter over hundreds of miles of the old bed of the lake.

Not a bird, bug, hare, or coyote [was] to be seen on this wide desolate waist. Nothing but man and he was out of his lattitude or his natural seane. There was a mountain in the middle of this vast plain and [it] appeard as though it had been surrounded by the lake at some past time. The wind blew cold and chilly as though it come off the watter towards us. This lake was in my old geography [named] Timpanagos and to the South to the Hela river was marked the unexplored regions.[50]

[By] evening the ground was a little soft and the horses fag[g]ed out. Stopt at some abandoned waggons. We were cold [and] pulled the waggons togeather, set them on fire and had a good warm.[51] Tied the horses [and] threw them the wood to eat. Rolled up in our blankets and the first night on the desert was gone.

The second day at noon, [we] left the bed of the lake and worried along until night whear there was som[e] little grass and some snow in drifts. The horses licked it up and so did we, for the watter was out.

Next day worried along and left one horse. [We] crost over a low mountain and struck watter.[52] And now for rest. We had some brandy

---

[50.] The Great Salt Lake and the Gila River are separated by more than five hundred miles; early mapmakers had no reliable information about the entire Great Basin. Blackburn clearly enjoyed being more knowledgeable about the West than his "old geography," which was probably Smiley's once universal but now rare *Easy Introduction to the Study of Geography* (1828). See Wheat, *Mapping the Transmississippi West*, 2:95, 234.

[51.] Utah's Department of State History investigated this site in 1986, prior to the attempt to lower the Great Salt Lake by the West Desert Pumping Project, which flooded much of the Salt Desert and its emigrant trails. They investigated five wagon sites and concluded, "This site represents one of the abandoned Donner-Reed wagons." They noted that "Captain James Brown's detachment of Mormon Battalion soldiers and Captain Howard Stansbury's party of government explorers are the only recorded parties to have burned abandoned wagons on the mud flats of the Great Salt Lake Desert . . . it is possible that both parties camped at the same site." See Hawkins, *Excavation of the Donner-Reed Wagons*, 71, 77–78, 137.

[52.] The party crossed the Cedar Mountains into Skull Valley, where they found water at Redlum or Hope Springs.

along and blew it in, which revived us excedingly. In the evening the horse we left behind come into camp. He thought it was a hard place to die and changed his notion. We forgot all about the desert and had a good super of boiled hare, crane, and wheat.

In the morning [we] went down into a wider plain and by the looks of the oposite mountain thought it was the Salt Lake Valley.[53] The canion and other points looked familiar to us and [we] thought our journey ended. Our boss says, "Toot your horn Gabriel! We are most there."

The weather thickend up and began to snow. Expected to come to the Jordan River every hour. Come to riseing ground [and] then we knew we were mistaken in the country. Followed the mountain north to the Lake. Turned around the promi[n]tory on the beach of the lake and camped under some shelving rocks, whitch shelterd us from the snow storm. Here we were on the shore of the great Timpanagos Lake, so named in the old geography. The sun rose clear next morning [and] we could [see] in the distance about twenty miles. The smoke of the chimneys and all else looked right. One of the boys said he could hear the chickens crow.

Changed a pack onto another [horse] that had a sound back and by the way he acted we thought he was an old pack horse. [We] did not find out [differently] until the crupper tightend on him a going down a hill and away he went. Tore a hole in the pack and spilt some wheat. We cau[gh]t him [and] scraped the wheat up clean for it was valuble in this far off land.

About three oclock we were on Jordons stormy banks and went up into the camp of the Saints, the New Jerusalem. Arived 16 November 1847 into verry comfortable quarters for the winter.[54]

They built a fort there for saf[e]ty, when a few women could have run the whole band of Goshutes [Goshiutes] out of the country with mop sticks.

Shortly after arriving in Great Salt Lake City, Blackburn and Lysander Woodworth brought Captain Brown before a church court for breaching a contract, indicating that Brown probably refused to pay them for their services during the return to Utah. On 27 November, the High Council, the ruling body that governed the Mormon colony in the absence of the church leadership, met to consider the matter. "Abner

---

[53.] The men rounded the Stansbury Mountains and entered Tooele Valley.

[54.] Blackburn's 16 November date matches President John Smith's statement that Brown "was gone three months and seven days," which described the time between 9 August and 16 November. See the Journal History, 6 March 1848.

Blackburn and Lysander Woodworth preferred a charge against Capt. James Brown for not supplying them with beef according to contract. Willard Snow spoke for the plaintiff and Abraham O. Smoot for the defendant. After the case was duly traversed it was voted unani[m]ously that Capt. Brown should furnish 400 lbs of beef to each and if that is not enough, he should furnish sufficient to last them till next spring."[55] Dale Morgan noted that Blackburn probably fared better through the winter than some of his fellow battalion veterans.

On 20 November, the High Council sustained Brown in his claim that "he had returned with authority to act as deputy quartermaster or agent in the disposal of government property in this valley and he was counselled to conduct the same upon honorable and righteous principles. He also stated that he had been gone three months and seven days and had been to some expense and trouble and thought he should charge the boys 10 per cent for getting and bringing their money."[56] John Steele's journal noted, "Captain James Brown returned from California, November 17, and knocked all our arrangements in the head, making us pay 10% for our money and wanting us to pay 6 cents per lb. for all the U.S. oxen that we have eaten since the 16th of July."

The High Council "also decided that Henry G. Sherwood and Capt. Brown should purchase the Goodyear place and property if it could be obtained on fair terms." Brigham Young had instructed that Miles Goodyear's establishment on the Weber River, the site of modern Ogden, should be purchased "if the means could be raised"; a committee only a few days before Brown's arrival had concluded that the money was not available. Tullidge wrote "that it was their soldier pay of $10,000 [sic] in Spanish gold, that furnished the first money in circulation in these valleys. Excepting these doubloons, and half-doubloons, with which Brown's detachment was paid off, there was probably not a cent of money in the country among the Mormons in the years 1847 and 1848."[57]

The trial before the High Council is the last-known encounter between Blackburn and Captain James Brown, whose reputation has fared so poorly in this study. Blackburn says not a word about his dispute with Brown, and he actually commented favorably on Brown's sense of humor and his ability to boost the morale of his men. The surviving journals and memoirs of other veterans of the sick detachment paint a picture of a strutting, humorless, and corrupt martinet, lacking consid-

---

[55] Journal History, 20 November 1847.
[56] Ibid.
[57] Tullidge, *Histories of Utah*, "Biographical Supplement," 111–12.

eration for his men and driven by extreme religious fanaticism. Brown's own Pueblo journal, which might mitigate this picture, was lost when he left it with his clerk, John Smith.[58] As it is, Blackburn's ambiguous but generally positive portrait of Brown is almost the only good news about the captain to appear in the battalion annals. Dale Morgan noted: "Blackburn's picture of Captain James Brown is the first to put a spark of humanity into him, and make one realize he was in fact a leader of men. In the Mormon chronicles, he is a personality as stiff and unlovely as a poker."

The money that Brown collected in California made possible the purchase of Fort Buenaventura. For $1,950 of the battalion pay, Captain Brown bought Miles Goodyear's fraudulent Mexican land grant, seventy-five cattle, seventy-five goats, twelve sheep, six horses, and a cat. The dairy products produced at Brown's Fort—or Brownsville as the settlement was called until 1850—provided critical supplies for the Mormons' first winter in Utah. "Just why Captain Brown should have fallen heir to all Goodyear's stock, and have exercised almost a proprietary interest in the Ogden lands, is far from clear. Certainly the money with which Goodyear was bought out did not belong to Brown, regardless of everything that has been written on the subject. Mormon Battalion funds were used, and only the extraordinary character of the contemporaneous Mormon social organization made justifiable such public use of funds which properly belonged to individual battalion members."[59] Tullidge wrote that Brown "retained only two or three hundred acres, allowing his fellow colonists, in whose interest as well as for himself the [Goodyear] claim was purchased, to settle in the country without price or question of their rights."[60] Traditions enshrined on local monuments state that Brown opened the lands around Ogden to any Pueblo veteran who wanted to settle on them, but few took his offer.

Brown went on to serve missions in Central America, England, and New York for the Mormon church, and he was an emigration agent in 1854. He served in the territorial legislature and on the Ogden city council. He died on his birthday in 1863, after losing an argument with a molasses mill. He was the father of twenty-four children.

[58.] Journal History, 29 July 1847.
[59.] Morgan, *A History of Ogden*, 18–19.
[60.] Tullidge, "Biographical Supplement," *Histories of Utah*, 111.

SEVEN

No Rest for Me

When Blackburn arrived in Great Salt Lake City in November 1847, he found that the new settlers included his twenty-two-year-old uncle Jehu (pronounced *jay-hugh*), Jehu's wife Julia Ann, and his grandmother, Elizabeth Bowen Blackburn, who at sixty-four may have been the oldest woman to cross the Mormon Trail in 1847. They had left Winter Quarters, Nebraska, on 21 June 1847 in the "Big Company," the second wave of the emigration, and traveled in John Nebeker's company of ten in Abraham O. Smoot's division. The family arrived in the Salt Lake Valley on 25 September and probably provided the "verry comfortable quarters" in the pioneer fort that Abner Blackburn stayed in during part of the winter of 1847–48. The beef he secured from Captain Brown very likely went into the family stewpot.

Blackburn, typically, was not about to be confined to the adobe fort. He embarked on a trading expedition to southern Utah with Thomas S. Williams and Ephraim Hanks. Blackburn returned from the trading expedition by late December.[1] The Salt Lake Valley, which enjoyed mild weather during the winter, was still in a wild state. On 28 January Robert Bliss reported "we have cought & killed more than 300 wolves this winter." Blackburn, again restless, left the valley early in March with a party carrying mail to the Mormon Winter Quarters in Nebraska. In addition to Blackburn, the group included David Marshall Stuart, Ammi R. Jackman, and battalion veterans Robert Bliss,

---

[1.] On 28 December, according to the minutes of the High Council, "The marshall reported that he took Thomas Williams, Charles Shumway and Ephraim K. Hanks and went as far south as the last large creek in the valley and turned back the five persons sent for." See Kelly, *Miles Goodyear*, 95.

Alva C. Calkins, Samuel Lewis, and William Garner, who was appointed captain.

William A. Garner was born 22 January 1817 in North Carolina and served as a private in Company B, messing with diarist Henry Bigler. He died 29 March 1892 in Council Bluffs, Iowa.

Robert Stanton Bliss was born 1 August 1805 in Connecticut and was sealed to Mary Ann Paine in the Nauvoo Temple on 29 January 1846. According to legend, parts of his remarkable journal were written with his own blood.[2] Bliss died in California in 1851.

Alva C. Calkins, a private in Company A, was born 30 September 1825 in Hartford, New York, and was one of four brothers to serve in the battalion. He died 21 July 1887 in Goodwater, Kansas.

Ammi R. Jackman was born 6 February 1825 at Genesee Falls, New York. Jackman reached the valley on 30 September 1847, with Charles C. Rich's company. He was the younger brother of the Parmenio Jackman who was mortally wounded on the Mojave with Thomas Williams in 1860, and the son of Levi Jackman, a member of the Salt Lake Valley High Council. Jackman married Mary Aurelia Eldredge in 1858 and had nine children. He made seven trips across the plains and took part in the southern Utah Black Hawk War. Jackman died 27 November 1899.[3]

David Marshall Stuart was born 8 March 1826 in Irvin, Scotland, and emigrated to the United States in 1845. He drove a team to Salt Lake Valley for John Benlow in 1847. Stuart served nine missions for the LDS church, including an 1855 mission to the California gold fields during which he attempted to sell land in San Bernardino for Amasa Lyman and Charles C. Rich. Stuart settled in Weber County and died 19 August 1898.[4]

According to Robert Bliss, Sunday, 5 March 1848, was

> a beautiful day warm like summer; while the People assembled for meeting at the Stand Prest L.W. Hancock myself & others

---

[2] Parts of the journal are written in a red-brown ink that does appear to be blood, but both forensic pathologist George Throckmorton and historian Everett Cooley have deep reservations about this story, which originated with Mrs. Oliver G. Workman, who claimed to have heard it from her husband. See Cooley, "The Robert S. Bliss Journal," 383.

[3] *Utah Genealogical Magazine* 4 (1913): 183.

[4] Stuart, *Life Story of David M. Stuart.* Stuart had two accounts of the 1848 mail journey published in his lifetime (see Appendix D), and certainly described the trip in his memoirs. Unfortunately, only a typescript prepared by a granddaughter survived, and she wrote, "I have left out all the truly personal parts, and have included just those incidents that pertain to the missionary work of those early days." See Bitton, *Guide to Mormon Diaries & Autobiographies,* 347. Such pious omissions have vandalized the integrity of much Mormon pioneer history.

met at Father John Smith[']s to receive his Benediction &
Blessing we found him in Excelent Spirits and were Blessed
with a Blessing indeed He said we should be prospered on our
Journey our Animals also we should enjoy Health be preserved from our enemies & go safely through & find our families Well.[5]

After a harrowing overland journey, Blackburn found his family living in Clay County, Missouri, and preparing to emigrate to California.
While there, he applied for the 160 acres of land due to Mexican War
veterans and sold the land to one William Butt.

On the return to Utah, Blackburn met his future wife, Lucinda Harris, who was traveling with her parents. In the narrative, Blackburn was
remarkably reticent about discussing family or personal matters. Blackburn stated that he traveled with his family, but did not mention meeting his bride-to-be. His granddaughter, Blanche Blackburn Corby, said,
"Lucinda Harris met grandpa in a wagon train while crossing the plains.
She happened to be in a train that he was guiding, and he fell in love
with her." In his 1897 letter to the *Deseret News*, Blackburn wrote, "My
wife came through [Great Salt Lake City] in 1848."

In another striking omission, Blackburn failed to mention that his
family traveled with the Brigham Young company that left the Elkhorn
River on 1 June. Along with later companies led by Willard Richards
and Amasa Lyman, the 1848 Mormon emigration totaled about four
thousand people.[6] On 11 June 1848, Thomas Bullock noted in his
journal: "By order of Prest Young, the Big Wagon was unloaded & distributed into others, Anthony Blackburn, John Harris, Samuel Meckam
and Stephen Taylor. the barbed grass was very plaguy both to men &
sheep. the fire fly flying about in great numbers. the mosquitos troublesome."[7] (The contents of the wagon were evidently church records.)

The Blackburns arrived in the Salt Lake Valley about 22 September,[8]
but while on the trail they had already received news that would

---

[5.] Levi Ward Hancock, who enlisted as a lowly fifer in Company E yet acted as
the spiritual leader of the Mormon Battalion, was originally selected as captain of the
mail company, but he backed out at the last minute. See Cooley, "The Robert S. Bliss
Journal," 394, 395.

[6.] Church Emigration Book 1830–1848, Vol. 1, LDS Archives. This estimate was
made by Andrew Jenson.

[7.] Thomas Bullock, Journal, LDS Archives. John Harris was Blackburn's future father-in-law.

[8.] The 31 December 1848 Journal History entry stated that the First Division "left
the Elkhorn River June 1st and arrived in G.S.L. City Sept. 20, 1848 and on the following few days."

change the course of American history and alter their own destinies: gold had been discovered in California.

THE NARRATIVE

The first settlers had a hard time the first winter here.[9] All their provision was brought from the Missouri River and their suplies ran verry low towards spring. And manny had to dig roots and hunt or trap for a liveing and [we] killed a great manny cattle. Every bone was mashed for the marrow and hides, hooves, and offall was eaten with a rellish.

Tom Williams,[10] Eph Hanks,[11] and myself fitted out for a trading scheme to barter with the Utas [Utes] on the head watters of the Severe River away to the south of Utah Lake. Come to Provo and had a palaver with Old Elk, the cheif of the Utahs.[12] Passed Spring Creek, Spanish

---

[9] Kate B. Carter, in a discussion of the sego lily, wrote that "Elizabeth Bone Bowen Blackburn relates, 'The winter of '48 was a very severe one. Only by living on short rations, sharing food with one another, eating raw hides, sego lily bulbs and thistles were these hardy pioneers able to survive.'" See *Treasures of Pioneer History*, 4:78. Carter is actually quoting from an anonymous typescript biography entitled "Elizabeth Bone Bowen Blackburn," which was probably submitted to the Daughters of Utah Pioneers in the 1920s or 1930s. The typescript referred to the winter of 1848–49. Copy given to Amy Gallagher Hoffman by Manasseh Blackburn; copy in editor's possession.

[10] Tom Williams, Blackburn's old companion-in-arms, later joined the gold rush and eventually became a prominent Salt Lake lawyer and merchant. He violently apostatized in 1856 after his daughter eloped with a son of Mormon leader Heber C. Kimball and he came into financial conflict with Brigham Young. Williams settled briefly in Weston, Missouri, where he ran a hotel. He returned to Utah in 1858 after the arrival of Johnston's army and became involved with the judicial crusade against the church in 1858–59. Williams was killed in the Mojave Desert, in very mysterious circumstances, on 18 March 1860.

[11] At twenty, Ephraim Knowlton Hanks had already seen the world on the ship-of-the-line *Columbus* and marched in Company B of the Mormon Battalion to California. Along with Blackburn, he worked on the Nauvoo Temple and crossed Iowa with the Saints. He led a company to California in 1850, participated in the handcart relief of 1856, and took an active part in the "so-called Echo Canyon war." He fought in three Indian wars, but was always proud that he had never killed an Indian. Hanks developed Mountain Dell in Parley's Canyon and died a Mormon patriarch in Pleasant Creek, Utah, in 1896. Charles Kelly, who called Hanks a "famous Danite," wrote that Blackburn's cousin, Howard Blackburn, told him in 1946 that "Eph Hanks was a very heavy drinker but an exceedingly hardy pioneer." See Kelly Papers, "Reminiscences of Howard Blackburn," Utah State Historical Society, 5.

[12] Provo would not be settled until the spring of 1849. The Ute warrior Elk, Big Elk, or Old Elk had sworn never to live in peace with the white man, and he "was brave, cool and determined, standing over six feet high." Captain Howard Stansbury wrote of Old Elk, "I knew the leader of the Indians to be a crafty and blood-thirsty savage, who had already been guilty of several murders, and had openly threatened that he would kill every white man that he found alone upon the prairies." See Tullidge, "History of Provo City," 236, 237. Blackburn will encounter Old Elk again.

Fork, and away to the south to the Seveare. Went up this stream to the head and found two trappers, Paker and Devous, a Frenchman.[13] They told us not to goe to the Indians, for the cheif had lost a son lately and he might want to send us along with his son to the happy hunting grounds of the great spirit. We soon seen through their story. They did not want us to goe there and get their trade. [We] went to the village and done as well as expected with [the] venture.

Returned to Salt Lake and stayed there until the seventh of March 1848.[14] A company fitted out to goe to the states and nine of us started with the mail and other matter.[15]

The first day [we] went up to the snow. The next morning [we] began to shovel snow. In places it was drifted deep. [We] did not goe more than three miles and camped. The next day the snow was deeper. Shoveld and worked up into a big snow bank. Lead up our pack horse. He went as far as he cared about going and I tied him to a bush. He commenced pulling back with all his might. The rop[e] broke and all we could see of him the next five minutes was a hole in the snow.

We gave it up [and] returned to the fort. Rested a day or two and a mountaineer told us we could goe out by way of Weaver [Weber] River canion and seven of us fools tried it on. It was winter and [we were] poorly supplied with every thing that was necessary for the trip.

Mad[e] another start in two days.[16] Come to the mouth of the canion. We followed the trail of some traders who had come in from Fort

---

[13.] Although the manuscript reads "Paker," this probably refers to mountain man Jim Baker, who was trading with the Sanpete Indians on the Sevier River in late 1847. See Morgan, "Miles Goodyear," 316.

[14.] According to the Early Church Information File, John Smith blessed Blackburn in Great Salt Lake City on 9 January 1848. The Robert Bliss journal described the mail company's departure on 6 March 1848, "came 6 miles from town to the mouth of the canion & encamped to wait for for [sic] some to find their horses at night we were exposed to a severe shower of rain which ended with a snow storm towards morning. Tues 7th March lay by for the boys to come up. Wed 8th March our boys came this morning." Cooley, "The Robert S. Bliss Journal," 395.

[15.] The total number of men in the company is variously reported as seven or eight. A page fragment at the end of Bliss's journal listed the participants as "Wm Garner Capt, R. S. Bliss Historian, Alvah C. Calkins, Abner L. Blackburn, Ami R. Jackman, Saml. Lewis, David Stuart." (This is the first document that uses Blackburn's middle initial.) Bliss wrote that an Armstrong departed the valley with the group and stopped at Fort Bridger. Hosea Stout reported that eight men arrived at Winter Quarters. Some reports listed William Garner under his own name and also as "Captain Gardner."

[16.] On 14 March, Bliss noted that "to day is again fine weather passed up the river through a difficult pass [Devil's Gate] through among the Rocks & Sides of the mt which opened into a fine valley [Morgan Valley]." Ibid., 396.

Bridger with suplies for the starving Mormons of Utah.[17] [We] folowed the [t]rail of the traders. There was considerable snow in places, but not enough to stop us. Went arround it to find more ahead. Crost the river manny times, but come through to Echo Canion, that noted place.[18] From here to Bear River, next the Mudy, and over to Ft. Bridger. Here we found two Missourians who had come out here to become mountaineers, but had their curiosity sattisfied and wanted to return home. They had a good outfit, good guns, and plenty of provisions, and wanted to return with us. We welcomed them to our company. They were fine apearing men. One of their names was Wheaty, the others name was Barlow.[19]

I helpt burry Wheatly in Carson Valley in 1840 [1850].

One cold windy morning we started. In fact, it is windy all the time in this altitude. Went down Ham [Ham's] and Blacks Forks and on to Green River. We kept larg[e] fires to warm by. Crossed Big Sandy and Little Sandy and come to Paciffic Springs. Come onto the South Pass. The snow was drifted deep. Crost over and found two soldiers in the willows. They had come from California the fall before. They stopt at Bridgers and secured some traps to ceath [catch] game with. They were nearly starved [and] had killed their horse and eat him and were trapping white wolves to eat. [They] were nearly naked and their feet were frosen and [they had] no shoes to wear, but wrapt their feet in rags. We took them along with us to Fort Larime.[20]

After we cros[sed] the South Pass some distance, a furious north east wind struck us. It picked up the snow and drove it in hollows in great piles. We could not face it and went to a small canion to avoid it. Found [a] kind [of] shelter for the animals. We went into a small cave,

[17.] Robert Bliss reported that, on 23 January 1848, a company started to Fort Bridger, and on 12 February "a company has just returned from Fort Bridger with Beef cattle they report the mts passable for Pack Animals but the snow is in places 8 or 10 ft deep." Ibid., 387, 390.

[18.] Bliss stated that they crossed the Weber River sixteen times in ten miles. Ibid., 396.

[19.] At Fort Bridger, Bliss wrote that "we were joined by a Gentleman who wished to go with us to the states," but he made no mention of a second man. On 12 April, Bliss provided the probable correct name for Blackburn's "Wheaty": "Through the acquaintan[c]e of Mr Wheatley who accompanied us from fort Bridger; we obtained 50 or 60 lb of fine dried Buffalo meat which was generously given us by the Gentlemen of the Post." Ibid., 397.

[20.] Bliss again provides confirmation: "Mon 27th March came about 16 miles & camped on Sweet water through a snow storm all the way . . . soon after we camped we found two of our boys who left the 15 Jan last they were in a deplorable condition one had froze his feet so he was unable to travel & they had killed their only horse to subsist upon." Ibid., 398.

built a fire and cooked dinner. The storm [was] rageing out side as strong as ever and [we] thought we had cheated the storm, but the hot fire heated the rocks and thawed out the snakes and we left the cave.[21]

Tried the wind again, [but] the horses would not face it. Tied up to some bushes and waited for the wind to lull. Towards sundown it slacked up and we went on until midnight to mak[e] up lost time. Went down the Sweet Watter two days and come to the Devils Gate. A few miles further was Independence Rock and at Sage Creek [we] halted two days to lay in a suply of buffalow meat. They were plenty here, fat cows and calves. Mountaineers kill no other kind.

I was crawling throu[gh] the brush to get a shot at a cow and come onto a wolf lying down. He raised up in his layer [lair] and looked at me and I grin[n]ed and snapt my teeth at him. He stept a few feet to one side and I passed on. I did not want [to] scare the cow. Gave the cow a center shot. The pack horse was loaded with fat buffalow meat. We had not gon[e] a hundred yards when the same wolf was at the carcas helping himself. We jerked the meat over a fire on some green poles and laid in a good suply and started for the North Platt River.[22]

Come across a band of Indians who appeard friendly. They appeard to be on the war path. They inquired if we had seen Indians. We told them no and gave them some meat and tobacco and they went on. We asked them what tribe they were after and [they] made us no answer. One of our men says, "May be they are after our tribe." Kept a close watch tha[t] night. Our guards seen what they called wolves prowling arround camp and one of the wolves shook out a robe and then he knew what they were. They shook their robes to stampede the horses, but our animals were pretty well worn out and did not scare good. The guard woke some help [and] took several shot[s] at the wolves and they went off on two legs.

The buffalow were thick. Killed one ocasionally to keep in practice. Lassoed a verry young calf. It made such lunges and bunted our legs that we let it go with its mother a bellowing close by.

Passed the Black Hills and come to Ft. Larime. The men at the fort knew we were comeing. The squaws have eyes like tellescopes. They do all the lookout buissness [and] they had seen us long before the others had. Bought a few things. Left the two men we had picked up at the

---

[21] On 28 March, Bliss simply noted that they "made a most disagreeable camp in the snow & storm." Ibid.

[22] Bliss wrote, "April 1[t] 1848 . . . about one hour after we had encamped one of our boys came in & reported he had killed a Buffalo we immediately took 6 Animals & dressed & packed it into Camp." Ibid., 399.

South Pass. They hired out to drive teams to the Missouri River for some traders and down the long Plat[te River] we went.

Come to Chimney Rocks and then to Scoch Bluffs [Scott's Bluff].[23] Hear one of our company took sick. He would cramp all up in a heap, hollow and groan. We done all we could for him, the poor fellow, and in the latter part of the night he died. James Carry was his name.[24] Laid him out. Wrapped some clothes around him. Found a gulch whear the watter had torn a hole about seven feet deep, wrapped a robe around him, and laid him away to rest. Said a few good words over the grave and come away. We had been eating wild segoes and he had eaten one that was poison. Some of them are poison.

Come to Ash Hollow.[25] Hear was campt several thousand Sioux Indians just strikeing camp and moveing north. Went into their midst. They were friendly. Gave them some presents. Pas[s]ed on a few miles. Our meat was out. We saw two buffalow at the edge of a steep bluff. All stopt. I took the best gun and crawled around to get a good shot. Come into some tall rye grass within sixty yards of them [and] cocked the gun. As I was about to take aim, a straw t[o]uched the trigger and off went the gun. The buffalow did not know whear the sound come from and ran strait at me in the rye grass. I threw up my gun and hat, yelled and ran at them. They passed each side of me. I did not have time to scare.

The clouds looked threatning and in the afternoon [it] began to rain mixt with snow. The wind was from the northeast and drove the storm in our faces. We stem[m]ed the cur[r]ent until the rain wet us to the skin [and we] could not face it anny longer. Turnd to the bluff of the river and found a half shelter from the storm. There was no wood and nothing but weeds and wet brush and [we] could not start a fire. Threw off our packs. Tied up the animals, drew on the blankets, and rushed togeather to keep from chilling to death.[26]

---

23. The company paused for breakfast at Scott's Bluff on 14 April and passed Chimney Rock the next day. Ibid., 402.

24. James Carry is not mentioned in the Bliss diary and is otherwise unidentifiable.

25. The reference to Ash Hollow indicates that the party traveled the south side of the North Platte River. Edwin Bryant described Ash Hollow in 1846: "This name is derived from a few scattering ash-trees in the dry ravine, through which we wind our way to the river bottom. There is but one steep or difficult place for the wagons in the pass. I saw wild currants and gooseberries near the mouth of Ash Hollow. There is here a spring of pure cold water." See Bryant, *What I Saw in California*, 97.

26. The last storm recorded in the Bliss journal took place on 9 April, three days before the party reached Fort Laramie. Blackburn inserted the description of the storm in the manuscript, indicating he may have accidently post-dated the time of the storm.

In the night the storm ceased. The morning found us hungry and [with] nothing but dried buffalow meat. The buffalow chips were all soaked with rain and snow so they would not burn. The animals found a little scanty feed and we all were in a miserable condition for travel. Went on a few miles, found good feed for the horses and camped. We found a few dried chips under a cliff, started a fire [and] baked some bread and made some royal coffee. Come to life again.

In a few miles [we] found plenty of buffalow and layed in plenty of jerked meat for the ballance of the trip.[27] The next morning we went right into the largest herd of buffalows in the West. Have heard of such droves before. They [were] going north and went on a fast walk. We were in the midst of them. We kept on our course and they kept theirs. They would come with[in] fifty yards of us and then goe around and come togeather again. There was miles of them. We were in the herd half an hour. This was the last we seen of the buffalow.

In a few miles further [we] saw something els[e] that raised the hair on our heads. There was about twenty five Pawnees Indians [who] charged down on us like the wolf on the fold. They come yelling like Devils. They were right onto us like a flash of lightning. They ar[e] the most savage looking Indians in the West.[28]

We soon seen we had no chance to fight. They commenced rolling us of everything they could lay hands on and threttend to cut our throats. We were not far from their camp. The old cheif and an Indian interp[r]eter come out to whear we were and told the Indians to stop robbing us. We went into their village and the cheif made them give

---

[27.] On Friday, 21 April, the party "came about 16 miles & camped on an Island to obtain wood to dry our Buffalo meat for our Journey the remainder of the way fo[r] we expect soon to be beyond game of any kind." They crossed to the north side of the Platte here or at Grand Island. During the day, they had crossed what Bliss called "Buffalo creek" and "sent one of our men to kill one he soon gave us a signal that he had killed one went to him and found he had killed one two years old we got him in camp about sundown & set up nearly all night to jerk it." Cooley, "The Robert S. Bliss Journal," 402.

[28.] Three bands of Pawnees had lived for three hundred years in territory that extended from Texas to South Dakota. Protestant missionaries, alternately benevolent and tyrannical, began working with the Pawnee in 1834. The tribe was decimated by a smallpox epidemic in 1838 and was continually tormented by the Sioux. The Pawnees alternately robbed and helped small bands of Mormon pioneers and became notorious for activities viewed by the emigrants as extortion, but which the Pawnees certainly saw as indemnification. Newspapers called them "pestiferous banditti," "Indians who have covered themselves with white blood," and "those grand rascals, the Pawnees," but the Commissioner of Indian Affairs in 1849 called them "a truly poor and persecuted people," noting that cholera had swept them off "like chaff before the wind." They were moved to Oklahoma in 1876, where about one thousand still reside on their reservation today.

back most of our loss, but the meat and tobacco we never seen afterwards. They had just made a treaty with our government and they thought it was not best to break it yet a while.[29]

Stayed there a while and started on. The Indian interp[r]eter said in four miles was a good camp whear we could stay all night. We went to the four mile place and twenty five miles further before we stopt. Would not trust those devils to anny thing.

We camped half way from the Platt to the Loup Fork, a verry treacherous, quicksandy stream.[30] Come to it in the morning. Started to cross and wallowed, mired down, rol[l]ed over, swam, waded, and managed to cross, but lost more provisions [and] some guns and was glad we were alive.[31] Built a fire and dried out. Comenced to think about something to eat. [We had] lost nearly all the provisions and our amunition. Went out to hunt something. Two went to hunt eggs, one to hunt ducks, and two went frogging down stream. They all returned after [a] while. Ther[e] was a lot of half ha[t]ched eggs, a dead duck, and a bunch of frog legs. [We] put them in a pot, boiled them down, stir[r]ed in some flour, and made slumgulion. If it was not clean, it was [still] nectar fit for the gods.

> We did not hanker after things,
> Had enough to do with out,
> And cooked our game with feet and wings,
> We lived from hand to mouth.

Kept down this stream and fell in with a band of Omahaw Indians agoing out after buffalows.[32] They enquired about the Pawneese and the buffalows and seeing our forlorn condition, commenced rolling us of every thing they could jerk away from us and left. We had nothing left, only what we had on our backs, but we were near to our journeys end.

[29.] A treaty stating that the Pawnee Nation "faithfully promised not to molest or injure the property or person of any white citizen" was dated 6 August 1848, but the *Daily Missouri Republican* stated that the treaty was made and the Pawnees were paid in the spring. The Pawnee war chief Sharitarish (White Wolf or Angry Chief) signed as chief of the Chauis. Iskatappe (Wicked Chief) and Chahikstakalesharo (French Chief) represented the Skidis.

[30.] From below Grand Island, the party traveled northeast from the Platte to reach the Loup Fork crossing located near modern Fullerton, Nebraska. The ford was exactly as dangerous as Blackburn described it.

[31.] It is possible to make out "lost 3 of our guns" on the last illegible page of Bliss's manuscript journal.

[32.] The Omahas were a Siouxan tribe closely related to the Poncas and occasionally allied with the Arikaras and Iowas. They successfully competed with the Pawnee until 1801, when that tribe carried a devastating smallpox epidemic into their midst from New Mexico.

Camped [and] hunted up more eggs and frogs. Made a meal out of them [and] lay down to sleep for the last time on this long and tiresome trip.

Crost the Elkhorn and in eighteen miles more arrived at Winter Quarters on the Missouri River and went in to comfortable quarters.[33] Lay on a feather bed, but could not sleep. It was something we were not acostombed to for years.

My parents lived in Clay County, Missoury and I went home.[34] They were glad to see me return. They never expected to see me again. They were getting ready to start to California and soon started. There was no rest for me. I must goe some place and this trip just suited me.

[We went to] St. Joseph and crost the Missouri River. [It was] a great place to lay in suplies for the plains and [we] started for the Platt. There were manny emigrants on the road, some [bound] for Oregon or California. Come to the Platt River and all stoped to organize into companys for saf[e]ty in crossing the plains. I shal[l] say but little about this journey, having just come across it.

There was manny companyes on the road, well organized and strong, [so] they could protect themselves from the Indians. And it was the same ro[u]tine of hi[t]ching up, camping, guarding, shoeing cattle and horses, quarreling, swearing and the diary of one company was like all the others. We saw few Indians on this trip. We had a verry easy and uneventful time. The feed was generally good.

Arrived at Independence Rock on the Sweet Watter. Here the companys divided up into small bands, the better to find feed and get along faster. While campt here we heard of the great gold discovery in California and manny that were going to Oregon changed their minds and went for the diggings and no one [was] going to Oregon from this [point] on.[35]

Our cattle and horses [were] worn down and we concluded to winter in Salt Lake Valley.

[33.] On 2 May, Bliss's journal ends, "crossed the [Elk] Horn by Swimming ourselves & animals over; then traveled 8 miles & camped to avoid a band of Pawnees who were verry saucy and impident to us stopping our Pack animals & holding our horses by the bits till they had took whatever they fancied." Robert Campbell's official journal at Winter Quarters, quoted in the Journal History for 3 May 1848, reported, "Captain Gardner, accompanied by Samuel Lewis, Alva C. Calkins, William Garner, Ami Jackson, David Stewart, Robert S. Bliss and Abner Blackman arrived at Winter Quarters from the valley, bringing many letters."

[34.] Blackburn sold a 160-acre land grant awarded for his Mexican War service while in Missouri. See Appendix D.

[35.] Sam Brannan dispatched four battalion veterans, William and Nathan Hawks, Sanford Jacobs, and Richard Slater, to carry word of the gold discovery east on 1 April 1848. The men went through Great Salt Lake City on 9 July, and met the Saints "west of Laramie" on 27 July. See Morgan, The Great Salt Lake, 216.

EIGHT

Gold Is Where
You Find It

I n the spring of 1849, Blackburn joined a pack train and left Zion
for the gold fields of California. Unfortunately, he gave little information about this party, and Mormon records provide few additional clues about its departure from Salt Lake or its composition. Patty
Sessions reported, on 17 March 1849, that "there are some people here
who are about to leave for the gold mines. Some for other places, but
most of them have the yellow fever." There were other reports of wagon
parties leaving Great Salt Lake City for the gold mines on 21 and 22
March.[1] On the next Sunday, "Prest Young spoke V.S. those who are
going to California for gold Dust."[2] Official Mormon attitudes toward
the opportunities offered by the gold fields were ambiguous: Brigham
Young condemned those who left Zion as "corrupt" and "rebellious
souls," but he could not turn a blind eye to the golden prospects that
California offered for raising money to support his struggling colony.
Leading church authorities "sponsored" church members to mine gold
for them in California, and on 13 April, Young sent Amasa Lyman,
Porter Rockwell, and twenty men to collect tithing and contributions
from the numerous Mormons who had remained in California.[3]

In 1849, Blackburn made what may well have been the first discovery of precious minerals in present-day Nevada and the next year wan-
dered into a controversy concerning white settlement of the Silver

---

[1] Journal History, 17, 21, and 22 March 1849.

[2] Brooks, *Hosea Stout*, 2:350.

[3] Davies, *Mormon Gold*, 109–14. Lyman also carried a bizarre letter from Brigham Young to Samuel Brannan, requesting payment of up to 100,000 dollars in
tithing and asking for an additional 20,000 dollars for Young and more for his coun-
selors; the request came with a thinly veiled threat, "a hint to the wise is sufficient."
See Schindler, *Orrin Porter Rockwell*, 191.

State. Due to the scarcity and inaccuracy of important source documents, the beginnings of modern Nevada history are more confused than the settlement of any other state in the Union. Blackburn provided a critical eyewitness account of these events.

The first of these controversies—who first discovered gold in Gold Canyon, site of the Comstock lode?—began with the muddled claim of another battalion veteran, William Prows (commonly misspelled as Prouse or Prowse), to a discovery in 1848.[4] Eliot Lord, writing for the U.S. Geological Survey in the early 1880s, described a California-bound Mormon wagon train in the spring of 1850, and he quoted an 1880 letter from William Prouse alleging that "he made a still earlier discovery of gold dust in this same creek bed, in the autumn of 1848, on his return to Salt Lake from the South Fork of the American River. He lingered behind his party in order to prospect, and on coming up with the train again told its members, Joseph Bates, Frank Weaver, and Rufus Stoddard, that he would 'show them a place, if they ever traveled that way again, where they could find gold.'"[5]

No contemporary account substantiates Prows's claim to have found gold in Gold Canyon as early as 1848. An analysis of his claim requires a close look at the organization of the 1848 companies of Mormon Battalion veterans who left California for Utah. The initial wagon party—which included diarists Henry Bigler, Ephraim Green, Addison Pratt, and Azariah Smith—left Pleasant Valley on 2 July 1848, followed on 12 August by Ebenezer Brown's wagon company, which included Prows and diarist John Borrowman. Both groups divided into pack and wagon parties—and most significantly, the pack train that separated from the Brown company left on 26 August, while the party was still in Carson Canyon. When the Thompson company camped at the mouth of Gold Canyon on 9 and 10 August, James Diamond and a calf were wounded by Indian arrows.[6] Borrowman also reported that the Brown

---

[4.] William Prows was born 11 June 1827, and was a private in Company C of the battalion. He pioneered southern Utah and served ninety days in the territorial penitentiary for illegal cohabitation. He died in Mexico on 24 May 1894.

[5.] Lord, *Comstock Mining and Miners*, 10–11. Lord cited Prows's claim in a footnote to his description of the Prows-Orr 1850 Gold Canyon discovery, giving his source as "Letter of William Prouse, December 14, 1880." Neither this letter nor any other firsthand account by Prows has survived, and Lord's footnote is the sole documentation for the Prows claim. Lord further confused the question by citing the diary of William Prouse for "May 15, 1859"; if Prows produced such a journal entry for 15 May 1850, it would not be authentic, since the Orr party did not reach Carson Valley until 15 June. No trace of any of these documents has been located.

[6.] See Bigler, *Azariah Smith*, 135–36; and Gudde, *Bigler's Chronicle*, 119–20.

party had trouble with Indians while camped in the area on 4 September. Given these circumstances, it is hard to imagine why Prows would want to linger and do a little prospecting. However, the memoirs of Joseph W. Bates demonstrate that Prows's story, if not an outright lie, could not possibly be true. Bates was a member of the pack train that left the Brown company behind in Carson Canyon and his memoir listed the ten men who made up the party—including himself and Rufus Stoddard. It would have been physically impossible for Prows to have overtaken a train including Stoddard and Bates as claimed in the Lord footnote, because they were far ahead of the Brown party that included Prows.[7]

Prows's claim must also be regarded with suspicion because of its origin. His letter to Lord was a direct attempt to gain credit for the first discovery of minerals in the area of the Comstock lode. Blackburn's 1849 story makes no such claim to a "first"; other historians have made that determination. Finally, a detailed Prows family history recounts three encounters with the "Three Nephites" (figures from Mormon folklore) and the loss of fifteen thousand dollars during the gold rush, due to a bad investment in hogs, but says absolutely nothing about an 1848 gold discovery in present-day Nevada.[8]

Adding fat to the fire, battalion descendant Allen Fifield wrote, in 1961, that "in this group was William Prows, the first man to wash gold in the Comstock. He later told his friend, Abner Blackburn[,] about his find, and Blackburn has long had the honor of being the discoverer of gold on the famed and rich Comstock Lode."[9] Fifield provided no sources for this assertion and presented no independent evidence that Prows actually made a gold discovery in 1848; his slander is nothing more than undocumented speculation.

Lord's own account of events in 1850 clearly contradicts Prows's claim to an 1848 discovery:

> The first wagon train which entered the [Carson] valley in the following spring [1850] was a noteworthy little caravan. Leaving Salt Lake in April they found fresh pasturage along the banks of the Humboldt River, and their cattle suffered little, though the heavy canvas-topped wagons were dragged slowly over an untried track, as the beaten trail was flooded by the

---

[7.] For Bates's autobiography, see Bagley, *Ephraim Green*, 45–46.

[8.] Xerographic copy of Prows Family History, provided to the editor by Norma Ricketts.

[9.] Fifield, "Wagons East Across the Sierra," 297.

swollen river. The party were nearly all Mormons, led by Thomas Orr, still living (1881), a hale, clear-eyed old man. . . . They were an orderly if somewhat stolid company, obeying orders without questioning why. . . . At the Sink of the Humboldt . . . some of the youngest and best mounted men rode forward rapidly to make the first trail of the mountain passes, and the main body followed by crossing the 40-Mile desert and ascending the valley of the Carson.

On the 15th of May they halted for a few hours, at noon, beside a little creek flowing down from the range of hills which bounded the valley on the east. The cattle were turned loose to graze upon the sage brush, and the women of the party prepared the simple dinner of bacon and potatoes. William Prouse, a young Mormon, meanwhile picked up a tin milk-pan, and going down to the edge of the creek began washing the surface dirt. After a few minutes he returned and showed his companions a few glittering specks on the bottom of the pan. The specks were gold dust, worth intrinsically only a few cents, thrown carelessly aside a few moments later, but they were then transformed into precious and fruitful seed, for this pinch of dust was positive evidence of the existence of gold in the deserts of Western Utah.[10]

If Prows already knew there was gold in Gold Canyon, his behavior as described by Lord did not show it. Thomas Orr, Jr., left a reminiscent account that casts more doubt on Prows's 1848 claim:

> Bill Prouse, who was working for General Sutter when gold was discovered by J. W. Marshall, had gone back to Utah with pack animals to meet his folks. He said he was familiar with all the stopping places on the emigrant trail and after joining our train was made pilot . . .
>
> We finally got across the desert and came to the Carson River. This river makes a bend around a desert twelve miles across and we reached the edge about noon. The locality is called Gold Canyon now, and is west [sic] of Virginia City. Prouse

---

[10.] Lord, *Comstock Mining and Miners*, 10–11. The borders of Utah Territory extended to the Sierra Nevada in 1850. Lord must be read closely to determine that the wagon train he described was traveling in 1850 and not in 1849. He quoted Thomas Orr, John Orr, and the 1880 Prows letter. Lord noted that Prows was living in 1881 in Kanosh City, Utah.

said the country there strongly resembled the California gold fields and a few of us went down with shovel and pan and dug a little pot hole the size of a post-hole and panned out two or three pans of dirt. Every pan showed color and we brought the gold for father's inspection. He was not much impressed by the find.[11]

The course of this wagon party will be examined in more detail in the next chapter. Orr's story makes a good case for an 1850 discovery, but gives no support to the story that Prows told to Lord in 1880.

At any rate, Blackburn's account must be read before doubting that his decision to prospect the eastern side of the Sierra Nevada was a completely original idea. The fact that he did not actually claim that his discovery was the first made in the Comstock validates his story. Blackburn simply related his experience, somewhat ruefully, without specifically claiming the historical glory (for whatever it is worth) of a first discovery. Finally, Blackburn's account received support in the story that H. S. Beatie told to H. H. Bancroft in 1884:

> Our party was the first to discover gold in Nevada. This Mr. *Abner Blackburn* was the first to find it. He made the discovery in July while I was gone over the mountains with his brother for supplies. When Abner Blackburn first went over the mountains it seems he had an idea that there was gold in the vicinity of what is now Virginia City; and while his brother & myself had gone over the mountains it appears that he went out prospecting and discovered gold, but got only a small quantity.[12]

After an early crossing of the Sierra that starved their horses and left some of the party snow blind, the pack train arrived in the gold fields. The California that Blackburn had seen in the fall of 1847 vanished forever when John Marshall, directing a party of former Mormon Battalion veterans in the construction of a sawmill on the South Fork of the American River, picked up a nugget of gold in the millrace. California, the continent, and finally the entire world went mad with gold fever. Blackburn paints an entertaining picture of the glory days of '49, adding his

---

[11.] Taylor, *Life History of Thomas Orr*, 19.

[12.] In his history of Nevada, Bancroft described the discovery of gold in Gold Canyon, identifying Blackburn by name, and noting, "There are various versions of the first discovery of gold in western Utah, but none more authentic." See Bancroft, *History of Nevada, Colorado, and Wyoming*, 66–69, 93. Beatie's story—the source of much confusion about the beginnings of white settlement in Nevada—is quoted in Appendix E.

own stories of fabulously rich diggings and relaxed camaraderie to the legends of the mines. Typically, rather than work through the summer, Blackburn and his brother Thomas decided to tour the mines, taking the narrative through Stockton, San Francisco, the southern mines, the forks of the American, and finally to the bars of the Yuba River. "We started out to see all the mines," Blackburn wrote, "and we did."

The mother lode—a term coined in the 1860s from concepts current from the early days of the gold rush—was a 120-mile-long system of gold-bearing quartz and schist that runs north-northwest from the town of Mariposa to El Dorado County, though actual gold deposits extended much farther north. A complex system of rivers drain the Sierra Nevada and flow into the great Central Valley of California, and over time this drainage system distributed gold throughout the foothills of the Sierra.

Early placer mining was based on panning (using everything from frying pans to water-tight native baskets) or on more efficient rockers or cradles, crude wooden machines four to six feet long with a cleat-lined bottom and a hopper at the end to trap gold. Both techniques depended on the action of water to separate gold from dirt, so the mining settlements naturally grew up along the banks of rivers and creeks.

In very simple terms, the river systems of the Central Valley are centered on the southern-flowing Sacramento and the northern-flowing San Joaquin. Both great rivers drained into the San Francisco Bay through an enormous delta to the west of Stockton. Generally, the northern mines drained into the Sacramento and its two major tributaries, the American and Feather rivers. Both rivers divided into North, Middle, and South forks, while the forks split into innumerable creeks such as the Dry, the Rabbit, and the Weber. The waters of the Bear and the Yuba flowed into the Feather.

To the south, the Consumnes and Dry Creek fed the Mokelumne, which mixed with the waters of French Camp Slough and the Calaveras before it debouched into the delta. The Stanislaus, the Tuolumne, the Merced, Bear Creek, the Mariposa, the Chowchilla, and the Fresno drained into the San Joaquin, and all this area—everything south of Placerville—was called the southern mines.

As Sacramento was the commercial center of the northern mines, Stockton was "the great mart through which flows the whole transportation and travel to the placers of the Stanislaus, Mokelumne, Maripose, Mercedes, Tuolumne, and Kings River."[13] The southern mines were largely settled by Spanish Americans, and Blackburn observed

---

[13.] Buffum, *Six Months in the Gold Mines*, 129. The Kings and Kern rivers flowed into now-vanished interior drainage systems.

that at Stockton there were "Brazilians, Cheleanians, Mexicans, Knakers and all the skum of the earth." The xenophobic prejudices reflected in Blackburn's comments were endemic among Americans, who felt that California had been seized by conquest and its gold revealed by Providence for God's newly chosen people, white Americans. To many, it was the simple working out of Manifest Destiny. H. H. Bancroft observed, "Those we have injured we hate; so it was with Mexicans and Americans in California; we had unfairly wrested the country from them, and now we were determined that they should have none of the benefits."[14]

In relative terms, the Latinos were perched at the top of the heap of white prejudices, as shown in this narrative. Blackburn expresses an appreciation (and even envy) of Californio culture—even though his descriptions can be read as either romantic or condescending. Compared with his contemporaries, Blackburn was a model of tolerance: Mormon Apostles Snow and Lyman could condemn "savage Spanish customs" without experiencing them.

Ranking just below the Spanish were the Kanakas—Hawaiians—who had migrated to California in some numbers before the gold rush. The Chinese, drawn to the phenomenon they called Gold Mountain, ranked even lower than the Hawaiians and were seldom treated as well as pack animals. The "Mongols" were viewed as exotic, depraved, and unredeemable pagans. By cooperative effort and persistence, they infuriated white miners by reworking claims that Americans had abandoned as worked out, often to considerable profit.

At the bottom of the pile were Native Americans, whose diverse tribes and cultures were virtually annihilated in the holocaust of the gold rush. Whites and Latinos made great fortunes by employing large gangs of Indians. They were thrown into a market economy gone mad. As the acorn trees that had sustained a fifth of America's native population were decimated, Indian miners developed a taste for oysters, dried codfish, and whiskey, and they died in droves.

Ironically, if any one class fell into Blackburn's "skum of the earth," it would be the Sydney Ducks, immigrants from Australia and the American's fellow Anglos. The Australians included numbers of hardened convicts who introduced their brand of skullduggery to the remarkably orderly early gold camps. In San Francisco, this group's specialty was arson, looting, and the harassment of the sizeable Chilean community. The "Australians banded in open defiance, and adopted blue shirts for a party color."[15]

---

14. Bancroft, *History of California*, 6:402.
15. Ibid., 6:403.

The rough democracy and common law of the mines did not extend to multicultural harmony. The eventual working out of placer gold exacerbated the situation, but as early as 1850 a Foreign Miners' License Law institutionalized Anglo prejudices with a twenty-dollar-per-month tax. To justify the tax, the California Senate finance committee noted that the state was filled with "the worst population of the Mexican and South American states, New South Wales and the Southern Islands, to say nothing of the vast numbers from Europe," for whom the tax would be a "small bonus for the privilege of taking from our country the vast treasure to which they have no right."[16]

Blackburn described one of the great wonders of the gold camps, the implementation of spontaneous mining law in a country that was completely lacking in organized government. The forty-niners were, by their own account, "a wild, heedless, wasteful, dissipated set of men," but they brought with them a deep appreciation of democracy and a nineteenth-century sense of fair play—at least for their white countrymen. They certainly regarded California as "a huge goose, to be plucked at will," and legally they were all trespassers, but very quickly they developed an unwritten "Miner's Code" that defined the size of a claim and the rights of the men working it. These rules were so effective that until 1866, no legislature passed any formal mining laws, though this is probably due in part to a realization that miners would ignore the laws. Historian J. S. Holliday noted, "During all that time when approximately $1 billion was mined without any congressional authorization, the regulations and customs of the miners constituted the only laws governing the mines and waters of the public land of the United States."[17]

Most American miners found brutally hard work but no fortunes, while tremendous numbers found disease, disability, and death. Blackburn recorded the death of miner James Riley from unspecified sickness and his wife's death from heartbreak in a long folk poem reminiscent of the classic Child ballad "Barbara Allen." Though rough poetry, it is forceful and truly felt. Pioneers like Blackburn, who would survive and raise a family as a farmer in the Golden State, remembered such events, counted the cost, abided poverty, and marveled at the experience of their youth.

THE NARRATIVE

In the spring, I joined a pack train for the gold mines and left my folks to come along after when the grass was good. We went by way of

16. Jackson, *Gold Dust*, 266.
17. Holliday, *The World Rushed In*, 400.

Bear River, crost the Maladd [Malad], and made a cutoff and come into the Callifornia road at the City of Rocks, allready discribed in a former trip.[18] There was the usual amount of wild Indians and the same shage brush, alkily, and one range after another of low mountains and it was verry monotinous to the view. About half way down the Humboldt, I was riding along side of William Lane and carrying our guns across our laps when his gun went off.[19] The bullet went through the edge of my pants, cut the stirrup leather off, and went through my horse and killed him. A pretty close shave. It was a fine horse, one that Lt. Rosecranz bought at the Pemo village on the Hele [Gila] River.[20] Saddled another horse and went on, ready for something els[e].

The Indians were verry poor this time of year. They would slip up and shoot arrows at the horses for to get them to eat. We met an Indian in the road. He had a sack on his waist fastend on a belt. We wanted to know what was in it. [He] untied the sack [and] it was full of ants. He motiond with [his] mouth that he was going to eat them.

We took him to camp to try to fill him up with grub, for there never was an Indian know[n] to have enough to eat. Built a fire and the Indian looked scared. He thought we were going to roast him for supper. Cooked our supper and eat it. We then began to stuff the Indian and gave him bread, bacon, coffee, beans, and crackers [and] the remains of a ham of meat. One of the boys gave him a bottle of pep[p]er sauce. He eat it and after this his gastric juices faild him. We concluded to let him shift for himself, for if he stayed with us long, he would clean out our larder.

[18.] Credit for pioneering the Salt Lake Cutoff goes to Samuel J. Hensley, who led a party around the north end of the Great Salt Lake after failing to negotiate the Salt Desert in the summer of 1848. (Hensley had been with the Stockton party that Blackburn met in the Goose Creek Mountains in 1847.) Hensley told the east-bound battalion men about the trail and they followed it into the Salt Lake Valley. See Korns, *West from Fort Bridger*, 248–68. Blackburn stated that some of these veterans were with his pack train.

[19.] Sixteen-year-old William P. Lane was born in Hamilton, Illinois, and entered Salt Lake Valley in 1847 with his younger sister, Mariah. He later settled with Lewis B. Myers and Nathaniel Fairbanks in Louisville, California. See Davies, *Mormon Gold*, 273, 275, 283. He may have been the son of Bishop William L. Lane, born 1797, a father of ten children, who died while crossing the plains, 8 July 1852. Blackburn's uncle, Elias, married Lane's daughter, Nancy.

[20.] George W. Rosecrans was born in Ohio on 6 February in either 1802 or 1812, and was a Seventy in the Mormon Church. Lieutenant Rosecrans took command of Company C after James Brown's departure with the sick detachment. He went from California to Utah in 1847, and may have encountered Blackburn in the Sierra with Brown's party. In 1850, he ran a hotel at Dolores Bar in Sutter County and probably owned the Rosecrans Quartz Lode mine. See Davies, *Mormon Gold*, 212, 375.

We had the usual amount of quarreling and swearing that all such companys have in crossing the plains. Arrived at the Sink [of the Humboldt]. There is a new rout[e] to California since I was here. It goes by way of Carson River.[21] Took the new road and crost the Forty Mile Desert of sand. Went up Carson River two days and stopt to recruit our animals.

Som[e] of our company had been to the mines before and I asked them why there was no gold on this side of the mountain. They sayed no one had looked for it. The next day, while they were playing cards, I took a bread pan and a butcher knife and went out in the raveins to prospect and found gold in small quantities in three places. Went to a larger raveine and whear the watter run down over the bed rock a little on the side of the gulch. Dug down in the slate and found a fair prospect and kept pan[n]ing for an hour or more. Went to camp and all hand[s] grab[b]ed up pans, knives, and kettles and started out. We scrached, scraped, and pan[n]ed until nearly sun down and took out nine or ten dollars worth of gold. Being without tools and nearly out of provisions, we were compeld to abandon the place, but calculated to return some time in the future. This place is Gold Canion. The Comestock [Comstock] and Vergina [Virginia] City [are] situated some distance above the place we prospected.[22]

We went on up the river and through the canion to the snow. It was verry deep on the mountain and [had] a hard crust on top. The horses seldom broke through. Could not find anny road and hunted around in some awful chasems. We were three days on the snow.[23] Our horses nearly starved and some of our party were snow blind. Decended a steep mountain and come to green grass and wild flowers. Took a general rest and laid over one day to look for the road, but could not find it. And followed the divide between the American River and the Mecoseme [Mokelumne] and made some steep assents and decents through brush [and] over rocks and chasems.[24] And began to think we were near the mines and all at once come onto some miners crevicing in a raveine for gold. We jum[p]t off our horses and began to do as they did and let our horses eat grass. We worked around in sev-

[21.] James Clyman opened a new route across the Forty Mile Desert after encountering the Mormon Battalion veterans who pioneered the Carson Pass trail in 1848.

[22.] This camp was in the vicinity of present-day Dayton, Nevada.

[23.] The party crossed Carson Pass and West Pass. West Pass, at ninety-five hundred feet, is the highest point on any emigrant trail in the United States.

[24.] The party actually crossed the divide between the American and Consumnes river drainages. The Mokelumne River is some distance south of the Mormon-Carson Emigrant Trail and Weberville.

eral small gulches wit[h] our knives and bread pans for about three hours and had coarse gold enough to buy some of [our] pressing needs.

Went over the ridge to [a] camp or town called Weaverville [and purchased] tobacco and whiskey with some other provisions.[25] We would have to goe to Sacramento or Suiters Fort to by our out fitt of tools and provisions [at] a distance of fifty miles.

The first work I done in Callifornia was to cut a door through Suiters Fort. It took but a short time with ax and pick to acomplish the task and [I] was paid one ounce for the job. Sold some of our horses and purch[as]ed provisions and tools for the mines. We heard of a big strike at Auburn Raveine and packed our horses with our outfitt and started up the north side of the American River for the diggings.[26] When we arrived there, [we] found the Sonoranians [Sonorans] and Chillanians [Chileans] had gutted the raveines of the cream. We dam[n]ed them some what and went down on the North Fork of the American River. The watter was high and we could not work the bars and we worked higher up until the watter fell. The company divided up, every one for himself.

Nat Fairbanks [and I] went up this river to prospect.[27] We found a little all along. Stopt in a reveine for lunch and we felt down in the mouth because we could not strike it rich and our luck had soured on us. We were sitting on a ledge of rocks in a dry raveine about twenty yards from the river. While eating, I looked down between my feet and see something yellow, about a half inch long. Picked it up [and] handed it to Nat. He sung out, "Gold! By my life!" Stoped eating just then. Searched arround and found plenty more. Commenced to make the gravel fly. Kept picking up peices of gold and panning out and found a pocket or two that was rich and worked untill sundown. [We] staked off two claims and started for camp. We took out in about five hours

---

25. Though listed in the 1850 census as Weaverville, the name of the camp is generally spelled Weberville after its founder, Charles Weber. Located at the confluence of Weber and Hangtown creeks, south of present-day Placerville, the town has vanished.

26. French prospector Claude Charnay discovered gold at the Dry Diggings in May 1848. When the camp was named Auburn Ravine, after a town in New York, in August 1849, it was comprised of three or four tents, but by 1850 Auburn and vicinity boasted 1,302 inhabitants. The town is now a California Historic Landmark.

27. Nathaniel Fairbanks was born 10 May 1823 in Queensbury, New York. He joined the Mormon church in 1843 and, like Blackburn, participated in the crossing of Iowa. In 1847, on the trail to Chimney Rock, Fairbanks survived a rattlesnake bite and entered the Salt Lake Valley with Orson Pratt's advance company on 22 July. He spent the winter in the valley, "participating in the hardships and trials of pioneer life." Fairbanks drowned in 1853 in a river near Sacramento, after being thrown from a mule. Mormon biographer Andrew Jenson commented, "Bro. Fairbanks was universally known among his associates as a brave man and a great hunter."

about four hundred dollars in coarse gold. Next morning, [we] told two friends [who] staked off two more claims. We worked the raveine to the river and four of us took out two thousand five hundred dollars in eight days and we left to find other diggings.

We heard they were shoveling it up rich in other places. We intended to come back here when the river was low. We went over to Coloma [and] bought some lumber to make rockers and crost over to Spanish Bar on the Mid[d]le Fork of the American River.[28] The miners were taking it out big over there. They had a bonanza. There we found a good placer and went to work. It pan[n]ed out good, all coarse gold and blue on the outside, caused by acid of some kind.

I heard my folks were comeing across the mountain and went to assist them and sold my intrest in the claim and started. Found them comeing down the mountain. Went to Sacramento and procured another out fitt for the mines. I took my folks up below Auburn and my father, brother, and I went up to my old raveine. The watter had fallen quite low and we found the ground richer than at first and we worked down into the river bed as low as possible and we were well sattisfied. We worked it all out and realised about eighteen hundred dollars from the place.

We then moved three miles above Auburn and camped on good grass. While here, two miners come up from the river to make preparation to goe home to Oregon. They told us they had been mining there for six weeks and had made verry well. They said we had better goe there, for they said they had been all over the mines. We looked like decent people and they said the miners down there wanted it all for themselves. In the evening, my brother and I went down and just as they were cleaning up their rockers we come in behind them. The bottom of their pans was coverd with gold. We seen enough to sattisfy the most greed[y] of mortals. We made two rockers and in the morning we were there before the miners had their breakfast.

We pitched in on the side of their works and they come chargeing down to us with pistols in hand to drive us off. We did not scare worth a cent and they gave us two claims joining theirs and wanted us to keep it quiet from others. Soon [we] were on good terms with them and were all good miners togeather.

[28.] Blackburn probably purchased this lumber at Sutter's Mill, the site of the discovery of gold on 24 January 1848. The mill had already been "transferred to other hands by Marshall and Sutter." Mormon miners opened the first placer on the Middle Fork of the American River at Spanish Bar in June 1848. The Middle Fork was "the richest of any in all that rich region, this one spot alone yielding more than a million of dollars." It was located about twelve miles northeast of Coloma. See Bancroft, *History of California*, 6:73, 354.

First day [we] cleaned off the top dirt [and got] ready to work. The gold was fine but not light. After we got started, [we] took out from eighty to one hundred and fifty dollars a day to the hand. The sun pourd down on our backs and [we] stood in cold watter. Some of the men were taken sick. We worked as long as we could, but had to lay off. The excitement of mining causes one to over work themselves.

These lines were composed in memory of a messmate who died in the mines of California in the year 1849. His wife was buryed by his side the following year.

JAMES D. RILEY OF TENNESSEE 1849

We had a messmate brave and true,
His hair was fair and curled.
As portly [a] man as you could see,
His wife he thought all the world.

By and by he was taken sick,
No docter here was found.
Tried every thing in our wits,
And no relief comes round.

Then geather arround his bed,
And watch for him to die.
His parting word has said,
Then cold in death he lies.

We dug his grave not far away,
Under some laurel trees.
Over the place the boughs did sway,
It was a loansome place to be.

And marked the place to keep,
For some might wish to see,
Or drop a tear and weep,
Over his sad memory.

On a board we wrote some lines,
So that his friends might see,
The place that he does lie,
His age and nativity.

To his poor wife in Tennessee,
We sent these sorrowful lines.
Her husband dear she nea could see,
For we buried him in the mines.

He beged of us to save his life,
While we were standing round,
And wanted to see his darling wife,
Before we put him in the ground.

In a few months his wife come round,
Her parents were by her side.
She wanted us to show the ground,
Whear her dear husband lies.

We led her up on top the hill,
To the lonely silent place.
With deep grief her heart was filled,
She wanted to see his face.

She wished to have a grave close by his side,
For she could not stay round.
She could not live and did decide,
She'd rather be in the ground.

In a day or two she was taken down,
And verry soon she died.
She said h[e]r wish was underground,
With her husband side [by] side.

We laid her near her husband dear,
The tears come in our eyes.
Her parents here were weeping near,
Whear their dear daughter lies.

They soon will be forgotten,
And no one seem[s] to care.
The boards will soon be rotten,
But the angels are watching there.

We sold our claimes for a good figure. Come up off the river and soon recruited up again. We made a very respectable pile of the needful.

My father located three miles north of Auburn and kept a miners store, boarding house, and a general trading station.[29] He was verry successful in his buisness. After resting from exposure, my brother and

---

[29] Bancroft reported, "Hereabout remained many Mormons, who forgot their destination, turned publicans, and waxed fat. . . . Blackman kept an inn at one of the fifty Dry Diggings, which, at the great renaming, became known as Auburn." Blackman is certainly Anthony Blackburn. See ibid., 6:73.

me with three chums thought we would see Callifornia and the mines. We fitted out in Spanish stile and started for Sacramento.

[We] stopt at all the places on the road. There was a bar for liquor, gold scales for weighing gold, cards and dice, [and] banking games of all kinds with players of all nations. Packers going to the mines, some on foot and [some on] horse back, and Chinamen with their bamboo poles loaded with all they could carry, Sonoraneans with their little mules, ox teams, horse teams, and a general mele. And all wanted to get there before it was too late. All appeard to be honest.

Come to Sacramento, or Embarkadero as some called it, and this place was the Cap Shief of all places. Everybody was in hot hast[e] about something. The great gambling houses were doing the best business. Monte was the favorite game, thou[gh] all kinds of games were played. Horses selling, men packing, vessels unloading saylors on a jambore. Outfitts [were] furnished for all parts of the mines. The gambling houses were the greatest attraction. A dozen ta[b]les with stacks of doubloons, Mexecan dollars, and gold dust by the sack. [There was] a band of music and liquor deliverd free to all the house. The tables were allways crowded with players at the games.

To Stockton was our next place to stop. There was little difference, but this place had more for[eig]niers than anny other. There was Brazilians, Cheleanians, Mexicans, Knakers, and all the skum of the earth. From here [we] went [to] San Francisco. The bay was crowded with shipping and foreighners from all nations and similar to the other towns we had been in. Ships would arrive [and] the crews would desert them and leave for the mines and the vessels [were] used for store houses and lodging places. The ships were stript of all furniture or anny thing they could be used for. A more conglo[mo]rate set of mortals was never seen on earth.

Nothing but clatter and confusion. We soon tired of the bedlam and concluded to have a change and started for the Spanish ranches. We wanted to purch[ase] some Sonorain mules. They are verry handy and nice to ride and hardy, easy to keep, and good travlers.

We struck out over the mountains to Sante Cruis [Santa Cruz] and then to the San Juan mission over amongst the Dons. Stopt at a large ranch, bought a few mules and some other Spanish notions, and rested several days. We were well treated and had a change whitch suited, torteles, chile colorow, penoche, wine, and so forth. We happend at a fandango which was a treat to us. The cabeleros come with all their jingling uniform[s] and appeard very elegant in their native custom. The sennretas were not [to] be outdone in their showy finery. They final[l]y started their dancing whitch consisted in walsing. They invited us to take a part in the dancing. We accepted their offer, but some of us made a sorry figure in the performance.

> They have the nicest seneretoes,
> At their dances or fandangoes,
> And they smoke their segarrettoes,
> While they dance to song and banjo.

We had a fine time. The wine flowed freely. The Hidelgoes were verry polite and the ladys apeared to the best advantage. They generaly have a row at their fandangoes, but this one was an acc[e]ption.

The natives eat drink and be merry—[they] have no thought for the morrow and do not exert themselves uselessly. They grow up in their native simplicity and have no aches and pains, with no lame backs or rheumatism to complain about. [They] are graceful, slender, and suple, and ready for a fandango at short notice.

After doing up our buisness, we started towards the southern part of the mines. Crost the Coast Range by way of Pecheco Pass.[30] Crossed the San Jaoquin River [and] went up the Merced River to the foot hills of the Siere Nevad[a] and followed along the mountain. There appeared considerable mining all along the creeks and the raveines. Crost the Tuolum[n]e River. This is a large stream and there was considerable mining on the bars and the creeks.

Nex[t] was the Stanislau River. Hear was the livest place we had seen and the richest in all the southern mines. Sonoro was the town of buisness and [there were] more foriginers here than any other place.[31] This was the richest place in the mines. The first miners here found gold by the sacks in places whear the watter had washed the bed rock clean. They often picked it up with out exertion, great quantities of it, [but there were] too manny cut throats here and we passed on towards the Calevas [Calaveras] River.

We come to [a] creek and here was an old man and his son. They had a rich claim and some Portugese miners were just making an attack

---

[30] Pacheco Pass in Merced County is still a gateway to the Central Valley of California. Marginal placers were discovered here in 1850.

[31] Sonora was one of the richest sites in the southern mines. Its 1849 population of five thousand had the only substantial number of women in the mines. William Perkins took a more progressive view of the camp than Blackburn: "Here were to be seen people of every nation in all varieties of costume, and speaking fifty different languages, and yet all mixing together amicably and socially; and probably not one in a thousand moralizing on the really extraordinary scene in which he was just as extraordinary an actor." See Morgan, *William Perkins' Journal*, 101.

on him to drive him off his claim. We interferd with their intensions and ran them off. The old fellow wanted us to stay with him and he would give us half of his claim. [We] accepted his offer and found the ground rich but shallow and worked it out in a week. We left. The old man said he would leave too. He had taken out several thousand dollars and his claim was nearly worked out. He said if he stayed there he would be murderd. He went with us for saf[e]ty.

Crossed the Caleveres and [saw] more mining generly. They were doing well. Kept on [and] crost Dry Creek and more mineing with the usual result, successful.[32]

The Mecosme River was the next and the whole face of the earth was being torn up and washed out. We thought the price of gold would come down there was such quantities taken out, but they were taking up the cream of the diggings. By and by the gold will be harder to find.

We heard of new diggings over on the divide between the Mecoseme and the American River. Went that way to see them and while we were crossing through we heard a noise off at one side in a raveine. Turned off the trail to see what it was and there was a lone man at [work] with his rocker a singing:

> O rock the cradle Lucie,
> Rock the cradle strong.
> O rock the cradle Lucie,
> And keep the baby warm.
>
> Mis Lucie had a baby,
> And she laid it on the grass.
> Every time the baby cried,
> She spanked it.[33]

And just before he finished the last word we burst right onto him. He trimbled all over and thought the Indians had him. The riffels in the rocker was nearly full of gold. We started on and he went with us over to the American River after provisions. Crost the river and thought we knew all about that stream and layed our course toward the Yuba and Feather rivers and explore[d] places that were new to us. We started

---

[32.] There are more than one hundred Dry Creeks in California, but Blackburn referred to the Dry Creek that now forms the border of Sacramento and San Joaquin counties.

[33.] On Mary Ream's typescript, Dale Morgan filled in the logical conclusion to this lyric: [on the ass].

out to see all the mines and did.

Crost Bear River but did not visit the mines, but higher up in the mountains were rich placers. Went over onto the Yuba River next. The bars of the Yuba were verry rich and some were taking it out by hand-fulls. We saw one man take out of a pocket fifteen hundred dollars in three pans of dirt. We had seen enough and did not goe to Feather River, though the mines of Feather River were amongst the best.

You might see a rough, brushy, rocky bar and in a week [there was] a town on it.

> The towns sprang up like mushrooms,
> On rivers raveines and bars,
> And women there it was too soon,
> We had no family jars.
>
> We had a visit from the fair,
> It was a grand surprise.
> The miners they did rend the air,
> To see a woman in the mines.
>
> And when she did come in to town,
> The miners gave a shout.
> The angels are comeing down,
> And gods are here about.

While looking around amongst the mine[r]s, watching them work, to my surprise I found Lou Devon, our pilot, and his wife, the Leaping Faun. They had arrived in the mines about two weeks before. They come on pack animals from Fort Hall on the Snake or Louis River. They were glad to see some one they knew before.

They had found a rich claim on the bar. He was stripping off the top dirt about a foot deep and underneath about six inches on top of the bed rock was rich in gold. His wife, or the Leaping Faun, was rock-ing out the rich dirt while he carried [it] to her in buckets. He gave me a pan to wash which come off the top of the bed rock, which looked nice. There was about one dollar and half in it, I suppose. He next gave me a pan of gravel which come out of a crevice in the bed rock. I set the pan in the watter and dashed some watter over it and the yellow stuff glitterd all over top of the pan. When the pan was washed out there was nearly an ounce of gold in the bottom of the pan. He told me to keep it and I give it to his wife and she put it in with the other dust in an old mockisson.

We eat dinner with them. The Leaping Faun had saved over some dried Buffalow and Elk meat from their trip from Fort Hall and the way she cooked it was most delicous to our taste. They had an increase in the family. There was running around a small half breed boy I had not seen before. He was quite dark colored and took after his mother. The little girl, the Sleeping Faun, was a lively little girl and could speak English verry well. She pourd watter on the dirt with a dipper while her mother rocked the miners cradle. They related over their adventures with Indian tribes in the buffalow land and the Rocky Mountains. After list[e]ning to their long narrative we bid them good bye and started home to our camp on the American River.[34]

Having visited the best portion of the mines, we returned to the place we started from. A company formed to turn the river across the bar whear we mined last on the river. There was a deep hole in the river [and] the miners thought the gold stoped in the hole. Cut the canal most through and my brother and I sould out for a good price. We found out that the gold does not stop in deep places like the Bible sayes. Gold is whear you find it.

[34.] Like Lou Devon's narrative, this section is inserted into the manuscript. This is a more logical location for Devon's tale, since both Devon and Leaping Faun tell part of the story.

If Devon was Louis Aimé Daunais, he vanishes from the historical record at this point. If, however, Devon was a free trapper who did not appear in the Columbia District accounts, one other intriguing—if unlikely—possibility exists. Assuming Blackburn actually remembered the trapper's name and rendered a close phonetic rendition of it, Lou Devon could be Louis Dauphin, "the 'famous hunter' connected with various posts of the Upper Missouri river. He was killed by the Sioux Indians in either 1864 or 1865 near the mouth of the Milk river." Other veterans of the Snake Country Outfit, including Richard Grant and Angus McLeod, later moved to Montana Territory, and this description of Dauphin seems to be in character for Lou Devon. See Hewitt, *Journal of Rudolph Frederich Kurz*, 206–7: and "Original Journal of James H. Chambers, Fort Sarpy," 292.

NINE

We Missed the Great Bonanza

One of the most extraordinary attributes of Blackburn's narrative is its blistering pace: not only does the story move along relentlessly, but it builds in significance and dramatic intensity. Having staked a claim to the first discovery of precious minerals in the Silver State, Blackburn provided one of two source accounts of the establishment of the first white settlement in modern Nevada. Before spinning this tale, he gave a colorful account of the 1850 Fort Utah fight.

As already indicated, Mormon attitudes toward Native Americans were extremely complex, and did not get any simpler when the Saints moved to the Far West. One of the themes of the Book of Mormon was that Indians were descended from disobedient sons of the prophet Lehi (including one Laman, the source of the Mormon name for Native Americans—Lamanites), who for their sins had been cursed with a dark skin. The Mormon scripture prophesied that the Lamanites would eventually join the church and play a key role in the Last Days and the establishment of the Kingdom of God, again becoming a "white and delightsome people." Levi Jackman was as perplexed as most Mormon pioneers at the problem that Indian realities posed for their millennialistic (and to modern eyes, racist) philosophy:

> We have considered it part of our duty to bring the Indians from there benighted situation and rais them as a branch of the house of Isreal to a knowled[g]e of the true and living God and establish them in the gospel of Christ. In this place we found a people to commence with. They have not ben poisoned with Sectarianism, nor were they but a little above the brutes in regard to intelligence. They live or rather exist in small bands

and are always at ware with each outher. They have no abiding place, but roam from place to place. And when they stop for a short time they fix them a lodge by sticking up sum poals and covering them with weeds or long grass so as to form a little she[l]ter. They live in constant fear of outher bands who each in turn kill them when they can. Some times however they have seasons of peace. They live on what little game they can get and roots and seads and crickets which are very large.

As to clothing it can hardly be said they have any. It consists mostley of old tattered and filthey skins of Buffelo, dear, Rabbit, etc. Finaly they are the [most] miserable, filthey, degraded set of beings that I ever saw in human shape. When I reflect and consider that they are of the house [of] Isreal and the children of the Covena[n]t sead unto whome belongs the Priesthod and the Oricals of God. And when I think of what they will be when they become a white and delightsum people, I say to myself O Lord who can do all this. But the decree has gon foarth and must be fulfilled.[1]

As unattractive as some of these beliefs might be to modern readers, the Mormons generally had a much better record in their relations with Indians than most whites, but nothing could change the fact that they were occupying key sites and destroying the resources that Native Americans depended upon for survival. As a contemporary military observer noted, "When the Mormons extended north and south, they encroached on hunting and fishing grounds, and the usual winter camping places, and scared off the game."[2] Conflict was inevitable. Four Indians were killed in a sharp fight with the Mormon militia in Utah Valley in March 1849, and in that same month the establishment of a Mormon colony located directly upon a traditional Ute fishing camp on the Provo River was a prescription for further trouble.

The pot began to boil when battalion veterans Charles Zabriskie, Richard A. Ivie, and John Rufus Stoddard left the new settlement at Fort Utah, "professedly to hunt cattle." They encountered an Indian called Old Bishop "on account of his appearance and gestures which

---

[1] Jackman, Memoirs, Utah State Historical Society, 65. In 1873, Wilford Woodruff, commenting on the church's Indian revelations, said, "When I see the power of the nation destroying them from the face of the earth, the fulfillment of that prophecy is perhaps harder for me to believe than any other revelation of God that I ever read." See *Journal of Discourses*, 15:282.

[2] Gunnison, *The Mormons*, 146.

somewhat resembled Bishop [Newel K.] Whitney's." Old Bishop was said to be wearing a shirt that Ivie claimed had been stolen from him, and he was shot through the head when the whites tried to reclaim it. The Mormons dragged the corpse to the Provo River and sank it near Box Elder Island.[3]

Settler Thomas Orr, Jr., told a different story in his memoirs:

> We made a treaty with the Utah Indians to keep them from stealing our cattle. By provisions of this treaty they agreed not to molest our cattle if we agreed not to kill the wild game which they depended on for a living. . . .
>
> One day after a four-inch fall of snow, Dr. [Doc?] Stoddard and Lorentzky [Zabriskie] left the fort and between there and Utah Lake scared up a dear unbeknown to the Indians, who were camped about a mile the other side of the fort. While the two men were out hunting they met up with an Indian who greeted them and asked what they were hunting. The whites replied nothing. In reply to a query the Indian said he was hunting deer.
>
> The Indian knew full well the whites were hunting deer and that they had violated the treaty. A quarrel between the Indian and the two men ensued. Dr. Stoddard stood with his rifle across his arm, prepared for action, and when the Indian started to kill Lorentzky, Stoddard fired first and the Indian dropped dead. His body was hid in a nearby creek caused for the most part by back water from the lake. After the dead body had been pulled up to the bank, one of the men stuck a knife into his belly and ripped him open so that his body would sink and efface all evidence of the crime. When the body was thrown into the water, instead of sinking, it floated downstream and caught against a limb of a cottonwood tree. Believing that the body had become immersed, the two whites returned to the fort.[4]

The Utes soon discovered the body. At the fort, Zabriskie and Stoddard openly boasted of the murder. Most accounts say that the men filled Old Bishop's body with rocks before sinking the body. "The

---

[3.] Journal History, 31 January 1850.

[4.] Taylor, *Life History of Thomas Orr, Jr.*, 17. No Mormon–Ute treaty on hunting survives, but an agreement regarding fishing rights was proposed about March 1848. See Christy, "Open Hand and Mailed Fist," 221, 223.

Indians assert that, annually, on the anniversary of his death, the old Bishop appears on the bank of the river, and slowly takes the rocks one by one out of his bowels and throws them into the river, then disappears. Some fishermen have watched in hopes of having an interview with the old Bishop's ghost."[5]

The situation worsened when War Chief Big Elk, who was sick with measles, came to the fort for medicine and was thrown out. The Indians retaliated by stealing three cows. On 2 February, Brigham Young authorized General Daniel Wells to call out volunteers from the Nauvoo Legion, the Utah militia. One hundred militiamen began assembling on the fourth, supported by regular army officers from Captain Howard Stansbury's Corps of Topographical Engineers surveying expedition. Stansbury "did not hesitate to say to [the Mormon leaders] that, in my judgement, the contemplated expedition against these savage marauders was a measure not only of good policy, but one of absolute necessity and self-preservation."[6] After a march through bitterly cold weather on 7 February, the "minute men" arrived at Fort Utah after midnight and assembled for battle early the next morning.

The Indians had fortified their heavily wooded campground a mile from the fort and up the Provo River. Entrenchments protected the Indian position, which was centered on a double-log house (two log rooms connected by a roofed porch). The Tumpanuwac Utes, under Chief Ope-Carry or Stick-on-Head and Big Elk, had about seventy warriors who possessed "arms equal to those of the expedition sent out against them," which were acquired through trade with California emigrants who had come through Provo the previous September. Stick-on-Head, seeing the imposing force arrayed against his people, came out to treat for peace, but Big Elk had his warriors open fire and the "engagement commenced in deadly earnest."[7]

The Utes held off their attackers through the first day's fight, wounding five or six whites. At a council of war held that night in the

---

[5.] Journal History, 31 January 1850. Brigham Young claimed that the story of the murder was concealed from him until 1854. In his Manuscript History, Young noted, "These facts, which were concealed from me at the time, explain to me why my feelings were opposed to going to war with the Indians, to which I never consented until Brother [Isaac] Higbee reported that all the settlers in Utah were of one mind in relation to it." However, Hosea Stout's journal for 8 January 1850 reported that a letter from Utah Valley was read to the legislature. "The Indians a[re] again committing depredations on the whites by stealing cattle Horses &c One Indian has been killed by the whites for attempting to shoot a man for attempting to take a shirt from him which the Indian had stolen." See Brooks, Hosea Stout, 2:359.

[6.] Stansbury, The Valley of the Great Salt Lake, 149.

[7.] Tullidge, "History of Provo City," 235, 237.

fort, Lieutenant George W. Howland of Stansbury's command, "who was experienced in methods of assault," recommended that they build a moveable battery, "which was forthwith constructed in the form of an A, with planks laid up edgewise on the top of the runners."[8]

The militia included Lot Smith, Eph Hanks, Orson Whitney, D. B. Huntington, Bill Hickman,[9] James A. Little, James Ferguson, Robert Burton, and William Kimball, many of whom would play a leading role in the 1857 Utah War. They determined to take the log house "at all hazards," and the second day's fighting, supported by artillery, lasted until nine o'clock at night. A cavalry charge, "complimented by Lieutenant Howland as being as fine as regular cavalry would make," was launched against the log house, supported by the infantry under Jabez Nowlan, which probably included Blackburn. The "battery did good service and had a good effect in frightening the Indians."[10] In a desperate fight, the Utes abandoned the log house and retreated to the cover of the riverbank. During the night, after "supplying themselves abundantly with the horse beef killed in the charge upon the log house," the Utes retreated, leaving behind several families who sought white protection at the fort.[11] Both Tullidge and Stansbury commented on the bravery of the Indians.

General Daniel Wells, "ordered not to leave the valley until every Indian was out," arrived at 3:00 A.M. on 11 February and directed a relentless pursuit. Wells told H. H. Bancroft in 1884 that Lieutenant Howland "got disgusted and came back about the time I went out."[12]

Howland had sent detailed reports to Wells on the eighth and ninth, reporting after the first day's fight that the Utes had "displayed a great amount of skill in selecting their position" and that "we were not able to get any advantage of them whatever." He complained, "The Cannon could not be used to with any effect." On the morning of 9 February, Wells sent instructions to Mormon Captain G. D. Grant to "erect a Battery upon wheels under cover to screen your men from arrows" and to "take *no hostile Indians as prisoners*, those friendly and for peace, take them under

8. Ibid., 238.

9. William A. Hickman provided the most colorful (and dubious) tale of the Fort Utah fight; by his account, the battle could not have been won without him. Hickman stated that he was in charge of the advance guard of the militia and reached Fort Utah about 9 P.M. on 7 February. He wrote that after the first day's battle, the "Indians set up such a yell of victory that one would think ten thousand devils had been turned loose." At the council of war that night, he "did not see one big feeling man" among the officers, who turned to Hickman for advice and "my plan was adopted without any opposition." Hickman gave a detailed description of the fight at the south of Utah Lake. See Hickman, *Brigham's Destroying Angel*, 56–70.

10. "Daniel H. Wells' Narrative," 125.

11. Tullidge, "History of Provo City," 239.

12. "Daniel H. Wells' Narrative," 126, 125.

guard and place them in the Fort, well guarded, and at no time leave the Fort unguarded . . . be *vigilant, be careful, and preserve the lives* of your men." Following the fight on the ninth, Howland wrote to Wells again, complaining about the comments of civilians at the fort. "Our men from the city are very much discouraged on account of the manner of *some* of the inhabitants of the Fort . . . it tends to put a damper on their courage and patriotism. It would have been far better for them to have gone and encamped close by the indians, than to have gone to the Fort and heard such remarks as 'I had sooner the indians should have my cattle than kill them for you to eat,' and 'I want them to go to California with.' such remarks as these are not calculated to inspire our men at all."[13]

The militia rested on Sunday, but the Utes, now divided into two bands, did not go far. Wells issued orders to unit commanders to "take no hostile prisoners" and "let none escape but do the work up clean."[14] He sent a small company to guard Rock Canyon, where they "found warrier Cheif Elk harn with a bull[et] hole through him."[15] His wife ("said to be the handsomest squaw in the Ute nation; she was also very intelligent") was killed in a fall while "scaling a precipice," probably trying to escape from the canyon.[16] Some of the Utes actually escaped over the mountains; thirteen of them returned in the spring, the only survivors of the seventy or eighty warriors who participated in the battle. Wells overtook the majority of the warriors south of Utah Lake, where the whites killed five and captured "15 or 20" in an assault at Table Mountain.[17] Seventeen warriors, "savage with their condition," were killed when they allegedly tried to escape the next morning, but J. W. Gunnison's journal stated that the prisoners were "taken about dark & kept under guard till morning, & forcibly disarmed—some tried to run off & were shot—The rest were also shot."[18]

[13.] See Howland to Wells, 8 and 9 February 1850, and Wells to Grant, 9 February 1850, Utah Territorial Militia, Correspondence 1849–1875, Utah State Historical Society.

[14.] Christy, "Open Hand and Mailed Fist," 225.

[15.] "Autobiography of Robert T. Thomas," 27. Lieutenant Gunnison (who was not an eyewitness) wrote that the skirmish lasted three days, and "the Indians decamped the third night for the mountain kanyons, now filled with snow; and the measles being among them, the exposure killed many. 'Old Elk,' the terror of the mountains, was found dead on the trail." See Gunnison, *The Mormons*, 146. Some sources state that Elk died of measles.

[16.] Tullidge, "History of Provo City," 239.

[17.] Blackburn does not appear to have participated in these subsequent actions, as his name appears on the "List of Detachment Left in Fort Utah Feby. 18, 1859." See Utah Territorial Militia, Correspondence 1849–1875, Utah State Historical Society.

[18.] Madsen, *Exploring the Great Salt Lake*, 265. Gunnison told the same story in *The Mormons,* noting that his informant "seemed disposed to paint it in as soft colors as possible."

Daniel Wells later recalled:

"During the whole expedition 27 warriors were killed. Their squaws, with their papooses and children, as is usual with them, threw themselves on the victorious party for protection and support; we brought them to the city, fed and took care of them until spring when they ran back to their Indian camps. Many of them died, not being able to stand our way of living."[19] Lieutenant Gunnison noted, "The captured Squaws are being distributed among the citizens for servants & the children to be taught to work for a living."[20]

Blackburn's grandmother Elizabeth and his uncles, Jehu and Elias Hicks, were among the 1849 Provo settlers. Jehu participated in the battle, but Elias was sick with measles. Both men later had remarkable careers in Utah Territory and represented opposite sides of the pioneer experience in Utah.

Frontier conditions hardened the Mormon pioneers. In May 1859, Jehu Blackburn's friend John D. Lee "met a large rattle snake. He offered fight and being the first snake I saw in 1859 and according to tradition to kill the first snake is equivalent to conquering your enemies that year. So I blowed his brains out with my revolver."[21] The people who settled the Great Basin were often deeply religious, but they were not plaster saints, and when they felt threatened they responded, often exactly as Lee did when confronted by a rattlesnake.

Following a family trade, Jehu Blackburn built the first sawmill in Utah County. On 1 February 1850, he became the father of a daughter, who was named Julia Ann after her mother, and he was appointed to the presidency of the Provo Stake. Shortly after the Fort Utah fight, General Wells sent twenty-three men to investigate a band of Utes camped at the southern end of Utah Lake and under the leadership of Chief Grocepene. "Hue" Blackburn and interpreter Allen Huntington were "sent ahead to see what the Indian wanted." Grocepene, whose warriors had discovered the mutilated corpses of the Indians the militia had killed at Table Mountain Point, struck Huntington, asking, "Why did you kill my brothers?" Drawing a pistol, Huntington prepared "to shoot the Cheif when Blackburn sna[t]ch[ed] the pistal from him."[22] This action averted a fight between the Mormon and Indian parties, which, since the companies were of equal size, the Mormons sought to avoid.

In January 1851, Julia Ann Blackburn died in childbirth; on 3

19. "Daniel H. Wells' Narrative," 126.
20. Madsen, *Exploring the Great Salt Lake*, 265.
21. Kelly, *Journals of John D. Lee*, 204.
22. "Autobiography of Robert T. Thomas," 29.

April 1852, Jehu married her sister, Susannah Jameson. On the same day he married a third woman, Mary Ann Hirons. Blackburn was elected Justice of the Peace of Utah County on 1 March 1851. In 1852, he was called to pioneer Parowan in southern Utah, and four years later he established a sawmill in Pine Valley, Utah.[23] Jehu Blackburn was listed on the 10 October 1857 muster roll of Company H of the Iron County Battalion of the Nauvoo Legion. During the previous month this force participated in the notorious Mountain Meadows Massacre.[24]

One family tradition indicates that Jehu Blackburn apostatized from the Mormon church after a dispute over property that was "consecrated" to the church, but southern Utah records indicate that Jehu was active in the Mormon church until his death.[25] After 1857 Blackburn lived on the edge of the Mormon frontier, settling in Minersville and Loa. Charles Kelly wrote that Jehu's nephew Howard told him in 1946: "Some of the pioneers of Loa bought children from the Indians. Howard Blackburn's uncle bought two."[26] Jehu had twenty children and died of pneumonia in Nephi, Utah, on 17 March 1879. Following his death, his brother Elias was notified that he had been rebaptized.[27]

Elias Blackburn became the first bishop of Provo and one of the most colorful pioneers of southern Utah. He participated in the 1856 relief of overland parties, acted as a quartermaster during the 1857 Utah War, ran a stagecoach service known as the Blackburn Express, and carried the mail between Great Salt Lake City and Nephi. Blackburn went underground when federal authorities sought him for questioning in the botched Aiken murders. He served a mission to England beginning in 1859, and acted as an emigration agent for six months in 1862. Elias Blackburn was bishop of the frontier settlements in the Fremont Valley and became a renowned frontier doctor, faith healer, and Mormon patriarch. He had five wives and thirty-nine children. Elias died on 6 April 1906 in Loa, Utah. His extensive papers are preserved in the Utah State Historical Society.[28]

About 16 April 1850, the DeMont-Beatie-Blackburn party of ap-

---

[23.] Burns, "Jehu Blackburn," 3, 4.

[24.] Muster Roll, 10 October 1857, Company H, 4th Battalion, Tenth Regiment of Infantry, Iron County Brigade, Nauvoo Legion, Utah State Archives, 3346.

[25.] Conversations with Phillip Blackburn, Anthony Blackburn, and Morgan Busch at the Blackburn Family Association Reunion, 3–4 August 1991.

[26.] Kelly Papers, "Reminiscences of Howard Blackburn," Utah State Historical Society, 3. These Indian children, who were apparently adopted into the family, appear in census records. Conversation with Morgan Busch, 5 August 1991.

[27.] Elias Hicks Blackburn Collection, Utah State Historical Society.

[28.] Voyle and Lillian Munson's *A Gift of Faith: Elias H. Blackburn* is a devout biography that provides much detail on the lives of Jehu and Elias Blackburn.

proximately eighty people left Great Salt Lake City, bound for the gold fields.[29] After a trip down the Humboldt that Blackburn found unremarkable, the company arrived in the Carson Valley at the edge of the snowbound Sierra Nevada. "It is an Oasis of great extent," Franklin Langworthy noted in the autumn, "green, romantic and beautiful, situated in the midst of vast deserts and barren mountains. The Carson river runs a serpentine course through the valley, the banks being everywhere fringed with a luxuriant growth of willows."[30] After the long march down the Humboldt and the desolate crossing of the sink, the journals of the emigrants were full of ecstatic descriptions of the valley's "rank and nutritious growth of grass," its bottom lands "covered with prairie grass and wild clover; wild buckwheat looked purple in the sun." Lorenzo Sawyer wrote, "I never found a more luxuriant crop of grass in my life than we found in this valley." It was watered by "the most beautiful spring branches, man, in any clime ever laid eyes on . . . clear as crystal and cold as heart could wish."[31] Joseph Pike found "the best timber I have seen since leaving Iowa and one acre of it worth more than [all the land] I have seen since I came into the great basen. And if I were going to settle anywhere between Fort Larryme and the Serenevada mountains it would be here on the west side of this valley."[32] The DeMont party "concluded to start a station for trade," at the site of present-day Genoa. Blackburn wrote, "There was no better place on the river."

With their head start from Great Salt Lake City, the Mormons were positioned to be the first overlanders to reach the gold fields in 1850. Unfortunately, the few accounts of the first Mormon companies are not coherent, let alone definitive, and it is even difficult to sort out how many parties are described in Mormon narratives; very likely, the composition of these companies shifted depending on trail conditions and

---

[29.] H. S. Beatie gave the number of the party and the departure date as 18 April, but placed the departure in 1849. Hosea Stout noted in his journal for 16 April 1850 that "large companies are also going now to the Gold mines." See Brooks, *Hosea Stout*, 2:367.

[30.] Franklin Langworthy reported that two hours before arriving at Mormon Station on 10 October, he "met a train of sixty Mormons, with four hundred horses and mules, on their way to Salt Lake. These Mormons . . . had killed and scalped six Digger Indians in revenge for thirty mules the Indians had stolen from them. They . . . did not know whether the Indians they had killed were those concerned in the theft, or otherwise." He also commented on "Erwin's trading post, ten miles south from Mormon Station," a probable reference to Edmond's Station. See Langworthy, *Scenery of the Plains*, 154–56.

[31.] Owens, "Archaeological and Historical Investigation of the Mormon-Carson Emigrant Trail," A:287, 206, 171, 286.

[32.] Joseph Pike, "Journal of 1850," California State Library.

rate of travel. The published diary of Louisa Barnes Pratt provided little information on the journey and no details of the Mormon camp in Carson Valley. The only other known contemporary account, a journal by Jesse Morgan, gave some intriguing insights into the composition of these 1850 California companies.

Morgan, who traveled to Utah with a Mormon emigrant party in 1849, "left Great Salt Lake City . . . in company with J. N. Spaulding and Wm. Prouse" on 22 April 1850. Along with "Barnes, Perkins, Smith," and men named Oliver Norton, Green, and Martin, Morgan joined "Capt. Ork's company" on 1 May—the Thomas Orr, Sr., party. At the Raft River, Morgan noted, "We had some difficulty in our course and six wagons and men left us and went on." On 30 May, the journal recorded that "Wm. Prouse and Roberts got married" at Matrimonial Bend on the Humboldt. On 5 June, in the area of the Big Meadows, "we overtook Captain Demont's company."[33] Unfortunately, Morgan did not specify whether the DeMont and Orr parties continued on to Carson Valley together, but he did note that the company camped on the river on 15 June, and "about seven miles back from this place, Wm. Prouse discovered gold in a Canion that came in from the north." The next day, "some men went back to examine the gold and reported favorably."[34]

The memoirs of Thomas Orr, Jr., gave additional, if confusing, insights into the founding of Mormon Station. Following his previously cited description of his party's rediscovery of Gold Canyon, Orr wrote:

> Half way across the plains below [present] Carson we met three Indians going that way and they told us the oxen could cross the mountains but the snow was too deep for wagons. We drove on to a little creek, with fine bottom land and stopped at a place near Lake Tahoe, now called Genoa. We were there three weeks waiting for the snow to disappear from the mountains. Some of us went up a canyon and felled trees. We used the poles in making up a corduroy road across a creek and in other places bridges would be constructed by men in our company.
>
> My Brother John, accompanied by men named Bill Prouse and Nick Kelly returned to prospect the place where Prouse had made a find of gold. My brother was lucky in the first hole, panning out a nugget which later showed a value of $8.25. This was the first piece of gold ever found on that side of the

---

[33.] Morgan, *A Trip across the Plains*, 20–25.
[34.] Ibid., 25–26.

mountains and my brother's sons living in Sonoma County, still possess this nugget . . .

After this delay we left Mormon Station (now Genoa) and heard that the men ahead of us were exacting a toll from travellers on the three bridges we had built across the Carson River. When we arrived at that point, we put an end to that practice and left the bridges open for the travellers following us.[35]

Whether this account records interaction between the Thomas Orr company and the DeMont-Beatie-Blackburn party is impossible to nail down. There are some parallels between the descriptions: both groups departed the Salt Lake Valley at about the same time and were about the same size (Beatie referred to eighty people, Orr to thirty-five families); both encountered Indians in the Carson Valley; and both arrived too early to take wagons across the Sierra. The Morgan journal indicated they traveled as separate parties above Big Meadows, but this is the only source that mentioned the other group; in fact, H. S. Beatie said specifically, "I did not see a white man for several weeks after we arrived there, nor did I hear of anyone in that country camping," which indicated that the two companies may have lost their distinct identities after crossing the Humboldt Sink. However, the parties seem to have arrived at Gold Canyon at different times. Blackburn's narrative noted that "there had been some miners there and [they had] worked out the best places" in Gold Canyon, which was a possible reference to the Orr company activities or other undocumented mining activities in the region in 1849. Amasa Lyman noted Blackburn's presence in Sacramento on 22 June 1850, while Orr and Morgan indicated that their party arrived at Placerville on 4 July.

The story of the founding of Mormon Station has long been based on reminiscent accounts collected by H. H. Bancroft in 1884, including an interview with H. S. Beatie, whom Blackburn called James Beaty and identified as the "secretary" of the 1850 party.[36] In an exhaustive survey of Mormon-Carson emigrant trail guides, journals, and reminiscences, historian Kenneth N. Owens has compiled a wealth of material painting a vivid picture of Mormon Station and one that requires a closer examination of the traditional view of Nevada's first white settlement.[37] Of

---

[35.] Taylor, *Life of Thomas Orr, Jr.*, 20–21.

[36.] It is not outside the realm of possibility that a man named Hampton Sidney would use the moniker "Jim." The complete text of Beatie's statement to H. H. Bancroft is quoted in Appendix E.

[37.] Owens, "Archaeological and Historical Investigation of the Mormon-Carson Emigrant Trail," Appendix A.

the eighty-four 1850 accounts collected by Owens, more than a dozen mentioned Mormon Station by name and almost all noted the presence of trading posts. By 2 July, David Wooster came

> to the site the Mormons have fixed up for a new settlement. They are building a large block house at the base of the mountain where there is plenty of timber, two miles from the river bank... There are now here about 100 Mormons. They have sent a train of pack mules to Sacramento for stores. The Israelites are flocking to this station from the Great Valley, and from the other side of the mountain. They are selling beef and other supplies to the emigrants at two dollars per pound.[38]

At the end of the month, emigrants reported several trading posts in the area and as many as five log houses in the midst of the pine grove at Mormon Station. On 30 July, William Kilgore arrived "at a mormon Station. Here we see some Log Houses and Six Families, Emigrants from Salt Lake. We learn that there are Gold mines in this vicinity, bot to what Extent has not yet been ascertained."[39]

Mormon Station was a single example of one of the phenomena of the overland experience, the spontaneous creation of trading stations along the trail that extended from California as far as Big Meadows on the Humboldt River.[40] At the Carson River crossing at the edge of the Carson Sink, emigrants described "Carson River City" and "Ragtown." In Carson Valley alone, "about every ten miles there is a Trading Post."[41] At the end of July, Thomas Christy observed that the traders "are running that business into the ground as fast as possible as too many cooks spoil the broth, as the saying is. There is too many at it to be very profitable."[42]

The journals paint a much different view of the station than either Blackburn or Beatie, neither of whom mentioned women at the settlement. William Kilgore wrote that six families from Salt Lake were living at Mormon Station in late July. William Rothwell described the station in mid-August:

[38.] Wooster, *Gold Rush Letters*, quoted in Owens, "Archaeological and Historical Investigation of the Mormon-Carson Emigrant Trail," A:164.

[39.] Muench, *The Kilgore Journal*, 54.

[40.] On 23 July, William Kilgore at "The Great Natural Meadow," probably near present-day Lovelock, noted, "There are men, at this place, hurding and recruiting givout Horses and agree to take them through for the Sum of twenty Dollars each." He also stated, "Some Indians are here. They are of the Shoshone tribe and engaged in helping the Emigrants prepare Hay." Ibid., 49.

[41.] Shepherd, *Journal of Travel across the Plains*, 35.

[42.] Becker, *Thomas Christy's Road across the Plains*, 84.

we passed through a Mormon settlement of several houses, established for the purpose of buying up broken down animals.
There were a dozen or more families. The neatly dressed
women, the prattling children, and the usual appearance of or-
dinary quiet life impressed upon my mind recollections of the
land of civilization.

This encampment is in one of the most picturesque and
beautiful spots I have ever seen upon the entire road. In all directions the scenery is delightful. On the West, towers a lofty ridge
whose summit reaches to the region of perpetual snow, timbered
from summit to foot with lofty pines many of which have a diameter of 5 feet. Down its rocky sides rush numerous little
rivulets of water fresh from the snows above. In front, and from
the foot of the mountain, stretches the meadow-like valley, 3–5
miles wide and no less than 25 miles long. Winding through this
grassy plain the river makes its way, marked by its usual growth
of cottonwood and willow. . . . It has been said that gold has
been discovered in the adjacent Mts., a thing quite probable.[43]

Like Rothwell, Andrew Hall Gilmore combined a description of the
scenery with an appreciation of the women. One of these women was
probably Thomas Blackburn's wife, Emily.

This is one of the most admirable situations I ever saw; it is
in a beautiful grove of large pine trees immediately at the base
of the mountain; in front lies the beautiful valley; while at the
rear the towering mountain shoots up and [is] densely covered
with a majestic forest.

At this station there were a good many handsome well
dressed women that added much to the beauty and pleasant-
ness of the place.[44]

James Abbey, like many emigrants, complained about prices at the
station, calling it "a perfect skinning post."[45] In early July, the traders

---

[43] Rothwell, "The Journal, Letters, and Guide," quoted in Owens, "Archaeological and Historical Investigation of the Mormon-Carson Emigrant Trail," A:251.

[44] Owens, "Archaeological and Historical Investigation of the Mormon-Carson
Emigrant Trail," A:296. In July 1849, David Cosad met a different group of Mormons
"a going to Salt Lake with their ox teams & families and the hardest looking Set of
Women I Ever Saw for white women. They had been to the mines & had plenty of
dust, but [I had] rather live without dust than live as they do." Ibid., A:49.

[45] Abbey, *California: A Trip across the Plains in the Spring of 1850*, quoted in Morgan, *The Humboldt*, 200.

were charging, per pound, two dollars for flour and sugar and a dollar for beef, while whiskey brought a dollar a pint and fifty cents per drink. High prices resulted in competition: by mid-July a second trading post opened, and by August there were five posts located along the Carson Valley road.[46] Byron McKinstry recorded declining, but still high, prices on 7 September 1850:

> Passed the Mormon Station and several others. This is a picturesque place. Fine pines, one very large one at the station, the camp under it. [Lewis] Lilley, [William H.] Clark and [Amos] Lyon sold out their team here for 50 dolls. per yoke and 10 dolls. for the wagon, and Lilley hired to go back for 50 or 60 m[iles] at 5 dolls. per day. Lyon sold Guise at 30 dolls. Flour is now down to 50 cts., and 37½ cts., pork and sugar at 75 cts., brandy 1.50 per pint.[47]

On 7 October 1850, the *Daily Alta California* published an item by R. Wilson, datelined 21 September 1850 at Mormon Station:

> Last summer, about twenty Mormons, from Salt Lake on their way to California, found gold on this side of the mountains, and built in Carson Valley two immense log houses, intending to winter here. Changing their minds, they sold out to a trader named More, from Stockton. Some have gone to the settlements in California, and others have returned to Salt Lake with stock purchased from the immigrants.[48]

An 1880 letter by Robert Lyon gave more information on prices and the women at the trading post.

> Californians spoke of Mormon Station as the principal trading-post east of the Sierra. . . . The Mormon Station (the present Genoa) was founded in June, 1850, by Salt Lake Mormons. I arrived at that station about July 20, 1850, and stayed there to rest one day. I sold a good American horse to the man who kept the trading post for thirty pounds of flour and fifteen dollars. Flour was $1.50 per pound, and he allowed me sixty dollars for my horse. There were two or three women and some children at the place, and I understood that they had settled there with the

---

[46.] Owens, "Archaeological and Historical Investigation of the Mormon-Carson Emigrant Trail," 90–91.

[47.] McKinstry, *Overland Diary*, 292–93. Bruce McKinstry repeated the 1849 founding date error in his annotations.

[48.] Quoted in Elliott, "Nevada's First Trading Post," 8.

intention of remaining permanently. . . . In regard to improvements there was one store where they kept for sale flour, beans, tea, coffee, sugar, dried peaches, sardines, tobacco, miner's clothing, overalls, shirts, etc., etc. There was also a grocery where they sold whiskey, bread, cigars and tobacco. They had a good-sized log-house completed all but the roof . . . the traders at that post were getting rich trading with the emigrants.[49]

The date of the settling of Mormon Station, the "first trading post in Nevada," was long a matter of controversy in Nevada history due to H. S. Beatie's error in dating its founding in 1849 rather than in 1850— a mistake infinitely compounded when H. H. Bancroft repeated it in his history of the state. Dale Morgan solved this problem in 1943 noting that "Abner Blackburn's reliable reminiscences establish 1850" as the correct date. Morgan showed that Beatie arrived in Utah with E. T. Benson's company on 28 October 1849, so that the founding of Mormon Station must have occurred in 1850.[50]

Despite Morgan's analysis, use of the 1849 date persisted in Nevada histories until as late as 1965.[51] Ironically, Bancroft could have forestalled the confusion had he listened more closely to one of his 1884 informants, John Reese, who eventually purchased Mormon Station:

> At this place [Mormon Station] in 1850 there was a trading post a little way off mine. The year that I went there [1851] there was but little emigration, but in 1852 it was a very good year. H. S. Beatie was there about 1850 with about ½ dozen most of whom came from the [Mormon] Battalion. They stopped a while, put up a trading post and went to California. They went with pack animals. They stayed there about two months and put up a cabin. They put in no ground. They came back here [to Great Salt Lake City] and Beatie told me about it, and that was why I went. I do not know of any[one] being there in 1849.[52]

---

[49] Angel, *History of Nevada*, 30.

[50] Morgan, *The Humboldt*, 199–200.

[51] Mack, *Here Is Nevada*.

[52] Reese, "Mormon Station," 188. An 1893 letter by one of Reese's 1851 employees, Stephen A. Kinsey, stated that prior to 1851 Mormon Station "was a tent used as a trading post." He wrote that when he arrived in 1851, "there was no one living there, no house, no ruins of a house, or the vestige of one to be found. Those who occupied the place in 1849–'50 [sic] had folded their tents like the Arab, in the fall of the last year and silently stolen away, leaving the torch of the Indian to efface any indication of their ever having been there." See Nevada Historical Society, MS/NC 344. In light of the numerous 1850 accounts of buildings at Mormon Station and Kinsey's interest in promoting his role in early Nevada history, his account must be regarded with some skepticism.

At any rate, after a supply trip to Sutter's Fort, Blackburn returned to work Gold Canyon. C. N. Noteware, who later became Nevada's secretary of state, may have encountered him.

> The writer passed the mouth of Gold Canyon on the third day of July, 1850, and on the divide between there and Empire, met a party of miners from California on their way with a mining outfit to work in the canon, where they said gold had been discovered the year before by a party of emigrants.[53]

Noticeably perplexed, at least sixteen journals of west-bound emigrants recorded an east-bound gold rush to the Carson Valley, describing parties of California miners who were either already in or packing to the canyons of the Carson Range. By whatever means it was made, the discovery of gold on the eastern side of the mountains was not long kept a secret; by 16 July, James A. Blood, crossing the Sierra, "met several small companies going to the Carson River, mining so they say. If so, it must be very rich mining, it being one hundred and fifty miles from Sacramento City." The next day, John W. Ellis "camped near where the Mormons are building a trading post. . . . Some gold found near here." He noted on the seventeenth, "We saw lots of gold hunters ranging over the mountains this afternoon."[54] The size of the rush is difficult to estimate, but it seemed large to the overlanders, who were themselves part of a tide of more than forty thousand west-bound emigrants. On 16 July, Lorenzo Sawyer recorded meeting "several trains a day bound for Carson river with provisions. Many . . . intend to prospect for gold."[55] On 31 July, William Kilgore described "meeting a great many miners who are going to those late Discoveries or mines about the Station."[56]

Most journals discounted the value of these mines, probably with encouragement from the miners themselves. Robert Lyon recollected stopping at Gold Canyon and encountering Mormon miners, who said "there was richer diggings near Hangtown, (Placerville), and unless they found better pay in a few days, they would return to California."[57] Still, contradictory reports circulated on the trail; after crossing the Sierra, Byron McKinstry heard that "they are digging gold in Carson Valley quite successfully."[58]

[53.] Angel, *History of Nevada*, 30.

[54.] Owens, "Archaeological and Historical Investigation of the Mormon-Carson Emigrant Trail," A:169, 176.

[55.] Sawyer, *Way Sketches*, quoted in Owens, "Archaeological and Historical Investigation of the Mormon-Carson Emigrant Trail," A:174.

[56.] Muench, *The Kilgore Journal*, 55.

[57.] Angel, *History of Nevada*, 30.

[58.] McKinstry, *Overland Diary*, 306.

The first Nevada gold rush that was described in the journals died within the year, after most of the miners, like Blackburn, "crevest around for a week or more and the men thought they could do better on the other side of the mountain." The great irony is that these parties were pecking at the edges of one of the richest mineral troves in the world, the Comstock lode, which would remain virtually undiscovered until 1859. Blackburn, writing in old age and poverty, dryly noted, "If we had known [of] the rich mines higher up the canion, the outcome would be different."

Yet another example of the historical depth of the narrative is Blackburn's accurate description of the obscure Georgetown Cutoff. This cutoff, a pack trail too difficult for wagons, entered the mountains about a mile below Mormon Station and skirted (without viewing) the southern edge of the Mountain Lake (later called Lake Bigler and Lake Tahoe), crossed the present Desolation Wilderness, and then followed the Rubicon River drainage to Georgetown. Nicknamed Growlersburg, Georgetown was located about ten miles due east of Auburn and had a population of five thousand in December 1849. Edmund Cavalieer Hinde met men promoting the cutoff on 20 July 1850:

> We seen some men from Georgetown and they offered to pilot us throug[h]. They say we can get through in 3 days. As soon as our company were acquainted with the men from Georgetown (a new town just started) we concluded to go throug[h] with them. We routed untill evening to go as far as the pass, where across it is about 7 miles. The[y] reported the Mormon station ten miles which is only six. When we reached the mountains we camped. On looking at the [Georgetown] road we concluded to keep to the old one.[59]

William Tell Parker's diary stated: "A mile below us is a cutoff to Georgetown, seventy-five miles distant, near Deer Creek. This is for packers."[60] On 27 July, Seth Lewelling described "a Mormon trading post. One mile further [on] is a pack trail made 3 weeks ago."[61]

Robert Chalmers took the Georgetown Cutoff on 25 August, leaving Mormon Station, one of "several stations at the foot of the gully that

---

[59.] Owens, "Archaeological and Historical Investigation of the Mormon-Carson Emigrant Trail," A:184.

[60.] Ibid., A:193.

[61.] Ibid., A:201.

leads up onto the mountains, a short cut off to the mines, or George-town." By Chalmers's mileage estimates, it was 112 miles from Mormon Station to Georgetown, across "a stony, hilly country" that took seven days to cross, counting one day "to recruit our animals." Near the crest of the Sierra, he "lost the path and could not find the right one for some time. There were so many paths that we thought we had arrived at the jumping off place." The rest of the journey was comparatively easy, though he noted: "There are plenty of grizzley bears here. We have not met any of them yet."[62] Georgetown is undoubtedly the correct reading for the "Jumptown" that confused Bancroft, in H. S. Beatie's "First in Nevada." Bancroft wrote that the men at Mormon Station "made another journey to the mines, this time with pack animals, and by the way of a pass three miles south of Beatie's claim, the adventurers crossing the streams on bridges and floats of logs."[63]

Although he wrote that in the spring of 1850, "My brother had married his girl and we were ready to leave the Saints for good," in the fall Blackburn returned to Zion again—probably drawn by the same force that had brought Thomas back in the autumn of 1849: love. Al-though the narrative does not mention a word about Lucinda Harris, Blackburn was counted in the 1850 census at Farmington, where the Harris family had settled.[64]

Increasingly bitter Indian fights dominate the last sections of Blackburn's narrative. In an 1897 letter, Blackburn called these conflicts "the carson war"—and from where he stood, it must have looked and felt like war. Desperate struggle replaces the romantic view of the tribes presented in the narrative of Lou Devon, building with a relentless and Homeric intensity toward the narrative's ultimate tragedy.

THE NARRATIVE

OCTOBER 20 1849

We started back on the road over the mountain[s] to help some of our relations that was on the road and were on the plains some

---

[62] Kelly, "The Journal of Robert Chalmers," 54.

[63] Bancroft, *History of Nevada, Colorado, and Wyoming*, 67. Bancroft confused the Georgetown Cutoff with the Carson Pass trail, noting, "This was probably the route opened by the returning Mormon battalion in the spring of 1848." Joseph Pike de-scribed using the cutoff in September 1850. Pike reported, "[We crossed] over creeks on bridges made by falling trees across and flatt[en]ing the top so that animals can stan[d] or travel on them. these were the only bridge[s] in the mountains."

[64] Blackburn was counted twice in the 1850 Utah census, at both Farmington and Provo.

place.[65] Went over into Carson Valley [and] enquired of the emegrants, but they did not know annything about them. Crost the desert
onto the Humbolt and heard they stopt to winter in Salt Lake valley. I
wanted to come back to Callifornia, [but] my brother was attracted by
a girl which drew his attension. We both went on and in twelve days
with our little Sonoranian mules reached our kindred in the valley.
And had a splendid time with our pockets full of the needful.[66]

We were just as good as the Elders of Israel. At least our gold was.
My brother was married on Christmas day.[67] We divided. I went south
to winter at Provo in Utah Lake Valley and winterd with my uncles.

The Utah Indians become verry troublesome and orderd the setlers
to leave. Of course, they would not. One thing brought another until
the Indians put on war paint and commenced hostilities and all the
available men in Utah were called out to fight [the] Utas.

The Indians selected a verry strong position on a river in timber,
logs, and brush. They barricaded their position well and were well
armed with rifels. We surrounded them and skirmished with them two
days with a few canon and small armes.[68] There were a few killed and
wounded on each side.[69]

[65.] Blackburn probably actually received this news in the fall of 1850; see his
comment, in Great Salt Lake City in the spring of 1851, that he left his "relation[s] to
come on with their slow cattle at their leisure." These relatives were probably Blackburn's sister, Eliza Jane, and her husband, John Pope Bainbridge. In 1964, Paul Gallagher interviewed his distant relative, Dorothy Fickus Johnson, who attended John
Bainbridge's funeral in 1889. Johnson told Gallagher that "the Bainbridges came overland from Illinois with the wagon train group headed by James Kinnon Giles and his
brother-in-law Samuel Powers of Decatur, Illinois late in 1850. . . . There is a family
story told that Eliza Jane (Blackburn) Bainbridge had another child (an infant girl)
with her on the wagon train, who was stolen by Indians while they were crossing the
plains en route to California in 1850." See Gallagher, "Bainbridge Family History,"
63, 143. The 1850 Illinois census for Carlinville listed a female infant in the Bainbridge family who apparently did not reach California.

[66.] On 28 October 1849, Abner Blackburn deposited 384 dollars in the Mormon church's gold accounts and Thomas deposited 200 dollars the next day. They
received Mormon paper money in exchange for their gold. See Davies, *Mormon
Gold*, 279; and Daily Transactions in Gold Dust, Brigham Young Collection, LDS
Archives.

[67.] Thomas Blackburn married Emily Bartholomew of New York. The marriage produced four children: Thomas Leroy, Alice Miranda, Emily Lucetta, and Perry Anderson.

[68.] Thomas Orr, Jr., stated that one of the cannons used in the Fort Utah fight
had fought in the Revolution and was brought across the plains from Iowa.

[69.] Joseph Higbee of the militia was killed, and about eighteen whites were
wounded. Howard Stansbury estimated that forty Indians were killed, while Daniel
Wells guessed twenty-seven warriors.

One of our men had a verry large nose. His wife told him in the morning if he was shot it would be in his nose. And sure enough he was, while charging a strong position held by the Indians. The bullet hit on the side of the bridge of his nose, which made a verry painful wound but not dangerous.[70]

We routed the Indians and they went in an almost inaccessable canion. We followed them up and killed Elk, the cheif, and a few others.[71] Captured some, but the most of them escaped to Spring Creek and Spanish Fork. We followed them up and at the south end of Utah Lake demolished them on the edge of the ice. The war was over and all went home.

A few days after the last batle with the Indians, a goverment surgeon wanted James Or and me to take a sley [and] cross over on the ice and secure the Indians heads, for he wanted to send them to Washington to a medical institution.[72] [We] hired a sley [and] crost over on the ice. The weather was bitter cold. The surgeon to[o]k out his box of instruments and comenced. It took him a quarter of an hour to cut off one head. The sun was getting low and [it was] frezing cold. Jim and me took the job in our own hands. We were not going to wait on the surgeons slow motion. Jerked our knives out and had them all off in a few minutes. They were frozen and come off easy in our fassion. The surgeon stood back and watched us finish the job.[73]

---

70. The Fort Utah battle was fought on 8 and 9 February 1850. Jabez Nowlan, a former corporal in Company C of the Mormon Battalion who had wintered at Pueblo with Blackburn, was wounded in the nose in the assault on the log cabin in the second day's fight.

71. This is the same Old Elk whom Blackburn met on his 1847 trading expedition. Bill Hickman claimed he "took off his head, for I had heard the old mountaineer, Jim Bridger, say he would give a hundred dollars for it." Hickman, *Brigham's Destroying Angel*, 68.

72. English-born Dr. James Blake served as scientist and geologist of the Stansbury survey party until disagreements with Stansbury caused him to quit without notice, taking a considerable part of the expedition's collections as collateral for his pay. Blake alienated Brigham Young when he sent the militia a bill for 123 dollars and lost a suit brought by Stansbury before the governor. For a complete account of this bizarre affair and strange character, see Madsen, *Exploring the Great Salt Lake*, 553–91.
James Orr was born 9 September 1828 at Cumbaslang, Lanark, Scotland, and arrived in Utah in 1847. Orr "was wounded by his own gun discharging accidentally" at the Fort Utah battle. See Brooks, *Hosea Stout*, 2:362. His family emigrated to California in 1850 and settled at Salmon Falls. Orr, a "whiskey-drinking [stage] driver," was twice held up by highwaymen. He "liked his nips and they said he sat with a shotgun and a keg between his legs, and a knife in his belt." Orr died 20 July 1891 in El Dorado County, California.

73. Epsy Jane Williams Pace wrote, "U.S. Surgeon Dr. Blake cut the heads off the Indians that were killed and brought them back to the fort. He had 40 or 50, and said that after the flesh was off he was going to take them back to Washington." See Pace, "History of Provo," Utah State Historical Society.

The surgeon shot some ducks, ten or twelve. [He] boxed them up, guts, feathers, and all, and told me to bring them down with the Indian heads in a week or two to Salt Lake City. Took them down according to agreement.[74] The weather turned warm and the ducks were green with rot. The Indian heads smelt loud. Drove to his office and told him the ducks were spoilt. He opened the box, pulled out a wing, smelt it and says they are just right. He settled up and invited me to super. I was not hungry and declined his offer.

In the spring of 1850 we made up a company to goe to Callifornia. It was not much work to find men to goe to the new Eldorado. In those times, California was the only magnet. My brother had married his girl and we were ready to leave the Saints for good.

Joseph Demont was our captain, James Beaty secretary, and [we] made the trip to Carson Valley with out anny thing happening of note.[75] Only camping, hitching up, going on, and stopping again. We stopt at the place I found the year before. It is now called Gold Canion, but there had been some miners there and [they had] worked out the best places.

One morning after we started a few Indians acompanyed us, they afoot, and kept along with the waggons. They would watch the wheels of the wagons to see the hind wheels run over the fore wheels. It was a great mistry to them. The fore wheels being the smallest, they thought the hind wheels being the largest ought to catch the front wheels.

The top of the Sirea Nevada mountains were in plain sight. We asked them by motion how long it would [take] to goe there. One of them could speak a verry little English. He stopt and pointed to the

---

74. On 22 February, Peter Conover, commanding at Fort Utah, reported to Major General Wells: "We called the roll yesterday and paraded the men. Found one absent by the name of Abner Blackburn. Report says that he started the day previous for the G.S.L. City without asking leave." See Utah Territorial Militia, Correspondence 1849–1875, Utah State Historical Society. Blackburn had an unassailable excuse for being AWOL.

75. Joseph DeMont is difficult to identify outside of the memoirs of Blackburn and Beatie. He participated in the great varmint hunt in Great Salt Lake City in December 1848, and apparently settled in San Leandro, California. Herb Hamlin wrote: "Jean Allen Latta, wife of California's noted historian, Frank Latta, is a descendent of Captain Joseph DeMont. . . . Her mother's name was Clarabell DeMont, born at San Leandro in 1876." *The Pony Express*, June 1966.

Hampton Sidney Beatie, born 31 December 1826 in Virginia, arrived in Great Salt Lake City in October 1849 with the Ezra Taft Benson party. During the winter, Beatie worked for merchants John and Enoch Reese. Beatie later settled in Salt Lake and joined the Mormon church. He became county coroner, a lieutenant colonel in the state militia, and a manager of the Church's cooperative store, ZCMI. One of his sons married a daughter of Brigham Young in 1872. Beatie died on 11 September 1887. See Esshom, *Pioneers and Prominent Men of Utah*, 181, 745, which spells his name as both Hampton and Hampden.

mountain and sayes, "A waggon, a waggon, a waggon, a waggon, a waggon." He would place one hand above another. That me[a]nt so manny camps. They went several miles with our company and went off to their wild home in the mountains. On leaveing their leader sayes, "Onda coche wappa honda."

Went to the [Carson] river [and] to th[e] canion. And the emegrants began to overtake us and said thousands and thousands were on the road comeing in every way. We concluded to start a station for trade [with] Ca[ptain] Dumont and four others, my brother and I included.[76]

I being the best ac[q]uainted with country, [I] took them back to wheare Genoa now is.[77] There was no better place on the river, [with] cold watter comeing out of the mountain and pine trees were plenty on the edge of the valley. There was oceans of good feed for stock. It was a choice place for our buisness. [We] built the first house for our stasion out of pine logs and a large log coral for stock and fixt for traffic.

I took several teams and started over the mountain after provisions and suplies for the station. On the other side of the mountain, teams had come up from Sacramento after snow.[78] It was selling for eighty dollars a ton in Sacramento and we loaded up with snow. [We] coverd it with pine boughs and waggon sheets. We killed two birds with one stone hauling down snow and carrying back provisions. Disposed of the snow. Layed in our suplies [and] returned to Carson Valley.[79]

The emegrants crowded the road. My partners wanted me to make

---

[76.] Juanita Brooks identified six of the seven men: Thomas and Abner Blackburn, Joseph DeMont, H. S. Beatie, and men named Carter and Kimball. See "The Mormons in Carson City, Utah Territory," 10–11. George Springmeyer, writing about Douglas County in Davis, *The History of Nevada,* 806, listed "men named Kimball, Carter, Pearson, Smith and Brown," but cited no source.

[77.] Mormon Apostle Orson Hyde renamed Mormon Station in 1855 because the steep Carson Range reminded him of the Italian coast behind Genoa. The Mormons abandoned Carson Valley in 1857, when Brigham Young recalled his extended colonies to defend Zion against Johnston's army. A reconstruction of the Blackburn-Beatie log house now stands at the historic state monument, located about a half-mile south of the original settlement.

[78.] Lorenzo Sawyer noted, on 17 July 1850, "We have met several wagons to-day bound to the mountains for snow to be hauled to Sacramento City, where it is said to be worth $1.00 per pound to cool sherry coblers for the Sacramentonians." Owens, "Archaeological and Historical Investigation of the Mormon-Carson Emigrant Trail," A:175. Leroy Kidder observed a "great number of teams were loading this and hauling it to Sacramento . . . and selling it in a wholesale way at twelve and a half cents per pound." Ibid., A:181.

[79.] Amasa Lyman noted, on 22 June 1850, "22 Saturday went to Sacrimento. C meet with br Blackburn from Salt Lake from whom we learned that they had trouble with the Indians of whom some 32 were killed." Amasa Lyman, Journal, LDS Archives.

up a company and goe back and work Gold Canion. They said they could carry on the station while I mined and have two strings to the bow. We fitted out with two teams and fourteen men with tools and started back.

On the afternoon of the first day we saw a band of about twenty Indians comeing from the mountain right towards us with bows and arrows and war clubs. They looked like a war party. We fixed our armes and all clome into the waggons and lay down to fool them, except two drivers on the outside. The savages come up close and began to surround us. We jumpt out of the waggons and faced them. They stood still and we the same.

They went back a ways and around a hill ahead of us to a narrow brushy place whear we had to pass. We could see their game. We left four men with the teams. The balanc[e] of us pas[s]ed around the hill and come in behind them and took the Indians [by] surprise. We fired on them, hit a few, and they disapeared in the brush. We completly surprised them. I never could understand their motive, unless it was we were going the wrong way to suit them. Their leader was the famous old Winemucca we found out afterwards.[80]

Continued on to the mines and worked several places with rockers and crevest around for a week or more and the men thought they could do better on the other side of the mountain. If we had known [of] the rich mines higher up the canion, the outcome would be different. We mist the great Bonanza and we come back to the station.

After we got started, trade flowed in onto us. It was hard to keep suplies on hand. Clos[e] to our place of business was the George Town cutoff. [It was] the nearest way to the mines and a great manny left waggons, harness[es], guns, and numerous other things and would pack over to the mines. Any thing to get there.[81]

The boys at the station would get on a spree. [They would] cut up

---

[80.] Chief Winnemucca of the Paviotso or Northern Paiute was born about 1805, near Humboldt Lake. He was also known as Mubetawaka and Po-i-to. In 1858, he complained that since the pine nuts his people depended upon had been exhausted by the white man, his tribe was forced to steal or starve. He was involved in the ghost dance movement, which originated in Nevada in the late 1870s. He blamed his final illness on his young wife's witchcraft. She was stoned to death with her child following Winnemucca's demise on 21 October 1882, at Copperton Station, Nevada. Winnemucca, Nevada, is named for him.

[81.] The journal of Joseph Pike provided contemporary confirmation of Blackburn's observations: "[On 10 September we] commenced asending the mountain over cragy rocks and precipetous clifts that [men] on any other buiseness than getting to California would think it impossible but men are after gold, and there is no danger that can stop them or da[u]nt their courage."

harness[es], bend guns around trees, run a lot of waggons togeather [and] set them on fire and run amuck gener[al]ly. There was no law or gospel to hinder them.[82]

We put in the sum[m]er and fall to good advantage. Divided the proceedes of our venture and all were satisfied.

My brother crost over to California, the others in various directions. I started to Fort Hall to trade off my stock to the next emegration. I had twenty five good horses and six mules. There was a company of nine in all. The Indians began to be very bad on the road. Renegades from other tribes come in on the Humbolt to rob and murder. They were well armed and clothed with plunder. All [the emigrants] we met advised us to return with them. We did halt and councild what was best to do and a few that had families in Utah wanted to goe ahead. And [we] went on and rued it afterwards.

I was taken sick on the Carson Desert and had to stop. The company stayed with me a while and left one man with me. Thought I was coming apart, my back and loins ached so bad. We fixt a way to ride lying down on the horse. Went on several miles and could goe no further and lay down on the sand to die. And told the one that was with me to goe to watter, but he stayed a while longer and I felt better. Clome into the saddle and in about an hour [?]. The company had given me up for dead. One of our company here, he was ailing the same as I was.

Continued up the Humboldt River about one hundred miles when the red devils come in sight. They [were] well mounted and clothed and had fire armes. They were not the natives of this river. They spied arround for a day or so and followed up. Tried to stamped[e] our horses at night.

One morning after going a few miles we saw about two hundred [Indians] on a hill close to whear we had to cross the river. The willows were thick with Indians [on] each side of the ford. They all come down off the hill and stationed themselves [on] each side of the road in the thick brush.

[82.] On 7 August 1850, James Shields recorded trading practices and high times at Mormon Station: "We traded off an odd ox for 25 lbs. of flour (a very good trade, so we think). The proprietor was very bussily engaged playing a game of Eucre and did not take a look at old Buck or he would not have bought him. Ever since we started this morning we have been traveling in what is termed Carson's Valley. Our road winds around at the base of the Sierra Nevada & passes neath the shades of a groves of pine trees some of which are 3 feet in diameter and from 100 to 150 feet in height. They make a dense shade. There is a Mormon settlement in the midst of this grove composed of 5 log houses. This is their 1st year and they have not made much improvement but if they are anything to their brother Salt Lake Mormons, next year they will have things nicely arranged. There are 2 trading posts within their settlement. I remained a few moments & they were playing cards & drinking liquor in fine stile." See Shields, "Journal," Beinecke Library, quoted in Owens, "Archaeological and Historical Investigation of the Mormon-Carson Emigrant Trail," A:224–25.

We dare not cross and kept up the side we were on. The Indians followed up. We come into raveins and thick brush and they had us fast.

They surrounded our party and commenced fireing. We returned the fire and killed some of them. We had two men wounded. They would crawl up in the brush and shoot. They had the advantage and they knew it.

By and by we began to get dry for watter. We could not stay here and started on again. Come to a verry steep brushy hollow and in trying to cross we become sepperated. And the Indians made a dash and captured nearly all our horses and seven pack animals loaded with our outfitt.

We had left one horse a peice and three packs. As soon as the Indians took our horses and packs, they left with the spoil. We went to the river after watter and were verry thirsty. Traveld as fast as the wounded men could stand it. One was wounded in the shoulder, the other in the arm. We escaped more by good luck than good management. There were too manny men with wives they were a going to see to stand much fighting. The next spring I had a good company and got even on the red skins, but never recoverd all my stock.[83]

We kept going until the wounded men could goe no further and camped. More than half our provisions was lost. [We were] on half rations and badly scared. By traveling at night and dodging the Indians, we come through all right. I had traveld up and down the Humbolt several times, but never saw the Indians as bad as this time.

[83.] The 2 November 1850 *Deseret News* reported the arrival of Blackburn's company in Great Salt Lake City. "A party of fourteen arrived from California about a week since, and report that near the centre of the big meadows, some 250 miles from this [place], they were attacked by 70 or 80 Boonack Indians, who surrounded them, shot and drove off a great portion of their horses, and it was several hours before they could make their retreat without loss of life, under a running fire, with the loss of most of their pack and animals.—There is reason to believe that very great depredations have been committed by the Diggers (Indians) on this route." Neither Blackburn's nor the article's mileage estimates provide much help in locating the site of the skirmish, but Blackburn's description of the ford makes it possible that the fight occurred about fifteen miles east of present-day Battle Mountain, Nevada, where the California Trail forded the Humboldt River.

TEN

Indian Wars of which I Have Had a Sad Experience

T he 1850 census counted 11,380 residents in the Salt Lake Valley, and by 1851 the newly formed Utah Territory had a population of 15,000.[1] Although denied statehood for Deseret in 1850, Brigham Young was appointed governor of the territory and, financed by the windfall of the gold rush, the Mormons were well on their way to establishing an empire in their mountain fastness.

On his return to Utah in the fall of 1850, Blackburn encountered a prejudice against Mormon Battalion veterans that was prevalent in the territory during the early 1850s. John D. Lee quoted Brigham Young on 11 March 1848: "I know that the lowest scrapings of Hell were in that Bot [Battalion], notwithstanding there was some good men among them." On 18 February 1849, Lee complained that "since returning from the Army, the most of them have become Idle, Lazy & indolent, indulging in vice, corrupting the Morals of the young Females."[2] Many battalion veterans did well in Utah, but as a class the "Battalion boys" were not much appreciated until growing conflicts with federal territorial officers resulted in their rehabilitation in 1855.[3]

By his own account, Blackburn was at some point "cut off" from

---

[1] Allen, *The Story of the Latter-day Saints*, 247, 258.

[2] Cleland, *John D. Lee*, 1:6–7, 92–93.

[3] At the "first general festival" of the battalion held in February 1855, blunt-spoken Brigham Young atypically minced words: "Some have imagined, as I have been informed, that the Battalion was not looked upon with sufficient favor. . . . Perhaps, in a few instances, there may have been remarks made about some members of the Battalion, from which it may be inferred that there might be persons who rather lightly esteemed those who went into the service of the United States. . . . I will say to you, that, according to the best knowledge I have of you, the course and conduct of many were not justified before the Lord, and a knowledge of these facts caused me to weep." Taylor, *Mormon Battalion*, 351–52.

the Mormon church "when i left Utah." Precisely dating this event is impossible, but in February 1849 a half-dozen battalion veterans rode into the Old Fort at Great Salt Lake City with their sweethearts before them on their saddles. This seemingly harmless prank outraged Mormon officials and caused five or six veterans to be "cut off" from the church. Blackburn commented on the practice, a custom called the "Spanish Rusty," referring to events in the spring of 1851. "When we went to a dance, the girl rode in the saddle and her pardner rode behind on the same horse. The boys did not care and the girls did not mind it. The authorities gave [us] a severe lecture. They said such indecent procedings must stop."

John D. Lee described what may have been the same events on 24 February 1849:

> 6 of the souldier Boys cut a Spanish Rusty by Riding into the fort with a young Lady sitting in the sadle before, & the man behind with his arms around the woman. One of the men was sawing on the violin. This they called Spanish manners or Politeness. Voted by the council that they all be cut off from the church & fined 25 dollars each & that the marshall collect their fine fourth with."[4]

Hosea Stout reported that the legislative council inflicted

> a fine of 25 dollars each on five young men named, Elias Pearsons, B Brackenbery, John F. Murdoc Jesse Earl & Frazier for unbecoming and demoralizing conduct.[5]
>
> They got up a party on the Cottonwood at Fraziers Mothers & they each selected their lady and marched their Spanish fashion with the Lady on before & they behind Staid all night & came home the same way. This and some more calculations of a worse nature still was the cause of their being fined. The subject was spoken of by A. Lyman & E. Snow, who also spoke at some length against all such proceedings & the introduction of other savage Spanish customs also against going to the gold minds, after which W. W. Phelps spoke & moved that those be

---

[4] Cleland, *John D. Lee*, 1:96.

[5] These men were Ephraim John Pearson, Benjamin Blanchard Brackenbury, John Riggs Murdock, Jesse Earl, and Thomas Leonard Frazier. All were battalion veterans, and despite being "cut off," Murdock, Earl, and Frazier returned to the Mormon fold.

cut off from the church who were fined as above, which was
carried unanimously.[6]

Although Blackburn places his "Spanish Rusty" escapade in 1851, it
seems possible, if not probable, that Blackburn was "cut off" in 1849
with the five men mentioned by Stout.[7]

As the narrative drew to a close, Blackburn made his most pointed
criticisms of the Mormon church, noting that at services "they would
talk business more than religion." He made a veiled reference to the
heavy-handed methods used by Young to rule the colony, commenting
that dissenters were threatened with being cut off from the church
"below the ears." The reformation observed by Blackburn in the spring
of 1851 grew in intensity until it nearly exploded into war in 1857. The
fanaticism generated by the revival did flame into horrendous violence
at a resting place on the Spanish Trail called Mountain Meadows.

In the spring of 1851 Abner Blackburn departed Zion for his seventh, last, and most violent trip down the Humboldt Trail. After two
boom years in 1849 and 1850, the California Trail went bust in 1851.
In one of the strangest statistical gyrations in history, the river of emigrants dropped from forty-four thousand in 1850 to a thin trickle of an
estimated eleven hundred souls in 1851, and then reached flood stage
again in 1852 with fifty thousand travelers.[8] Blackburn worked as a
teamster for Utah merchant John Reese, who sent a dozen wagons to
the Carson Valley in hopes of reaping profits from thousands of emigrants who never showed up. The Bannocks and other Shoshone tribes
had also moved in to take advantage of the same opportunities. Traveling with a party more amenable to fighting Indians than the family men
who had endured the Indian raids of the previous fall, Blackburn exacted revenge and actually recovered some of his lost stock. His account of the running battle with the Indians is among the most vivid
and detailed in the annals of the overland emigration.

After arriving at Mormon Station, Blackburn decided against
spending another season at the trading post and went into the winter

---

[6.] Brooks, *Hosea Stout*, 2:343.

[7.] No records have been located placing such an event in 1851. Given Blackburn's general accuracy, however, it is possible the practice was revived to "pester"
the Mormon authorities. Blackburn's 1894 statement that "when i left Utah they cut
us all off from the church i suppose they dropt me too," fits no other set of events
described in the narrative. Juanita Brooks wrote that this custom, which was "offen-
sive to orthodox Mormons who believed that the girl should always ride behind the
man, was a common practice among the Californians." See Cleland, *John D. Lee*, 1:96,
128.

[8.] Unruh, *The Plains Across*, 120.

mountains on a vain gold hunt. Following his return to Carson Valley, he crossed the Sierra to California.

By 1851 the Blackburn family was scattered across California. Anthony, Hester, and Matilda were counted on the 1850 census in San Diego County, which at that time included San Bernardino. Anthony had left his prosperous innkeeping enterprise in the gold fields to answer Amasa Lyman's call to find a gathering place for the Mormons in southern California. John and Eliza Bainbridge were possibly living with other members of the Bainbridge family in El Dorado County. In mid-October, Thomas and Emily Blackburn were living near Placerville, running a hotel.[9] In the winter or spring of 1851, they followed the Gold Bluff excitement to northern California.

On 23 July 1850, Apostles Amasa Lyman and Charles C. Rich wrote to Brigham Young:

> We come to the conclusion that the interest of the church require a resting place in this region for the saints and the portion of California described by Mr. Rich in his letter to you, is the only place that is now open for settlement with all its advantages . . .
>
> Acting upon the conclusion to which we have arrived at we have sent Bro. J. C. Hunter (who has been confirmed in his former appointment as Indian Agent) to settle in the re[g]ion, together with Bros. Crisman & Blackburn to secure by settling on the same and looking out for the best points and direct and influence others who may settle their to do the same until Bro. Rich shall be there to direct in person the settlement of those who may chose to make that country their home.[10]

Lyman had left San Francisco with Jesse D. Hunter, a former battalion captain, and Charles Crisman on 8 February. The party reached San Pedro on the twentieth, and at least part of the company proceeded to San Bernardino, where they discussed the purchase of Rancho del Chino with Isaac Williams. Lyman departed San Pedro for San Francisco on 2 March.

Tracking Anthony Blackburn's travels depends on a close analysis of a few journal entries and a reliance on the 24 July 1850 census, which placed him in San Diego County. Amasa Lyman's journal stated

---

[9.] The 1850 census for San Diego County, taken 24 July 1850, listed Blackburn, Anthony, 48, Laborer, PA.; Hester, 48, PA.; Matilda, 24, PA. The census for El Dorado County, taken 14 October 1850, listed Blackburn, Thomas, 26, Ohio, Hotel, and Emily, 18, N.Y, as living at the "new town" of Mud Springs, now El Dorado.

[10.] Lyman and Rich to Young and Councell, 23 July 1850, LDS Archives.

that he "went to br. L, meet with br Blackburn"[11] on 19 May. Ten days later, C. C. Rich noted that "to Day visited Br. Blackburn staid ovr night traveled 9 miles."[12] On 16 July, Rich met "Br. [Jesse D.] Hunter and Blackburn," and Lyman wrote: "traviled slowly up the river to Sacramento where we met brs. Hunter & Blackburn who were ready to go below."[13] This single entry pinpointed Anthony Blackburn's departure to immediately after 16 July, leaving only eight days for him to reach San Diego and to be counted by the census. This was a quick trip, probably by steamer down the Sacramento and thence by ship to San Diego. Anthony Blackburn may have purchased land or made some financial commitment to southern California during his stay in 1850, since most of the family would settle in San Bernardino in 1851.

Early in 1851, Anthony Blackburn, perhaps determined to gather the family together again, returned to San Francisco to discover that Thomas had been swept up in the "vapid Gold Bluff excitement."[14] Sparked by tales of beaches littered with gold dust, thousands of miners flocked to the mouth of the Klamath River late in 1850 and into the spring of 1851. There actually were fine particles of gold scattered in the sands of Gold Bluff, but there was no practical way to separate the two and the rush dissipated into the backcountry of Trinity County.[15]

Thomas and Emily Blackburn followed the miners into the hills and, in typical Blackburn fashion, went into business:

> In the spring of 1851, to accompany the travel between Trinidad and the Salmon river mines, a ferry across the Klamath some five miles below the mouth of the Trinity was established on the regular road to Bestville. The proprietors were Gwin R. Tompkins and Charles McDermit.[16] This ferry was placed in the charge of a man named Blackburn and was usually known as Blackburn's ferry.[17]

[11.] Lyman, Journal, LDS Archives.

[12.] C. C. Rich, Diary, LDS Archives.

[13.] Lyman, Journal, LDS Archives.

[14.] Rasmussen, *San Francisco Ship Passenger Lists*, 2:96, named A. Blackburn as a passenger on the steamer *Constitution* that arrived in San Francisco on 29 January 1851.

[15.] Bancroft noted, "The auriferous sand was estimated to yield from 10 cents to $10 per pound. . . . Over 2,000 miners were lured from El Dorado and Calaveras alone, it was said." See Bancroft, *History of California*, 6:364–65.

[16.] "Captains" Gwin and McDermott were described as founders of Happy Camp, "the first settlement made within the limits of Del Norte" county. See *History of Humboldt County*, 121.

[17.] *History of Siskiyou County*, 126.

Here, in late June, the family experienced the tragedy that precipitously ends Abner Blackburn's narrative.

THE NARRATIVE

We spent the winter with the Saints and they were real good while our money lasted, but they did not like the gay uniform of the Spanish Hidelgo whitch the California boys brought with them. The boys took delight in pestering the leaders with their California customs.

When we went to a dance, the girl rode in the saddle and her pardner rode behind on the same horse. The boys did not care and the girls did not mind it. The authorities gave [us] a severe lecture. They said such indecent procedings must stop. They cannot come in here to winter here and bring in their vulger customs from a half civilised country. It is a disgrace to the Saints to have their daughters chapperoned about in such fas[h]ion and is a bad example to the rising generation and must be stopt at once.

W. W. Phelps was the last to speak.[18] Sayes he, "The California boys puts me in mind of a young lady, a gentleman, and a dandy. They were conversing about what they would like to be in the future life. The lady said she would like to be a lilley of the valley for all to admire. The gentleman sayes he would like to be a far off twinkling star in the vast universe of worlds. The dandy sayes he would like to be the left horn of a womans saddle."

Now, I would like to know which was the worst, the Callifornia boys or brother Phelps. This conversation took place before thousands of people.

The Saints were haveing a great revival and tried to live perfect before the Lord. Meet togeather, pray, and exort the breathern to works of righ[t]eousness and [they] would talk in unknown tounges. Anny one in the meeting that they understood it would interpit what was said by the power of the spirit.

At another meeting for exortation [and] prayer there was an Englishman right raw from England. He would say anny thing that come on his toung. He would blirt it right out. "My brothers and sisters may

---

[18.] William Wines Phelps was born 17 February 1792 in New Jersey and joined the Mormon church in 1831. He came to Utah in 1848, where he was a legislator, journalist, university regent, and composer of still-popular hymns. According to the Journal History, Phelps preached on 16 March 1851 to a congregation in the Bowery, which may have included an offended Abner Blackburn. Phelps died in Salt Lake in March 1872.

the Lord bless you all. I am glad to be with you tonight to talk over our troubles and trials through life. We cannot be perfect, but we can try. And this puts me in mind of a jaunt I took up the canion the other day. I went to seek some house logs and they looked strait and sound. Come close up [and saw] some were crooked, others forked or snarled and twisted. Saw one higher up, a nice strait tree without limbs, and com[m]enced to cut it down and low, it was hollow at the butt. My beloved brethren, I am affraid that is the case with manny of you. A great manny appear to have no blemish, but are like the tree—they appear well, but will not bear inspection."

The Saints meet togeather every Sabbath to hear the word of the Lord from Brigham or some of his apostles and they would talk business more than religion, for their belief was an ac[k]nolliged success, as they thought. If there was any member that did not [do] his duty, he was roasted with the most severe language. If anny one comited anny crime, they [were] threatend to be cut off [from] the Church, below the ears.

The most bigoted in the cause of the Church were apointed Bishop. They would call on their members for tithing and tenth besides their regular taxes.[19] They have some verry good business regulations. The whole business centerd in Brigham and anny one outside of the Church is ostracised or b[o]ycotted. This was no place for them.

In the spring I joined a company under Jef Edmons and started west to California and left our relation[s] to come on with their slow cattle at their leisure.[20] I thought if I could pass through once more, I

---

[19] This statement may be a backhanded reference to Blackburn's uncle, Elias Blackburn, the first bishop of Provo. Between 20 March 1851 and 1 January 1856, Elias "Received and Dispursed according to the orders from G[eneral] T[ithing] Offices $56,150.34. I taken it in Person to Prst Young. he Seemed Satisfied with my Report of the Tithing." See Elias Hicks Blackburn, Journal, 9 March 1856. However, what appears to be a copy of the report is inserted in the journal and indicates that the sum only included $108.20 in cash, most of the balance being paid in "Produce & Labor Tithing."

[20] John Reese's company consisted of a herd of livestock and "10 or 12 wagons" loaded with seed stock and trading goods. Jefferson Edmonds was an associate of Orrin Porter Rockwell. The two men ran the Deer Creek House in the California gold fields. See Davies, *Mormon Gold*, 370. Edmonds was in John D. Lee's company in the "war of extermination against all the ravens, hawks, owls, wolves, foxes, etc. now alive in the valley of the Great Salt Lake." See the Journal History, 24 December 1848. C. C. Rich camped on 25 August in Carson Valley at "Edmonds Station," a name often ascribed to Mormon Station but probably a separate enterprise located ten miles away. See Charles C. Rich, Journal, LDS Archives. The *Deseret News*, 31 October 1855, 50, reported Edmonds as the leader of a group of Mormons returning from Carson Valley. The relations mentioned by Blackburn were probably John and Eliza Bainbridge.

would quit the plains for ever.[21] Started the 10th of April 1851 and nothing happend until we pas[s]ed the City of Rocks.[22] One of our company was out hunting. We heard a shot and then a bellow. Went out to whear he was. He set his gun down in a bush and when he drew it out the gun went off and shot him through the bowels. We took him to camp and in the night he died.[23]

We heard of trouble ahead of us. The first companys had skirmished with the Indians. They lost some stock and three men wounded. They sent back for help. We come up in a few days with the advance company and they wanted us to goe ahead. We took the lead willingly, for we had an old grudge against those red skins.

Come to the Pallaccades. Campt [and] put the animals on good feed. Put four men on guard with the animals. In the morning, about daylight, heard yelling and hooping and there in plain sight was forty warriors mounted and charging on our herd of horses. The snow was coming down thick, mixt with rain. The[y] had chosen the best time to make an attack on us.

Our guard fired on them and ran for camp. We had two horses staked, is all we had left, and before we could get ready to persue, the Indians had left with our horses. They left the cattle. We persued [t]hem, some [of] us barefooted, and [it was] snowing, mixt with rain. Our amunition got wet. Our feet [were] bleeding. The guns would not goe off [because] the powder was damp.

The Indians ran into a canion. Clome up on the rocks and told us to come on. Under the circumstances we were compeled to retreat. It [s]nowed all day.

We concluded to fit out ten men, well armed [and] with provisions and persue them on foot and spi out their camp and surpris[e] them in the latter part of the night. We did not care how many there was of them. We felt desperate.

[21.] In later life, Blackburn said he had made seven trips across the plains; this statement reveals that he meant crossings of the Great Basin. Blackburn left Great Salt Lake City and returned from California in 1847, 1849, and 1850, and left in the spring of 1851, for a total of seven trips.

[22.] The Journal History, quoting Thomas Bullock's journal for 10 April 1851, noted, "Col. Reese started out 10 or 12 wagon loads of flour to Carson Valley to feed the gold diggers." The *Deseret News* of 3 May 1851 recorded that "the last of the spring emigration from this place (among whom was Col. Reese,) bound for Carson valley, with bread, flour, and merchandize, passed the ferry on Bear river on the 22d inst. Many of these emigrants have informed us they design trading with travellers at Carson valley, and returning to our city to winter."

[23.] This is the third gun accident described in the narrative. The estimated four hundred emigrants Indians killed during the antebellum era were certainly a mere fraction of those killed in gun accidents. See Unruh, *The Plains Across*, 345–49.

We followed several miles to wheare they had killed a mule of mine and eat it. Went on about ten miles further, wheare they camped and eat a horse of Edmonds, our captain. We seen by sighns they kept a lookout to know wheather they were followed. Found a sly place and spent the night and fixt for the morrow.

In the morning [we] followed the trail. We looked ahead from the top of the hill and saw their lookout. We left the trail and made a circle around them and come in [on] the trail behind them. Slipped up on them, captured them, and made them goe along with us. Here we waited a while in the thick brush. After [a] while, [we] seen two more coming. Dare not shoot them. We spring on them, tied and gaged them. We took a detour and spied their camp. Sneaked arround and come in behind them, clos[e] to their horses. Slip[p]ed around their animals. When they saw us, the whole camp was in motion in a minute. We fired on them. Sent four men to round up the horses and six to hold the Indians in check. They were badly frightened and could do nothing, while we pourd in a deadly fire on them.

[We] started the horses [and] all mounted and struck out for our camp. The Indians were completely demoralized. A few Indians followed, but our long ranged rifels sent them back. We los[t] twenty seven and recoverd seventeen [horses]. We put the horses through to camp with out stopping. They did not ceath [catch] us napping anny more. We knew they would follow us up and try to ceath us off our guard. We swore by the holy hide of Apis that we would get even on them and we did and by all the gods at once.[24] That they should [remember us], we smote them hip and thigh from here on. [We] did not miss taking a shot at them.[25]

We made an other start. The company behind said we could have all the glory. Continued down the river nearly to the place I lost my horses the fall before in a fight with Indians. One morning we [were] strung out on the road, some a foot, others riding a mile ahead. Saw two Indians riding dow[n] off a hill whear they had been on the lookout for us. They rode down to the river and verry soon seen eighteen of them all mounted on good horses comeing towards us. The men in advance dropped back until there was nine of us a mile ahead of the wagons. The Indians rode close up to our line and had their guns cocked and we did the same. The Indians began to jabber and one would not

---

[24.] Apis was the divine bull worshiped by the Egyptians.

[25.] This encounter took place in the vicinity of Gravelly Ford, about five miles east of present-day Beowawe, Nevada, a site notorious for fights between emigrants and Indians.

trust the other. I seen some of my horses. I lost one verry fine horse of mine [and] an Indian was sitting on [it]. I took the horse by the bridle and both partyes commenced shooting. It was too close quarters for the Indians and they ran, but left four of their number on the ground. We had one killed and three wounded. I recoverd two of my horses.

We persued them and em[p]tied our revolvers in their backs. They would stop and take their wounded on behind them. We followed them to the willow brush and had another bout with them and drove them from the river. They were armed and clothed with murderd eme-grants propperty. They did not like to be hunted. We searched them out and drove them off the river.

From here to the sink, [we] made good progress and cleard the road of all danger. Crost over the desert to Carson. Continued on to Genoa, our old trading post. The snow was so deep [we] could not cross the mountain with wagons for some time. Some of my ac[q]uaintence come over the mountain with an old Indian who said he could lead them to a place whear they could find all the gold they wanted in a day or two. We asked them about the Indian, for we did not goe much on them. They said he was a good fellow and [they] were willing to trust him. They wanted two of our company to goe along to make the party stronger.

We started with seven men and one Indian made the number. Crost Washo[e] Valley, past Steamboat Hot Springs, onto Trucky River and [went] away to the north into an unexplored region and wild Indi-ans.[26] The old Indian began to be affraid. The wild ones would kill him and [he] would say, "Sia sia." That means bad. He would stop and point to a high peak away off in the distance. He marked out a canion head-ing in the mountain. We wanted him to goe on. He shook his head and all we could get out of him was, "Sia sia." The boys said they could find it and let the old sia stay back. I suspected the old sinner and wanted to take him along. The others said he was most frightend to death and let him goe. The boys had paid him well and he knew if there was no gold found he would suffer and he would crawfish out in time. He had a coyote grin on him that gave him away.

Come to the foot of the mountain and campt. Next morning started out to explore the place. Went up the canion the old devil pointed out to us and prospected several places and looked in several creeks, but the collor of gold we did not find. The boys were furious, as the old devil had lied and we were sold. If he had been here, the boys would have strung his hide on a bush.

[26.] Located ten miles south of modern Reno, Steamboat Springs became a bathing resort in the 1860s and "a favorite place of Comstockers to cure hangovers."

We returned to Carson Valley and made preparation[s] to cross over the mountain. Went up to the snow, [but] could not follow the road. The snow was verry deep in places and the stock broke threw the crust. Turned to the right and crost that awful gorge at Tradg[e]dy Springs and come into the road and made a cuttoff and soon come to the end of our trip.[27]

I went to San Francisco to see my parents. While there I heard of my father being murderd on the Klamath River by the Indians. I went on the nex[t] steamer, going up the coast and landed at Trinidad. My brothers wife was here. She was brought here for saf[e]ty. My brother was on the Klamath River guarding his propperty with some others. I went out with a pack train to assist him to move away from there.

T[homas] R[ose] Blackburn went up the coast at the Gold Bluff stampede not far from the mouth of the Klamath in the spring of 1851. The Bluff did not turn out as well as expected and most of them scatterd out, some to Rouge River, Trinity River, and the Klamath bars.

My brother and his pardner started a ferry on the Klamath to ferry miners and their pack trains across.[28] The Indians objected to the rope that was strec[t]hed across the river to ferry with. They said it kept the fish back from comeing up the river, but that was only an excuse. They began to be ugly and rob, steal, and murder the miners.

My father come from San Francisco to see his son on the Klamath River. He come out from Trinidad on a pack train. The train stopt at Elk Grove for the night. Father continued on alone and arrived close [to] the ferry about dark, not over one hundred and fifty yards from the ferry. The Indians attackted and murdered him in a horrible manner, those at the ferry knowing nothing about it at the time.[29]

At the ferry was a large canvas house for a store and five men sleeping in it. Brothers house was allmost joining. It was made out of redwood boards split out of logs. He and [his] wife lived in it. About ten oclock at night, the Indians cut through the canvas house and murderd

---

[27.] Tragedy Spring was the site of the murder of Salt Lake-bound Mormon Battalion veterans Ezra Allen, Daniel Browett, and Henderson Cox on 27 June 1848. The epitaph carved in a fir tree above their grave made the springs a well-known landmark on the Carson Pass road. Blackburn left the only extant account (albeit a very short one) of an 1851 crossing of Carson Pass. According to Owens, "Archaeological and Historical Investigation of the Mormon-Carson Emigrant Trail," 112, "not a single diary, trail journal, or later reminiscence documents the [1851] trip across the Mormon-Carson Emigrant Trail."

[28.] The ferry was five miles west of modern Weitschpec, California, at a site identified as "Marten's Ferry" on the map in *History of Humboldt County* and as "Martin's Ferry" in the text.

[29.] Family tradition tells that the Indians skinned Anthony Blackburn.

the inmates in their beds. Their cryes was dreadful. Two of them ran to the river and were killed on the bank.

The noise and the screams awakend my brother and his wife. They fastend the door and barricaded it, none too soon. The savages were trying to enter, but met a warm reception. He had several fire arms in the house and his wife loaded the guns while he fired them. Some were hurt and they drew back.

They next tried to burn the house. That made a plain mark to shoot at. [The Indians] had to quit. Next, [they] tried to [k]nock the house down with rocks and come verry near it. While they [were] at work, some got picked off.

The moon rose and enabled him to see better how to shoot. Next, [the Indians] rol[l]ed large boulders from the top of the bluff to mash the house down. Brother ran in the canvas house and picked up a six shooter. The Indians did not see and [he] increast his store of arms.

They rol[le]d logs of fire from the bluff. While at that work he shot their cheif. They went off to howl a while. The last ruse was for them to give themselves up and [they] sent a squaw that had been to work at the ferry. They knew if they give up, death was their portion. Daylight began to appear after the sun rose. The Indians went off.

A pack train come along but as soon as they saw what hap[p]end, they left. My brother next fixt up the ferry boat to goe down the river and was putting his things [in it] when a large train come in sight and stayed with him.

They said they found a man murderd on top of the bluff clos[e] by. [Thomas] went up and found his father murderd by the Indians. We made war on the savages. The miners had no mercy on them and cleand the bad ones all out. After we settled up our business, we returned to San Francisco and our family went to southern California.

To be continued.

So ends the narrative.

In addition to Abner Blackburn's tale, there are contemporary accounts of the events at Blackburn's Ferry in the *Alta California* and the journal of Joseph Banks. Three reminiscences also described the events. In one of them, a participant, A. E. Raynes, left an account based on his personal experiences and the memories of Emily Blackburn, Thomas's wife.

The *Daily Alta California* of San Francisco told the story of the fight on Sunday morning, 6 July 1851. It was taken from a letter dated 30 June 1851, which four men in an open boat had carried from Trinidad to Bodega. The letter reported that Indians had murdered five men and had "attacked many ranches on the road to the mines and killed quite a large number of persons. On the evening of the 26th two packers were attacked by the Indians and one killed." The survivor carried word to Young's Ranche and then the following took place:

> As there were but two guns at the ranche and expecting an attack every hour, a message was despatched [sic] to Tompkin's Ferry, two miles below for arms and men. Upon arriving at the Ferry he found four men murdered. The Indians had made an attack just at daybreak, cutting the canvas, entering the tents and cutting their throats while asleep. A short distance from this tent was a house occupied by Mr. and Mrs. Blackburn. The Indians after murdering those in the tent attacked the house. There were two rifles in the house: Mrs. B. loaded while her husband shot four of the Indians. They attempted to fire the house, but Mr. B. shot them down as fast as they advanced. The Indians finding they were losing many without a chance of entering the house soon retreated. Mr. Blackburn's father (who had just arrived from San Francisco) was found the next morning wounded within an hundred yards of the door. . . . These facts were obtained from Mr. Raynes, who was the messenger sent to the ferry. . . . Names of persons killed: J. Bender; Owens Scott of Mo.; Anthony Blackburn of San Diego; I. T. Jarnagin; John Dudley.

These events achieved some notoriety in the mines. By 5 September 1851, word of Anthony's death had reached the Blackburns' old residence at Auburn. John Banks noted in his diary the story he was told:

> Saw Mr. Veazey, one of [John S.] Giles' company on the trip to Klamath. . . . They left on account of Indians. There the natives are a fierce, manly, warlike set of fellows. Near Giles' camp a Mr. Blackburn kept a trading post. His house was built of clapboards. The Indians resolved to plunder and destroy this place. Five men encamped near there were murdered in their beds. Blackburn heard the noise and awakened his wife. He had two rifles in readiness. The Indians immediately made the attack. The night was dark, but Blackburn fired by the noise, his wife loading. Four Indians rushed towards the house with torches in hand to fire it, but each fellow carried death in his hand, the light making a sure aim. Day began to dawn, and

Blackburn singled out their chief. This ended the fight. The squaws were seated on the bluff above the scene of the carnage, baskets in hand to carry off the spoils. Fourteen Indians were killed. This was not the end of the tragedy for Blackburn. A packer told him a man was lying dead in the road a short distance back and ought to be buried. They went to perform this last, sad office for the stranger, as they supposed. But judge Blackburn's horror when he found his father covered with *gore*. The unfortunate old man had left one of the southern valleys to visit his son. This was surely a sad but true picture.[30]

Walter Van Dyke, a pioneer of Klamath County, wrote a reminiscent account of the massacre for the August 1891 *Overland Monthly*. A tattered copy of this article was photostated with the manuscript and influenced Blackburn's account of the fight at the ferry.

In the summer of 1851,—I am unable to give the exact time, as I have preserved no data of the event,—the little town of Trinidad was startled by a report that all the whites at Thompkins's Ferry had been murdered by Indians. The Ferry at the time was run by a Mr. Blackburn. He was a married man, and had his wife with him, a rare thing at that time and place. . . . There were half a dozen men or so besides Blackburn connected with the little camp at the Ferry. The buildings were merely posts, with canvas sides and top, except that Blackburn had erected a small house of logs and shakes, a little off from the others, for himself and his wife. The camp was located on a little plateau on the southerly side of the river.

Late in the day preceding the massacre quite a large party from the mines, going to Trinidad, were ferried across the river. Instead of stopping over night there they pushed on for Elk Camp. On the way up, they met an elderly man on foot,— who, it was afterwards learned, was the father of Blackburn of the Ferry. The people at Elk Camp tried to dissuade him leaving so late, but he was anxious to see his son that night.

His paternal desire was never gratified. The hostiles in the plot had no doubt watched every movement. They had seen the last party pass the Ferry without stopping, thereby leaving only the few men who were connected with the post. This was their opportunity, and they only had to wait the hour of night,

---

30. Scamehorn, *The Buckeye Rovers*, 168–69.

when their intended victims should be sound asleep. In the meantime they had intercepted and murdered the elder Blackburn on the trail not far from the Ferry.

As the white men retired to their bunks or beds in the canvas houses or tents they occupied, every movement could be seen by the outlying savages, and each one's position located. The Indians at that time used no firearms, but in addition to their bows and arrows had long, ugly knives, and some few had obtained hatchets. The evidences of their bloody work showed that they had cut through the canvas of the tent and cloth houses, and murdered the inmates while asleep, or before sufficiently awakened to defend themselves.

Some noise, however, happened to awaken Blackburn, and he looked out just as the Indians, who seemed to him to cover the whole plateau, were turning towards his little cabin. As if by inspiration, he took in the situation at a glance. Seizing a gun, of which he had several on hand ready for use, he fired at those in advance. They fell back a little, but more soon appeared, and they met a like reception. By this time Blackburn's wife was at his side loading the guns as he fired. The Indians, failing on this line, stole around and approached from other points. Small openings in the cabin, however, allowed the inmates to discover their movements, and the blazing rifles would salute them from whatever direction they came.

Towards daylight the Indians disappeared, going up the river. In the morning, seeing the coast clear, Blackburn ventured down to the river bank, found a canoe, and with his wife, escaped down the river, and subsequently reached Trinidad in safety. It was learned later that he had killed a number of the hostiles, including some of their leaders, and many more were wounded.

It was towards noon before anyone reached the Ferry, when a party from the mines arrived on the opposite bank of the river. Seeing no movement to bring the boat over for them, and receiving no answer to their calls, some of the party hunted up an old canoe and crossed over for the boat. The horrible sight presented at the little camp explained the situation of affairs. From the fact that Blackburn and his wife were missing, it was supposed they, too, had been murdered in trying to escape, and at first it was so reported. All the other whites there at the time, however, fell victims to this first Indian outbreak in that section. For reasons already stated, I cannot give the exact number killed.[31]

The tales passed down in the family grew more colorful and less accurate. In 1950, Blackburn's nephew Daniel Fabun stated: "Tom [Blackburn] and his wife held the Indians at bay three days, Tom doing the shooting, his wife moulding bullets and loading the guns. On the third night they escaped down the river on a raft. Later, Abner and Tom killed many of the Indians."[32] Herbert Hamlin, in a typically error-filled note, wrote, "When Klamath Indians later killed his father and brother [sic], Abner took a toll of Redskins equal to ten to one."[33] Abner Blackburn, typically, did not boast of his prowess as an Indian fighter. In his 1894 letter to Utah relatives, he said simply that his memoirs described "indian wars of which i have had a sad experience."

It is impossible to determine Abner Blackburn's role in the revenge exacted on the Indians: even he seems to have preferred to forget about it. In contrast to the several accounts of the Blackburn massacre, the indiscriminate massacre of Indians that followed was described in scant detail. Walter Van Dyke remembered: "Swift retribution followed upon this unprovoked massacre. From Humboldt Bay, Trinidad, and the mines men gathered. Most of them were schooled in frontier life, and all well armed. Not many days elapsed, therefore, before the rancherias, or Indian villages, from Thompkins's Ferry to the mouth of the Trinity, were pretty much all wiped out, and many Indians belonging to them killed."[34]

The *History of Humboldt County*, part of a series not noted for its sympathy towards Native Americans, commented:

> Indian difficulties will be treated of in the order of their occurrence, and facts and causes related with as close an adherence to truth as is possible when information is drawn solely from the testimony of the whites. It will be seen, however, that even then the record is by no means creditable to our boasted civilization. . . . The Indians were interrupted in their fisheries; lands were plowed up where they had obtained their grass,

---

[31.] Van Dyke, "Early Days in Klamath," 178–79. For a more accurate account Van Dyke wrote for H. H. Bancroft in 1878, see Appendix F.

[32.] Fabun, "Abner Blackburn, Pioneer, Scout, Indian Fighter."

[33.] *The Pony Express*, September 1944, 8. Hamlin, possibly repeating a family legend but with a typical disregard for accuracy, stated that in northern California Blackburn "killed 45 Indians in a single battle." Ibid., June 1942, 2.

[34.] Van Dyke, "Early Days in Klamath," 178–79.

seeds and roots; their game was killed; trees and shrubs were burned, which furnished nuts and berries, and last but not least, says the Times of that date [1854]: "They are ill-treated and abused, bad white men ravish squaws and whip and beat the men."[35]

The same history placed these people in the *To-lick Si-li-qua* language group and noted that "the Klamath River Indians were the finest specimens of physical manhood to be found among the natives of California, powerful and fierce, and gave the whites trouble from the time they first placed foot on their hunting grounds."[36] It described the fate of the Klamath River Indians:

> Three men volunteered to push through to Trinidad for assistance to administer to the Indians chastisement they would not soon forget, while Blackburn and his dauntless wife remained on guard at the cabin. They lost the trail in the darkness and lay all night in the redwood forest, until daylight enabled them to again find the trail and push on for help. Arriving at Trinidad the next day, they were joined by only ten men and the little party of thirteen started back to the ferry to attack at least three hundred savages.
>
> A number of miles above Trinidad lies a body of water on the low land between the mountains and the sea, known as the Big Lagoon. When the party arrived at this point they came upon a large number of Redwood Creek Indians in canoes, whom they decided to attack. They therefore fired upon the canoes, when the savages jumped into the water and swam ashore. A brisk battle was maintained for some time, the men using their animals for protection. The superiority of guns over bows and arrows was soon demonstrated, and the Indians withdrew with the loss of two or three braves.[37]

By another account, this party then went to Durkee's Ferry near the mouth of the Klamath and made an attack on a "large rancheria of the

---

[35.] *History of Humboldt County*, 152. Describing the founding of Happy Camp, this history made a possible reference to the Blackburn Massacre and its aftermath. "Notwithstanding all the precautions taken by the company, three young men of the party were killed by Indians. In return an attack was made on an Indian village, and it is believed all were murdered." Ibid., 121.

[36.] Ibid.

[37.] Ibid., 153.

Klamath River Indians, the same who had made the attack upon Blackburn's place." The attack only resulted in the killing of two or three Indians because Durkee, who was "living with a squaw from this rancheria," warned the Indians of the attack.

Two or three weeks after the Blackburn killings, a party including McDermot, Thompkins, Alisha Swain, and possibly Abner Blackburn launched a second assault on the Indians. This group killed two Indians at the Blackburn cabin, but found "the Indians had retreated to the recesses of the mountains, beyond the reach of the avenging arm."[38] On 4 August, the Blackburn brothers left Trinidad on the lumber schooner *Alexander*, arriving in San Francisco on the sixth.[39]

In 1897 Blackburn gave several relics, including a pistol, to the Pioneer Jubilee Committee. On 7 May, he wrote an alternate account of the massacre, in response to a letter "requesting me to give [a] sketch of their history":

> The pistol has been in manny an encounter with the savage tribes of the west. The most noted event of the trials was on the Klamath river in that remarkable scrimage with the indians. I loaned the pistol to my brother to goe to the gold bluff excitement at the mouth of the Klamath and while there they wear attacted by the indians about ten oclock at night. They cut through a cloth house [used] for a store and murdered five of the inmates. They then came to my brothers house a few feet away where him and his wife were living. They had heard the cries of the massacre and were prepared and well armed. They bolted the door. The whole plateau was black with indians. They tried to break the house down but met a warm reception. They then tried to set fire to the house and that made a fair mark to shoot at. The indians next rolled large boulders from the top of the bluff to knock the house down. His wife loaded the guns while he fired. The savages kept trying the whole night to get him out, and sent a squaw to have them surrender, but they knew death was their doom if they did.
>
> My father had come the evening of the fight from Sanfrancisco to see his son and was within sixty yards of the house of my brother when the indians murdered him. My brother and wife were all that was left alive in those parts. My pistol was used in this scrimage. Also in the Klamath war and in the car-

---

[38.] *History of Siskiyou County*, 127.

[39.] Rasmussen. *San Francisco Ship Passenger Lists*, 2:187.

son war and also the Provo war with old Elk the Chief besides several trips across the plains in an early day with manny encounters with wild tribes of the west.[40]

With this letter, Blackburn's voice fell silent. Though the final words of the narrative are "to be continued," no epilogue is known to exist.

[40.] Gibson, *Blackburn and Allied Descendents of John Blackburn, Sr.,* 404. Gibson noted that the letter was "contributed by Mrs. Ruth Towle Blackburn, Mayer, Arizona. Original on file in the Central Company DUP Office." The Abner Blackburn file has vanished from the Daughters of Utah Pioneers collection in Salt Lake City.

To Lay My Bones
to Rest

The abrupt ending of the narrative supplied no reason for the move to San Bernardino. Blackburn's motives are difficult to divine, but they were probably related to his father's journey to southern California in 1850. In his last annotation to the Blackburn narrative, Dale Morgan cited the LDS Journal History summary of Amasa Lyman's July 1850 letter to Brigham Young, stating that "the only place which appeared suitable for a location for the brethren was Southern California; whither Elder Rich and he had instructed Brother J[esse].D. Hunter,[1] Indian Agent, also Brothers Charles Crismon and Blackburn to locate; Brother Lyman added that to strike hands with a man in California having the spirit of God is a rare treat, and was like a fruitful shower in a parched land."[2]

Although Anthony Blackburn probably stayed with the Mormon faith until his death, his son was already disenchanted with Mormonism. In describing his departure from Great Salt Lake City in 1850, Abner Blackburn wrote, "We were ready to leave the Saints for good." Given the hostility and even disgust that Blackburn displayed toward the Mormon church at the end of the narrative, why did he choose to settle in the most thoroughly Mormon town in California? One answer may be that Hester Blackburn remained committed to the faith; she was

---

[1.] Hunter, born in Kentucky in 1804, was a veteran of the Missouri troubles and a captain in the Mormon Battalion. He had been army commandant at San Diego and Indian agent at the San Luis Rey Mission, but journeyed north to work in the mines. Shortly after arriving in southern California, Rich and Lyman reported that "we visited Bro. J. D. Hunter to solicit his aid in the buisness of procuring a location for the Saints but we obtained no help." By 1853, Hunter was living in Los Angeles, where he died on 27 August 1872.

[2.] Journal History, 23 July 1850. The San Bernardino *Weekly Times,* 30 September 1876, memorial to Hester Blackburn stated that she came to the valley in 1850.

referred to as "Sister Blackburn" in San Bernardino journals, indicating that she maintained her membership in the church at least through the early period of the settlement. Arrangements or obligations made by Anthony before his death may have influenced the decision. A more complex solution to the puzzle lies in the appeal that San Bernardino must have exercised as a community made up of old friends and familiar faces. The raw boomtowns of the gold rush were lawless, lonely places, and the attraction of a society made up of former neighbors from Missouri and Illinois and companions-in-arms from the Mormon Battalion may have been irresistible, even for a skeptic like Abner Blackburn.

In early San Bernardino, Mormon history repeated itself. The rise and fall of the Mormon colony is an intriguing story of utopian dreams, frontier conflict, and, finally, defeated idealism. As early as May 1847, Captain Jefferson Hunt of the Mormon Battalion wrote to Brigham Young from San Bernardino, "We have a very good offer to purchase a large valley sufficient to support 50,000 families."[3] Blackburn's own Company C had been stationed at Cajon Pass and battalion veterans carried tales of the rich land and mild climate to Utah in the fall of 1847. Apostles Amasa Lyman and Charles C. Rich lobbied Brigham Young to establish a California outpost. The Mormons sought a snow-free route to Zion for converts from Australia and the South Seas and even hoped that a direct trail to the Pacific would provide for English converts an alternative to the arduous trip across the Great Plains.

On 23 February 1851, Brigham Young authorized Rich and Lyman to establish a colony in lower California.[4] When Young went to Payson to bid farewell to the departing colonists, he was angered to find that instead of the anticipated twenty-five volunteers, almost five hundred people with one hundred fifty wagons had seized the opportunity to leave Utah for California. Young wrote, "I was sick at the sight of so many of the saints running to California, chiefly after the god of this world, and was unable to address them."[5] One colonist noted, "Heber [Kimball] Preached & Discouraged many from going."[6]

Blackburn's future father-in-law, John Harris, was part of the company and left a diary describing the 1851 trek from Salt Lake to San Bernardino. Harris was born in Pennsylvania on 2 December 1808 and married Lovina Eiler (born 17 December 1807 in Montgomery County,

    [3] Arrington, *Charles C. Rich*, 155.
    [4] Ibid., 157.
    [5] "Manuscript History of the Church, Brigham Young Period, 1844–1877," 20 March 1851, LDS Archives.
    [6] Kartchner, "Autobiography," 36.

Ohio) on 5 January 1831. Lucinda, their second child, was born 13 November 1832 in South Bend, Indiana. Harris's diary began on 20 February 1846 with the departure from South Bend, bound for Nauvoo. The family consisted of three sons and four daughters. The youngest child, Joseph, died during the journey in Warren County, Illinois. On 29 March, "John Harris and Lavina Harris was baptis into the church of latter day saince in the Mississippi River at Nauvoo." On 9 May, they crossed the river and began their journey west. A month later, the family "come to the grand river. stopt and our fore [oldest] children was baptised in gran river, Daniel, Jacob, Lucindy, Angeline."

The journal did not cover the Harris's 1848 plains crossing in company with the Blackburns. The family settled in Farmington, where Harris served in the bishopric.

On 11 March 1851, the Harrises "started on our journey from Salt Lake vally," bound for southern California. The route essentially followed the Old Spanish Trail, one of the most treacherous and waterless desert passages in all the dry Southwest. This journey has been justly called "one of the most arduous pioneer treks in American history."[7] After a month on the trail, Harris noted, on 13 April, "today we went to meeting and family scolds becaus so many wane going to Calafornia on there one buck." After recuperating at Mountain Meadows, the party descended to the Santa Clara River and began a backbreaking journey down the "rio virgin." The worst part of the journey began as the party prepared to cross to Las Vegas and the Mojave Desert. On 11 May, they "came to the Vegus and watter. come on 50 miles drive without watter or feed. carried som watter along to give the oxen and horses." Harris commented, with eloquent understatement, "this is hard."

It got harder. On the fourteenth they hit "the rufis road that I ever see. stony sharp flint stones." Indians began to harass the cattle, shooting arrows into the mules and oxen. On the

> 44 mile desert . . . we startet after breakfast and drove till noon when we stopt and watterd our cattel with what littel we had with us. we started and 3 miles and my ox gave out and I went 1 mile ahed left my waging and put boath teames on one waging and drove on till sunset. my oxen laid down and I staid with him a while. got up and started on and drove them a mile farther. they laid down and I could not git them up any more. I started for my wagions but lost them and got ahed of them 3 miles before I mad anything of them being most chkt for wat-

---

7. Lyman, "The Rise and Decline of Mormon San Bernardino," 46.

ter. I went on to 12 miles farther. lucinda and angeline had gon to watter by the aid of brother wood with the horses and I got there at daybrak to the bitter springs. the wagans came there at sun up. this was ouer seres time. watter watter [w]as the cry but we are at the spring.

The spring was "a miserable plase without feed anuf scarsely to ceap the cattel alive. the cattel so far axosted that we ware obleag to lay still and rest our team."

   The party pushed on to the Mojave, and by 31 May it had found good feed and water. On 11 June, "we came to the valley in open daylight of Callafornnia witch looks like living." On the twelfth, they "campt at the mouth of Calhoon pas under a butiful Sickamore grove" where Blackburn's son Levi would later be born.[8] The Mormons stayed at the grove while Lyman and Rich negotiated a land purchase. Harris used the interval to go back to the desert to retrieve tools he had left behind, only to find them "destroid."

   On 23 July the party "moved on." Three days later, "we came home."

> From the 24th of August till the present time thire was nothing acurd wourth notis but a hard living and several trips to the coast and other plases of camping out a liveing on bred & watter. Oct. 28—We moved into the ranch of St. Barnadeane and comments bilding a house and I was verry on well with piles for seven weeks. On the 13th of November Daniel Harris came home. on the 5 of December we got into a house without a flore, dors or windas. rumer of a indin ware was raist and we commenst to fortefy ourselves with a packit wall inclosing ten akers of ground with three mane gat[e]s. One on the southeast noth and northwest northeast. the fort lying [in] the shape of a tryangel. by this time the rains came and we commenst soing are grain. the grans commenst groing very fast.
>
> In January 1852 and february our time ocupide in soing our gran. March 1852 and April—bilding fens and publick works, making roads, scool houses and other thing.
>
> April 28, 1852, Lucinda Harris was married to Abaner Blackburn.[9]

---

8. "Abner Blackburn Made Seven Trips into the West," *San Bernardino Sun*, 4 December 1938, 11. This article stated that Lucinda Harris arrived in San Bernardino at "about the same time as Abner Blackburn did."

John Harris returned to Utah after 1857 and eventually settled in Arizona. He died 4 May 1899 in Tucson.

In 1847, trapper Isaac Williams offered to sell Jefferson Hunt the vast Rancho Santa Anna del Chino for 500 dollars down and payments that could be met by selling off the ranch's livestock. Williams thought it over, and on 19 December 1850 he raised the price to 150,000 dollars.[10] Upon the arrival of the Mormons, however, Williams withdrew the offer, leaving the colonists—who were broke and had relied upon selling Williams's cattle to finance the ranch purchase—to find another property. The apostles finally bought the Rancho San Bernardino from the Lugo family. The ranch supposedly consisted of 80,000 to 100,000 acres, and the Mormons paid 77,500 dollars for the land. This presented a serious problem, since the total cash assets of the entire pioneer company consisted of only 800 dollars.[11] Lyman and Rich borrowed the 7,000-dollar down payment from sympathizers in northern California at a gold rush interest rate of 3 percent per month. These complex financial transactions saddled the colony with an enormously troublesome mortgage.[12] Even worse, the boundaries of the rancho were only vaguely established, and the Lugos did not have clear title to the entire claim.

Lyman and Rich concluded negotiations for the ranch on 22 September 1851.[13] Blackburn's obituary stated that "when the Lugos went to Chino to receive the purchase price of the Rancho San Bernardino, Mr. Blackburn was a most interested witness of this momentous transaction which turned over to go ahead Americans this inestimable possession."[14] Assuming that the 22 September date matches the event to which the obituary refers, Blackburn had arrived at the colony by late summer.

Abner and Thomas Blackburn are listed as occupants of Fort San Bernardino in 1851. The fort, built in response to rumors of an impending Indian attack, was "the most elaborate fortification ever attempted in southern California."[15] A plat of the fort indicates that the Blackburn brothers shared a cabin on the southwest wall of the stock-

9. "A Copy of the Diary of John Harris," Feldheym Library, San Bernardino, California.

10. Rich, "Early Land Purchase and Settlement in San Bernardino," LDS Archives. This document quotes the Williams letter describing the size and stock of the ranch.

11. Arrington, *Charles C. Rich*, 163.

12. Lyman, "The Rise and Decline of Mormon San Bernardino," 46–47.

13. Beattie, *Heritage of the Valley*, 182.

14. *San Bernardino Sun*, 3 November 1904, 6.

15. Brown, *History of San Bernardino*, 1:40.

ade. The entire Blackburn clan was located in San Bernardino, except for Eliza Bainbridge, who possibly visited the colony with her husband John in 1852. Matilda Blackburn married schoolmaster, lawyer, and choir director William Stout on 7 October 1851.[16]

Abner Blackburn was elected constable for San Bernardino township on 20 November 1851, as noted in Mormon clerk Richard Hopkins's official journal:

> An order having been granted by the County Court that this Township should have Two Justice of the Peace and Two Constables. In compliance with which an Election was held to day which resulted in the choice for Justice of the Peace. Jesse D. Hunter of San Bernardino and Louis Robidoux of Europa [Yucaipa]. And for Constables Abner Blackburn of San Bernardino and Antonia Preeta [Donaciano Prieto] of Jurupa. Weather mild and pleasant and no indications of rain.[17]

No details of Blackburn's service as constable are available; given that upon entering the valley all of the Mormons had sworn not to appeal to civil authority to resolve disputes, the office should have been a sinecure.[18] San Bernardino separated from Los Angeles County in 1853, and the first county elections were held in June; Gilbert Hunt replaced Blackburn about the time this reorganization took place.

During his term as constable, Blackburn may have lived at the strategically important Sycamore Grove on Lytle Creek at the head of Cajon Pass. Levi Anthony Blackburn, his oldest son, was born at the Sycamore Grove on 15 May 1853.[19] Sarah Pratt Miner's diary entry for 6 November 1852 contained the following cryptic information:

[16.] Stout, a distant relative of Mormon lawman and diarist Hosea Stout, was the erratic *Brooklyn* pioneer whom Sam Brannan removed as head of the New Hope colony. Lyman and Rich used him to interpret the complicated Lugo deed, and they "had undoubtedly been negligent in not having the fine print of the documents examined by someone more competent in Spanish than William Stout." Lyman, "The Rise and Decline of Mormon San Bernardino," 47. Matilda and William Stout would divorce in the late 1850s, remarry, and later separate again. Stout, unfortunately, had never bothered to divorce his first wife, an omission that would surface during the probate of his will in 1886. See San Bernardino County Clerk's Office, Book B of Wills, 578.

[17.] Hopkins, "Journal of the San Bernardino Branch," LDS Archives.

[18.] At a two-day religious conference shortly after their arrival at Sycamore Grove, "all affirmed" Rich's proposal "that this people as a body covenant that they will not fellowship any that belong to the church who will go to law, brother with brother, seeking redress of the laws of the land." See Arrington, *Charles C. Rich*, 165.

[19.] *San Bernardino Sun*, 4 December 1938, 11.

> Start before day break & drive about 6 miles stop to feed
> & breakfast road good to the summit of Cahone pass then
> down a very bad hill sand rocks in the Kanyon—arrive at a
> place to camp 3 p.m. find Mr. [John] Brown [Sr.] there, meet
> Bainbridge & Blackburn—10 miles.

Miner's diary had an even more ambiguous entry for Sunday, 21 November: "lesson in the evening—call at Mrs Blackburns just before dark account of the death of Gen. Bean story of the woman who was shot in the road."[20]

Hopkins kept a tithing record, with facing pages marked DR (Donation Received?) and Contra. The Blackburns are not credited with paying any tithing, but Thomas R. Blackburn and Abner L. Blackburn each borrowed ten dollars in cash on 22 March 1852. On 13 April 1853, "Esther" Blackburn borrowed "By Cash" ten dollars.[21]

Amasa Lyman married Abner Blackburn and Lucinda Harris on 28 April 1852. Richard Hopkins's journal noted only that the "weather [was] cool and cloudy with slight Shower in fore noon."[22] Hiram Blackwell, writing to C. C. Rich on 17 May 1852, commented, "Abner Blackburn and Miss Harris have entered into the *all-glorious* state of matrimony."[23]

By all accounts, the first years of the colony were idyllic; but in one minor contrary incident, Blackburn, James Button, and George Swarthout were subpoenaed on 2 June 1854 to appear in the "grass burning case" of George Day. The complaint stated that Day "on or about the 28th day of October 1853, set on fire the grass, brush and timber" of one George Garner, burning his fence and peach trees. The trial was held 11 November 1854, with Jefferson Hunt acting as prosecutor. Blackburn, a witness for the prosecution, testified that he "saw the fire. Saw [George] Lord [illegible] a fire & supposed it was set on fire. Day told witness 2 weeks before the fire that the woods ought to be burnt & it would injure others worse than him." Under cross-examination, Blackburn admitted that he had not seen Day start the fire. The jury found Day guilty and fined him 280 dollars.[24]

The story of the disintegration of the Mormon colony at San

[20.] Sarah Pratt Miner, Diary, LDS Archives. Bainbridge is very likely John Bainbridge, husband of Blackburn's sister Eliza. "Gen. Bean" was J. H. Bean, who organized a company of volunteers to counter the Indian scare in 1851.

[21.] Tithing Office Account Bk, 1852–1853, 114, 117, 118, 138, LDS Archives.

[22.] Hopkins, "Journal of the San Bernardino Branch," LDS Archives, 87.

[23.] Charles C. Rich Papers, LDS Archives.

[24.] San Bernardino County Historical Archives, Case 8, Box 10.

Bernardino is a variation on the theme that led to the destruction of Mormon utopias in Ohio, Missouri, and Illinois, and repeated the common early Mormon experience (by some of the same participants) of settlement, prosperity, conflict, and flight. Until 1854 the colony was a model of cooperation and agrarian success. Spurred on by extraordinarily wet years and communal discipline, the Mormons were able to cultivate bumper wheat crops. The burden of the mortgage in the face of the depression that wracked California from 1854 to 1857 and the leadership's demands for political conformity and fiscal support eventually led to cracks in the colony's solidarity. One Mormon loyalist would later comment on "the History of Paying for San Bernardino. Please allow me to Omit as Reflection would be unprofitable."[25]

The colony's troubles were rooted in the vagueness of the Lugo deed. Within a year of the purchase, it became clear that the original land grant actually consisted of only thirty-five thousand acres, less than half of the amount that the apostles assumed they were purchasing. In 1853, they were given the right to select their acreage from the original eighty thousand acres, but the final boundaries were not determined until 1856, when the apostles abandoned ground they had worked out and laid claim to better-watered land. Assuming that they were on government land, settlers had already taken up holdings on these properties, and such moves resulted in bitter conflicts.

Shortly after the purchase, Lyman and Rich established a private corporation to manage the real-estate deal. They viewed the mortgage, however, as a community responsibility, and made heavy demands on the settlers to meet critical mortgage payments—including sending off heads of family to work in the gold fields. They traded stock to raise money until William Warren wrote that "some have turned out their last cow to the Ranch."[26] Resentment was inevitable.

By this time San Bernardino was a magnet for disillusioned Mormons from harsher settlements. The settlement provided an escape route for those who disliked polygamy and chaffed under the authoritarian rule of Brigham Young. C. C. Rich complained to Brigham Young that "men who will not be governed in one place will not be governed in another."[27]

Richard Hopkins described the defection of one dissenter early in 1856: "Ned became disgusted and followed of[f] the Pacific Circus which for a time astonished the natives in this region. The Circus I

---

[25] Kartchner, "Autobiography," 37.

[26] Arrington, *Charles C. Rich*, 202.

[27] Lyman, "The Rise and Decline of Mormon San Bernardino," 54, 60, 61.

mean not Ned."[28] William Warren, damning with faint praise, wrote Amasa Lyman in December 1855, "The only thing that would make our community better would be less drunkeness, gambling, Horse racing, swearing and their natural products."[29]

Serious conflict began when disenchanted Mormons ran a ticket in opposition to the official Mormon party. On 21 April 1855, colonist Henry G. Boyle noted in his diary:

> This day our election for supervisors comes off. . . . These men came out in opposition to Amasa's nomination, contrary to council and exhibited a regular mob spirit. This is the first opposition we have had in elections since we came into the country. I will here insert some of the names of those that vote the opposite tickets: B. F. Grouard . . . Ruben Heron . . . Wm. Stout, Thomas Blackburn.[30]

By 29 April, "Brothers Heron, Grouard, and Vanluven . . . were cut off from the Church," creating a core of opposition to church leadership.

"Brother Heron" was Rube Herring, Blackburn's old acquaintance from Fort Pueblo who was now known as Valentine Johnson Herring. As superintendent of schools, Herring oversaw 206 students in the settlement's two adobe schools, filing a report for November 1853 whose literary style was described as "quaint" and "pithy." He also served as county assessor, and although "generally considered a strictly honest man," his assessments did not sit well with the Mormon leadership, who refused to pay in full for his services. Outraged, Herring opposed the Mormon election ticket and was excommunicated. Like John Brown, Sr., he played a leading role in San Bernardino's spiritualist community.[31] Herring briefly served as sheriff after the Mormons abandoned San Bernardino. He died on 30 September 1869, "at his residence north of Roubidoux, between Agua Mansa and Jurupa," now West Riverside, California.[32]

Two other Pueblo mountain men, James W. Waters and John Brown, Sr., the "Medium of the Rockies," played critical roles in the disputes generated by the unsettled land question. James Waters would

---

28. Charles C. Rich Research Files, Leonard J. Arrington Papers, LDS Archives, Hopkins to Lyman, 30 January 1856, LDS Archives.

29. Arrington, *Charles C. Rich*, 203.

30. Boyle, Autobiography and Diary, LDS Archives. This is the only known document that directly links the Blackburns with the Mormon dissidents.

31. LeCompte, "Valentine Johnson ('Rube') Herring," *Mountain Men*, 9:208–9.

32. John Brown, Jr., Diary of 1869, Sherman Library, Corona del Mar, California, 9.

become one of San Bernardino's richest men and leading citizens, but his fortune was based on the ruthless trading practices of the frontier. On 26 April 1854, Mormon diarist Thomas Brown met

> a small train of goods and droves of horses owned by Mr. Watters—a mountain trader, who it appeared was on his way to Gt. Salt Lake City to sell them, having left his brother with a small portion of the goods at Parowan. . . . [Ute Chief] Walker was with Watters, one of his squaws and a son. Watters had received a present of a fine Indian boy, apparently about 8 years of age and had given Walker one of the best horses in his drove with goods amounting to about $200. Thus they evade the penalty imposed on those who trade Indians by the laws of the Territory of Utah."[33]

Porter Rockwell and several San Bernardino Mormons, including Charles Crisman, accompanied this trading party.[34]

Waters bought thirteen five-acre lots in San Bernardino from Lyman and Rich about 1853 and loaned them much-needed cash. In 1855, Richard Hopkins wrote that "Captain Watters moves to the upper country this week though his wife remains here it is a kind of mutual split"—indicating a final parting with Candelaria.[35] In February 1856, he married Luisa Margetson, an English Mormon convert with whom he had a large family. He continued to range up the coast and across the mountains, driving stock in 1853 and 1856 with John Brown from San Bernardino to Waters's ranch at Mariposa. Waters was not in San Bernardino during the most serious period of the Mor-

---

[33.] Brooks, *The Diary of Thomas D. Brown*, 11–12.

[34.] One of the men sent to southern California with Anthony Blackburn, Charles Crisman never earned the trust of Lyman or Rich, who wrote Brigham Young a dark letter warning the Prophet about Crisman: "Bro Charles Crisman leaves with [James Waters's trading] company. He is the man that built the first saw mill in City Creek. Should he pay liberal tithing, by his liberality he might live. As it is, it is doubtful. . . . P.S. Per aullusion to Bro. C was for yourself merely to let you know that what ever he may have done for himself he has been of no assistance to us." See Lyman and Rich to Young, Arrington Papers, 23 March 1854, LDS Archives.

[35.] Hopkins to Rich, 4 May 1855, Arrington Papers, LDS Archives. Augusta Joyce Crocheron remembered Waters ("an American stock drover") and "Condelario." Crocheron wrote: "The name Condelario well became [her] large proportions, benevolent heart and good natured face. . . . I loved to lean around and study the enormous filagree gold earrings, necklace and bracelets, compared with the satin like tresses, listening meanwhile to the stories she told of saints, and flirts, and duels." Crocheron wrote that Waters abandoned his wife due to her extravagances. See Crocheron, "California Memories," 286–87.

mon conflict, but in 1858 he returned to the valley and purchased the Rancho del Yucaipa. Waters became a powerful landowner and cattleman, with herds in San Diego County, the Mojave, and Montana. He served as a county supervisor and built the city's opera house in 1881. He died in San Bernardino, on 20 September 1889, and is buried in the Pioneer Memorial Cemetery near his old friend, John Brown, Sr.

Of the three old trappers, John Brown, Sr., played the most significant role in the Mormon conflict. Brown joined the Mormon church in 1852, shortly after his arrival in San Bernardino.[36] He played a prominent role in the community, serving with Herring as an associate justice of the Court of Sessions.[37] His autobiography records his spiritual healing of one of Amasa Lyman's sons. Like James Waters, he lent money to the Mormons and took up residence in Yucaipa.[38] Brown's conflict with the church may have begun when he had the temerity to ask Lyman and Rich to pay back a thousand-dollar loan on 11 July 1853.[39] He assumed his Yucaipa homestead was outside the land claimed by Lyman and Rich, but in March 1856, the Lugos "offered the General [Rich] a large amount of Cattle, if he will rent them the [Yucaipa] valley, where Brown is, but they want him removed."[40] Rich ordered Brown to pay back rent and purchase the ranch or leave the property in ten days, and he "forwarded a Bill for over four years use of Yukypu and San Bernardino Ranche $1500.00 giving him Dr. [credit] for $30.00 paid in 1853 to help pay taxes." An enraged Brown came to talk to Rich about this demand

> and expressed a determination to remain without so much as paying taxes. Bro Rich talked to him and requested him to come to the office in the morning and would converse further on the subject. Brown thought the matter over during the night and the next morning proposed that if Bro Rich would sign an article releasing him from indebtiness and give him more time

---

36. Lyman, "The Rise and Decline of Mormon San Bernardino," 56. Amasa Lyman's journals refer to Brown as "Br.," an appellation used for fellow church members.

37. "Minutes of the Court of Sessions of San Bernardino California," LDS Archives. On 7 August 1855, the court tried and convicted "Ramon Gillardo for Assault and Battery upon the person of John Brown."

38. Beattie, *Heritage of the Valley*, 239.

39. Amasa Lyman, Journal, LDS Archives. Brown was dunning Lyman again in August 1854. On 16 November 1854, Lyman noted he had raised five hundred dollars for "Mr. Jas. Waters."

40. William Warren to Lyman, 3 April 1856, Arrington Papers, LDS Archives.

he would move his stock. . . . Brown started home in the eveng
and circulated the report that [in] the night he was attacked in
the Canyon and shot at three times. This he attributed to the
Mormons.[41]

Brown told his neighbors that "if they did not take a stand the Mormons would drive them from the country." Brown circulated a "remonstrance" aimed at Rich, which was signed by the leading Mormon dissidents. "Brown waited about a week and not hearing anything from the General concluded that he was laying a deep plot to swallow him Ranch cattle and all . . . and left with his stock for the Tularys."[42]

Into this tinderbox the Mormon leadership threw a lighted match. In May, Bishop Nathan C. Tenney was ordered on a mission to the Cahuilla Indians. Almost immediately, the dissident party, now known as the Independents (or, to Lyman, as the "factionalists"), reported "that they were informed that the Indians had lately been taught by the Mormons that the Mormons were the Indians' friends, and the Americans were their enemies; and that the Mormons were calling upon the Indians to be baptized by them, and assist them to conquer their common foe."[43] There could be no more inflammatory charge on the frontier. John Brown (returned from the "Tularys") got Juan Antonio, the Cahuilla chief, to swear an affidavit confirming this statement. A meeting of dissidents moved to "utterly condemn the course taken by an incendiary villain known as Bishop Nathan Tenney . . . in preaching treason and sedition." Tenney denied these charges in print, stating that Juan Antonio had publicly confirmed his denial. United States Army Captain H. S. Burton, however, reported to his superior on 15 June 1856 that Juan Antonio had told him "that the Mormons are our friends, and that the Americans are our enemies; they are fools, liars, bad people, and . . . that soon the Mormons will whip the Americans, and then they and the Indians will live happy."[44]

[41.] Arrington Papers, Hopkins to Lyman, 2 May 1856, LDS Archives. On 27 January 1878, John Brown, Jr., described a Sunday drive to Yucaipa in his diary. In what is now probably Reservoir Canyon, "we saw the place where the Mormons shot at Pa." John Brown, Jr., Diary of 1878, courtesy of Dean Painter and Arda Haenszel.

[42.] Arrington Papers, Hopkins to Lyman, 2 May 1856, LDS Archives.

[43.] Beattie, *Heritage of the Valley*, 248.

[44.] House Executive Document No. 76, Vol. 9, serial no. 906, quoted in Beattie, *Heritage of the Valley*, 250–51. The resemblance to Blackburn's summary of a similar Indian controversy during the Missouri Mormon troubles is not coincidental. Mormon historians avoid this issue, but the participants recognized it as a long-standing problem. On 30 December 1851, Rich reported "Marshalls Confession who was hung at San Diago. he implicates us [and] I shall reply to it. it is the same old story—the Mormons being friendly to the Indians." See Arrington Papers, LDS Archives. Periods added.

On 1 July 1856 Hopkins wrote to Amasa Lyman, telling the Mormon side of the story about Tenney's mission to the Indians.

> Rube [Herring] and others privitely swore that [Tenney] should not [preach to the Indians], that he would preach treason. Br. Tinney made the Indians one visit. Was by them kindly received and they were anxious to have them teach them. Amediately after this Homer Chapman D G Weaver and others went to work to tamper with the Indians and put lies in their mouths. After this they gave the Indians a feast of some 12 or 15 head of cattle. (stolen) and got the thing all right, Sparks Andrews and a few kindred spirits met long after at Chapmans house. held a secret meeting and expressed their fears that Tinney had been tampering with the Indians. And appointed a committee to visit the Indians [and] take their affidavits. (of course previously prepared) and forward them with such other *proof* as they could get to the Governor, and solicit his aid and protection.[45]

San Bernardino divided into two camps, Mormons and Independents, and each party held separate Fourth of July celebrations, complete with competing liberty poles. The conflict simmered through the summer. In the spring of 1857, apostate Jerome Benson fortified his ranch at Jūmumba to resist a court-ordered eviction from lands claimed by Lyman and Rich. Remarkably, beyond a drunken knife murder in 1857, the conflict never flamed into open violence. Ultimately, the situation was defused when the Mormons abandoned San Bernardino.

John Brown went on to organize the Union League during the Civil War, to develop a toll road through Cajon Pass, and to become the much-beloved first president of the San Bernardino Society of California Pioneers. In 1872, Blackburn's son Levi was the treasurer of the Association of Spiritualists, successor to the Brotherhood of Kindred Manifestation; Brown was the moving force behind these organizations. After his death on 20 April 1899, an honor guard of young women dressed in flowing white robes attended the huge white casket at his funeral.[46]

Blackburn's part in the fall of Mormon San Bernardino is obscure. He must have been a member of the Independents. The known facts

---

45. Arrington Papers, Hopkins to Lyman, 1 July 1856, LDS Archives.
46. Belden, "John Brown," *Mountain Men*, 7:53–56.

and several vague but persistent family legends link him with more than simple vocal opposition to the church. A key piece to the puzzle is a deed transferring all of Blackburn's San Bernardino property—a farm with three frame houses, fruit trees, and a pump house—to his mother for five hundred dollars. Richard Hopkins executed the deed on 28 February 1856, after Abner Blackburn personally appeared before him. William Warren recorded the deed on 14 December 1857, at the request of Hester Blackburn.[47]

In the summer of 1855, Blackburn's father-in-law, John Harris, was sent on a two-year gold-mining mission to raise money to pay off the Rich and Lyman mortgage. Leaving his family in San Bernardino, Harris lived at Coloma and worked for Mormon sympathizer Peter Wimmer, one of the men present at the discovery of gold in 1848. His stark and enigmatic journal painted a striking picture of a troubled Lucinda Blackburn:

> Friday 16 [May 1856]. I hode in his grape vine til towards night when I was cald to the house by ellen. she said a man had cam to see me [and] I must cam quick. when I cam to the house to my grate saprise I found Abaner Blackburn. he was hunting me.
>
> Sunday 18. I went with Blackburn my suninlaw to white rock Springs and found lucinda and the children w[e]ll. lucinda culd not speek to me for som time for crying. She held me by the hand and leand on me for more then ten minnets before she could speake. I never seen her in such a way before.
>
> munday 19. I left white rock and my children . . .
>
> Sunday 15 [June]. I went with Brother hardey to texix hill. he was going to the Citty of Sacramento for goods. I went to whiterock Springs to Blackburns. I found them all well.
>
> munday 16. I staid with Lucinda all day . . .
>
> firday 4 [July]. I felt verrey well and startid for white rock springs to see lucinda and Abaner Blackburn. I found them all well and he has Bou[gh]t a place for Fore hundred Dollers in cattel . . .
>
> wensday 10 [September]. I chored it round in the gardin till Brekfast when drecly after my Brother william harris and his wife come to visit me and lucinda misses Blackburn my Daughter was with them and hir two littel Boys. I was fild with Joy to see hir. after an interduction to mr and miss wimmer

---

[47] Deeds, Book A, 340, 341, San Bernardino Archives.

the[y] was kindly receaved with good treatment. the[y] spent the day with me and my frens till towards night wen the[y] left for there home.

Sunday 5 [October] I startid from Wimmers Before day and went 23 miles and Back the same day. when I got to Blackburns she had just got two letters from home stating that [my daughter] Susannah was married to Clarke Fabun.[48] I dont think that I ever was more supprised at any thing that ever transspired thrue all [my] wandering in life than did the noos of this marrig . . .

thursday 10 [December]. I startid with william harris teamster for fulsim. it was cold and chilley and he[a]vy fog till nearly night. I went to the forks of the road then left the team for whiterock Springs to my saninlaw and found them all well with a yo[u]ng son in the fameley. he was barn November 21 1856 and waid 7lb. I got verry wet Before I got there. it raind very hard this eaving.

friday 11 [December]. Stade with lucinda all day. we were left to ourselves the most of the day and we had sattisfaction to talk over the church matters consarning her coming away with him and I Blest hir as she requested of me.

Satterday 12 [December]. I tuck leaf of my childrin and my dautter with a Brokin hart to Part with and come to Coloma.[49]

This remarkable document offers the only insights into a crisis in the Blackburn family. It was a "grate saprise" for Harris to see Blackburn, whom he must have assumed would be in San Bernardino. Blackburn arrived in May 1856, shortly after the Brown–Rich land conflict. Lucinda, a few months pregnant, was upset enough about events to be unable to speak for ten minutes upon meeting her father.

The most likely interpretation of these events is that Blackburn was in trouble for siding with the Independents in their conflict with Rich and Lyman. After selling their property to Hester Blackburn and driving their stock to the northern gold fields, the family moved to a community of disillusioned Mormons who would be sympathetic to

---

48. Clark S. Fabun was a disenchanted Mormon who had lost two wives in childbirth.

49. John Harris, Gold Mission Journal. Mary L. Lewis transcribed part of a copy of the original in her possession and sent it to the editor. Additional quotations were taken from a typescript journal found by Amy Hoffman in the Ruth Towle Blackburn papers. As the typescript contains obvious typos, the two sources have been combined for readability, with periods added.

their plight. Harris's use of the phrase "church matters consarning her coming away with him" is a key to understanding Lucinda's situation: By following her apostate spouse to the god-forsaken North, she too had turned her back on the covenant and would be cut off from faith and salvation with her husband. Small wonder that her faithful father had "a Brokin hart."

The journal of Frederick William Hurst, a Mormon convert from New Zealand who was serving a mission to the California gold fields, painted a colorful description of White Rock Springs:

> On Monday, June 1st [1857], we went to White Rock Springs but owing to so few coming togeather at their request we postponed the meeting, etc. But such an evening I never wish to spend again as long as I live. [I] understand that these had not renewed their covenants, they talked about Brother Brigham, the twelve, etc., concerning the evil that existed there. One of them said if he met a certain Brother, calling him by name, that he would put his knife into him. To speak plain I never want to be in greater Hell than to be with such characters.[50]

Given Hurst's account, White Rock Springs was a hotbed of apostasy and a likely haven for an outcast like Blackburn. In 1857, Blackburn purchased the Halfway House, an inn about a half-mile west of White Rock Springs, one-quarter mile shy of the midway point on the Sacramento-Placerville Road. One of the oldest inns in the gold fields, it was originally named the Wellington House and was "a favorite stopping place for teamsters."[51] According to Sacramento County records, Blackburn was assessed taxes on a 160-acre ranch and an inn called the Half Way House on the Hangtown Road.[52]

A persistent legend that Blackburn crossed paths with the Danites, the secret police of early Mormonism, must be factored into this background. Daniel Fabun, Blackburn's nephew, told this story:

[50] Frederick William Hurst, Diary, LDS Archives. The editor is indebted to his aunt, Cleo Hurst Bailey, for permission to use the typescript copy of her great-grandfather's fascinating and detailed journals that her parents, Samuel H. and Ida Hurst, compiled in 1961.

[51] Cross, *The Early Inns of California*, 206.

[52] Assessment Roll, 1857, Sacramento County Records. The assessment was: "Possn of tract of Land on Hangtown road known as the 'half way house' and Ranch 25 miles from City," which was "occupied as tavern & Farm." The land and improvements were valued at 300 dollars, personal wealth at 590 dollars, for a tax liability of 25 dollars.

"Abner and seven other men did not belong to the Church. Brigham told them to join up or else. That night, the eight men left for California. Brigham sent his destroying angels to bring them back. The Angels did not return."[53] Herb Hamlin claimed to have heard a similar tale from Jess Blackburn, Abner's son, and dated it to the early 1850s: "Brigham sent three Danites from Salt Lake to bring back Abner Blackburn from San Bernardino dead or alive. The Danites never went back."[54]

Recounting a family legend, Cyril Grohs, widower of Blackburn's granddaughter Margaret Fredricka (Freddie), said that Brigham Young ordered Blackburn to take six mules to southern Utah. Blackburn never delivered the mules and claimed that renegade Indians stole them, though Grohs believed that Blackburn sold the mules and pocketed the cash. Jesse Blackburn told him that seven Danites "were sent out. And from what I gathered none of them ever showed back up. Two . . . were put away by the Indians up there, the Navajo. . . . No one ever knows what happened to the horses and mules. . . . They disappeared. Well, I think one of the horses showed up in San Bernardino because they were branded."[55]

None of these conflicting legends much resembles history, but they may preserve a kernel of truth. Perhaps Blackburn's conflict with the church was rooted in a livestock deal gone bad; maybe he was responsible for the failure of three Danites to return to Utah. The Danite story may even have some connection to the most difficult problem in his biography: When did Blackburn make his sea voyage?

Blackburn's 1894 letter to his Utah relatives is the only surviving reference to what must have been a remarkable nautical adventure. Blackburn wrote that he "travled the Pacific Ocean from [the] Bering Straits to Valporazo the South Sea islands and sowed my wild oats [and] have settled down in this semi tropic clime to lay my bones to rest." The itinerary suggests that Blackburn sailed on a whaling ship; his subsequent practice of the cooper's trade may have been learned at

---

[53.] Fabun, *Pioneer Cabin News*. Fabun's story seems to refer to Blackburn's departure in 1851 from Salt Lake City, but the narrative provides no indication that Blackburn had trouble with Danites on any of his departures from Utah.

[54.] *The Pony Express*, June 1946, 1. Hamlin, maintaining his standards of inaccuracy, wrote that in 1848, Blackburn "lured his folks away from the Mormon Church, which was one of the reasons why Brigham sent 3 Danites after him to bring him back dead or alive, but the Avenging Angels never returned to Zion." See *The Pony Express*, September 1944, 8.

[55.] Interview with editor, 6 October 1990. Grohs reported that he had heard the story "about 15 times" from two sources: Jesse Blackburn and Mary Chapman Blackburn, the widow of Abner's son Fred.

sea.[56] The reference to "wild oats" indicates that he made the voyage in his youth, probably in the late 1850s.[57] Jess Blackburn may have told Cyril Grohs that Abner left from San Francisco on a whaling voyage.[58]

Meanwhile, the Mormon colony in San Bernardino collapsed. One element that has never been factored into the causes of its demise is the role played by spiritualism. The detailed diaries of Caroline Barnes Crosby, sister-in-law of missionary and diarist Addison Pratt, paint a graphic picture of day-to-day life in San Bernardino in the 1850s, describing its singing and writing schools, library association, earthquakes, and even visits by circuses. Crosby also told of a surprisingly widespread interest in spiritualism—she called the practitioners "Harmonialists"—including an intriguing reference to Blackburn's mother, Hester:

> Frid. 22nd [February 1856]. Just before 12 came sisters Pratt and Blackburn to spend the P.M. with me. We enjoyed it finely. Sis Blackburn read some in Nichols Journal concerning Spiritualism. I discovered that she and sister P[ratt] were inclined to believe considerably in the system, but I had very little to say on the subject.[59]

On 9 October 1856, Crosby noted, "Evening we were invited to Wm Mc'[Gary?]s to a little dance we went over, found bro. Blackburn and wife there," which was a reference to Thomas and Emily. Crosby's journal recorded an interest in doctrines other than spiritualism. On 21 March 1856, she wrote, "Br [Charles] Hill dined with us, and preached his doctrine of Spiritualism and Freelovism."

Although Brigham Young "spoke in tongues" during his first meeting with Joseph Smith, the practical prophet was no fan of the popular mystical practices such as seances and phenomena like "rappings" that swept the country in the early 1850s. In 1853, Lyman and Rich re-

---

[56.] The voyage described by Blackburn would have exceeded twenty thousand miles. In 1857, three ships are listed as hunting the "Coast California." The bark *Carib*, Captain Reynolds, hunted the Pacific Ocean after departing from San Francisco on 9 May 1857. The *Carib* sailed again on 17 May 1858, and "sailed 1859; Easton, captain, returned 1860 with 600 whales." See Starbuck, *History of the American Whale Fishery*, 558–59, 566–67.

[57.] Blackburn appeared on the "Delinquent Tax List of 1857" in Sacramento County records for failing to pay his twenty-five dollars tax assessment, perhaps because he was sailing the Pacific. The voyage fits into no other period of his life.

[58.] Interview with editor, 6 October 1990. A previous conversation with Russ and Amy Hoffman may have influenced Grohs's statement.

[59.] Caroline Barnes Crosby, Diaries, Utah State Historical Society.

ported to Young, "We have had some curious manifestations under the head of Spiritual communications by working table tip[p]ing and writing but the people are generally satisfied that God is not in the whirlwind nor the storm but in the spirit that whispers to the contrite heart."[60] Lyman was not being completely honest, since he was sympathetic with spiritualist beliefs and encouraged their practice. Along with many of the leading figures in the community, Lyman participated in weekly "prayer circles" that communicated with "spirits."[61] He was eventually excommunicated from the church for his liberal beliefs and participation in seances. Rich was less involved; he said he was not "led away by these rapping spirits," and according to Richard Hopkins, "he did not object to the exercising of spiritual gifts but urged the Saints to be shure that they were directed by the spirit of God."[62] Spiritualism may not have been a major source of conflict in the Mormon colony, given the participation of a large part of the Mormon leadership, but it is worth noting that most of the anti-Mormon party were associated with the Harmonialists.

In Utah, Brigham Young had his hands full during the fall of 1857 contending with the United States Army advancing across the plains under the command of Albert Sidney Johnston. Even before news of the army arrived, Young called on Rich and Lyman to serve European missions, thus removing the two main pillars of the California community. Young may have considered moving the entire church to San Bernardino when he was faced with famine in 1855—"Perhaps we may have to take our line of march to your point in order to save ourselves from starvation"—but he held a deep-seated distrust of the colony and his policies ensured its demise.[63] In Salt Lake, Young said, "If Bro. Lyman were to tell you the situation in that place he would tell you that Hell reigns there and it is as much as any Mormon can do to live there, and that it is about time for him and every true Saint to leave that land."[64] The Mormon leaders in San Bernardino received the message recalling them to Utah on 30 October and announced the news in church on 2 November. Approximately fourteen hundred of San Bernardino's three thousand inhabitants packed up, sold out, and moved to Utah.[65] One colonist complained in his autobiography that

60. Arrington, *Charles C. Rich*, 179.
61. Amasa Lyman, 1854 Journal, LDS Archives.
62. Arrington, *Charles C. Rich*, 189.
63. Ibid., 187.
64. *Deseret News*, 17 June 1857.
65. Lyman, "The Rise and Decline of Mormon San Bernardino," 60.

"we Received Little or Nothing for our Places & Many Could Not Endure the Sacrafice of Property & Remained Their & many died there &
all who Staied became Cool in the Gospel."[66] By 1859 it was "well
known that there are not twenty Mormons in this county."[67]

Once the church had abandoned San Bernardino, probably after
the conclusion of his sea voyage about 1859, Blackburn returned to
southern California. He was certainly living in San Bernardino again by
1860. His obituary in the *San Bernardino Sun* credited him with being
one of the men—including leaders of the 1857 anti-Mormon party—
who worked for Abraham Lincoln's election in 1860. Blackburn's son,
William Byron, was born 7 April 1860 in San Bernardino. In 1861,
Abner Blackburn and a Mrs. Blackburn were among the founding
members of the Union League, supporters of the federal cause during
the Civil War.

The 1860 and 1870 censuses listed the extended Blackburn family
in San Bernardino, including Thomas's family and (for 1860) his
mother Hester, and Blackburn's occupation is recorded as farmer. In
1860, Abner had no property except a cow.

Blackburn's brother, Thomas, died on 15 June 1863. Family tradition held that he went mad every year on the anniversary of his father's
death.[68] Emily Blackburn married Isaac Hawley, and with him ran
"Hawley's Station" on the San Bernardino and Death Valley road near
the Calico Mine.[69]

Late in life, Hester Rose Blackburn sat for a portrait, which is a
classic photograph of the heroic pioneer woman. Adorned with only a
silver belt buckle and spectacles, she seems almost frail, but a close
look at the work-worn, eloquent hands reveals enormous strength.
Here was a woman of immense experience and—from her portrait—
vast patience. A dual image of spiritualist/healer and survivalist frontier
businesswoman emerges from the scant records of old San Bernardino.
According to entries in Caroline Crosby's diaries, she worked as a nurse
or healer in the Mormon colony during the 1850s. John Brown remembered her and fellow spiritualists in his peculiar autobiography:

---

[66] Kartchner, Autobiography, 39.

[67] Beattie, *Heritage of the Valley*, 315.

[68] Blanche Blackburn Corby, Testimony, Robert A. Allen Papers, Nevada Historical Society. Conversation with Amy Hoffman, 3 June 1990. No cause of death for
Thomas is listed in any Blackburn material.

[69] John Daggett, "Mrs. Isaac Hawley," 4:12. Daggett was lieutenant governor of
California. For a description of Hawley's Station, "a popular and well-regulated station," see King, *Once upon a Desert*, 188.

As with magic power, my arm reached out, my hand took up the pen . . . and began writing things to me most wonderful. It wrote the names of [Henry D.] Sherwood, [Zina G.] Ayres, [Frederick] Van Leaven, [Valentine Johnson] Herring, Mrs. [Barbara Ward] Heaps and Mrs. Blackburn; those whose conditions have ripened and changed, like the egg which conditions have disrobed of its shell and sent forth like a beautiful, aerial songster.[70]

On a more practical side, on 30 January 1865 she was listed as "Wd. Blackburn" on the "Report of the East Upper Dam Ditch" water record, and she took part in a water suit against A. J. Cox in 1872, along with her old acquaintance Ellis Ames, who had dropped the "E" from his last name since he had warned the Blackburn family on Shoal Creek of the Haun's Mill Massacre.[71]

Anthony Blackburn may have come to California for gold, but his widow discovered real estate. The only sample of her handwriting is a letter to A. J. Chase from "San Barnadino June the 2 1868." It has distinct similarities to her son's writing, including the use of the small "i" for the personal pronoun when it occurs within a sentence, and a direct, no-nonsense style:

I set down to anser your letter as soon as con veiant. i do not want to make sale of my part of them lots un til the devide is made. i own 30 of them. when my part is set of[f] then i will sel as good ofers present. I hope Mr Chase wil soon push through. we are all bound up un til it is done. excuse my riting. i can hardly hold my pen for the cramp in my hand.

/s/Hester Blackburn[72]

In 1874, Mrs. Blackburn paid taxes on property worth three hundred dollars and had two hundred dollars "Raised on Notes—Personal property."[73]

---

[70] Brown, *The Mediumistic Experiences of John Brown, The Medium of the Rockies*, 61. Different printing houses published Brown's book four times. Its success may have encouraged Blackburn to write his narrative. Note that the men listed were all prominent Independents.

[71] San Bernardino County Historical Archives, Case No. 179, Box 40.

[72] Copy of original letter and typescript courtesy of Amy Hoffman. Original in Ephraim Morse Manuscript Collection, California State Library. Periods added.

[73] San Bernardino Tax Assessor Rolls, 1874, San Bernardino Historical and Pioneer Society.

After a long illness, Hester Blackburn died on 17 September 1876. She left one hundred dollars to her daughter Eliza, and in her will, wrote that "the balance of my estate I give to my daughter Mrs. Matilda Stout, my son Abner, and the four children of my son Thomas now dead." She had appointed George Lord and Ralph Shelton as executors of the estate and asked them to "settle up and distribute my estate without any procedings of or in the Probate Court or any other Court or tribunal."[74] Blackburn delivered his mother's will to Ralph Shelton. Ironically, the will went through probate, in part to approve the request to avoid probate, and Shelton distributed the $850 estate after being appointed executor on 31 May 1877. Perhaps significantly, battalion veteran Lucas Hoagland later wrote that her son's "chronic Deafness and general breaking down in health . . . was incurred on or about the year 1876 or 1877."[75]

The San Bernardino Grange No. 61 passed a resolution of respect on her death. "She was among the first settlers of this valley in 1850, beloved and respected by all, she was ever instructive, genial, and companionable, noted for her honesty and integrity, with a kind word for all."[76] Hester Blackburn was buried in the southwestern corner of the Pioneer Memorial Cemetery in San Bernardino.

In the 1860s San Bernardino was as fiery, colorful, and tough a town as existed on the western frontier, enlivened with gunfights, floods, Indian wars, and a local gold rush; but Blackburn's life in those years consisted mostly of hard work. Between 1860 and 1890, Blackburn worked as a farmer, millhand, miner, and cooper; but almost nothing is known about his life during these decades. During 1863 he worked at the James-Rowland sawmill located at the head of the Mormon Sawmill Road.[77] The 1874 San Bernardino tax rolls show that Blackburn owned real estate worth $200.00, one wagon and one carriage valued at $100.00 each, four Spanish horses, and two American cows with a total value of $575.00, on which he paid a tax of $5.17½ on 31 October. The rolls for 1877 listed a "Coopershop" worth $100.00, and tools and a sewing machine each worth $25.00.

In 1873, the last of ten children completed the Blackburn family. Twins Levi Anthony and John Franklin were born at the Sycamore

---

[74] San Bernardino County Clerk's Office, Book B of Wills, 46 *et seq.*

[75] Pension Files, National Archives, Mexican Department, Pension No. 9150.

[76] San Bernardino *Weekly Times*, 26 September 1876. See the 23 September issue for a death notice.

[77] La Fuze, *Saga of the San Bernardinos*, 1:75. La Fuze quoted from the James Mill Account Ledgers.

Grove, on 15 May 1853. One child died and John Franklin Blackburn, born 4 December 1854, was given the name. Siblings followed at irregular intervals: Charles, 21 November 1856; William Byron, 7 April 1860; Ella Lucinda, 13 April 1862; Arnetta Matilda, 6 March 1864; Mary Adelia, 17 May 1869; Jesse O., 21 October 1871; and Frederick Abner, 30 October 1873.

In May 1881, Blackburn and his son, Levi, developed elevated reservoirs for the Mojave Gravel Placers in Holcomb Valley to wash auriferous gravel. "Levi Blackburn informs us that he has completed arrangements in Holcomb Valley for hydraulic mining on a considerable scale. He says his men will average five to ten dollars per day."[78] At about the same time, "a number of men were assisting the Blackburn brothers clean out the old Green Lead in preparation for working its rich veins again."[79] In the 1880s, the Blackburns used Coxey and Luna Springs in the San Bernardino Mountains as summer pastures for their cattle.

Blackburn's nephew, Daniel Fabun, wrote that his uncle established a home (which Fabun later called a ranch) on east Mill Street. The ranch was located along the Santa Ana River, on land now covered by Norton Air Force Base. According to Fabun, his uncle followed "his trade of cooper" and sold the ranch before moving to a home at 390 Mt. Vernon.[80] The move was made after Blackburn sold land, probably the Mill Street ranch, to Kate Hatherly in February 1887 and purchased a lot that had been part of the Fabun Ranch from his sister-in-law Susannah Fabun. Here, he built the house on Mt. Vernon Avenue that would be the Blackburn homeplace until Lucinda's death.[81]

The minutes of the San Bernardino Society of California Pioneers, kept by Secretary John Brown, Jr., the son of Abner's old friend,

---

[78] *San Bernardino Valley Index*, "Mining News," 13 May 1881, 1. LaFuze reported the Blackburns's claim to one thousand flowing inches of the Holcomb branch of the Mojave River.

[79] La Fuze, *Saga of the San Bernardinos*, 1:198. The wealthy Greenlead (rhymes with *seed*) mine was located in West Holcomb Valley and produced several hundred thousand dollars during its long life.

[80] Fabun, *Pioneer Cabin News*. Fabun wrote, "I could tell many interesting tales about this hardy Pioneer as I remember him well."

[81] San Bernardino deeds indicate that Blackburn purchased land from Alva Downey (May 1866) and David Seeley (June 1866) and sold land to A. B. Wise (February 1869). In March 1874, he sold land to Mary Crawford and, along with his mother Hester, bought land from A. D. Boren. In July 1877 and April 1878, he purchased land from J. S. Searles et al., and in February 1878 he sold land to Henry Peake. A land boom exploded in San Bernardino in the 1880s, and in June 1885 he sold land to C. H. Golding. In poor health, Blackburn deeded all his property to Lucinda in April 1900. Summary of deeds provided by San Bernardino County Archivist James Hofer.

recorded Blackburn's admission to the society on 9 March 1889. At the society's 16 March 1889 meeting, Brown reported, "A sketch of the life and experiences of Abner Blackburn was then read and on motion received and Pioneer Blackburn [was] request[ed] to complete said sketch and bring the same down to his experiences in San Bernardino County."[82] This is the earliest indication that Blackburn was at work on his memoirs, and it suggests that he continued his narrative with an account of old San Bernardino. An extensive search for this document has turned up no clues as to its fate or location; it is possible that Blackburn never wrote it at all. Since no account of the Mormon colony by an apostate is known to exist, such a record would be significant. The garbled accounts of Lucinda destroying the "first draft" of the narrative may actually refer to the destruction of this record; it is also possible that his daughter Nettie consigned it to the flames.

The 1894 Great Register of San Bernardino voters provided a physical description of the "retired" Blackburn at age sixty-seven, listing a light complexion, gray eyes and gray hair, and giving his height as five feet, ten inches tall.

Blackburn's old age was not comfortable. Mexican War pension records in the National Archives provide detailed information on his last eighteen years, telling a sad story of poverty and ill health.[83]

On 20 February 1886, county clerk William F. Holcomb, the man who started the rush to Holcomb Valley following his discovery of gold, filled out Blackburn's "Declaration for Service Pension War of 1846 with Mexico." It listed his occupation as "Farmer." Blackburn's former comrades in Company C, Hamilton Swartout and William Ezra Becksted, swore that they "saw him in the army Traveled together messed together Eat and camped together." On 3 September 1887, Lucas Hoagland completed a Survivor's Affidavit of Witness, testifying that "Abner Blackburn is disabled by reason of Chronic Deafness and general breaking down in health." Hoagland had this knowledge "from my living neighbor to him and being on intimate terms with him having observed his deafness coming on and his failing health." Blackburn was granted a pension of eight dollars per month in January 1889.

On 1 February 1893, Blackburn applied for a pension increase, stating, "I am troubled with heart and Kidney disease and general debility." On 30 December 1894, Blackburn described the state of his health,

---

82. Record Book A of the San Bernardino Society of California Pioneers, 172–73, 176, San Bernardino Historical and Pioneer Society.

83. Pension Files, National Archives, Mexican Department, Pension No. 9150. These documents include service records, pension applications, testimony from witnesses supporting the applications, legal-fee payment records, and medical reports.

which was terrible. The form reported that on 5 January 1893, "a specialist" performed an operation for what was supposedly "a cancer of the anus." It still had the "feeling and appearance of recurring." The operation did more harm than good, destroying his sphincter and causing a prolapse of the rectum, "which at times produces great pain" and must always have been uncomfortable.[84] The operation made Blackburn "totally disabled from the performance of manual labor." His property consisted of one acre of land with "four small wooden buildings" not exceeding in worth $1,200.00. "I have no income from any source whatever, save the annual rents and profits of said property together with the Mexican war pension of $8.00." This income "is the only means of support for myself and my said family consists of a wife and two minor children aged respectively 16 and 17 years of age all of whom are wholly dependent upon me for their support." He stated, unarguably, that this was insufficient to support "myself and said family with the necessities of life." Dr. Jefferson T. Colliver wrote that he had treated Blackburn for the last two years while he was suffering from cancer and "it is not at all probable that the same will ever be cured."

On 6 December 1893, three medical officers gave Blackburn a physical examination. He weighed $147\frac{1}{2}$ pounds and had a pulse rate of 68. He described his cancer and stated, "I suffer pain in my hips and back. My bowels protrude causing great misery. My heart is instable. Have great trouble to pass water. I urinate 4 times daily and once at night. I do not do any manual labor." Upon examination, the doctors discounted most of these claims, finding that he was well nourished and had a "functional irritability of the Heart," but no organic heart disease or kidney disease. They noted the 1893 "Surgical Interfearance by 'Plaster,'" which caused the rectal prolapse that was "2 by 2 Inches. No other disabilities were found to Exist." From this description, it is likely that Blackburn suffered from prostrate trouble.

In March 1896, Blackburn again petitioned for an increase in his pension. He spent a week at the Soldiers Home in Los Angeles County and reported, "I am now wholly disabled from old age Deafness G.S. wound of left thigh and disease of rectum. I own no property and have no income except my pension of $8 per month which is insufficient to procure the necessaries of life." Surgeon H. E. Hasse affirmed that Blackburn was "wholly incapacitated for the performance of manual

---

[84] A prolapse is "a falling or dropping down of an organ or internal part." The condition terminated Blackburn's career as a horseman, but it would not have been exceptionally debilitating.

labor." On 26 March 1896, Blackburn's pension was raised from eight to twelve dollars per month.

Blackburn completed a Department of the Interior questionnaire on 11 December 1901, stating that he was married to Lucinda Harris on 27 April 1852 by Amasa Lyman when "they had no records." When asked, "Were you previously married?" Blackburn replied tersely, "Never was maried but once." When Lucinda applied for widow's benefits, the government would want more proof.

In the spring of 1897, Utah prepared to celebrate the fiftieth anniversary of the arrival of the Mormon pioneers with a spectacular jubilee. On 13 April, Blackburn wrote to Spencer Clawson:

> Dear Sir: By reading the Deseret News I understand that you want all the pioneers of 1847 to be on hand in Salt Lake City on July 24 of this year. There is a few of us here that would like to come under the conditions named by the Deseret News.
>
> California is not a land of gold and we are nearly all poor. I am a member of the Nauvoo Legion and enlisted in the Mormon Battalion at Council Bluffs returning under Lieutenant Willis to the Pueblo on the Arkansas. I then started to California with Captain Brown by way of the South Pass falling in with Brigham Young's company of pioneers at Fort Laramie and journeyed with him into Salt Lake Valley arriving there on the 24th day of July 1847. There we stayed until the 9th of Aug. 1847 when I went with Capt. Brown and Samuel Brannan for California.
>
> I would like very much to come and wish you could give me the particulars [on] how to come. I would like to know if pioneers of 1848 are also included. My wife came through there in 1848 and would like to know if she could accompany me.
>
> Hoping these lines will be sufficient I will close.
>
> —Abner Blackburn[85]

Blackburn's complaint about his poverty was unfortunately all too true. He was at a loss to explain his current straits; how could a man

---

[85.] Carter, *Our Pioneer Heritage*, 4:441–42. As in his memoirs, Blackburn made the improbable assertion that he had joined Brigham Young's Pioneer Company at Fort Laramie.

with such a golden youth arrive at such a poverty-stricken old age? A history of the forty-niners asked the rhetorical question, "Why are so many of the Old-timers so poor?" It observed that "for being here at the first, when the mines were so rich, the gold so easy to get, and all kinds of business so good, they should all be wealthy by now." The book answered the question with the irrefutable argument that they had spent all their money, and the conditions of the gold rush "had the effect to destroy all habits or ideas of economy."[86] A fortune in gold dust had slipped through Blackburn's hands in California's "palmiest days," but he had spent a life of backbreaking labor in raising nine children, only to find himself reduced to living on a twelve-dollar monthly government pension in his decline. California was not a land of gold. Blackburn was only rich in memories.

The organizers of the 1847 Utah Pioneer Jubilee sent Blackburn a registration form that he signed and returned. These registers were bound into a fascinating and heartbreaking curiosity called "The Book of Pioneers," which now may be found at the Utah State Historical Society. The forms are frustrating because they asked the surviving pioneers for artifacts and not for information; they provided a single line at the bottom of the form for "Remarks." Blackburn stated—this time correctly—that he had arrived in Salt Lake Valley on 29 July 1847 in the company of "Captain James Brown of the Mormon Battalion." He offered to donate "an old pistol and my portrait one pamphlet. a buckskin purse one old key and tin box." On the single line left for "Remarks," Blackburn wrote, "if the rellicks are not acceptable please return them." Blackburn, like many other pioneers, clearly had a lot more he could have remarked upon, while the relics so zealously collected have vanished—including the portrait, probably a painting or drawing, which, Blackburn wrote, "was taken near Prarie DuChene in the year 1845 by a frenchman Du Shong, not a very good likeness. It has been rolled up most of the time."[87]

Blackburn attended the Pioneer Jubilee and, along with the other survivors of '47, was presented with a gold medal. On 24 July, George E. Anderson photographed the "Veteran Pioneers of 1847" congregated in front of the Assembly Hall on Temple Square. Abner Blackburn appears to be standing directly under the American flag at the back of the picture. The pioneers paraded down Main Street and witnessed the unveiling of the Brigham Young monument between the temple grounds

---

86. Haskins, *The Argonauts of California*, 260, 262.

87. The "rellicks" were acceptable and Spencer Clawson sent Blackburn a receipt and asked for details. For Blackburn's full reply, see Appendix B.

and Zion's Bank. It was "a grand affair eclipsing all former celebrations. At the Big Tabernacle there was Pioneer speeches, songs, music by the Bands and choirs, a monster Prosesion 8 miles long." Ten thousand people attended the festivities, which lasted four days, concluding with a grand display of fireworks. "Many interesting relicks were shown from Nauvoo, and early Pioneer days. Many old friends met and renewed their acquaintance that had not seen each other for 30, 40 and 50 years."[88]

The celebration was probably Abner Blackburn's last hurrah. By 18 October 1902 Lucinda Blackburn reported to her fellow pioneers that "Abner is in a feeble but hopeful condition."[89] On 4 January 1904, the San Bernardino *Daily Times-Index* noted, "The San Bernardino Society of California Pioneers enjoyed their first meeting yesterday in the new, commodious hall of the Native Sons on 3rd Street. . . . Great-grandmothers Bottoms, Glenn, and Blackburn were able to ascend the stairs and enjoy the proceedings."

Abner Blackburn died at 6:45 A.M. on 2 November 1904.[90] The *Daily Times-Index* published an obituary on the same day, headlined, "Abner Levi Blackburn Dead; Another Rugged Pioneer Leaves the Fast Thinning Ranks; Helped Survey the City of Salt Lake and Took an Active Part in the Building Up of the San Bernardino Valley." The obituary incorrectly reported that "when Pioneer Fred T. Perris laid out the city of Salt Lake Mr. Blackburn carried the chain for that eminent surveyor and otherwise aided in making Utah and its fair capital attractive to all arrivals."[91] It noted, "In his latter years Mr. Blackburn frequently suffered severely from physical affliction of a cancerous nature, becoming especially at those times an object of veneration and fraternal solicitude."

The *San Bernardino Sun* published an obituary on 3 November under the title "Pioneers Cross Over," which lifted much of its text from the *Times-Index's* notice:

> When about 19 years of age, Mr. Blackburn enlisted in the Mexican war. After arriving at the front, he was detailed as a member of a scouting party, which was sent to Monterey, Cali-

[88] Larson, *Diary of Charles Lowell Walker*, 2:849–50.

[89] Record Book, April 12, 1902–October 12, 1907, San Bernardino Society of California Pioneers, San Bernardino Historical and Pioneer Society.

[90] Blackburn's death certificate, signed by D. W. White, M.D., listed "Malignant Ulcer of the Rectum" as the primary cause of death and "inuition"—general wasting away—as the secondary cause.

[91] As already noted, this is a likely reference to Blackburn assisting H. G. Sherwood's 1847 survey.

fornia in 1847. . . . In the early fifties he came to California, which has since been his home.

Shortly after his arrival in California, Mr. Blackburn joined an emigrant band of settlers and miners who battled successfully with the Klamath Indians and secured permanent peace.

Finally, becoming a true San Bernardinoan and chiefly engaging in agricultural pursuits, he soon rose to the front rank in this progressive community, and was ever ready with sage council and excellent example . . .

For some time prior to his death Mr. Blackburn was physically unable to meet with his argonaut associates on their weekly sessions, but his devoted wife has never failed to inform the interested attendants at Native Sons Hall of the condition of this venerable invalid at her home, which Mrs. [Matilda Blackburn] Stout, although herself feeble, has brightened by her presence.

The pioneer society and a committee from the Native Sons of the Golden West conducted Blackburn's funeral at 2:00 P.M. on 3 November at his home. "A large number of the valley Pioneers and Native Sons, and many friends of the late Abner L. Blackburn gathered at the family residence at Mt. Vernon avenue and Fourth street yesterday afternoon, to take a last look at the features so long familiar and so dearly loved by every loyal citizen of San Bernardino." Baptist minister Mark Shaw preached the funeral sermon. John Brown, Jr., led the mourners in the singing of "In the Sweet Bye and Bye" and read the pioneer burial service at the graveside.

Following her husband's death, Lucinda Blackburn went through a long and tedious process to secure widow's benefits. She had to submit affidavits proving she was actually married to her husband of fifty-two years. On 1 February 1905, she swore, "In the last few years before the death of my said husband, we had no means of usbsistence [sic], except the pension that my said husband drew from the Government of the United States, and since the death of my husband I have had no means of subsistence, whatever, and I have been living on what we saved out of his pension." On a form filed in January 1905, Lucinda Blackburn indicated that she "has been disabled since January A.D., 1897 by old age and hard labor." Judge Horace C. Rolfe, Lucas Hoagland, and D. L. Aldridge testified that they had known Lucinda Blackburn for more than fifty years. Lizzie Fabun swore, "Lucinda Blackburn is not able to and does not do any labor. The only property that said Lucinda Blackburn owns is her home place, close to where I live, something less than one acre of ground, with a common dwelling house on the same." Mrs. Blackburn was granted the pension, but may never have received it before her death, while the lawyer who processed the forms got twenty-five dollars.

On 11 October 1905, Lucinda Blackburn died at her home at 9:00 P.M. Her obituary in the next day's *San Bernardino Sun* noted, "She well remembered the early days of this valley. . . . Though her later years have been clouded by illness and the death of her husband a year ago, yet she has ever shown a remarkable fortitude and patience through it all. The death of her husband weighed heavily upon her mind and she has gradually failed since that time."

Blackburn's daughter, Nettie West, was appointed as "Administratrix of the estate." The estate consisted of personal property worth 221 dollars, a house, and four lots. The estate was valued at 2,721 dollars. The children deeded the land to Nettie on 15 March 1906.[92]

The Blackburns were buried next to their daughter Delia in the Pioneer Memorial Cemetery. Eventually, most of their other sons and daughters joined them.

----

[92] Microfilm Probate Records, Probate Case 2598, San Bernardino County Clerk's Office. The site of Blackburn's last home is across Mt. Vernon Avenue from the smokestack of the old Santa Fe Railroad repair shops. A highway overpass has obliterated the site.

An Account of My
Past Misdeeds

The fate of Abner Blackburn's narrative is almost as intriguing as the story of his life. It involved some of the leading western historians of the 1930s and 1940s—including Charles Camp, Carl Wheat, Herbert Bolton, Irene Paden, Charles Kelly, and Dale Morgan. Paden, Kelly, and Morgan all expressed a desire to edit the memoir at one time or another. The reasons the narrative was suppressed for so long, and the ultimate loss of the manuscript, comprise a sad cautionary tale for anyone who manages historical resources or simply loves history. The story involved so many twists and turns that Dale Morgan, who was seldom stumped, wrote, "I am damned if I know all the ins and outs of that manuscript."[1]

After his death, Blackburn's manuscript "byography of my Adventures" took on a life of its own. Lucinda Blackburn objected "strenuously to it ever being published, and . . . instilled in her daughter, Nettie, a feeling that it must be guarded, more than read."[2] After Lucinda Blackburn's death, the narrative and a trunk full of family papers, photographs, and heirlooms came into the possession of her daughter, Arnetta Matilda Blackburn West—Aunt Nettie to the rest of the family. The trunk was stored in 1942 in San Bernardino. At some point, Aunt Nettie let her niece, Blanche Blackburn Corby, make a typescript of the manuscript.

[1.] Dale Morgan to Charles Kelly, 19 January 1951, Charles Kelly Collection, Utah State Historical Society (hereafter cited as CKC). Information about the discovery of the Blackburn narrative in the 1940s is taken from correspondence between Morgan and Charles Camp, Mary Ream, and Robert A. Allen in the Dale L. Morgan Collection, Bancroft Library (hereafter cited as DLMC), letters from Morgan and Irene Paden in the CKC, and letters and documents in the Robert A. Allen collection in the Nevada Historical Society (hereafter cited as NHS).

[2.] *The Pony Express*, July 1948, 5.

In 1943, Dr. Charles L. Camp, a paleontologist and western historian at the University of California, gave this account of the discovery of
the narrative:

> Carl Wheat told me about this manuscript years ago and I
> tried unsuccessfully many times to see it. The people who
> owned it were Mormons and they had some curious idea that it
> was scurrilous so they would not let anyone read it. All we
> could do was to sit in the living room and listen to some tanta-
> lizing extracts. Finally I sicked Herbert Hamlin, Editor of the
> Pony Express Courier on this and he spent some six months
> tracking down the original. He is very anxious to work on it
> and use it as a thesis.[3]

Herbert Hamlin gave a somewhat different account in 1941.

> In 1933, Dr. Charles Camp, of the University of California,
> first ran into this diary, or obtained knowledge of its existence.
> Mrs. Corby's Aunt Nettie, who then resided at Fresno, was on a
> visit to Palo Alto. She was present at the time Dr. Camp called on
> Mrs. Corby. She objected seriously to Dr. Camp reading the man-
> uscript. She did, however, consent to Mrs. Corby reading ex-
> cerpts of it to Dr. Camp who sat across the room. Dr. Camp told
> Carl Wheat of the California Historical Society of the existence of
> this important document. Mr. Wheat went to Palo Alto and also
> listened to parts of it which were read to him. Both of these men
> consider Abner Blackburn's memoirs of great historical value.[4]

Herbert Samuel Hamlin was born 29 October 1888 on the Sioux
Indian Reservation in South Dakota.[5] After the murder of Sitting Bull
in 1890, fear of an Indian uprising caused his family to move to Salt
Lake City, where his father became a contractor and state legislator.
Hamlin was, by his own 1942 account, "raised in Salt Lake City
amongst the Mormons. . . . Since I carried Buffalo Bill's bags at the Al-
bany Hotel in Denver, the early part of this century, nearly 40 years
ago, I have always been interested in the Wild West."[6] Hamlin worked

---

[3.] Charles Camp to Dale Morgan, 31 August 1943, DLMC.
[4.] Blanche Blackburn Corby, Testimony, NHS.
[5.] Hamlin often used "Skyhawk" as a middle name and claimed it was derived
from an Indian princess in his mother's family, the Van Scoyaks.
[6.] Herbert Hamlin to Dale Morgan, 22 August 1942, NHS.

for Utah Senator George Sutherland to pay his way through George-town University and was later employed by the U.S. Geological Survey and mining companies in Montana.[7] During the depression, Hamlin sold coal and ice boxes in Hanford, California.[8] He moved to Berkeley and found himself at loose ends after separating from his wife, Lily Lee, in the late 1930s. Planning to write a biography of Sam Brannan, a kindred spirit, Hamlin had visited many Mormon historical sites, but despite this project and being raised in Utah, he had only a dim un-derstanding of Mormon history.

The Pony Express Courier magazine was founded by Herbert Brame in 1935 and published in Placerville, California. Hamlin was hired in early 1939 as advertising manager, and by July he had purchased the magazine. Hamlin changed the name in 1944 to *The Pony Express*. The magazine became the official organ of E Clampus Vitus, a group of his-tory aficionados who had revived a gold rush fraternal organization.

Hamlin had a hard time making ends meet as an editor. In 1941, he went to work for the Nevada State Highway Department. "During 1941–42," Hamlin later wrote, "the writer worked for the State of Nevada, rooting into its early history . . . the work was done under the supervision of [State Highway Engineer] Robert A. Allen, one of the state[']s colorful historians. The considerate Allen, and Governor Carville, who was also interested, gave the writer free rein."[9] An avid amateur historian, Allen also used his office to employ Mary Ream as a clerk to gather historical information on old trails.[10]

In an undated note, Hamlin wrote Allen about the Blackburn "diary" that Charles Camp had described to him in 1939. "I have a line on this diary. The grand daughter has an 8 years start on me, and has married since. She now lives near Redding, California. Or, did 3 years ago. If I get this diary I want you to make me head rodman on a road survey."[11] While on a collecting trip to northern California in the fall of 1941, Hamlin peppered Allen with breathless letters and telegrams de-scribing his progress. At Red Bluff, after "some 'Pinkerton work' locat-ing her," he stumbled onto Mrs. Corby and her copy of the narrative.

---

[7] Hamlin, while a member of the university track team, raced against Olympian Jim Thorpe. In old age, Hamlin took an active part in the movement to restore Thorpe's Olympic medals.

[8] Hamlin's nephew Jack Walker stated, "Herb could sell an icebox to an Es-kimo." Interview with editor, 15 March 1991.

[9] *The Pony Express*, November 1957, 2.

[10] Mary L. Ream was born in Indiana in 1897 and taught in Nevada schools be-ginning in the 1920s. Technically, the Nevada State Highway Department employed her as a draftsman. She died in Carson City 10 April 1984.

[11] Herbert Hamlin to Robert Allen, NHS.

On 2 December, he met and interviewed Blanche Blackburn Corby.[12] He sent Allen a scrawled postcard promising, "you get what I got."[13]

Hamlin talked Mrs. Corby out of the typescript she had made of Blackburn's memoirs. He now had the truly important part of his quest in hand—the text of the narrative—but he was obsessed with artifacts, and he began tracking down the holographic manuscript. Five days after the interview, the Japanese bombed Pearl Harbor, diverting Hamlin's attention and restricting his ability to travel.

On 29 December 1941, Hamlin wrote Robert Allen:

> Herewith, is the manuscript of Abner Blackburn which was copied several years ago from the original manuscript by his granddaughter, Blanche Blackburn Corby, and turned over to me on December 2, 1941 at Anderson, California.
>
> Mrs. Corby's aunt, Nettie Blackburn West, who lives in Los Angeles, has the original. Mrs. Corby told me that in due time we can expect to get it. We may have to wait until Mrs. West dies, but she doesn't think so. Next time she calls on her she is going to try to obtain it.
>
> According to Dr. Charles Camp of the University of California and Carl Wheat of the California Historical Library, this document contains information of no small value. It is a contribution in itself to Western history, filling in many unknown gaps and the only reason why it has waited all these years, hidden from human eyes, is because "Aunt Nettie," his sixth child, objected seriously to its publication. Mrs. Corby, Abner's granddaughter, thinks it is rather silly to withhold the information any longer, regardless of the few or many derogatory remarks about the Mormons, which are mild in comparison to other things that have been written or said.
>
> I don't think I have ever enjoyed musing over any history more than I have this lengthy account of Abner's travels.[14]

Allen justly believed that he had some rights to the Blackburn manuscript, since he—or the state of Nevada—paid Hamlin to find it. Even Allen was confused about the precise ownership: in 1942 he wrote Dale Morgan that "I have paid for the gathering of this information and the

---

[12.] Hamlin took five pages of "testimony" from Blanche Corby. The interview is full of tales about Blackburn, but it is laced with misinformation.

[13.] Herbert Hamlin to Robert Allen, 2 December 1941, NHS.

[14.] Herbert Hamlin to Robert Allen, 29 December 1941, NHS.

Abner Blackburn narrative is now the property of the State Highway Department, or to be exact, yours truly."[15]

In April 1941, Dale Lowell Morgan, who was at work on his first book, *The Humboldt*, wrote to Mary Ream at the recommendation of his friend, Utah historian Charles Kelly. Morgan later observed that Miss Ream "displays an intelligent interest and a happy resourcefulness in questions about Nevada history."[16] Morgan's book made him vitally interested in Nevada's past, and the two began a fascinating correspondence on western-trails history that, on 19 January 1942, turned to Abner Blackburn's reminiscences.

Morgan was just beginning the work that would make him one of the most respected and prolific western historians. Deafened by spinal meningitis at fourteen, Morgan had trained as a commercial artist before turning his talents to historical writing. By 1941 he had authored most of the Work Projects Administration's *Utah: A Guide to the State* series and several historical monographs. As assistant state project director for the WPA, Morgan gained a wide knowledge of Mormon journals and memoirs. Since his immediate task was a book on the Humboldt for the Rivers of America series, Morgan was intrigued when Ream informed him that "Abner tells about the journey to San Francisco with Captain Brown to get the payroll in 1847."[17] Morgan immediately responded, "I'm interested in what you say about the Abner Blackburn Reminiscence. Can you tell me whether this is published or unpublished, and where I could get a copy?"[18]

Ream replied that the only copy was in the possession of Robert Allen. She recommended that Morgan write directly to Allen, and added, "I think you would enjoy reading it. Too bad Abner's wife insisted that he delete and tone down his original memoirs when he copied them. The wife seems to have been afraid of offending the Mormons."[19]

Morgan wrote to Allen, asking to see the memoirs:

> It is my intention, presently, to write a history of the Mormons with some claims to definitiveness, and in pursuance of

---

[15.] Robert Allen to Dale Morgan, 15 July 1942, DLMC. Emulating Louis XIV, Allen believed, "The state, that's me" when it came to the Highway Department. The typescript and a photostat of the original manuscript wound up in Allen's papers, which eventually came into the possession of the Nevada Historical Society. Allen made an abridged edition of the Blackburn memoirs, which was never published. See Abner Blackburn File, Utah State Historical Society.

[16.] Dale Morgan to Robert Allen, 12 April 1943, DLMC.

[17.] Mary Ream to Dale Morgan, 19 January 1942, DLMC.

[18.] Dale Morgan to Mary Ream, 22 February 1942, DLMC.

[19.] Mary Ream to Dale Morgan, 1 April 1942, DLMC.

this intention, I have been gathering all the facts possible, from every source, well knowing that any historian is the sum—or the product—of his facts. In the last four years I have amassed several million words about the Mormons, including about 650 life sketches, journals, and autobiographies, which range from a page to eight 600 page volumes, but I find the more I find out, the more I need to find out. . . . In view of these facts, you will understand my interest in Blackburn.[20]

Morgan provided Allen with a description of Blackburn's accidental shooting in Iowa, and asked to see and copy the reminiscences. Allen replied, "Since you have been so nice to our Miss Ream, we will see to it that you get a copy of the Blackburn manuscript." He held out hope of "getting the uncensored original" and explained his involvement in the project. "My interest in all this is personal. I love history, particularly of this part of the country and naturally being in that frame of mind, I am always willing to let the other fellow enjoy some of the things we collect. You may be looking for your copy of this diary shortly."[21]

On 6 May, Mary Ream sent Dale Morgan the thirty-four-page copy she had made of the Blackburn-Corby typescript.[22] She wrote, "It seems that Abner's wife prevented him from expressing himself too strenuously in regard to the Mormons when he was writing up the narrative. I wish she had encouraged him to write more in detail." Noting William Prows's claim, she added that "we will have to accord Blackburn the honor" of discovering Gold Canyon.[23]

The next day, Morgan wrote, "I have just spent two of the enjoyable hours of my life, reading and re-reading Abner Blackburn's manuscript. This is altogether one of the most delightful memoirs I have anywhere encountered." He promised to send

> some extended notes on the manuscript which I'm sure will interest [Robert Allen] and you also; I should like to say

---

[20.] Dale Morgan to Robert Allen, 12 April 1942, DLMC.

[21.] Robert Allen to Dale Morgan, 28 April 1942, DLMC.

[22.] Before his death, Morgan gave part of his Mormon life-history collection, including the Mary Ream typescript with his notes, to Madeline McQuown. It is now found in her papers in Special Collections at the Marriott Library.

[23.] Mary Ream to Dale Morgan, 6 May 1942, DLMC. Ream added: "The story of [Lou] Devon and the Leaping Faun I did not copy. It is quite long but if you are interested in it I'll make a copy for you. Neither did I type the lengthy poem relating to James D. Riley. There were about fifteen verses . . . and to me they didn't seem important." She also omitted the poem "Early Dayes in California."

right now, however, that Abner's narrative is amazingly accurate for a reminiscent account, and it fills in certain gaps about Mormon history generally, and the movements of certain Mormon parties particularly, that have interested (and provoked) me for several years past. Captain Brown's 1847 company is a particular example of this; very little has been known of this trip to California and return; I have been reduced to piecing the merest threads together . . . under such circumstances, Abner Blackburn is a treasure indeed! I had no idea that his manuscript was one of such detail—and I never anticipated the altogether unexpected informal charm of his style.[24]

On 12 May, Mary Ream penned a note to Dale Morgan, while her typewriter underwent spring cleaning, warning, "Please keep the Blackburn narrative under *your* hat. Publication rights are owned by Herbert Hamlin who is in the employ of the Highway Dep't. I am sure you will keep the journal confidential." In response to Morgan's question—"What happened to Abner finally, do you know? When did he die, and where? And whom did he marry?"—she answered, "Yes, I know the details concerning Abner's later life, marriage, death etc but can't give this info. out yet."[25]

On 3 June 1942 Morgan sent five tightly typed pages of annotations that reflect his wide-ranging knowledge of Mormon history and his ability to analyze the material in depth.[26] Morgan wrote,

I have many Mormon narratives, but nothing at all resembling Abner's. His merry heart, his love of wine, his shrewd eye and keen wit—these are attributes all too rarely come upon in narratives of this kind, and you may be sure that I appreciate such a person when I come across him. What I would give to have been able to talk with Abner, even for an hour or two! To me he perfectly typifies the spirit of Nevada, so different from the spirit of Utah (which while most admirable in its own way nonetheless sometimes grinds terribly on the nerves).

24. Dale Morgan to Mary Ream, 7 May 1942, DLMC.
25. Mary Ream to Dale Morgan, 12 May 1942, DLMC.
26. Morgan restricted his notes "more or less to [Blackburn's] involvement in Mormon history, and [I] do not venture to comment on the specifically California elements of the manuscript."

Morgan was completing his Humboldt book and planned to move to the East Coast "to finish in the great libraries there the research job which began for me so laboriously in the Mormon archives four years ago," but promised to organize his Nevada Mormon bibliography for Allen "to reciprocate your courtesy."[27]

On the same evening Morgan wrote Mary Ream, "I should very much like to incorporate a few paragraphs relative to the Humboldt River into the final draft of my book. If you and Mr. Allen do not mind, I shall write to Mr. Hamlin and request of him this privilege. . . . I more especially would like to quote Abner on the Brannan-Brown troubles. . . . What would be Mr. Hamlin's reaction to [such] a request. . . ? It is about midnight, and my family is protesting about my typewriter, so this must be enough for now."[28] On 30 June, he sent Miss Ream corrections to the annotations, which reflect his concern with detail and precision, and again he asked if he should approach Hamlin directly.

Ream suggested in reply that Morgan write to Hamlin in Placerville. "I think he is on the trail of some historical material in California," she said, which was an understatement since just two weeks earlier, Hamlin had acquired the original Blackburn manuscript. "You would enjoy Mr. Hamlin—he is always on the trail of something big."[29]

By March, Hamlin had tracked down the manuscript. He wired Allen:

NELLY [sic] BLACKBURN WEST AGED DAUGHTER OF ABNER PROMISED DONATE ORIGINAL MANUSCRIPT TO MUSEUM IS IN STORAGE HER TRUNK SAN BERNARDINO ALSO EARLY PHOTOGRAPHS AND OTHER EFFECTS.[30]

Hamlin photographed General John Henry "Gatling Gun" Parker, a Spanish-American War veteran, standing next to the impressive Blackburn gravestone. Hamlin wrote that he and "the late General Parker paid a call upon Mrs. West. It was perhaps through the persuasion of the General (to whom she took a liking) as much as the writer's, that she agreed to let us have the journal for publication."[31] Ream repeated Hamlin's claim that he had negotiated a deal for the literary rights to the manuscript.[32]

---

[27] Dale Morgan to Robert Allen, 3 June 1942, DLMC.

[28] Dale Morgan to Mary Ream, 3 June 1942, DLMC.

[29] Mary Ream to Dale Morgan, 8 July 1942, DLMC.

[30] Herbert Hamlin to Robert Allen, 13 March 1942, NHS.

[31] *The Pony Express*, July 1948, 5.

[32] According to Hamlin, Therese José Hamlin purchased the Blackburn holographic manuscript. Hamlin wrote that he "gave them the copy [at the Nevada State

Herbert Hamlin returned to California in June to purchase the manuscript and to interview Jesse O. Blackburn, Abner's only surviving son, whom he thought had possession of the memoirs. According to the story he told in *The Pony Express*, Mrs. West gave him a note instructing her brother to release the journal for publication. Hamlin found Jesse "to be a real chip off the old block. He was chuck full of the old Blackburn humor that burned so gloriously in his frontier and venerable sire. He could see no sense in hanging so tenaciously onto his father's manuscript, and agreed with his aunt [sic] that it should be given to posterity."[33]

Hamlin was only telling part of the story. By 23 June he had discovered that Dale Morgan had the Ream typescript and ran into a further complication. As he wired Robert Allen:

WIRE ME ROSSLYN HOTEL NAME OF PERSON IN SALT LAKE TO WHOM MARY REAM SENT INFORMATION AND COPY OF ABNER'S DIARY. FAMILY GAVE SAME TO FREDERICK MORRISON THINKING IT WAS FOR ME FOR PUBLICATION HE LEFT NO ADDRESS.

Hamlin, about to make the collecting coup of his acquisitive life, was blindsided by the unknown Frederick Morrison, and he suspected Morgan. Hamlin panicked. Allen wired Morgan's address by the next day, and on the twenty-sixth, Hamlin sent Allen a postcard from San Jacinto, indicating that he had visited Jess Blackburn and had a letter from him requesting the return of the memoirs. Blackburn had mailed the manuscript to Morrison "thru error—and have only loaned. . . . How Morrison found out he had it is still a mystery to me as well as Blackburn."[34]

Hamlin tracked Morrison to Los Angeles. He later wrote that

the trail led to the fastness of the high San Jacinto Mountains, 50 miles South of Riverside, after it had disappeared from an

---

Highway Department], which I secured after many years search, and the original is owned by Mrs. Hamlin. In addition to this I have several testimonies from Blackburn's relatives pertaining to the memoirs." See *The Pony Express*, August 1947, 12. Hamlin wrote that "on December 1st, 1941, a copy of the much sought after diary was located, and publication rights obtained from a worthy niece of the stalwart frontiersman." He later claimed that he had "exclusive publisher's rights" to the memoirs. See *The Pony Express Courier*, June 1942, 2, and September 1943, 14. Hamlin's vanished papers make it impossible to determine the exact nature of this deal. The claim probably had no legal foundation, but it forestalled publication of Blackburn's memoirs for decades.

33. *The Pony Express*, July 1948, 5.
34. Herbert Hamlin to Robert Allen, 26 June 1942, NHS.

old trunk in San Bernardino, and ended in Los Angeles, between the Southwest Museum and Huntington Library, at 10 o'clock Saturday morning June the 27th. The latter institution is known to pay high tributes for such documents . . . nothing in their confines equals in color, or value, the recently discovered records of Abner Blackburn.

Hamlin gave Mrs. Richard José and others "credit for finding this rare western gem."[35]

In 1942, Hamlin married Therese Shreve José, the widow of Broadway star Richard José, "the world's greatest ballad singer," who popularized "Silver Threads among the Gold." Therese was born in Carson City, Nevada, on 10 July 1868, and was raised by Therese and Tiburcio Parrott, her aunt and uncle. Therese inherited an estate in San Mateo and considerable wealth from the Parrott and Shreve families. She married José in July 1898 and managed forty-two transcontinental tours for the singer. She was also a "religious teacher," practicing a "cross between Christian Science and common sense," and a "homeopathic" Red Cross nurse during World War I. José recorded for the Victor company and eventually became a California state real estate commissioner.[36] Carlo DeFerrari, a friend of Hamlin, described him as "wrapped up" in José; Hamlin and Therese wrote an unfinished series of articles on the singer.

José died in October 1941. Therese kept José's name after marrying Hamlin and worked as associate editor of *The Pony Express* for twenty-seven years. Therese was in her mid-seventies in 1942, and she cut a formidable figure that can only be described as matronly.

Meanwhile, Morgan was finishing his Humboldt book. He had already written Allen asking for permission to quote from the narrative, and he wrote to Hamlin on 11 July with a similar request. No correspondence with Hamlin survived in Morgan's extensive papers, but Hamlin's reply to this "kind letter" indicated that Morgan had tried flattery to cajole Hamlin.[37]

On 15 July, Robert Allen wrote Morgan to say that since he had paid to get the information, "I can see no reason why you cannot quote parts of the narrative, giving the acknowledgement to me as State Highway Engineer for the courtesy." He then let the cat out of Hamlin's bag:

[35] *The Pony Express*, June 1942, 2.

[36] For information on Richard and Therese José, see *The Pony Express*, November 1957; January 1958; July 1969; and January-February 1978.

[37] Herbert Hamlin to Dale Morgan, 22 August 1942, NHS.

"It might be of interest to you to know that we will shortly have the original of the Blackburn narrative in our possession."

Morgan sent his thanks to both Mary Ream and Robert Allen. Then, in words that would ring with bitter irony, he wrote, "I am glad to hear that the original Blackburn manuscript is to be acquired by you, for I am sure it will be carefully preserved, and so as nearly insured for loss as any document well can be."[38]

In August, Hamlin wordily denied Morgan's request. "The writer would, with pleasure, be willing to grant you this privilege were it not that others are interested in this manuscript besides myself. It was obtained through 9 years of struggle, and 6 years of that endeavor were put in by two others. . . . I only wish it were possible to give you the permission." Hamlin added, "The field of history is very long, and very wide, as you doubtless know, and a man's years are very short."[39]

In late September, Morgan had an unexpected visitor. "Hamlin was in town and looked me up," he wrote Robert Allen on 5 October. Hamlin told a different story in *The Pony Express Courier*. "One of the members of our staff made a trip to Salt Lake City expressly to ask him not to use the Blackburn material which was inadvertently sent to him by a Carson City clerk with whom it had been entrusted to read only. One of the obtainers of the Abner Blackburn journal did not wish it to be passed out by 'piecemeal.'" Hamlin preceded this with a slam against Morgan's Humboldt book: "We have not seen it, but had heard it was pretty good. I don't think the author had done much travelling around, but he is reputed to be a good writer—much better than the average WPA writer." (This remark followed a letter to the editor from James Abel, which said, "The historical side of [*The Humboldt*] seems fairly accurate; it has little literary merit. The interpretation is extremely poor.")[40]

---

[38] Dale Morgan to Mary Ream and Robert Allen, 20 July 1942, DLMC. Morgan ended the letter by asking them to "tell me a little of the historical program of the State Department of Highways." Mary Ream replied, on 12 August, that she "would be stepping out of bounds if I were to answer this request," but in a handwritten note at the top of the letter she wrote, "Off the record & for your private information, I devote my time to historical research, principally concerned with old trails." Morgan clearly had hit on a politically sensitive subject. Allen replied on the twenty-eighth about "who carried on historically in this State. The Department of Highways . . . has investigated numerous historical leads, has amassed quite a bit of information on the history of the State of Nevada. . . . Of course, the prime interest of the Highway Department is to develop more travel over the roads of the State. This can be done when people know of the historic things that are to be seen along the highways and on the by-ways of the State."

[39] Herbert Hamlin to Dale Morgan, 22 August 1942, NHS.

[40] *The Pony Express Courier*, September 1943, 14.

Morgan told a different story about this "rather curious situation." He had already sent the manuscript to his publisher when he received Hamlin's August letter. "I brought up the subject of the Blackburn manuscript," he wrote Allen. He tried to persuade Hamlin that since Hamlin was about to publish the memoirs and *The Humboldt* would not be out until at least March, Hamlin should add his permission to Allen's:

> Well, Hamlin is a very nice fellow, but he is an enthusiast, and his mind does not stick long to any one subject; his ideas bounce all over space and time, and although I brought the subject up a half a dozen times, he always got off on some tangent, and I swear that when we parted at 1:30 A.M., I was hardly wiser than was in the beginning.[41]

Morgan placed the decision as to whether he could use the Blackburn quotes in Allen's hands, offering to pull the Blackburn material from the galleys. Allen made no such request and replied, "I was particularly interested in your remarks about an enthusiast who visited you and agree with you heartily that his ideas bounce all over space and time. If he can be nailed down some time and kept on the subject, his work might be useful."[42]

In 1951, Charles Kelly wrote Morgan about his plan to publish Blackburn's 1847 Salt Desert account in an article for the *Utah Historical Quarterly*. Morgan summarized his experience with the manuscript for Kelly:

> Robert Allen stuck up the money to finance Hamlin's chasing around, and Hamlin finally ran the manuscript to earth in southern California. What he got, to begin with, was a typewritten copy of the original made by Blackburn's granddaughter. Either this or a copy of it was given to Allen, and Allen had a new copy made from this which he sent to me. Later, so I understand from the P. E., Hamlin got the original of the manuscript.[43]

Morgan described to Kelly Hamlin's response to his quotation from the Blackburn narrative in *The Humboldt*: "I've never heard directly

---

[41.] Dale Morgan to Robert Allen, 5 October 1942, DLMC.
[42.] Robert Allen to Dale Morgan, 4 December 1942, DLMC.
[43.] Dale Morgan to Charles Kelly, 22 February 1951, CKC.

what Hamlin's reaction was, but Rod [Korns] summed it up for me with a knife-cutting-throat gesture."[44]

In August 1947, Robert Allen "was displaced through a political move and is no longer on the job."[45] This fact led to a turn of events that Irene Paden explained to Charles Kelly:

> Robert Allen, of Carson City, Nevada, paid Herbert Hamlin to collect certain documents, of which Blackburn's was one. When the business deal came to an end Mr. Hamlin reserved Blackburn's, which was the most exciting, and said that he had collected it on his own time. This Mr. Allen denied. But Mr. Allen was at that time State Highway Engineer and Mr. Hamlin edited the Pony Express Courier. A man in politics cannot afford to lock horns with the editor of a paper. This affair was allowed to drop temporarily. When Mr. Allen went into business for himself he said 'the heck with that' or words to that effect and told me to go ahead and use it. I placed it in the Bancroft Library—that is, I placed a copy. Mr. Hamlin retained the ms. I may have requested that the material be kept sealed—not for public use—until further notice. I don't remember.[46]

Hamlin "fiddled around with the manuscript for years, and after much teasing of the customers began to serialize it in the Pony Express" in July 1948.[47] He made a hash out of it, and abruptly stopped publication of the manuscript in September, ending when the Missouri volunteers "threw up the sponge and went home." Hamlin published several more Blackburn articles containing his bizarre annotations, including one ridiculing Mormon temple ceremonies, and then abandoned the project entirely, without explanation, having published only about a fifth of the narrative. One clue concerning why he stopped is a letter from Dr. Ray Fisher, a disgruntled Mormon reader. "Blackburn was one of those early adherents of the Mormon faith who could not stand the sacrifice necessary in the early years of that now great institution which

---

[44.] Dale Morgan to Charles Kelly, 19 January 1951, CKC.

[45.] *The Pony Express*, August 1947, 12.

[46.] Irene Paden to Charles Kelly, 31 January 1951, CKC.

[47.] Dale Morgan to Charles Kelly, 19 January 1951, CKC. Morgan commented that Hamlin published more notes by himself, "and rather sad notes," than Blackburn manuscript. Hamlin may have delayed publication of the narrative until the death of Nettie West in 1947 or feared that Allen would ignore his fraudulent claim to the "literary rights" and publish on his own. He credited the "help of Dr. Charles L. Camp of the University of California, and with typist help at Bancroft Library through the kindness of Dr. George P. Hammond, Director." See *The Pony Express*, July 1948, 3.

has a million followers." Hamlin noted that "a million members is not to be sneezed at," and it is likely that Fisher was not the only angry Mormon who wrote Hamlin.[48]

Despite Hamlin's intimate involvement with western lore, he was not much of a historian. After visiting Israel Smith, leader of the Reorganized Church of Jesus Christ of Latter Day Saints, Hamlin announced that polygamy was an invention of Brigham Young. He published an article stating that Sam Brannan formed the Mormon Battalion in Honolulu. His mistakes in summarizing the Blackburn material between 1942 and 1948 are, to paraphrase Dale Morgan, too numerous to note, and his botched attempt at editing the narrative probably did Blackburn's reputation more harm than good.[49]

Hamlin continued to edit *The Pony Express* into the late 1970s, but his strange career careened into disaster. An Ex Sublime Noble Grand Humbug of E Clampus Vitus and past president of the California Historical Society remembered that Hamlin and Therese "moved to Sonora, and had a great collection of Western material—mostly just piled around their large house—and basement."[50]

Therese José died on 14 February 1969, at age 101.[51] Much of her fortune had been lost to bad investments or spent on Hamlin's western collection. After his wife's death, Hamlin came under the influence of "Christian Crusader" and right-wing evangelist Billy James Hargis. Hargis gave Hamlin room at his American Christian College in Tulsa, Oklahoma, to house Hamlin's collection as the "Pony Express Museum and Library," and he permitted Hamlin to lecture to students and to spin tales. Hamlin gave the college the personal papers he had donated to and then reclaimed from the University of the Pacific, papers that possibly included the Blackburn manuscript. In October 1974, a sex scandal involving Hargis came to light. A male student confessed to the college's vice president, David Noebel, by whose account "Hargis had conducted a wedding for the student; on the honeymoon, the groom and his bride discovered that both of them had slept with Hargis." Hargis, who reportedly seduced a boy of fifteen or sixteen, blamed his conduct on "genes and chromosomes." He briefly retired to his Ozarks farm due to "ill health" after ex-

---

48. *The Pony Express*, November 1948, 9.

49. Russell R. Elliott expressed the frustration of many historians when he noted Hamlin's *Pony Express* articles on Blackburn: "These 'Reminiscences' are not very useful to the researcher since they are not published verbatim forcing the reader to rely almost entirely on the editor's evaluation." Elliott, "Nevada's First Trading Post," 9.

50. Albert Shumate to editor, 30 April 1990.

51. *The Pony Express*, February 1969, 10.

torting the proceeds from a 72,000-dollar life insurance policy and a 24,000-dollar annual stipend from the college.[52] He returned to Tulsa in February 1975, to continue to manage his far-flung religio-political snake oil operations, but the college collapsed in the wake of the scandal and Billy James's reputation has not been the same since.[53]

Hamlin, broken by the scandal, returned to Utah and then California. For a time he lived in a trailer house at Columbia, in the midst of the wreckage of his collections.[54] Enamored of reactionary politics throughout his career as an editor, the destitute Hamlin finally became a ward of the state in the custody of Robert Louis, conservator of the Tuolumne County Public Guardian's office. Louis spent a week in Tulsa sorting through an enormous storage space that Hamlin had rented: "Every box you opened up was a surprise package. It was like going through a museum." There were books, manuscripts, coins, bags, furniture, artifacts, and an antique saddle. Louis made some attempt to recover the books and papers that went to the American Christian College, but declared that he was unsuccessful.[55] Public Guardian Maureen Hamilton eventually placed Hamlin in a nursing home and recalled throwing away the debris that littered his trailer.[56] Hamlin died in Sonora at age ninety-three, in September 1982; according to his sister,

---

52. "The Sins of Billy James," *Time*, 16 February 1976. See also Edward E. Plowman, "The Rise and Fall of Billy James," *Christianity Today*, 27 February 1976.

53. Hamlin's family believes that he was swindled out of the fortune he inherited from Therese José by Billy James Hargis and financed his old age by selling off his antique collection in San Francisco. Interview with Margaret Walker Paetz, Margaret Hamlin Walker, and Jack Walker, 24 March 1991. Hamlin's nephew, Stephen Walker, said that Hamlin, lacking storage space, once left a five-foot Ming vase on a friend's porch for five years. Phone interview with editor, 23 March 1991.

54. According to Hamlin's niece, Margaret Walker Paetz, Hamlin purchased two trailers and planned to move his sister, Margaret Hamlin Walker, into one of them. Mrs. Walker declined, and Hamlin filled the two trailers with his collections. When he was moved into a nursing home, the trailer was repossessed and its contents discarded. Interview with editor, 24 March 1991.

55. Phone interview, 8 May 1990. Carlo DeFerrari, Sonora historian and Tuolumne Museum member, remembered that Hamlin's personal papers went to Oklahoma. Much of Hamlin's material disappeared, including his book collection, and the remainder was sold at auction. DeFerrari reported that nothing much was left by the time of the auction, but that at one time Hamlin "had it all." Phone interview, 30 May 1990.

56. Phone interview, 8 May 1990. Hamilton reported that by the time she worked with Hamlin, "things were in sad shape." The materials the county acquired were not manuscript quality, but just a "cluttered personal mess." Some of the material was turned over to Hamlin's daughter Pat, who died in 1990. Hamilton also stated that Hamlin engaged in "questionable" deals; following his wife's death, he pawned Therese's jewelry to finance one such deal.

he rode horseback the day before he died.[57] His western collection vanished like the morning dew.[58]

Hamlin's friends, associates, and relatives universally state that he was "quite a character," likeable but eccentric and always working an angle. His nephew, Jack Walker, remembered, "My Uncle Herb was the original flimflam man." Edith Walker reported that on meeting Herb, she thought, "People like this are only in the movies."[59]

The fate of Hamlin's Blackburn notes, interviews, and manuscripts is a complete mystery. Paul Gallagher saw the manuscript in Sonora, in Hamlin's possession, about 1965. In June 1966, Hamlin wrote that "in The Pony Express Library and Museum reposes [Blackburn's] interesting narrative of the west." An immensely frustrating search for the manuscript has led to the reluctant conclusion that it was lost in the chaos of Hamlin's last days and probably came to rest in the Tuolumne County dump.[60] The possibility exists, however, that Hamlin sold or gave the manuscript to a responsible collector; so some slight hope remains that it will eventually reside in a credible western-history research institution.

Hamlin's claim to "exclusive literary rights" kept the narrative off-limits to all but a select few research historians. In 1990, there were only a handful of copies of Blackburn's narrative: photostats of the manuscript at the Nevada Historical Society and the Bancroft Library, and typescript copies at BYU, the Utah State Historical Society, the LDS Archives, and the Marriott Library. These copies carried restrictions that had been in place so long that no one remembered why they were restricted. Because these restrictions were coupled with the standard archival practice of not permitting copies to be made from a copy of an

---

[57.] Phone interview with Margaret Hamlin Walker, 17 March 1991.

[58.] Letters to every historical society and museum in Oklahoma have produced no information about the fate of the Pony Express Museum and Library. Albert Shumate reported, "I believe his money and his collection was lost in the Tulsa misfortune . . . my guess is the Tulsa college 'cleaned him out.'" Letter to editor, 30 April 1990. David Noebel was told that Hamlin, after breaking with Hargis in about 1976, took his collection when he returned to Sonora and it was sold to pay his nursing home bill. Noebel does not believe that either the college or Hargis retained any part of Hamlin's collection. Phone interview, 9 March 1991.

[59.] Interviews with editor, 13 and 15 March 1991.

[60.] After Hamlin was placed in a rest home, he failed to make payments on the two house trailers used to store his collection. The trailers were repossessed, and probably their contents were hauled to the dump. Hamlin's family believed that Billy James Hargis may have acquired his collection, and Hamlin's heir noted that if Hargis got the Blackburn manuscript, "you may have an easier time finding the ten commandments." Lee Fairchild to editor, 31 March 1991. Hargis, however, denies knowing what happened to the manuscript. Billy James Hargis to editor, 17 April 1991.

original manuscript, it became extremely difficult to study the narrative. Still, Blackburn's stories found their way into numerous western histories.

After eighteen years of silence on the subject, Herbert Hamlin published Blackburn's account of discovering Gold Canyon in the June 1966 issue of *The Pony Express*. The man whose self-aggrandizement and incompetence was responsible for obstructing publication of the narrative for decades now stated, without defining how it would come to pass, that "some day a copy of this manuscript will be published."

Continually entertaining, extraordinarily significant, often moving, and always human, Abner Blackburn's memoirs provide a ground-level view of some of the most interesting events in the settling of the West. In his last surviving letter, Blackburn wrote; "I have [written the] biography of my adventures from 1843 to 1851 containing about thirty thousand words. I am awaiting to find some suitable schollar to assist me with the prepareing it in shape."[61] Blackburn never found his suitable scholar. This work hopes to give his story a new life.

[61.] Gibson, *Blackburn and Allied Descendents of John Blackburn, Sr.*, 404.

Abner Blackburn to "Niece," 17 April 1894

S ince the institution of the temple ceremonies in the early church, Latter-day Saints have been encouraged to study their genealogy to identify relatives who can have posthumous temple endowments performed for them. On 13 April 1897, Blackburn's uncle, Elias Hicks Blackburn, noted in his diary, "Wrote to California to Abner Blackburn for Genealogy as I am assisting the Marshall Association in Geneology. Plisint day." Abner Blackburn's response, directed to "Dear Niece," appears to be a reply to this letter. Why Abner directed the letter to his niece is a puzzle: perhaps it is a family joke, since Abner was almost a year older than his uncle. Possibly, one of Elias's daughters drafted the letter, although the complimentary close is from "your Nephew."

The letter, now in the Elias Hicks Blackburn Collection at the Utah State Historical Society, and Blackburn's form, in the society's "Book of Pioneers," are the only extant holographic examples of Blackburn's handwriting, and they identify the hand that composed the narrative as that of Abner Blackburn. The punctuation and spelling are very similar to that in the narrative. The letter is reproduced exactly as written, to provide an example of Blackburn's unedited text. It provides a wonderful summary of his life, details of family history, and the only reference to Blackburn's adventure in the Pacific.

San Bernerdino California Apr. 17. 94

Dear Niece,

i received your welcome letter yesterday and feel happy to answer it to day. My mothers name was Hester Rose she was married to my Father April 25, 1821 She died September 17, 1876 Matilda was married in 1844 and left her husband in

1845 they had one child a boy whitch died young She was
maried again Oct the 7 1851 to William Stout he died about 8
years ago they had no children my brother Thomas died in
1863 the 15^t of June his wifes maiden name was Emily
Bartholomew they had four children the first Thomas Leroy.
The second Allice Maranda the third Emily Lucetta the last—
Perry—their is about two years difference in their ages

Eliza Blackburn was married Jan 27, 1844 to John Bainbridge they had four children the oldest—Jean a boy the second Sara the next Bell. Clarence the last—i think their is some
dead those named are alive [but] they live at a distance and i
am not well informed concerning them

I was married April 28^t 1852 to Lucinda Harris we have
nine children all liveing the oldest Levi Anthony born May 15,
1853 John Franklin December 4^t 1854. Charles Novem 21
1856 William Byron April 7 1860 Ella Lucinda April 13 1862
Arnetta March 6, 1864. Mary Adelia May 17 1869 Jesse October 21, 1870 Freddie Abner October 30 1873 i can give more
family dates because i have the dates

if their is any more information [you need] please let me
know and i will freely inform you to the best of my ability—for
i am glad to correspond with a persons that can think further
than yesterday i feel intrested in Utah for all my young days
werre spent in Mormonism from Jackson County to far west
and Nauvo to Salt Lak i have ben in the employ of Joseph
Smith and Brigham Young and have went through most all the
early exciting times of the Mormon Church

I am not an acomplished scholar but have abandoned
hard work and ocupy myself in other ways more beneficial to
old age I have been writing a byography of my Adventures in
an early day containing an acount of transacions in the Mormon church from 1836 to 1851 also an acount of the mexican war which i was in and indian wars of whitch i have had
a sad experience in—with seven trips across the plains
through hostile indian bands and in the mines of California
in her palmiest days have travled the Pacific Ocean from
[the] Bering Straits to Valporazo the South Sea islands and
sowed my wild oats [and] have settled down in this semi
tropic clime to lay my bones to rest and have ben wrighting
up an acount of my past missdeeds containing about thirty
thousand words

When it is convenient i would like to make [a] visit to
Utah for i am acuainted with nearly all the first settlers it is
over forty two years since i left their

I wish you would please wright me some information concerning Jehu and Elias and their familyes i would have written
long ago but when i left Utah they cut us all off from the
church i suppose they dropt me too i suppose uncle Jonathan
Rachel and Aunt Becky are dead and gone their is no way for
me to hear only from Utah

Give my regards to Elias and his and Jehues familyes hoping these line will not be to tedious i remain your Nephew

/s/Abner Blackburn

Abner Blackburn to Spencer Clawson, 7 May 1897

S pencer Clawson, an organizer of the Utah 1847 Pioneer Jubilee
Committee, was in charge of collecting pioneer artifacts for a
state historical museum to be built at Main Street and South
Temple in Salt Lake City. Despite a two-thousand-dollar donation from
the LDS church, the museum was never built; and the collected relics,
which were displayed at the Jubilee, have been lost or dispersed into
the collections of the Daughters of Utah Pioneers, the Sons of Utah Pioneers, and the LDS church. A search for the Blackburn relics has
yielded nothing but suggestions that they might be in someone else's
collection.

San Bernardino May 7th 1897

Mr. Clawson
Dear Sir:

I have received your receipt for the last relicks a portrait
and pistol and requesting me to give sketch of their history.

The pistol has been in manny an encounter with the savage tribes of the west. The most noted event of the trials was
on the Klamath river in that remarkable scrimage with the indians. I loaned the pistol to my brother to goe to the gold bluff
excitement at the mouth of the Klamath and while there they
wear attacted by the indians about ten oclock at night. They
cut through a cloth house [used] for a store and murdered five
of the inmates. They then came to my brothers house a few feet
away where him and his wife were living. They had heard the
cries of the massacre and were prepared and well armed. They
bolted the door. The whole plateau was black with indians.
They tried to break the house down but met a warm reception.

They then tried to set fire to the house and that made a fair mark to shoot at. The indians next rolled large boulders from the top of the bluff to knock the house down, His wife loaded the guns while he fired. The savages kept trying the whole night to get him out, and sent a squaw to have them surrender, but they knew death was their doom if they did.

My father had come the evening of the fight from Sanfrancisco to see his son and was within sixty yards of the house of my brother when the indians murdered him. My brother and wife were all that was left alive in those parts. My pistol was used in this scrimage. Also in the Klamath war and in the carson war and also the Provo war with old Elk the Chief besides several trips across the plains in an early day with manny encounters with wild tribes of the west.

My portrate was taken near Prarie DuChene in the year 1845 by a frenchman Du Shong, not a very good likeness. It has been rolled up most of the time.

I have [written the] biography of my adventures from 1843 to 1851 containing about thirty thousand words. I am awaiting to find some suitable schollar to assist me with the prepareing it in shape.

Yours truly,

/s/ Abner Blackburn[1]

---

[1] Gibson, *Blackburn and Allied Descendents of John Blackburn, Sr.*, 404, noted that the letter was "Contributed by Mrs. Ruth Towle Blackburn, Mayer, Arizona. Original on file in the Central Company DUP Office." The Abner Blackburn file has vanished from the Daughters of Utah Pioneers Collection in Salt Lake City.

Documents Related to the 1847 Return to Utah

T he following appendixes are parallel and corroborative documents that enhance and support Abner Blackburn's narrative. They consist of sources that are very difficult to access.

This appendix contains a 6 August 1847 letter by James Brown to one of his wives, describing the purpose of his trip to California; the Jesse Brown–Edward Tullidge account of the return of the Brown party in the fall of 1847 to the Salt Lake Valley; and instructions that Lansford W. Hastings gave to Samuel Brannan, outlining the trail Hastings recommended that Brannan follow from the settlements in California to Fort Bridger. While Brannan did not take this route, the Brown party followed it on their return to Utah.

JAMES BROWN, LETTER, 6 AUGUST 1847

Before departing Salt Lake Valley for present-day California on 9 August 1847, James Brown received powers of attorney from "all" of the Mormon Battalion sick detachment to secure their discharges and collect their pay in California.[1] On 6 August, Brown wrote to one of his wives, Abigail Abbott Brown, who had been left behind at Council Bluffs in 1846:

> I wish you to come to this beautiful valley with the first company next spring. I have not been able to assist you but a very little since I enlisted. I was detached last October at Santa Fe and sent to Pueblo in command of 107 souls. Since that time Lieut. Willis and Captain Higgins have reported to me

---

[1.] Roberts, *The Mormon Battalion*, 61.

with their detachments, making in all 170 souls. My expenses have been high and I have not been able to draw my pay in time to assist you to come last spring. You must wait with patience and I will assist you all in my power—I arrived here with my command on the 28th of July, one week after the Twelve. I was close on their heels and communicated with them from time to time after we got to Fort John. I have quartered my company in this beautiful valley where there is salt water and sweet water cold water and hot water in abundance and the plain looks very much like the one the Lord speaks of in the scriptures where the Lord's house was to [be] built in the tops of the mountains and I hope I shall soon see you together with the rest of our friends flowing to it.

I should have returned this fall with the Twelve, if I had been counselled to assist you on your journey to this place. I am counselled to take eight men and report myself at San Francisco Bay, on the Pacific Ocean, and meet the Battalion that is near that post. It is eleven hundred miles from this place. I want to return to Salt Lake this fall or early in the spring. Brother Brannon, from near the Bay, is here and is going to pilot me; then my business will be to get a discharge for my men and draw their pay and transact other business of importance for the good of the Church.[2]

THE TULLIDGE ACCOUNT OF THE 1847 RETURN TO SALT LAKE

Abner Blackburn gave the only direct account of the Brown–Brannan expedition by a participant. James Brown's grandson, Moroni Brown, used information provided by Jesse Sowel Brown to write the account published by historian Edward Tullidge in 1886. The Brown–Tullidge account substantially corroborates Blackburn's version of these events, and provides some new details. As Dale Morgan noted, this was the only information available on the journey until the discovery of the Blackburn narrative.

> Captain Brown prepared to return to Salt Lake City, and could get but four men to join him in the return trip, among whom was his son, Jesse S. Brown. Came to Sutter's Fort,

---

[2] James Brown, Letter to Abigail Brown, 6 August 1847, Salt Lake Valley, LDS Archives. Andrew Jenson entered these comments in the margin of the letter: "Copied from original in possession of M.A. Abbott, Richfield, Utah/Co, Utah, June 16, 1907." Abbott was the grandson of Abigail Brown. No evidence has been found describing what "other business of importance for the good of the Church" Brown was to conduct in California.

which place the small company left with twenty-three days' provisions—expecting to accomplish the journey from that point in the same length of time that it had required to go from Salt Lake City to Sutter's Fort [that is, twenty-three days]. The journey, however, required forty-eight days to be accomplished, hence Captain Brown and his company came near starving to death on the way back. Were pursued by twenty-five Indians while on the Truckee River. The Indians came upon them on the third day of their pursuit very early im the morning—just as a grayish twilight began to deck the eastern horizon. Samuel Lewis, who was one of Captain Brown's party, had served as picket or guard that night; and when in the dim twilight he beheld the stalwart forms of about twenty-five Indian warriors, making rapid strides on foot towards the camp, he gave the signal to his comrades: "Captain, the Indians are upon us!" The Indians evidently expected to attack the camp when the men were all asleep, but the outpost had frustrated their design. By the time that the Indians had approached to within a short distance of the camp it became broad daylight; Captain Brown advancing toward them, gave signs that they were to halt. The Indians were prompt in obeying the order, but began to make peace-signs, stating that they were "Shoshones," which, of course, was false. This was simply a stratagem of theirs to deceive. The fact of the Shoshones being friendly towards whites, accounts for this band of warriors claiming to be of that tribe. In the meantime Captain Brown, had given orders for his boys to prepare for moving, which they were busily carrying out. Finally at the solicitation of Captain Brown, ten of these redmen advanced to within a few spaces of where the small camp of scared whitemen were. They (the Indians) indulged in a mumbling conversation with each other as they stood gazing upon the proceedings of Captain Brown and his men, their talk would occasionally develop into a chuckling among themselves, characteristic of such people when they have gained a victory over an enemy.

The Indians became very insolent in a few minutes, and even attempted to steal ropes, spurs, provisions, etc., and one young buck attempted to steal a horse right from under the gaze of the men. He jumped on one of the horses and started on a keen gallop toward a clump of brush that grew close by. Captain Brown raised his rifle and was in the act of taking aim at the Indian when his comrades called for him to return. He quickly complied and brought the horse back.

When the boys were ready to proceed on their way Captain Brown gave orders for the Indians to clear the way, and the small company filed out toward their destination, at the same time each man had his hand upon the trigger and his gaze centered upon the Indians.

The Indians followed to the first crossing of the Truckee River, where an episode occurred which caused them to abandon their pursuit. Captain Brown gave signs that they were not to cross the river; after the five men had landed safe on the opposite bank, they beheld that their pursurers [sic] were nearing the first shore. They paused a moment on the brink of the stream, and then, with an air of persistency, waded into the river, and when the whole band were in the middle of the stream, Captain Brown's rifle leveled at the squad of Indians, was followed by one of the number being borne out of the water by his comrades. It was never learned by this party of travelers whether the shot proved fatal or not. Their course thence for about twelve miles extended along the Truckee River (which stream they had occasion to cross several times) after which a desert about forty miles in width was spread out before them. They rode to the edge of this desert, and encamped for breakfast shortly before noon. One of the Indians followed on foot for several miles, evidently with the intention of finding where the party of white men might camp the next night. However, he soon abandoned the pursuit. After breakfasting at this place, they prepared to launch out into the desert, and when they packed a large mule with the flour which was to last them on their trip to Salt Lake City, that amiable quadruped took occasion to stamp and scatter the flour for two or three hundred yards through the sage-brush. After this the boys had to subsist on boiled wheat until they reached the valley. Leaving their last camping place, they traveled the remainder of that day and nearly the whole of the following night, and camped on the desert without water for their animals or themselves; and it was nearly noon the next day before they found water.

They had completely foiled the enemy in thus making a long march, and the latter, not having horses or firearms, were unable to cope with even this small number of men who were supplied with both.

Thence they proceeded to the "sink of the Humboldt River," and agreeable with directions which they had received from a surviving member of the Hastings company of emigrants, most of which (as before stated) perished at Lake Donner, they left the old Fort Hall route, and took what was called the "Hastings' cut-off."[3] They had been informed that by taking this course they would reach Salt Lake City with at least two hundred miles less travel. This course led them southward across what was known as the "Seventy-five-mile Desert."

By the time they reached the Humboldt their provisions had entirely given out, and their horses being considerably reduced in flesh they were unable to travel very fast, and the county had not proved as prolific in game as they had expected. They had yet to encounter their greatest foe. It was this desert of seventy-five miles in width. The weather was getting very cold, and light snow storms had not been infrequent from the time they left the Humboldt region. This had rendered the country in a condition greatly to impede travel. They had supplied themselves with nothing in which to carry any quantity of water to speak of, and when they came to the desert they simply had to stem the hideous foe by launching out into this stretch of alkali bed with a determination to get through.

Three days were consumed in accomplishing the journey across the desert. They found water the third day about 2 o'clock. Some of the animals had given out, and had been left on the desert. For three days these five men had subsisted on three very lean geese which Jesse had killed the day before the company arrived on the desert; and during that length of time they had no water. One or two members of the party gave out, and were so weak they had to be assisted on their horses by their emaciated comrades. They arrived in Salt Lake City about the 1st of December, 1847 [sic], in an exceedingly broken up condition. This trip had reduced Captain Brown from 200 weight avoirdupois to 150, and the other members of the company were proportionately reduced.

---

3. Tullidge was confused about the composition and fate of the Hastings companies, which included the Donner party. Tullidge wrote that the Brown party "was the first company traveling westward, to view the remains of the celebrated Hastings company who perished at that memorable lake (Donner) the previous winter." Tullidge, "Biographical Supplement," *Histories*, 103. The Donner party lost thirty-five members in the Sierra, a fraction of the total number of emigrants who followed Hastings.

Captain Brown had succeeded in procuring the soldiers'
pay—$10,000—which he brought with him to Salt Lake City,
and distributed among his company. He also brought with him
4½ bushels of wheat and half a bushel of corn, the first grain
planted in Weber County.[4]

LANSFORD W. HASTINGS, INSTRUCTIONS TO SAMUEL BRANNAN, 1847

A long-lost Lansford Hastings document written in 1847 sheds
new light on—and raises new questions about—the route taken by the
James Brown party on its return to Utah. On 8 July 1847, Mormon pioneer Thomas Bullock noted in his journal that he had copied a map
and waybill of the country between the Salt Lake Valley and Sacramento, which Sam Brannan had carried on his journey from California
to Green River. Bullock wrote that he "made a copy of Hastings directions from Bridger's Fort to the Settlements in California also a map of
the route—returning the originals to brother Brannan." Bullock's journal entry prompted historians Dale Morgan and Roderick Korns to
search for the Hastings material. They noted in *West from Fort Bridger,*
"This waybill and map have been searched for in the archives of the
Historian's Office without success."[5] In July 1991, LDS archivist
Michael L. Landon found the file containing the waybill and map. The
file contains a single sheet of instructions in Hastings's handwriting,
measuring approximately 12 by 8.25 inches, and Bullock's copy of the
map, which is titled "Hastings Map." It shares the page with "Miles
Goodyear's map," which is dated 12 Jul 1847.

The road via the Salt Lake intersects the old road, on
Mary's River about 230 M. above the sink. Leaving the old road
at this point you continue up the South fork of Mary's river
about 20 M. to a point where the road bears almost directly
south. At this point or near this, you will observe an opening,
or gaps in the mountain at the east, through which you will
pass instead of continuing around the point of the mountain at
the south. By this course you will save fifty or sixty-M.

When you pass the south [end?] of the Salt Lake, you will
take the right hand road leading directly east, over the mountain instead of bearing to the North up Weber's River.

[4.] Ibid., 103–5. Tullidge wrote that this account is "from the pen of his grandson,
Moroni F. Brown." Page 103, however, stated that "Jesse S. Brown, who was a member of this small company, gives a most interesting account of this journey," without
indicating if it was a written or oral account.

[5.] Korns, *West from Fort Bridger,* 118.

After crossing Weber's River (the 1st river of any importance after passing the Salt Lake) you will continue up a small fork of that River coming in from the East. When you leave this fork be sure to take the left hand road, as it is much the nearest and best.

Be sure to Examine the mountain laying at the north, about midway up this "long drive."

/s/ L.W. Hastings[6]

Written one year after Hastings led his unfortunate followers across the arduous "cutoff," the instructions provide some insight into his knowledge of the trail. It told Brannan, who was traveling east from California, how to locate the Hastings Cutoff and how to get through the Wasatch Mountains from the Great Salt Lake. The first sentence locates the intersection of Hastings Cutoff with the California Trail, about 230 miles up the trail from the Humboldt Sink. Hastings provided specific instructions on how to find "an opening, or gaps in the mountain at the east" to cross the present Ruby Mountains. This is undoubtedly present-day Harrison Pass, since going twenty miles up the South Fork of the Humboldt would bring a traveler to a location somewhat south of present-day South Fork Reservoir, from which it would be difficult to see the only possible alternative route, Secret Pass. Harrison Pass also cuts off about sixty miles of the wagon road through Overland (or Hastings) Pass, the route actually followed by the 1846 wagon parties.

Hastings provided no explanation of how to cross the difficult country of eastern Nevada and the Salt Desert, but gave detailed instructions on how to locate the route (the "right hand road leading directly east") that the Donner-Reed party used in crossing the Wasatch. Once in the mountains, Hastings recommended following Echo Canyon, "the nearest and best" route to the high plains of what is now Wyoming. The crude map that accompanied the instructions described this country.

Like many trail documents, the instructions raise more questions than they answer. Why didn't Hastings recommend that Brannan turn south at the North Fork of the Humboldt and cross Secret Pass, the route Hastings had followed in early 1846 with James Clyman? This would have saved twenty-five more miles from the Harrison Pass route. Why didn't Brannan take Hastings's recommended route? And finally,

---

6. Lansford Warren Hastings, "Instructions, 1847," LDS Archives.

how did the original waybill, which Bullock returned to Brannan, wind up in the LDS Archives?

A Brannan letter written at Fort Hall, on 18 June 1847, provides a possible answer to the second question. He reported that he and his three companions were not "able to travel the regular route due to the high waters."[7] While this may simply indicate that Brannan had to follow high ground on the flooded California Trail, it may be that May floodwaters on the South Fork spared Brannan a perilous (or even fatal) detour on the Hastings Cutoff.

Although Brannan did not follow the Hastings instructions, it precisely describes the route taken by James Brown and Abner Blackburn in the fall of 1847. Both the Blackburn and the Tullidge accounts vaguely indicated that they got directions from "emigrants." Blackburn noted how difficult the road was to locate and wrote, "We found it by directions of an emegrant," although no emigrants are known to have used the cutoff in 1847. The Tullidge account more specifically recorded that they found the cutoff "agreeable with directions which they had received from a surviving member of the Hastings company of emigrants."[8] Could that "surviving member" have been Hastings himself?

James Brown was almost certainly aware of the Hastings instructions; even if Brannan had failed to show them to Brown, it seems unlikely that Brigham Young would have dispatched Brown to California without knowledge of the "waybill" copied by his clerk, Thomas Bullock. Certainly the strongest indication that Brown knew of Hastings's instructions is the fact that the returning company followed the directions to the letter.

While Brannan may have returned the instructions to Bullock before departing for California, it is possible that Brown carried the original instructions with him on his return to the Salt Lake Valley, where they found their way to the church historian's office.

---

7. *The Millennial Star* 9, 15 October 1847.
8. Tullidge, "Biographical Supplement," *Histories*, 104.

Supporting Accounts of the 1848 Salt Lake to Winter Quarters Trip

I n addition to Blackburn's narrative, participants Robert Bliss and David Stuart left accounts of the journey from Great Salt Lake City to Winter Quarters. Robert Bliss was the official historian for the company. The portion of the Bliss journal published in the *Utah Historical Quarterly* in 1931 breaks off in the middle of a word in the 13 January 1848 entry. Historian Everett Cooley discovered the rest of the journal—which had been literally torn in half—when the records of the Mormon Battalion Monument Commission and the State Society of Daughters of the Mormon Battalion were transferred to the Utah State Archives in 1958.[1] The Bliss account was published in the October 1959 *Utah Historical Quarterly*. David M. Stuart left two surviving accounts of the journey, while the family of Ami Jackman wrote short accounts of his participation.

This appendix also includes the text of the deed by which Blackburn transferred his Mexican War bounty lands to one William Butt.

DAVID M. STUART 1878 ACCOUNT

I got [Father John Smith's] blessing in the spring of 1848, when he called upon me with others to carry the mail back to Winter Quarters on the Missouri river, "For," said he, "President Young and the Saints will be anxious to hear from us."

Accordingly, a company of seven men, all members of the

[1.] Cooley, "The Robert S. Bliss Journal," 380–404. The holographic manuscript of the last section of the journal is now in the Utah State Archives. Two of the pages are generally illegible, but appear to describe a stay on Grand Island in the Platte and the crossing of the Loup Fork.

"Mormon Battalion" except myself, were detailed for the mission. My companions were among those who had planted victoriously the flag of our country on the Pacific slope, and they were now to return with the first mail from the Rocky mountains under its protection. We started on the sixth day of March to cross the Big mountain, but found the snow too deep, and returned to the valley.[2] We then went up Weber canyon, following an Indian trail to Echo canyon, where we struck the wagon road our emigrants had made and followed it through the snow, more or less, until we crossed the Black Hills.

We were taken by a band of Sioux Indians on the Laramie plains, who were out hunting buffalo. They detained us for all day and filched our trappings, our powder and ball, but feared to touch the mail when we told them the great father of our country would be angry and send an army to punish them if they detained us or injured the mail. They let us go in the evening, and we traveled all night, fearing they might follow us. We had no more trouble until we reached the Loup Fork of the Platte, where we found we had to swim our animals. Our captain, William Gardner [sic], could not swim, and came very near drowning. He lost his gun in the river, and barely got out himself. All our animals got across but an old Spanish horse that got down on a sand bar in the middle of the river and could not get up. We feared that he would remain there and die, and were about to leave him to his fate, when we remembered that the Patriarch, Uncle John Smith, blessed us and predicted that we should all get through alive and that we should not lose an animal. After talking the matter over, we concluded to make another effort to save the old horse and fulfil Father Smith's prophecy; so those of us who could swim went back, believing that the Lord would assist us as He had previously protected us.

We found the old horse in the quicksand, unable to move or make an effort to help himself; so we concluded to leave him to his fate, when someone suggested that we drown him, the water being about two feet deep where he lay. So we crowded his head under water, when he made a spring to save his life and floundered out in the deep water. He then swam ashore, to our great joy, thus fulfilling Father Smith's prediction.

---

[2] Stuart's reference to Big Mountain indicates that the party first attempted to leave the valley by Emigration Canyon.

We arrived safely in Winter Quarters on the 11th of April, and received a hearty welcome from President Young and others of the Twelve, who took us to their homes where we enjoyed their hospitality and blessings, which to me have ever been more than meat or drink.[3]

DAVID M. STUART 1897 ACCOUNT

In the spring of 1848 Uncle John Smith, the Patriarch of the Church, and the President of the first Stake in the [Salt Lake] valley, called on me while at work sawing logs with the whip saw, and said he wanted me to take a mission back to Winter Quarters, with letters to Brigham Young and the brethren "for," said Uncle John, "they will be anxious to hear from us, and many others want to send letters to their friends, and this may be considered the first mail east from Great Salt Lake Valley. Several of the Battalion boys are going back for their families, but the number is too small to make it safe, and as you are a young man you can go with them just as well as not."

I said, "Brother Smith, I am at your service, to go, or come, or stay just as the spirit prompts you." Said he, "Go, you shall be spared by the way and will not lose an animal." The company was organized as follows, William Garner, president; Robert Bliss, Abner Blackburn, Abner Kaulkens, Samuel Lewis, David M. Stuart. We started on the 6th day of March with twelve horses, six to ride and six to pack our bedding. Our provisions consisted of a little flour; we trusted to killing game for meat. By the way, the Indians took us at Ash Hollow and kept us in their camp two days, but finally let us go, after getting most of our ammunition—we had but little for them to pilfer—and although they were on the warpath, the Lord softened their hearts, and they gave us a quantity of dried buffalo meat and let us go. In crossing the Loop Fork of the Platte we had to swim our horses. Brother Garner could not swim, he caught his horse by the tail and lost his gun in the operation, but saved his life. One old Spanish mare that wore the bell, got down on a sand bar and made no effort to get up. After making a fire and drying our clothes we determined to return with

---

[3] D. M. S., "Early Experience of an Elder," *The Juvenile Instructor* 13 (1 January 1878): 3.

poles and help the mare up so as to fulfill Uncle John's prophesy, that we would not lose an animal. After laboring for a long time we lost hope, for she would make no effort to save herself, so we concluded to drown her by forcing her head under water, there being about two feet and a half feet of water where she lay. As soon as we had her head under water she made a struggle for dear life and rolled into the deep water and swam out, to our great joy and the fulfillment of Uncle John's prophesy. We had no other serious mishaps or sickness by the way, although we had to pass through snow more or less, to where Cheyenne city is built. We killed an old buffalo bull near Independence Rock, on the Sweetwater, and had a rare feast; arrived in Winter Quarters on the 11th of April[4] safe and sound, with all our animals in tack, but jaded like ourselves.[5]

JACKMAN FAMILY ACCOUNTS

Levi Jackman described his son Ammi's experiences in memoirs written about 1851:

> Notwithstanding the little disentions and covitisness that was among us, take[n] as a whole we enjoyed our selves and was a hapy a people as could be found in any place. On the 12th a Compeny of Seven men Started for winter Quarter with the Mail. Ammi was one of them. It was a hard and hasidus undertaking, Over a thousand miles to go at this Season of the year, without an inhabitant only at Bridger and Larema, liable to loose ther way in the Mountains or on the Plains or to be killed by the Indians. But the Mail must go. I felt bad for him under such circumstances, but I believed the Lord would presirve them allth[ough] they might have to suffer much.
> Both did take place, they narrowley escaped deth by the

[4.] Stuart is incorrect in his departure and arrival dates. The party actually arrived in Winter Quarters on 3 May 1848. The Hosea Stout diary for 11 April 1848, however, recorded: "Three men arrived here today from the Valley. The news from their was good." This refers to a company that, according to the Bliss journal, left Salt Lake Valley on 12 January. Unfortunately, none of the men in this party is named in any Mormon source. See Brooks, *Hosea Stout*, 1:309.

[5.] David M. Stuart, "A Pioneer's Experience," *The Millennial Star* 59 (27 May 1897): 323. See also the *Deseret News*, 4 May 1897. Despite Stuart's wonderful story about the old Spanish mare, Robert Bliss wrote on 18 April that "we left one of our animals which gave out" at Ash Hollow. Bliss said nothing about meeting the Sioux at Ash Hollow, but described an encounter with the Pawnees in the illegible pages of his journal.

Indians, and friezing and by Starvation, yet they got through a
live and were Joyfuley rece[i]ved by the Presidency and all the
Saints. I felt rather loanley for a while not having any connection within one thousand miles. Yet in [the] main I enjoyed
myself well.[6]

Finally, in 1905 Mary A. Jackman wrote this account of Ammi Jackman's experience:

> In March 1848, he, with six others, started back to winter
> Quarters to carry the mail—the first to be taken back from
> here.
> The party went on ponies with no provisions except what
> they could carry in their saddle bags—depending on their guns
> to supply them with food. They were taken prisoner by the In-
> dians who robbed them of the few provisions they had—of
> their blankets, guns and ammunition. Twice again they were
> captured but managed to escape.
> During the last thirty days of the journey they lived en-
> tirely on roots, herbs and reached winter Quarters in a starving
> but satisfied condition because they had accomplished their
> purpose.[7]

ABNER BLACKBURN DEED TO WILLIAM BUTT

In 1848, Blackburn found his family living in Clay County, Missouri, preparing to emigrate to California. While there, he applied for
the 160 acres of land due to Mexican War veterans and sold the land to
one William Butt.

> Land Grants in the United States Archives, from applica-
> tion for land of Abner Blackburn. Private in Captain Brown[']s
> Company, Mormon Battalion, Volunteer 23480.
> Land Grant No. 18974 for 160 [acres] issued 3 July 1848
> and sent care of William Butt—Linden Missouri. State of Mis-
> souri Atchison Co. on the 8 May 1848 Abner Blackburn made
> application for "Land Grant" of 160 acres. This land grant was
> given by [the] United States Government, for Military Service
> in the Mormon Battalion. He was mustered into service at

---

6. Levi Jackman, "Memoirs," Utah State Historical Society, 66.
7. Mary A. Jackman, "Ammi R. Jackman," Utah State Historical Society.

"Council Bluffs Missouri." by Lieutenant Colonel J. Allen on the 16 July 1846. for the term of one year and was discharged at Utah Valley in Upper California on the 16 July 1847. By reason of expiration of time of service. I never received any discharge the Battalion to which I belonged was mustered out of service. The Certificate of a commissioned officer of the company to which I belonged cannot now be had.

Sworn to and subscribed before me the day and year above written.

[s/] Abner Blackburn

[s/] Thomas Tanner Justice of Peace[8]

---

8. This information is taken from a handwritten transcript copied by Frances Callahan in the National Archives, January 1947; copy in editor's possession.

"The First in Nevada": The Bancroft-Beatie 1884 Interview

In 1884, H. H. Bancroft and Mormon historian Franklin D. Richards interviewed Hampton S. Beatie about his experiences in establishing the first white settlement in Nevada at Mormon Station. Beatie's account substantially parallels and confirms the story told in Blackburn's narrative, but he made numerous small errors and consistently predated the events by one year. Although Bancroft had John Reese's account, which indicated that Beatie's 1849 dates were in error, he accepted Beatie's date. The complete interview is reproduced here.

THE FIRST IN NEVADA
H. S. BEATIE 1884

I was born in Washington County, Virginia in 1826. I left there in 1836 in company with my Father and went to Boone County, Missouri, and from there to Lexington, M., in the following year, '37. Remained in Lexington and La Fayette County until the Fall of 1840. I then went to Kentucky and remained there that Winter, and from there went back to Virginia to College where I was till Sept. 13, 1843, but did not graduate. During that time my Father had remained in Missouri, and I joined him in Andrew County. I was not connected with the [LDS] Church until I came here [to Great Salt Lake City]. I came here in company with Mormon Emigrants in C. T. Benson's company on the 26th of October (1848) [sic]. I married in Missouri. My first thought on coming here was the thought that if I had ever struck a country town I did when I struck Salt Lake—nobody but my wife & family and a few of the Company. I acted as Clerk of the Company coming here. The people seemed to have scattered off in different settlements. I stayed here until the 18th of the next April when I started with a company under Captain DeMont for California. I went with my own outfit. There were 80 souls in the Company and I was elected clerk of it. None of the teams took anything but supplies. My idea, as well as that of the Company, was to go there and mine for a short time and then come back. I did not belong to the Church then, though some of the company did, but most of them did not. The Mormon portion of the company went to mine temporarily, leaving their families here. I don't think they asked the advice of the Church authorities before going.

Mr. Ban. wished to know if this kind of thing was sanctioned by the Church leaders—that is the Mormons going away to seek gold and mine.

F.D.R. As a rule this was not sanctioned. There was a company of brethren went one time to California on business to get some seed &c., and while there they may have done a little mining as each of them brought a little gold back with them. But the advice of the authorities in those days to the people was for them not to go after gold, but to settle down here and make homes for their families, and not suffer themselves to be lured away after gold mining &c. Prest. Young said that everyone who stayed at home and worked would in 5 years be able to buy out all those who went off for gold & then came back.

H.S.B. There were two Mormons by the name of Smith & Brown from Farmington and another named Parson. Most of the Mormons were from Farmington. There were 15 of the party that I went out with that Spring [that] returned that fall. I also came back in the Fall. On our way to California I took up some land and built a house in Genoa. We got there sometime early in June 1849.[1] There were 7 of us started there—DeMont, Blackburn, Carter and the others I can't think of their names. There was no other white man in the region when we arrived there. Plenty of traders came over during the Summer. I did not see a white man for several weeks after we arrived there, nor did I hear of anyone in that country camping. The traders that came in were from the west and not from this way. Each of the 7 had

---

[1.] Dale Morgan noted, "Beatie's account should be examined with the understanding that he is one year off in his dates; he came to Utah in 1849, and his company therefore left in the spring of 1850, as Blackburn says."

one team. When we got the house built I and Mr. Blackburn were appointed to go over the mountains and bring supplies back as we began to learn that there was going to be a heavy emigration. We went over to Placerville with our teams. In Genoa we settled right west of Reese's place, where he afterwards built his sawmill. My place was about 50 yards from the place where [Reese later] built his trading post. We put up a log cabin. It was not standing when I went back there [in 1853?]. Timber was very plentiful. I left there in September and we sold out to someone named Moore. I think Reese bought this man out. We did no fencing or planting. We went to make a station for the purpose of supplying provisions to the emigrants who came along. We built a corral there to keep the stock in. The cabin was a double-logged one story house about 20 by 60 feet containing two rooms. We put no roof on nor a floor as it did not rain that season—at that time we did not know but what we would winter there when we would have to put a roof on. I don't recollect the object of our putting up the log house only we had nothing to do so we put a house up. We had no trouble with Indians.

Mr. Blackburn & myself took 6 yoke of cattle and disposed of half of them and with what money we raised we loaded the team with flour, dried fruit, bacon, sugar & coffee. We went through Carson Canyon & over the mountains—the old emigration route. We then came back & disposed of our stock and started again for California. We took 15 pack animals and went over what was known as the Jumptown [?] route which strikes over the mountains 3 miles S. of Genoa. We passed [over] all the streams on a log. That was my last trip to California.

On the whole we done very well down there. Traded for horses, mules, and anything that was needed. Our principle trade was horses & mules. People from California would come in the Valley & dispose of their stock and then go back—there were none from this way. None of them built cabins during my stay there. They had their wagons & tents but mostly pack mules—I don't know of anyone else camping farther off. My house was the first one built in the Valley and I think in Nevada.

Our party was the first to discover gold in Nevada. This Mr. *Abner Blackburn* was the first to find it. He made the discovery in July while I was gone over the mountains with his brother for supplies. When Abner Blackburn first went over the mountains it seems he had an idea that there was gold in

the vicinity of what is now Virginia City; and while his brother
& myself had gone over the mountains it appears that he went
out prospecting and discovered gold, but got only a small
quantity. No other mining was done by our party at that time.
Flour at that time was worth $2.00 a lb., fresh beef $1.00,
Bacon $2.00. A friend of mine went of [over?] the mountains
and left a yoke of cattle with me, and one day I got a thousand
dollars for one of those oxen in the shape of beef. We had not
sufficient flour to sell out in large quantities and therefore we
used to deal it out in small quantities thereby benefitting more
people. One time a Captain of a train of emigrants came along
& wanted to buy 500 lbs of Flour @ $2.00 a lb but I refused
him not having sufficient to deal out in such large amounts.

There was a good deal of emigration that year & a great
amount of suffering. For a few loaves of bread I could get a good
horse. I had friends over in Sacramento where I got my supplies
from, and should have made all the money I wanted that year if I
could have got the provisions, such as flour, sugar, &c. Demont
& Kimball went over to California and I never seen them since.
That left 5 of us and 10 more came from California making 15 in
all, and we journeyed together back home [to Great Salt Lake
City]. We came back with packs. We had a [great] many horses
but we sold a few of them and brought the others along—we had
over a 100 head. We traveled independent—every man for himself. Went over the Indian Road over the Humboldt. On the 4 or
5th of Oct. as we were traveling along we discovered that a man
had been killed, his body laying on the ground. We stayed there
about ¹/₂ an hour & looked around, and 3 Indians came up who
could talk a little English. We found out afterwards that they were
just a reconnoitering party sent to discover how we were armed
&c. We went on to an open piece of ground where we stayed all
night. Next morning we saw a band of Indians on a high knoll
several miles ahead. We knew then that they calculated to make
an attack upon us. We crossed the river & dismounted and there
engaged in a little fight with them. Most of the Indians were on
horseback and they encircled us round. Only one Indian was
killed as far as we know and some horses. None of our party were
struck at all. We then desired to make peace with them, and one
man of our party volunteered to go out to meet them & obtain
peace if possible, but they shot at him & killed the horse under
him, so he returned. While we were catching wild animals the Indians came & drove all our band of horses off and we did not get

them again, as we did not go after them not wishing to have any more trouble. The Indians were Bannocks. No more trouble after then with Indians. They also took all our possessions except a little sugar & coffee. When we got to Bear River there was a camp there, and after an amount of talking &c. we got a 50 lb sack of flour for $50.00. This camp were on their way to Fort Hall with provisions for that place. The first house we struck in Utah was at Brigham City I believe. We got in here the 19th of Oct 1849. Before the Winter was out a clerk of Col Reese's came and asked me to go into his (Reese's) store, and I went & clerked for him, stayed there till sometime in 1853.

Utah Lake was frozen over at the time of the Indian trouble at Provo.

In 1853 I went out to Carson Valley with an escort with Marshall Hayward and Judge Stiles who were going for the purpose of organizing Carson as a County in pursuance of an act of the Legislature the winter before. *Enoch Reese* went with the Company and I was in his employ. Took 30 or 40 head of mules and disposed of them in the Sacramento mountains. Took provisions from here for the Colonel's station out there.

Then I found houses built extending through the whole length of Carson Valley—frame houses, blacksmith shop and a mill had gone up. There were no mines in the country then unless there were some in the hills that were not known. Farming and stock raising was the principle trade. The Indians that came in were friendly disposed and would help to get in the harvest &c. Produce was sold to the emigrants still. There was about a dozen houses in the valley at that time. No house anywhere else. There was a trading post called Ragtown on the emigrant line E. of Genoa, which was trading with emigrants. In connection with Hayward & Styles & Orson Hyde went over to California and we separated at Placerville.

F.D.R. My impression is that Marshall Hayward, Judge Stiles & Orson Hyde were the three Commissioners appointed by the Government to run that line & organize that County.

H.S.B. I came back the same Fall and did not go out again. Christopher Markley, Jesse M. Perkins, Reuben Perkins, Shepherd & Hutchins went out there as Missionaries and stayed several years.[2]

[2.] H. S. Beatie, "The First in Nevada," *Nevada Historical Society Papers* (1913–1916): 168–71.

Accounts of the Death of
Anthony Blackburn

In addition to Abner Blackburn's two accounts of his father's death and the accounts quoted in chapter 10, eyewitness A. E. Raynes, Judge Walter Van Dyke, and two histories of Humboldt County recounted the story.

Van Dyke's Statement

Thirteen years before his version of the death of Anthony Blackburn was published in *The Overland Monthly*, Judge Walter Van Dyke provided H. H. Bancroft with the following account.

Statement of Recollections on
Matters Connected with Early Years
of Cal. & Oregon, 1849–63, by Judge Van Dyke,
Furnished to Bancroft Library, 1878.

I was chosen District Attorney for Klamath County in the Spring of 1851. In that Spring we had some Indian difficulties. There was a massacre at Tompkins's Ferry, on the trail between Trinidad and Klamath River. Trinidad became the post of supply for that part of the country, the river communication having failed, and Uniontown, now Arcata, was the post for lower Trinity River. Both of those places were very flourishing trading posts during '51 and '52. White women were very scarce in that country. There was a man and his wife by the name of Blackburn living at Tompkins's Ferry. They had a little shanty for themselves, but the men lodged in a canvass house. It was a little trading post and ferry on the trail to the mines. The night before the massacre occurred, old Mr. Blackburn, the father of the young married man, was on his way up from Trinidad to visit his son. He left the last camp, which was Elk Camp, on the hills this side of the ferry, in the afternoon, and after the massacre occurred his body was found this side of the ferry station, mutilated by the Indians. They killed him before he got to the place, and that night, with long knives, they cut holes through the canvass house and went in and killed the men, three or four, who were sleeping in the tent. The noise roused Blackburn and his wife, who were in the temporary house nearby. He looked out and saw the Indians all mounted, and coming to his house. He had two or three guns, and he commenced blazing away, and they scattered at once, and he thus kept them at bay. They had no fire arms, but had long knives and hatchets. His wife loaded the guns, and he kept firing, and kept them off until the next morning at 8 or 9 o'clock, when a large pack train returning from the Klamath and Salmon Rivers came down to the ferry and crossed, on their way to Trinidad, and the Indians scattered. When they got there, they found the conditions of things, of course, and found that Blackburn and his wife were the only ones left. That created quite an Indian excitement. The whites became ugly, and the Indians became ugly; up to that time they had always been friendly.

A. E. RAYNES ACCOUNT

An item preserved at the California State Library gave A. E. Raynes's version of "one of the most stirring incidents of Pioneer days." This account is more accurate in many details than that of Walter Van Dyke. Sometime, probably in the 1880s, Raynes had received a photograph of Emily Blackburn Hawley which

> revived in Mr. Raynes memory some of the details of the incident which brought fame to Mrs. Blackburn and which aroused the fighting blood of the early settlers from Trinidad to Yreka, and this is the story as Mr. Raynes tells it:
>
> In 1851, I was riding express from Trinidad to Salmon River and Yreka. My route crossed the Klamath River at what was known as the Blackburn Ferry. At this point Mr. Blackburn had a large tent in which he kept a limited stock of flour, bacon, etc., and he had several men employed about the place.

Mr. Blackburn and his wife lived in a little shake house a short distance back of the tent.

About five hundred yards back from the river there was an Indian rancherie occupying a large flat. These Indians were supposed to be friendly, but had this supposition been true, this story of treachery and bloodshed would never have been told.

On my regular trip from Trinidad with the express, I camped one night about two miles above the ferry at a little ranch. Early the next morning I saddled my mule and started down the river to the ferry. Mr. Blackburn saw me and came across with the boat, exclaiming as soon as he got within talking distance: "Raynes, I'm mighty glad to see you. Everybody but myself and wife have been murdered by the Indians." We crossed back and Blackburn showed me the work of the murderous red men. In front of the tent lay the body of a young man almost hacked to pieces. Another of the men lay dead at the back of the tent and the third one we found down the river.

Blackburn told me that the night before the Indians made a sudden attack on his camp. Mr. and Mrs. Blackburn were barricaded in their little shack and while Mr. Blackburn kept up a steady fire through a hole in the shakes, Mrs. Blackburn loaded the rifles, of which there were two, with bullets that she had moulded that evening. They succeeded in holding the Indians at bay until morning when the whole band disappeared, going back into the mountains. Investigation showed that all his men had been killed.

While I reconnoitered along the river, Blackburn carefully crept back to the big flat where the Indians had the rancherie, and found it deserted, but he saw the body of a white man lying there. As all of his men had been accounted for, he examined the body to see if he could identify it, and was horror stricken to discover it to be his own father whom he had not seen for years.

It transpired that his father had come from Trinidad to visit his son, and being anxious to get to the ferry, left the pack train encamped two miles away and made his way alone to his son's place, only to be murdered within sight of his destination. . . . The memory of that brave woman moulding bullets and loading rifles for her husband and in a fight against such a fierce raid should be preserved for the younger generations.

In 1851 she was wife of Mr. Blackburn of the Klamath River ferry mentioned in the foregoing article, and it seems they both left the Klamath region later and took up their residence in San Bernardino where he died. "John Daggett"[1]

Raynes stated that he "left Blackburn and his brave wife, and hurried back to the little ranch, and told the story. Then with two others, Bill Little and Bill Young, I pushed on through to Trinidad to give the alarm and secure assistance, while the other members of the pack train stayed at Blackburn's to await our return." Raynes returned with twelve men who took revenge on local Indians.

INDIAN MURDERS AT MARTIN'S FERRY

The most dramatic account of the "Blackburn Massacre" appeared in a history of Humboldt County. It gave special emphasis to the bullet-molding story and described the revenge of the whites in florid Victorian prose.

In 1851, Blackburn, his wife and three men were in charge of the above ferry. Blackburn and his wife occupied a small shake shanty on the river bank. One day Mrs. Blackburn, a noble woman of the brave pioneer class that have been led by love to follow the footsteps of their idol into the very heart of the wilderness, noticed that the stock of bullets had become exhausted. She immediately moulded a large quantity, and by this prudent act and afterward her heroic conduct, saved the lives of herself and her husband that self-same night. No trouble had been experienced from the Indians for some time by the occupants of the ferry-house, and they retired to rest that night with little thought of the bloody deed the savages proposed to commit. As the shadows of night blended into a universal gloom, the Indians gathered in the forest about the abode of their intended victims, and waited until their eyes were closed in peaceful slumber and the place was wrapped in a mantle of silence.

When the night had sufficiently advanced to assure them that their victims were asleep and that they would not be inter-

---

[1] "John Daggett, Blackburn, Mrs. Isaac Hawley—Part in Indian Fight at Blackburn Ferry." This article, from an unidentified magazine or newspaper, is preserved in Daggett's Scrapbook, vol. 4:12, California State Library Collections.

rupted in their hellish deed by the appearance of belated travelers, they crept stealthily to the tent where the three men lay sleeping, and commenced the work of death. Two of the men were killed instantly, while the third sprang to his feet and rushed from the tent with a cry for help. He had taken but a few steps when the cry was hushed upon his lips, and he fell to the ground dead beneath the knives of his pursuers. The agonizing cry of the wounded man awoke from their slumbers the occupants of the ferry house, who knew too well its dreadful import. Hastily barricading themselves, they prepared for defense. Their arms consisted of two rifles and a revolver, and with these, Thomas L. Blackburn kept the savages at bay through the long and terrible night, his noble wife reloading the weapons as fast as he discharged them.

With the coming of morning there appeared on the opposite bank of the river A. E. Raynes, William Young, and William Little, who had stayed that night at a cabin a few miles distant, and had come at the request of the occupants to see if Blackburn had any extra arms, as they feared an attack by the Indians. Blackburn made his appearance from the house and greeted them with a sad voice, saying: "I'm glad to see you boys; they are all killed but myself and wife." When he had ferried them across the stream they went to the scene of the conflict.

Sad Meeting of Father and Son

They saw a body lying about 100 yards from the house and hastened to the spot. When the body of the dead man was turned so they could see his face, Blackburn sprang back with the cry: "Great God, it is my father, Anthony Blackburn," and so it was, killed by the heartless savages in sight of the cabin of his son, whom he had not seen for ten years. . . . The old gentleman had accompanied a pack train from Trinidad, and when they encamped for the night some ten miles from the ferry, he pushed on alone, and had fallen before the knives of the Indians that lay concealed in the forest, awaiting the time for the attack upon the cabin.[2]

[2.] *History of Humboldt County*, 152–53. The *History of Siskiyou County, California*, 126–27, repeated the story verbatim. See also, Irvine, *History of Humboldt County, California, with Biographical Sketches*, 66.

Sources

O nly a very naive scholar would attempt to edit Abner Blackburn's memoir. It covers so much territory that very credible historians have taken the narrative for a forgery, and searching for corroborative evidence of Blackburn's stories of the fur trade, early Mormonism, the Mexican War, the overland emigration, and the gold rush constituted a superlative challenge. Unraveling the narrative's mysteries required much hard—but very rewarding—detective work. Since many of the events described were obscure and Blackburn's version of events often ran against the established historical grain, the task demanded extensive documentary and archival research. Yet the narrative's contrariness had its own rewards, since contemporary journals, newspapers, and documents often confirmed Blackburn's tale.

This bibliography cites first editions, but most books have been reprinted and some are available in later editions. Archival manuscript number citations refer to numbers current in 1992, and may change as collections are reclassified.

Blackburn's memoirs have had some impact on western history and already have a limited publishing history. A California high school student, Michael Witt, made a typescript of the Blackburn narrative as a history class project in 1966. Witt lived in Red Bluff and probably had access to a copy of the Blackburn-Corby typescript. In 1990, a primitive heat-transfer copy of Witt's paper was the only version of the narrative in the LDS Archives. Kate B. Carter of the Daughters of Utah Pioneers published a surprising selection from Blackburn in 1968, in the volume of *Our Pioneer Heritage* devoted to the Mormon Battalion. No documentation was provided with the section, but Carter probably used the Witt typescript as her source. Leonard J. Arrington, *The Mormons in Nevada* (Las Vegas, Nevada: Las Vegas Sun, 1979) devoted a chapter to a summary of Blackburn's adventures. Arrington made several unfortunate errors, including killing off Blackburn in 1894. J. Kenneth Davies, *Mormon Gold: The Story of California's Mormon Argonauts* (Salt Lake City: Olympus Publishing Company, 1984), contained a summary of the Blackburn narrative. While Davies did much pioneering work in reinterpreting Mormon attitudes toward the gold rush and provided good documentary background on Blackburn's story, his book is incorrect in many details. For example, he inexplicably failed to connect Anthony and Abner Blackburn as father and son. Blackburn was also quoted in histories of the Mormon conflict in Missouri and in accounts of the settling and exploration of Utah and Nevada. He even made a brief appearance in Boyd Gibbons, "The Itch to Move West," *National Geographic* 170 (August 1986).

The Archives of the Historical Department of the Church of Jesus Christ of Latter-day Saints (cited as LDS Archives) contain an immense amount of material closely related to the narrative, including contemporary letters, journals, documents, and memoirs. The Journal History is a chronological collection of letters, newspaper clippings, magazine articles, reminiscences, journal entries, and miscellaneous Mormon documents and contains information of special relevance to Blackburn's narrative. A xerox copy is available at the Library Division of the Church Historical Department, the Church of Jesus Christ of Latter-day Saints, Salt Lake City, Utah (cited as LDS Library).

Herbert Hamlin perpetuated a vast amount of misinformation about Abner Blackburn, which complicated the process of distinguishing Blackburn myth from history. Hamlin's magazine was published as the *Pony Express Courier* from 1935 to May 1944 and, as *The Pony Express*, from June 1944 to June 1978, with sections of the Blackburn memoir published during 1948 and 1949. The July 1948 issue introduced Hamlin's abortive effort to publish the "diary," and included photographs of Charles and Jesse Blackburn, Blanche Blackburn, and the "late Mrs. Nettie West." Hamlin acknowledged that he was "indebted to Jesse O. Blackburn, Nettie Blackburn West, and Blanche Blackburn Corby for stories and testimonies," and then published an article that seems to prove he had never read the entire narrative. Nonetheless, the loss of Hamlin's photograph and manuscript collection, which included these Blackburn family photographs and interviews, may be as significant as the loss of the holographic manuscript of Blackburn's narrative.

Family histories provided much information about the Blackburns. They included William J. and Lucy E. Burns, "Jehu Blackburn, Utah Pioneer of 1847," LDS, Library; Evelyn D. Gibson, *Blackburn and Allied Descendants of John Blackburn, Sr.* (Lincoln, Nebraska: Anchor Printing Company, 1978); and Paul E. Gallagher, "Bainbridge Family History" (unpublished manuscript, ca. 1966, in the possession of Amy Hoffman). Gibson's data was largely taken from Ruth Towle Blackburn, wife of Abner Blackburn's grandson Chapman, while Paul Gallagher was a grandson-in-law of Blackburn's sister Eliza Bainbridge. Gallagher and Ruth Blackburn engaged in an interesting correspondence (now in the possession of Amy Gallagher Hoffman), which included this story in a 10 February 1965 Ruth Blackburn letter.

> I was at the (California Historical Society) Library last summer hunting for another Journal that I know was written by Abner because I read it and the one we received years later was just not the same. It starts out "I was named Anthony Abner Blackburn but was always called Abner because there were so many Anthonys." The copy of the one I have starts; "My parents were born in Bedford Co. . . ."

This is a direct statement that Mrs. Blackburn actually read an alternate "journal," perhaps a contemporary account that Abner Blackburn used to compose his memoir. No one would be more delighted than the present editor to see such a document, but unfortunately this letter raises more questions than it answers. Where and when did Ruth Blackburn see this document, and why was she looking for it in San Francisco? A close examination of the rest of the letter reveals several errors of fact and much speculation. Finally, the assertion that Blackburn's *real* name was Anthony Abner Blackburn is apparently a family tradition impossible to verify in the documentary record. Without explanation or attribution, Herb Hamlin wrote in *The Pony Express* that Blackburn's full name was Anthony Abner Blackburn, but Hamlin also dated Blackburn's death as taking place in 1908, an error he seems to have picked up in his 1941 interview with Blanche Corby. No documents contemporary with Blackburn himself, however, support the belief that Blackburn's first name was Anthony. The Robert S. Bliss diary of 1848, San Bernardino tithing records from the 1850s, and Blackburn's headstone all use the middle initial L, while *Abner Levi* is the name reported in his obituaries. Amy Gallagher Hoffman argues that Blackburn took the name Abner when he joined the Mormon church, but this was not Mormon practice.

This conundrum points to a fundamental problem evaluating the interaction between Herbert Hamlin and the Blackburn family. The record is now so confused that it is impossible to tell whether Hamlin got his misinformation from the family, or if Hamlin's misinterpretations corrupted the family tradition.

Blackburn's granddaughter Fredricka Blackburn Grohs wrote Gallagher on 22 November 1968, "Blanche Corby gave me some priceless Blackburn heirlooms just before she died. Many of these include papers, clippings and partial histories of various members of the Blackburn family. . . . I am framing and displaying many of these heirloom items in my home." Grohs left many of the Blanche Corby artifacts with Barbara and Amy Blackburn of Prescott, Arizona, before her death, and the sources she described in her letter to Paul Gallagher may eventually turn up in their possession.

Voyle L. and Lillian S. Munson synthesized and generally corrected much of this family information in their biography of Blackburn's uncle, *A Gift of Faith: Elias Hicks Blackburn* (Eureka, Utah: Basin/Plateau Press, 1991). Blackburn's nephew, Daniel Fabun, wrote a legend-soaked reminiscence for the San Bernardino Pioneer Society's newsletter, "Abner Blackburn, Pioneer, Scout, Indian Fighter," *Pioneer Cabin News* (October 1950).

Important manuscript sources for the Blackburn narrative are in the Robert A. Allen Papers at the Nevada Historical Society, which include two photostatic copies of the narrative manuscript, Dale Morgan's 1942 annotations, Herb Hamlin's December 1941 interview with Blanche Blackburn Corby, and correspondence between Allen and Hamlin; the Elias Hicks Blackburn Collection, MS B-61, and "The Book of Pioneers" of 1897, at the Utah State Historical Society, which contain the only surviving holographic copies of Blackburn's handwriting; and the Ephraim Morse Manuscript Collection's Hester Blackburn to A. J. Chase letter at California State Library.

Two manuscript journals by Blackburn's father-in-law, John Harris, have survived. "A Copy of the Diary of John Harris," in the Feldheym Library, San Bernardino, California, is an anonymous typescript prepared by the John Harris–Lovina Eiler Family Association and donated to the library by Karen Purvis. (The association newsletter indicated that Mrs. Dale Brown of Phoenix, Arizona, made the typescript.) The "Gold Mission Journal, 1855–56" survives in a typescript, in possession of Amy Blackburn, and a xerox copy of the original, in the LDS Archives. These documents describe Blackburn family events that are documented in no other source.

Several general works have been of much use in identifying individuals named in the narrative. The great Hubert Howe Bancroft histories, *History of California*, 7 vols. (San Francisco: The History Company, 1886–1890); *History of Utah, 1540–1886* (San Francisco: The History Company, 1889); and *History of Nevada, Colorado, and Wyoming, 1540–1888* (San Francisco: The History Company, 1890) are classics, and the "Pioneer Register and Index" in volumes 2–5 of *History of California* has a wealth of information on early Californians, as does John A. Sutter, *New Helvetia Diary* (San Francisco: The Grabhorn Press, 1939). The vast literature of the Daughters of Utah Pioneers is full of family data about pioneer Mormons, but it is honeycombed with errors and is often bowdlerized. Daughters of Utah Pioneers publications include Kate B. Carter, *Heart Throbs of the West*, 12 vols. (Salt Lake City: Daughters of Utah Pioneers, 1939–1951); *Treasures of Pioneer History*, 6 vols. (Salt Lake City: Daughters of Utah Pioneers, 1952–1957); *Our Pioneer Heritage*, 20 vols. (Salt Lake City: Daughters of Utah Pioneers,

1958–1977); and Daughters of Utah Pioneers Lesson Committee, *An Enduring Legacy*, 12 vols. (Salt Lake City: Daughters of Utah Pioneers, 1978–1989).

Other sources used to identify individuals include Davis Bitton, *Guide to Mormon Diaries and Autobiographies* (Provo, Utah: Brigham Young University Press, 1977); Frank Esshom's "mug book," *Pioneers and Prominent Men of Utah* (Salt Lake City: Utah Pioneers Book Publishing Company, 1913); Andrew Jenson, *Latter-Day Saint Biographical Encyclopedia*, 4 vols. (Salt Lake City: Andrew Jenson History Company, 1901); Carl V. Larson, *A Data Base of the Mormon Battalion* (Providence, Utah: Kieth W. Watkins and Sons Printing, 1987); Brigham H. Roberts, ed., *History of the Church*, 7 vols. (Salt Lake City: Deseret News, 1932); and Dan L. Thrapp, *Encyclopedia of Frontier Biography*, 3 vols. (Glendale, California: The Arthur H. Clarke Company, 1988).

LeRoy R. Hafen, ed., *The Mountain Men and the Fur Trade of the Far West*, 10 vols. (Glendale, California: The Arthur H. Clarke Company, 1965–1972); and Dale L. Morgan and Eleanor Towles Harris, eds., *The Rocky Mountain Journals of William Marshall Anderson: The West in 1834* (San Marino, California: The Huntington Library, 1967) has Morgan's wonderful "Galaxy of Mountain Men." Carl I. Wheat, *Mapping the Transmississippi West*, 5 vols. (San Francisco: The Institute of Historical Cartography, 1957–1963) is the classic reference work on early maps of the West.

James B. Allen and Glen M. Leonard, *The Story of the Latter-day Saints* (Salt Lake City: Deseret Book Company, 1976), is a standard Mormon history. Three recent histories, Richard E. Bennett, *The Mormons at the Missouri* (Norman: University of Oklahoma Press, 1987); Peter L. Crawley, ed., *The Essential Parley P. Pratt* (Salt Lake City: Signature Books, 1990); and Stephen C. LeSueur, *The 1838 Mormon War in Missouri* (Columbia: University of Missouri Press, 1987) contain much information about the early church. Alphonso Wetmore, *Gazetteer of the State of Missouri* (St. Louis: C. Keemle, 1837), describes the bitterness of contemporary attitudes toward the Mormons.

Accounts of the Haun's Mill Massacre can be found in Alma Blair, "The Haun's Mill Massacre," *BYU Studies* 13 (Autumn 1972); Brigham H. Roberts, *The Missouri Persecutions* (Salt Lake City: George Q. Cannon and Sons Co., Publishers, 1900); and Pearl Wilcox, *The Latter Day Saints on the Missouri Frontier* (Independence, Missouri: 1972). Olive Ames, wife of Blackburn's neighbor Ellis Eames, left an account of the massacre published in *The History of the Reorganized Church of Jesus Christ of Latter Day Saints*, 8 vols. (Independence, Missouri: Herald House, 1967–1976), 2:234–37, but she did not mention her Blackburn neighbors.

The best account of Joseph Smith's life remains Fawn Brodie, *No Man Knows My History: The Life of Joseph Smith the Mormon Prophet* (New York:

Alfred A. Knopf, 1945), but Donna Hill, *Joseph Smith: The First Mormon* (Garden City, New York: Doubleday and Company, 1977), provides a Mormon view of his life. Linda King Newell and Valeen Tippitts Avery, *Mormon Enigma: Emma Hale Smith* (Garden City, New York: Doubleday and Company, 1984), discuss the Prophet from his wife's perspective. Leonard J. Arrington has written the best Mormon biography of *Brigham Young: American Moses* (New York: Alfred A. Knopf, 1985), but a comprehensive biography of Young from a non-Mormon perspective remains to be written.

For accounts of Nauvoo, see Robert Bruce Flanders, *Nauvoo: Kingdom on the Mississippi* (Urbana: University of Illinois Press, 1975), and Samuel W. Taylor, *Nightfall at Nauvoo* (New York: The Macmillan Company, 1971).

In addition to the typescript translation of the original French Joseph Sire Journal at the Missouri Historical Society, information on steamboating, the voyage of the *General Brooke*, and the early fur trade is taken from Hiram Martin Chittenden, *History of Early Steamboat Navigation on the Missouri River: Life and Adventures of Joseph LaBarge, Pioneer Navigator and Indian Trader for Fifty Years Identified with the Commerce of the Missouri Valley*, 2 vols. (New York: 1903); Louis C. Hunter, *Steamboats on the Western Rivers: An Economic and Technological History* (Cambridge: Harvard University Press, 1949); James T. Lloyd, *Lloyd's Steamboat Directory, and Disasters on the Western Waters* (Cincinnati: James T. Lloyd and Co., 1856); Donald Jackson, *Voyages of the Steamboat Yellow Stone* (New York: Ticknor and Fields, 1985); and John E. Sunder, *The Fur Trade on the Upper Missouri, 1840–1865* (Norman: University of Oklahoma Press, 1966).

A comprehensive modern history of the Mormon Battalion does not exist, but John Yurtinus, "A Ram in the Thicket: The Mormon Battalion in the Mexican War" (Ph.D. diss., Brigham Young University, 1975), makes a good start. Yurtinus has published "Images of Early California: Mormon Battalion Soldiers' Reflections during the War with Mexico," *Historical Society of Southern California Quarterly* (Spring 1981). The classic (though not concise) history is Daniel Tyler, *A Concise History of the Mormon Battalion in the Mexican War, 1846–1847* (Salt Lake City, 1881). Brigham H. Roberts, *The Mormon Battalion, Its History and Achievements* (Salt Lake City: The Deseret News, 1919) is a concise history. Charles S. Peterson, John F. Yurtinus, David E. Atkinson, and A. Kent Powell, *Mormon Battalion Trail Guide* (Utah State Historical Society, 1972), identify battalion trail sites, while David L. Bigler, ed., *The Gold Discovery Journal of Azariah Smith* (Salt Lake City: University of Utah Press, 1990), is by far the best account of this unique American military organization.

The number of firsthand Mormon Battalion journals and reminiscences is truly astounding. Milo Milton Qauife, ed., *The Diary of James K. Polk during His Presidency, 1845 to 1849*, 4 vols. (Chicago: A. C. McClurg and Co., 1910), amplifies the political background. *The Conquest of New Mexico and California* (New York: G. P. Putnam's Sons, 1878), is commander Phillip St. George Cooke's reminiscence. Published journals include Ralph Paul Bieber, ed., "Cooke's Journal of the March of the Mormon Battalion, 1846–1847" in *Exploring Southwestern Trails, 1846–1854* (Glendale, California: Arthur H. Clarke Company, 1938); J. Cecil Alter, "The Journal of Robert S. Bliss," *Utah Historical Quarterly* 4 (October 1931); Everett L. Cooley, "The Robert S. Bliss Journal," *Utah Historical Quarterly* 27 (October 1959); Frank Alfred Golder, Thomas A. Bailey and J. Lyman Smith, *The March of the Mormon Battalion from Council Bluffs to California, Taken from the Journal of Henry Standage* (New York: The Century Co., 1928); Erwin G. Gudde, *Bigler's Chronicle of the West: The Conquest of California, Discovery of Gold, and Mormon Settlement as Reflected in Henry William Bigler's Diaries* (Berkeley: University of California Press, 1962); and Wanda Wood, "John W. Hess, With the Mormon Battalion," *Utah Historical Quarterly* 4 (April 1931).

Manuscripts of Battalion journals consulted include Robert S. Bliss, "Journal," Utah State Archives; Henry G. Boyle, "Reminiscences and Diaries, 1846–1888," MS 1911, LDS Archives; James Allen Scott, "Diaries," MS 1398/1–2, LDS Archives; Joseph Skeen, "Reminiscences and Diary," 1846 July–1847 May, MS 1551, LDS Archives; Joel Judkins Terrell, "Diary, 1846–1847," MS 1672, LDS Archives; Hayward Thomas, "Recollections and Journal, 1848–51," MS 1434, LDS Archives; and George Deliverance Wilson, "Journal," MS A 1005, Utah State Historical Society.

Two sources exist for John Steele's accounts: "Reminiscences and Journals, 1846–1898," MS 1847, LDS Archives, and "Extracts from the Journal of John Steele," *Utah Historical Quarterly* 6 (January 1933). Steele's published journal is actually a memoir, edited by J. Cecil Alter, who included asterisks to denote "omissions of slight historical interest." No manuscript source is available to evaluate these omissions. The memoir was derived from Steele's actual journal, now in in the LDS Archives, from which it differs in substantial detail. Quotations from Steele's memoir (cited as "Extracts") are from the *Utah Historical Quarterly*, while quotations from the journal (cited as "Journal") are from the LDS Archives.

"Mormon Battalion Correspondence Collection, 1846," MS 2070, LDS Archives, is a remarkable collection of letters, mostly written from the Mormon fort at El Pueblo. James Scott's Christmas 1846 letter to his cousin, R. A. H. McCorkle, provided one of the best descriptions of the location of the Mormon settlement available—though he omitted an exact unit of measure following "quarter." From other sources, it is reasonable to assume that Scott meant "mile." For a discussion of problems locating the Mormon fort, see LeRoy R. Hafen and Frank M. Young, "The Mormon Settlement at Pueblo, Colorado, During the Mexican War," *Colorado Magazine* 9 (July

1932); and Janet LeCompte, *Pueblo, Hardscrabble, Greenhorn: The Upper Arkansas, 1832–1856* (Norman: University of Oklahoma Press, 1978). LeCompte wrote, "Somewhere in the great rockbound archive of the Church of Jesus Christ of Latter Day Saints at Salt Lake there must be a description of the location of Mormon Town—may it soon come to light!" Another overlooked source is Julia Farnsworth, "Scrap Book for the Daughters of the Mormon Battalion for the Years 1905–22," Mormon Battalion Monument Committee, Newspaper Clippings, B100J3, Utah State Archives. Two documents of interest are "Mormon Battalion, James Brown Detached Company, Descriptive Roll, 1847"; and "Soldiers' Pay Record, 1847," MS 9126:2, LDS Archives.

Other sources related to the sick detachment's winter at El Pueblo and the settlement's remarkable collection of mountaineers are Harvey Lewis Carter, *Dear Old Kit* (Norman: University of Oklahoma Press, 1968); Howard Louis Conrad, *Uncle Dick Wootton: The Pioneer Frontiersman of the Rocky Mountain Region* (Chicago: W. E. Dibble and Co., 1890); Leroy R. Hafen, "Mountain Men Who Came to California," L. A. Westerners Brand Book 5 (1953); Andrew Jenson, "Manuscript History of Pueblo, Colorado," MS 4029/3, LDS Archives; Francis Parkman, *The California and Oregon Trail: Being Sketches of Prairie and Rocky Mountain Life* (New York: George P. Putnam, 1849); and Arthur Woodward, "Jim Waters," Keepsake of the Los Angeles Corral of Westerners, Publication No. 23, 1954. The works of George Frederick Ruxton, *Life in the Far West* (Edinburgh: William Blackwood and Sons, 1849), and *Ruxton of the Rockies* (Norman: University of Oklahoma Press, 1950), are available in excellent editions by LeRoy R. Hafen. Dean A. Painter supplied the editor with information from the 1869 diary of John Brown, Jr., (3d Memoranda, 9, Sherman Library, Corona del Mar, California), which provided the remarkable birth and death dates of "Old Rube" Herring.

Finally, the Pension Files, National Archives, Mexican Department, contain information on many battalion veterans. Blackburn's pension file, No. 9150, is full of gruesome details about his old age.

Descriptions of the 1847 Mormon pioneer trek are available in Thomas Bullock, "Journals," MS 1385:1–4, LDS Archives; Howard Egan, *Pioneering the West, 1846 to 1878* (Richmond, Utah: Howard R. Egan Estate, 1917); Richard K. Hanks, "Eph Hanks, Pioneer Scout" (Masters thesis, Brigham Young University, 1973); Sidney Alvarus Hanks and Ephraim K. Hanks, *Scouting for the Mormons on the Great Frontier* (Salt Lake City: Deseret News Press, 1948); Edward and Ruth S. Jacob, eds., *The Record of Norton Jacob* (Salt Lake City: The Norton Jacob Family Association, 1949); Andrew Jenson, "Church Emigration Book 1830–1848," Vol. 1, LDS Archives, and "Day by Day with the Utah Pioneers 1847," *Salt Lake Tribune* (June, July

1947); William L. Knecht and Peter L. Crawley, eds., *History of Brigham Young* (Berkeley: MassCal Associates, 1964); Hal Knight and Stanley B. Kimball, *111 Days to Zion* (Salt Lake City: Deseret Press, 1978); and Wallace Stegner, *The Gathering of Zion* (New York: McGraw Hill Book Company, 1964).

Horace Kimball Whitney's "Journal," LDS Archives, MS 1616, is an unexplored gold-mine of information on the 1847 Mormon pioneer company, demonstrating that new material can be found on the most shopworn subjects.

Trying to determine the veracity of "Lou Devon's Narrative" has been far and away the most difficult challenge posed by the Blackburn narrative. Excellent source accounts on the Mandan tribe in the early 1830s include George Catlin, *Letters and Notes on the Manners, Customs, and Conditions of the North American Indians*, (London: 1841), and *O-kee-pa: A Religious Ceremony and Other Customs of the Mandans* (London: 1867); and Alexander Philip Maximilian, Prince of Weid, *Travels in the Interior of North America, 1832–1834* (London: Ackerman and Co., 1843), republished as Reuben Gold Thwaites, ed., *Early Western Travels, 1748–1846*, 34 vols. (Cleveland: Arthur H. Clarke Company, 1906), vols. 22–24. For a summary of Maximilian's expedition, see Joseph C. Porter, "Marvelous Figures, Astonished Travelers," *Montana* 41 (Autumn 1991).

Annie Heloise Abel, ed., *Chardon's Journal at Fort Clark, 1834–1839: Descriptive of Life on the Upper Missouri; of a Fur Trader's Experiences among the Mandans, Gros Ventres, and Their Neighbors; of the Ravages of the Small Pox Epidemic of 1837* (Pierre: Department of History, South Dakota, 1932), is far and away the best source on the epidemic of 1837 and the years immediately thereafter. Michael K. Trimble, "Epidemiology on the Northern Plains: A Cultural Perspective," (Ph.D. diss.: University of Missouri–Columbia, 1985), closely tracks the progress of the epidemic and analyzes Chardon's information. Chardon gave an interesting account of the disaster to naturalist John James Audubon in 1843, which is available in Maria R. Audubon, ed., *Audubon and His Journals*, 2 vols. (New York: Charles Scribner's Sons, 1897). J. N. B. Hewitt, *The Journal of Rudolph Friederich Kurz: An Account of His Experiences among Fur Traders and American Indians on the Mississippi and Upper Missouri Rivers during the Years 1846 to 1852* (Washington: United States Government Printing Office, 1937), and Henry A. Boller's unvarnished *Missouri River Fur Trader: Letters and Journals* (Bismarck: The State Historical Society of North Dakota, 1966), are eyewitness accounts of the Mandans after the period described in Devon's narrative.

Martha Warren Beckwith's *Mandan and Hidatsa Tales* (Poughkeepsie, New York: Vassar College, 1934), and *Myths and Ceremonies of the Mandan and Hidatsa* (Poughkeepsie, New York: Vassar College, 1932), provided evidence that there might be reality behind Lou Devon's story.

The Minnesota Historical Society microfilms of Gilbert Livingston Wilson's 1913 and 1918 reports included two versions of the Butterfly winter count and Buffalo-Bird Woman's commentary on it. Clark Wissler of the American Museum of Natural History employed Wilson, a Presbyterian minister, to gather ethnological material, and Wilson delivered annual reports to the museum between 1908 and 1918. Wilson's papers include a notebook by his artist brother, Frederick N. Wilson. This collection provides a wealth of information about Mandan and Hidatsa survival, but shows how difficult it can be to interpret such data. Wilson seems to have had limited historical knowledge (or even interest) about the Mandans and Hidatsas, but his informants painted a detailed picture of an active tribe of hunters and warriors. The 1837 smallpox epidemic seemed to have had surprisingly limited effects on tribal culture and traditions. Butterfly's winter count described verifiable events, like the disappearance and annihilation of thirty Mandan warriors in 1836. These accounts provide support for a belief that some of the Mandans and Hidatsas abandoned their traditional homeland in 1839 and moved to the "Crow Country" for at least two winters. Wilson's interpretation of his Hidatsa informants' geographical names, however, is open to question; for example, there is no Rose River in North Dakota. This study used vols. 13, 14, 16, 22, which are the "Hidatsa-Mandan Reports—Fort Berthold Reservation" for 1913, 1914, and 1918.

Anthropologists dominate Mandan scholarship. The classic anthropological accounts are G. F. Will and H. J. Spinden, *The Mandans, A Study of Their Culture, Archaeology and Language* (Cambridge, Massachusetts: Peabody Museum of American Archaeology and Ethnology, 1906); Robert H. Lowie, "Notes on the Social Organization and Customs of the Mandan, Hidatsa, and Crow Indians," *Anthropological Papers of the American Museum of Natural History* 21, Part 1 (1917); and Alfred W. Bowers, *Mandan Social and Ceremonial Organization* (Chicago: University of Chicago Press, 1950). Gilbert Livingston Wilson, "Hidatsa Eagle Trapping," *Anthropological Papers of the American Museum of Natural History* 30 (1929), puts Lou Devon's eagle hunt into a historical perspective. More recent works include Edward M. Bruner's essay on the Mandans in Edward W. Spicer, ed., *Perspectives in American Indian Culture Change* (Chicago: University of Chicago Press, 1961); John C. Ewers, *Indian Life on the Upper Missouri* (Norman: University of Oklahoma Press, 1968); and W. R. Wood, ed., *The Selected Writings of Donald J. Lehmer* (Lincoln: J and L Reprint, 1977).

Roy W. Meyer, *The Village Indians of the Upper Missouri: The Mandans, Hidatsas, and Arikaras* (Lincoln: University of Nebraska Press, 1977), and Joseph H. Cash and Gerald W. Wolff, *The Three Affiliated Tribes: Mandan, Arikara, and Hidatsa* (Phoenix, Arizona: Indian Tribal Series, 1974), are secondary sources on the Three Tribes. General works include Edward S.

Curtis, *The North American Indian*, 20 vols. (Seattle: E. S. Curtis, 1907–1930), and John R. Swanton, *The Indian Tribes of North America* (Washington: Smithsonian Institution Press, 1984). Brigham D. Madsen, *The Northern Shoshoni* (Caldwell, Idaho: The Caxton Printers, Ltd., 1980), is an excellent history of the tribe.

The number of captivity narratives is shown by the Garland Library of Narratives of North American Indian Captivities, selected by Wilcomb E. Washburn of the Smithsonian Institution. The series includes 311 narratives in 111 volumes. For surveys of captivity narratives, see Richard VanDerBeets, *Held Captive by Indians: Selected Narratives, 1642–1836* (Knoxville: University of Tennessee Press, 1973), and *The Indian Captivity Narrative: An American Genre* (New York: University Press of America, 1984); and James Levernier and Hennig Cohen, eds., *The Indians and Their Captives* (Westport, Connecticut: Greenwood Press, 1977). *A Narrative of the Captivity and Adventures of John Tanner (U.S. Interpreter at the Sault de Ste. Marie,) during Thirty Years Residence among the Indians in the Interior of North America. Prepared for the Press by Edwin James, M.D.* (New York: G. and C. and H. Carvill, 1830), has striking parallels to Devon's story.

Dated descriptions of Fort Hall are available in Richard G. Beidleman, "Nathaniel Wyeth's Fort Hall," *Oregon Historical Quarterly* 58 (September 1957); Louis Grant, "Fort Hall under the Hudson's Bay Company, 1837–1856," *Oregon Historical Quarterly* 41 (March 1940); and T. C. Elliott, "Richard ('Captain Johnny') Grant," *Oregon Historical Quarterly* 36 (March 1936). Note, however, that none of his contemporaries ever called Richard Grant "Captain Johnny."

Lou Devon still eludes positive identification, despite a search of the records of the Columbia District in the Hudson's Bay Company Archives in the Provincial Archives of Manitoba, a hunt through George P. Hammond, ed., *The Larkin Papers*, 11 vols. (Berkeley: The University of California Press, 1951–68), and a survey of 1850, 1860, 1870, and 1880 U.S. census records for California, Washington, Oregon, and Montana. Harriet Duncan Munnick, *Catholic Church Records of the Pacific Northwest*, 7 vols. (St Paul, Oregon: French Prairie Press, 1987), contains much information on several Snake Country men, but little on the most likely candidates, Louis Aimé Daunais and Francois Proulx. Elizabeth Arthur, ed., *Thunder Bay District 1821–1892* (Toronto: University of Toronto Press, 1973); "Original Journal of James H. Chambers, Fort Sarpy," *Contributions to the Historical Society of Montana* 10 (1940); and Raymond W. Settle, ed., *The March of the Mounted Riflemen* (Glendale: Arthur H. Clarke Company, 1940), suggested some intriguing possibilities. A wealth of information about the activities of the Honorable Company in the West can be found in Hartwell Bowsfield, ed., *Fort Victoria Letters, 1846–1851* (Winnipeg: Hudson's Bay Record Society, 1979); E. E.

Rich, ed., *McLoughlin's Fort Vancouver Letters, Third Series 1844–46* (London: Hudson's Bay Record Society, 1944); William R. Sampson, ed., *John McLoughlin's Business Correspondence, 1847–48* (Seattle: University of Washington Press, 1973); and Glyndwr Williams, *Hudson's Bay Miscellany 1670–1870* (Winnipeg: Hudson's Bay Record Society, 1975). Two works by Richard H. Dillon, *Fools' Gold: The Decline and Fall of Captain John Sutter of California* (New York: Coward-McCann, 1967), and *Siskiyou Trail: The Hudson's Bay Company Route to California* (New York: McGraw-Hill, 1975), give an excellent analysis of the Honorable Company's activities in California.

Two journals demonstrate the fickleness of the historical record. "Alexander Lattie's Fort George Journal, 1846," *Oregon Historical Quarterly*, 54 (September 1963) begins the day the bark *Vancouver* crossed the Columbia Bar, possibly carrying Lou Devon to California. Thomas Lowe, "Private Journal kept at Fort Vancouver on the Columbia River, 1843–1850," Provincial Archives of British Columbia, Typescript E/B/L 95 A, is the record of a young Hudson's Bay Company clerk and is full of colorful detail. Lowe would probably have commented on the arrival of Lou Devon on the *Janet* in November 1847 (he commented on the ship's imminent departure on 30 November), but Lowe accompanied that year's York Factory Express and did not return to Fort Vancouver until 21 November.

Finally, George Louis Curtis, "The Last Lodges of the Mandan," *Harper's Weekly* 33 (30 March 1889), suggests a possible source for Devon's story: it was published just two weeks after a draft of Blackburn's memoirs was read to the Society of Pioneers.

Sources related to the Brown-Brannan journey to California include Anonymous, *A Sketch of the Life of Com. Robert F. Stockton* (New York: Derby and Jackson, 1856), and Vardis Fisher, *Idaho, A Guide in Word and Picture* (Caldwell, Idaho: The Caxton Printers, 1937). Douglas C. McMurtrie, ed., *Overland to California in 1847: Letters written en route to California, West from Independence, Missouri, to the Editor of the Joliet Signal by Charles Ingersol* (Chicago: Black Cat Press, 1937), and Charles L. Camp, "William Alexander Trubody and the Overland Pioneers of 1847," *California Historical Society Quarterly* 16 (June 1937), contain almost everything that is known about the 1847 California Trail companies. Bruce R. Hawkins and David B. Madsen, *Excavation of the Donner-Reed Wagons: Historic Archaeology along the Hastings Cutoff* (Salt Lake City: University of Utah Press, 1990), describe the site where Brown's company burned the Donner-Reed wagons. For accounts of the Donner-Reed party, see George R. Stewart, *Ordeal by Hunger* (New York: Henry Holt and Company, 1936), and J. Roderic Korns, *West from Fort Bridger: The Pioneering of the Emigrant Trails across Utah, 1846–1850* (Salt Lake City: Utah State Historical Society, 1951; printed as *Utah Historical Quarterly* 19).

Sam Brannan has long eluded a competent biographer: Abner Blackburn captured his spirit as well as anyone has since. Dismal attempts include Paul Bailey, *Sam Brannan and the California Mormons* (Los Angeles: Westernlore Press, 1943); James A. B. Scherer, *The First Forty-Niner and the Story of the Golden Tea-Caddy* (New York: Minton, Balch and Company, 1925); and Reva Scott, *Samuel Brannan and the Golden Fleece* (New York: The Macmillan Company, 1944). Even Eugene E. Campbell, "The Apostasy of Samuel Brannan," *Utah Historical Quarterly* 27 (April 1959), repeated myths Brannan promoted himself. However, Lorin Hansen, "Voyage of the *Brooklyn*," *Dialogue: A Journal of Mormon Thought* 21 (Autumn 1988), has written an admirable account of the 1846 Mormon voyage to California. Brannan's for- mer business partner, William Glover, *The Mormons in California* (Los Angeles: Glen Dawson, 1954), has little good to say about his former associ- ate, and neither does James Skinner, "Autobiography," MS 6587, LDS Archives.

Material on the California missions is taken from Stanley Young, *The Missions of California* (San Francisco: Chronicle Books, 1988), and Zephyrin Englehardt, *The Missions and Missionaries of California*, 4 vols. (San Francisco: The James H. Barry Company, 1915).

Source accounts of overland trails include Robert H. Becker, ed., *Thomas Christy's Road across the Plains* (Denver: Old West Publishing Company, 1969); Edwin Bryant, *What I Saw in California* (New York: D. Appleton & Co., 1848); Charles Camp, *James Clyman, Frontiersman* (Portland, Oregon: The Champoeg Press, 1960); John C. Frémont, *Report of the Exploring Expedition to the Rocky Mountains in the Year 1842 and Oregon and Northern California, 1843–44* (Washington: Gales and Seaton, 1845), reprinted as Allan Nevins, ed., *Narratives of Exploration and Adventure by John Charles Frémont* (New York: Longmans, Green and Co., 1956); Sarah Winnemucca Hopkins, *Life among the Piutes: Their Wrongs and Claims* (Boston: Cupples, Upham and Co., and the author, 1883); Charles Kelly, "The Journal of Robert Chalmers," *Utah Historical Quarterly* 20 (January 1952); Franklin Langworthy, *Scenery of the Plains, Mountains and Mines: A Diary Kept upon the Overland Route to California, By Way of the Great Salt Lake* (Ogdensburg: J. C. Sprague, Book-Seller, 1855); Leander V. Loomis, *A Journal of the Birmingham Emigrating Company* (Salt Lake City: 1928); Joyce Rockwood Muench, ed., *The Kilgore Journal of an Overland Journey to California in the Year 1850* (New York: Hastings House, 1949); Henry M. Naglee Papers, MR-129, Bancroft Library; David Morris Potter, ed., *Trail to California: The Overland Journal of Vincent Geiger and Wakeman Bryarly* (New Haven: Yale University Press, 1945); William R. Rothwell, "The Journal, Letters, and Guide of William R. Rothwell, Being the Narrative of His Trip Across the Plains in 1850," tran- script in the Beinecke Library, Yale University; Sarah Royce, *A Frontier Lady:*

Recollections of the Gold Rush and Early California (New Haven: Yale University Press, 1932); Lorenzo Sawyer, *Way Sketches Containing Incidents of Travel across the Plains from St. Joseph to California in 1851* (New York: Edward Eberstadt, 1926); Lee Scamehorn, Edwin P. Banks, and Jamie Lytle-Webb, eds., *The Buckeye Rovers in the Gold Rush: An Edition of Two Diaries* (Athens: Ohio University Press, 1965); J. S. Shepherd, *Journal of Travel across the Plains to California, and Guide to the Future Emigrant* (Racine, Wisconsin: Mrs. Rebecca Shepherd, 1851); and James G. Shields, "Journal of a Trip across the Plains from Indiana to California in 1850," manuscript in the Beinecke Library, Yale University. Joseph Pike's wonderful journal in the California State Library includes a description of an abortive attempt to cross the Georgetown Cutoff. Martha M. Morgan, *A Trip across the Plains in the Year 1849 with Notes of a Voyage to California by Way of Panama* (San Francisco: Pioneer Press, 1864), contains the only known contemporary mention of the DeMont-Beatie-Blackburn party. While Martha Morgan is listed as the author, the trail journal was kept by her husband, Jesse Morgan, who was killed shortly after arriving in Sacramento.

Classic secondary trail histories are Thomas H. Hunt, *Ghost Trails to California* (New York: Weathervane Books, 1974); Charles Kelly, *Salt Desert Trails* (Salt Lake City: Western Printing Company, 1930); Charles Kelly and Dale L. Morgan, *Old Greenwood* (Georgetown, California: The Talisman Press, 1965); Merrill J. Mattes, *The Great Platte River Road* (Lincoln: Nebraska State Historical Society, 1969); George R. Stewart, Jr., *The California Trail: An Epic with Many Heroes* (New York: McGraw-Hill Book Company, 1962); and John D. Unruh, Jr., *The Plains Across: The Overland Emigrants and the Trans-Mississippi West, 1840–1860* (Urbana: University of Illinois Press, 1979). Charles Kelly, "Gold Seekers on the Hastings Cutoff," *Utah Historical Quarterly* 20 (January 1952) quoted Blackburn's account, while Rush Spedden, "Who Was T. H. Jefferson?" *Overland Journal* 8, No. 3 (1990) provides unique insights into the Hastings Cutoff. Excellent trail bibliographies are Merrill J. Mattes, *Platte River Road Narratives* (Urbana: University of Illinois Press, 1988); Lannon W. Mintz, *The Trail: A Bibliography of the Travellers on the Overland Trail to California, Oregon, Salt Lake City, and Montana during the Years 1841–1864* (Albuquerque: University of New Mexico Press, 1987); and John M. Townley, *The Trail West: A Bibliographic-Index to Western Trails, 1841–1869* (Reno: Jamison Station Press, 1988).

Kenneth N. Owens's study of the Carson Pass route across the Sierra, "Archaeological and Historical Investigation of the Mormon-Carson Emigrant Trail, El Dorado and Toiyabe National Forests," Vol. 2, History, and Appendix A (Placerville: U.S. Forest Service, 1990), is a model of trail research that should generate substantial revisions to several historical subjects.

Norma B. Ricketts, *Tragedy Spring and the Pouch of Gold* (Sacramento:

Ricketts Publishing Company, 1983), did pioneering work on the Mormon Battalion's opening of the Carson Pass trail. For an excellent account of the rediscovery of the Johnson's Ranch site, see Jack and Richard Steed, *The Donner Rescue Site: Johnson's Ranch on Bear River* (Sacramento: Graphic: Publishers, 1991).

Primary accounts of the gold rush include E. Gould Buffum, *Six Months in the Gold Mines* (Philadelphia: Lea and Blanchard, 1850); Chauncey L. Canfield, ed., *The Diary of a Forty-Niner* (Boston: Houghton Mifflin Company, 1920); Charles D. Ferguson, *The Experiences of a Forty-Niner during a Third of a Century in the Gold Fields* (Chico, California: H. A. Carson, 1924); C. W. Haskins, *The Argonauts of California* (New York: Fords, Howard and Hulbert, 1890); Stephen C. Massett, *"Drifting About," or What "Jeems Pipes of Pipesville" Saw-and-Did* (New York: Carleton, Publisher, 1863); Rodman W. Paul, *The California Gold Discovery: Sources, Documents, Accounts and Memoirs Relating to the Discovery of Gold at Sutter's Mill* (Georgetown, California: The Talisman Press, 1966); Georgia Willis Read and Ruth Gaines, *Gold Rush: The Journals, Drawings, and Other Papers of J. Goldsborough Bruff, Captain, Washington City and California Mining Association, April 2, 1849–July 20, 1851*, 2 vols. (New York, Columbia University Press, 1944); William T. Sherman, *Memoirs of General William T. Sherman*, 2 vols. (New York: D. Appleton and Company, 1876); and Bayard Taylor, *El Dorado or Adventures in the Path of Empire* (London: Bohn, 1850).

Secondary gold rush sources are William S. Greever, *The Bonanza West: The Story of Western Mining Rushes 1848–1900* (Norman: University of Oklahoma Press, 1963); Erwin G. Gudde, *California Place Names* (Berkeley and Los Angeles: University of California Press, 1969), and *California Gold Camps* (Berkeley and Los Angeles: University of California Press, 1975); J. S. Holliday, *The World Rushed In, The California Gold Rush Experience: An Eyewitness Account of a Nation Heading West* (New York: Simon and Schuster, 1981); Donald Dale Jackson, *Gold Dust* (New York: Alfred A. Knopf, 1980); Joseph Henry Jackson, *Anybody's Gold: The Story of California's Mining Towns* (New York: Appleton-Century Company, 1941); Laurence I. Seidlemen, *The Fools of '49* (New York: Alfred A. Knopf, 1976); and Charles Howard Shinn, *Mining Camps: A Study in American Frontier Government* (New York: Alfred A. Knopf, 1948).

Blackburn's narrative has already had an impact on Nevada history, but the origins of white settlement of the state remain dismally confused. Other primary accounts are John Reese, "Mormon Station," *Nevada Historical Society Papers* (1913–1916), and Stephen A. Kinsey, "Letter to Worlds Columbian Exposition," 1893, Nevada Historical Society, MS/NC 344. Myron Angel, ed., *History of Nevada* (Oakland, California: Thompson and West, 1881), and Sam P. Davis, ed., *The History of Nevada* (Reno: The Elms Publishing Company, 1913), provide additional information, but almost no documentation about the events of 1850. After Dale Morgan solved the problem with Beatie's 1849 date for the founding of Mormon Station in *The Humboldt*, Juanita Brooks, "The Mormons in Carson City, Utah Territory," *Nevada Historical Society Quarterly* 8 (Spring 1965), and Russell R. Elliott, "Nevada's First Trading Post: A Study in Historiography," *Nevada Historical Society Quarterly* 13 (Winter 1970), did much to resolve the confusion, but traditionalists such as Effie Mona Mack and Byrd Wall Sawyer, *Here Is Nevada: A History of the State* (Sparks, Nevada: Western Printing and Publishing, 1965), remain confused.

Equally troublesome is the task of assigning blame for the first discovery of precious minerals in the present Silver State. Eliot Lord, *Comstock Mining and Miners* (Washington: Government Printing Office, 1883), is the single ambiguous source for the William Prows 1848 discovery claim. John Townley made the best possible case for Prows, in "Trail to the Comstock: An Accidental Bonanza," *Overland Journal* 9 (Number 1, 1991): 22–30, but he relied heavily on notably unreliable sources, including mythologist Allen Fifield and family traditions. Townley concluded that either Blackburn or Prows was lying (with Blackburn being his most likely candidate), but a more charitable interpretation would be that both men believed the stories they told. A complete aberration, Allen Fifield, "Wagons East across the Sierra," *The Historical Society of Southern California Quarterly* 43 (September 1961), first alleged that Prows told Blackburn about his 1848 discovery, which enabled Blackburn to make and fake his 1849 discovery. Fifield's article is an undocumented fantasy: his Blackburn slander is simply the final whopper in a series of tall tales that a serious historical periodical should never have published. For example, Fifield claimed that Brannan crossed the Sierra in April 1847 by Carson Pass, which would require relocating the Donner-Reed party camp visited by Brannan. Fifield blamed Joaquin Murietta for the murder of three battalion veterans at Tragedy Spring—a completely laughable assertion. According to John Townley, in an unpublished manuscript, "Allen Fifield cited a now-lost letter in which Prows claimed he told Blackburn about the strike before Blackburn went west in 1849." In addition to this lost letter, no Lord-Prows correspondence is known to exist, and "whatever journals or records Prows might have kept from his earlier travels were lost when his widow, Louisa, and her fellow LDS settlers at Colonia Juarez, Mexico, returned to the United States." Allen Fifield's collection of family papers disappeared following his death in 1973. The loss of these alleged documents makes it impossible to substantiate Fifield's assertion that Blackburn jumped Prows's claim, or even to determine if Fifield actually had documentation (which seems unlikely) or simply based these statements on a string of ill-informed assumptions. Fifield's speculations are the historical equivalent of gossip.

For an examination of the sources related to the 1848 Mormon emigration from California to the Salt Lake Valley, see the editor's *A Road from El Dorado: The 1848 Trail Journal of Ephraim Green* (Salt Lake City: Prairie Dog Press, 1991). Lillie Jane Orr Taylor, *Life History of Thomas Orr, Jr.* (published by the author, 1930), and Betty Yohalem, *I Remember: Stories and Pictures of El Dorado County Pioneer Families* (Placerville: El Dorado Chamber of Commerce, 1977), contain the Thomas Orr, Jr., accounts of the 1850 discovery of Gold Canyon.

Territorial Utah history is explored in the works of Juanita Brooks, including *The Mountain Meadows Massacre* (Stanford, California: Stanford University Press, 1950); *On the Mormon Frontier: The Diary of Hosea Stout*, 2 vols. (Salt Lake City: University of Utah Press, 1964); *Journal of the Southern Indian Mission: The Diary of Thomas D. Brown* (Logan, Utah: Utah State University Press, 1972), and Robert Glass Cleland and Juanita Brooks, eds., *A Mormon Chronicle: The Diaries of John D. Lee 1848–1876*, 2 vols. (San Marino, California: The Huntington Library, 1955). Two works by S. George Ellsworth, ed., *Dear Ellen: Two Mormon Women and Their Letters* (Salt Lake City: University of Utah Library, n.d.), and *The Journals of Addison Pratt* (Salt Lake City: University of Utah Press, 1990), bring details of early Utah history to life.

Unpublished sources on early Utah include "Daily Transactions in Gold Dust," Brigham Young Collection, LDS Archives (available by special permission); Levi Jackman, "Memoirs," A-1-1, and Mary A. Jackman, "Ammi R. Jackman," B-289, Utah State Historical Society; Charles Kelly Papers, "Reminiscences of Howard Blackburn," B-114-10, Utah State Historical Society; "Muster Roll, 10 October 1857, Company H, 4th Battalion, Tenth Regiment of Infantry, Iron County Brigade, Nauvoo Legion," Utah State Archives, 3346; Epsy Jane Williams Pace, "History of Provo," A 1376, Utah State Historical Society; "Autobiography of Robert T. Thomas," Harold B. Lee Library, Brigham Young University; and "Utah Territorial Militia, Correspondence 1849–1875," Utah State Historical Society, A-384.

Published sources on early Utah history include J. W. Gunnison, *The Mormons, or, Latter-day Saints, in the Valley of the Great Salt Lake* (Philadelphia: Lippincott, Grambo & Co., 1852); William A. Hickman and J. H. Beadle, *Brigham's Destroying Angel: Being the Life, Confession, and Startling Disclosures of the Notorious Bill Hickman, the Danite Chief of Utah* (New York: Geo. A. Crofutt, 1872); Charles Kelly, ed., *Journals of John D. Lee, 1846–47 & 1859* (Salt Lake City: Western Printing Company, 1938); Charles Kelly and Maurice L. Howe, *Miles Goodyear, First Citizen of Utah* (Salt Lake City: Western Printing Company, 1937); A. Karl Larson and Katharine Miles Larson, eds., *Diary of Charles Lowell Walker*, 2 vols. (Logan, Utah: Utah State University Press, 1980); Brigham D. Madsen, ed., *A Forty-Niner in Utah, With* the *Stansbury Exploration of Great Salt Lake: Letters and Journals of John Hudson, 1848–50* (Salt Lake City: Tanner Trust Fund, 1981), and *Exploring the Great Salt Lake: The Stansbury Expedition of 1849–50* (Salt Lake City: University of Utah Press, 1989); Howard Stansbury, *Exploration and Survey of the Valley of the Great Salt Lake* (Philadelphia: Lippincott, Grambo and Co., 1852); David Marshall Stuart, ed., *Pioneer Missionary: True Life Story of David M. Stuart* (Bountiful, Utah: Family History Publishers, 1988); David M. Stuart, "Early Experience of an Elder," *The Juvenile Instructor* 13 (1 January 1878), and "A Pioneer's Experience," *The Millennial Star* 59 (27 May 1897); Edward W. Tullidge, "History of Provo City," *Tullidge's Quarterly Magazine* 3 (1885); *History of Salt Lake City* (Salt Lake City: Star Printing Company, 1886); *Histories of Utah, Vol. 2: Northern Utah and Southern Idaho Counties* (Salt Lake City: The Press of the Juvenile Instructor, 1889—note that there is no Vol. 1); and Daniel H. Wells's Narrative, in *Utah Historical Quarterly* 6 (October 1933). The *Journal of Discourses*, 26 vols. (London: Latter-Day Saints Book Depot, 1854–1886), contain the colorful sermons of early Mormon leaders. Harold Schindler, *Orrin Porter Rockwell: Man of God, Son of Thunder* (Salt Lake City: University of Utah Press, 1966), is the single best account of territorial Utah.

Mormon–Indian relations still cry out for a comprehensive (and courageous) study, but good sources include June Lyman, Norma Denver, Floyd A. O'Neil, and John Sylvester, *Ute People: An Historical Study* (Salt Lake City: Uintah School District and the Western History Center: 1970); Floyd A. O'Neil, "A History of the Ute Indians of Utah until 1890" (Ph.D. diss., University of Utah, 1973); Floyd A. O'Neil and Stanford J. Layton, "Of Pride and Politics: Brigham Young as Indian Superintendent," *Utah Historical Quarterly* 46 (Summer 1978); and Ronald W. Walker, "Toward a Reconstruction of Mormon and Indian Relations, 1847–1877," *BYU Studies* 29 (Fall 1989). Howard A. Christy described the Fort Utah fight in "Open Hand and Mailed Fist: Mormon–Indian Relations in Utah, 1847–52," *Utah Historical Quarterly* 46 (Summer 1978), and in "'What Virtue There Is in Stone,' and Other Pungent Talk on the Early Utah Frontier," *Utah Historical Quarterly* 59 (Summer 1991).

Accounts of the death of Anthony Blackburn are found in the *Daily Alta Californian*, 6 July 1851; *History of Humboldt County* (Wallace W. Elliott & Co., 1881); Leigh H. Irvine, *History of Humboldt County, California with Biographical Sketches* (Los Angeles: Historic Record Company, 1915); [Harry L. Wells], *History of Siskiyou County, California* (Oakland, California: D. J. Stewart, 1881); Walter Van Dyke, "Statement of Recollections, 1878," Bancroft Library, and "Early Days in Klamath," *The Overland Monthly* 28 (August 1891); and John Daggett, "Mrs. Isaac Hawley," Daggett's Scrapbook, vol. 4, 12, California State Library Collections.

Compared to the narrative's wealth of detail, the last fifty-three years of Blackburn's life must be pieced together from scattered references in journals, local histories, census records, newspapers, tax rolls, deeds, legal documents, Mormon Battalion pension records, and (most unreliably) family legends. Blackburn's role in many events is ambiguous at best, and the summary of his life in his 1894 letter provided the only description of episodes and careers that covered years or even decades.

Tracking Abner Blackburn's course across California in the 1850s was helped by Ralph Herbert Cross, *The Early Inns of California, 1844–1869* (San Francisco: Lawton Kennedy, 1954); Samuel H. and Ida Hurst, "The Diary of Frederick William Hurst" (self-published, 1961: typescript copy in the possession of Frank Don and Cleo Bailey, Salt Lake City, Utah; original MS, 1861, LDS Archives); Amasa Lyman and Charles C. Rich to Brigham Young, 23 July 1850, Brigham Young Papers, LDS Archives; Louis J. Rasmussen, *San Francisco Ship Passenger Lists*, 4 vols. (Colma: San Francisco Historical Records, 1972); Alexander Starbuck, *History of the American Whale Fishery* (Secaucus, New Jersey: Castle Books, 1989); and "Assessment Roll, '57" and "Delinquent Tax List of 1857," Sacramento County Records.

Primary sources on old San Bernardino include the Leonard J. Arrington Papers, Charles C. Rich Research Files, MS 4212, LDS Archives; George Washington Bean, "Journal, 1854 Dec–1856 Mar," MS 7805, LDS Archives; John Brown, Sr., *The Mediumistic Experiences of John Brown, The Medium of the Rockies* (Des Moines: Moses Hull and Co., 1887); John Brown, Jr., and James Boyd, *History of San Bernardino and Riverside Counties*, 3 vols. (Chicago: Western Historical Association, Lewis Publishing Company, 1922); Augusta Joyce Crocheron, "California Memories," *The Contributor* 6 (May 1885); John Codman, *The Round Trip* (New York: G. P. Putnam's Sons, 1879); Eliza Persis Russel Robbins Crafts, *Pioneer Days in the San Bernardino Valley* (Redlands, California: 1906); Caroline Barnes Crosby, "Diaries," Vault Manuscript B 89, Utah State Historical Society; Ephraim Green, "Diary, 1852 Oct–1856 Sep.," MS 4511, LDS Archives; David Hollis Holladay, "Diary, 1855 Jul–Aug," MS 1128, LDS Archives; Richard R. Hopkins, "Journal of the San Bernardino Branch of the Church of Jesus Christ of Latter Day Saints," LR 1594, Folder 1, and "San Bernardino Tithing Office Account Bk," LR 1594/22, LDS Archives; Luther A. Ingersoll, *Ingersoll's Century Annals of San Bernardino County, 1769 to 1904* (Los Angeles: L. A. Ingersoll, 1904); William D. Kartchner, "Autobiography," MS 3267, LDS Archives; Amasa Lyman, "Journal," MS 2757, LDS Archives; Sarah Pratt Miner, "Diary," MS 7270, LDS Archives; Edwin Pettit, *Biography of Edwin Pettit* (Salt Lake City: The Arrow Press, n.d.); Eliza Ann Graves Rich, "Correspondence, 1851–1877," MS 5338:1, LDS Archives; Ezra C. Rich; "Early Land Purchase and Settlement in San Bernardino," LDS Library; Mary Ann Phelps Rich,

"Autobiography," MS 4520, LDS Archives; H. C. Rolfe, "The Early Political History of San Bernardino County," H. C. Rolfe Scrapbook, San Bernardino County Library; Louisa Brown Waters, "Trail Blazers of Cajon Pass," *Westways* (January 1939); and Marjorie Tisdale Wolcott, *Pioneer Notes from the Diaries of Judge Benjamin Hayes, 1849–1875* (Los Angeles: 1929).

The great history of the San Bernardino Valley is George William Beattie and Helen Pruitt Beattie, *Heritage of the Valley: San Bernardino's First Century* (Oakland, California: Biobooks, 1951). Biographies of Mormon leaders provide much information about the settlement's early days. Leonard J. Arrington, *Charles C. Rich: Mormon General and Western Frontiersman* (Provo: Brigham Young University Press, 1974), can be supplemented by Rich's "Journal," MS 889, and "Letters, 1855–1868," MS 5338/3, available by special permission in the LDS Archives. Amasa Lyman lacks a good biography, but Albert A. Lyman, *Amasa Mason Lyman: Trailblazer and Pioneer from the Atlantic to the Pacific* (Delta, Utah: Melvin A. Lyman, 1957), exists, and Loretta L. Hefner, "From Apostle to Apostate: The Personal Struggle of Amasa Mason Lyman," *Dialogue: A Journal of Mormon Thought* 16 (Spring 1983), is an excellent summary.

Good local histories are Larry Burgess, "Fred T. Perris: Pioneer and Energizer," *Heritage Tales*, San Bernardino Historical Society (1979); Arda M. Haenszel, *Historical Cajon Pass: A Self-Guided Driving Tour in Three Parts* (Redlands, California: San Bernardino County Museum Association, 1976); Arda M. Haenszel and Jennifer Reynolds, *The Historic San Bernardino Mission District: A Self-Guided Driving Tour* (Redlands, California: San Bernardino County Museum Association, 1975); Patricia King, *Once upon a Desert* (Barstow, California: Mojave River Valley Museum Association, 1976); Pauliena B. La Fuze, *Saga of the San Bernardinos*, 2 vols. (San Bernardino: San Bernardino County Museum Association, 1971); and "Tales of the Old Santa Fe and Salt Lake Trail to California," *The Santa Fe Magazine* 8 (March, 1914). Francis J. Johnston, "The James Bros. in California," *Odyssey: Published Quarterly by the San Bernardino Historical and Pioneer Society* 8 (Fall 1986), lends some credibility to Blanche Corby's statement to Herbert Hamlin that her father, Charles Blackburn, "saw Jesse James several times around San Bernardino and Frank James, too."

Documents consulted on old San Bernardino include Microfilm Probate Records, San Bernardino County Clerk's Office; "El Rancho San Bernardino Deeds," MS 4652, LDS Archives; "Book B of Wills," San Bernardino County Clerk's Office; "Case No. 179," San Bernardino County Historical Archives; "Minutes, 1853–1855," San Bernardino Court of Sessions, MS 5163, LDS Archives; "Record Books of the San Bernardino Society of California Pioneers," and "San Bernardino Tax Assessor Rolls, 1874," San Bernardino Historical and Pioneer Society.

Scholarly works on San Bernardino are M. Guy Bishop, "The Mormon San Bernardino Colony," *The Californians* (Sept.–Oct. 1987); Eugene E. Campbell, "The Decline and Fall of the Mormons in San Bernardino: A Second Look," paper presented at the meeting of the Mormon History Association, 1967, LDS Library; Edward Leo Lyman, "The Demise of the San Bernardino Mormon Community," *Southern California Historical Quarterly* 65 (Winter 1983), and "The Rise and Decline of Mormon San Bernardino," *BYU Studies* 29 (Fall 1989); and Joseph S. Wood, "The Mormon Settlement in San Bernardino, 1851–1857" (Ph.D. diss., University of Utah, 1967).

Newspapers consulted include the *San Bernardino Sun, San Bernardino Times-Index*, and *San Bernardino Weekly News*. Specific articles included "Death of Captain Weaver," *San Bernardino Guardian*, 27 July 1867; "Mining News," *San Bernardino Valley Index*, 13 May 1881; "Abner Blackburn Made Seven Trips into the West," *San Bernardino Sun*, 4 December 1938; and Buff Belden, "Mountain Road Costs Miners $2,000 in Gold," *San Bernardino Sun-Telegram*, 6 September 1959.

Only the vagaries of research could bring a historian to the antics of a modern evangelical scoundrel, but filling this void are Edward E. Plowman, "The Rise and Fall of Billy James," *Christianity Today*, 27 February 1976, John Harold Redekop, *The American Far Right: A Case Study of Billy James Hargis and Christian Crusade* (Grand Rapids, Michigan: William B. Eerdmans Publishing Company, 1968); and "The Sins of Billy James," *Time*, 16 February 1976.

Finally, the works of Dale Morgan are in a class by themselves: they inspired the spirit of this book. In addition to his own work, Morgan deserves much of the credit for J. Roderic Korns's classic *West from Fort Bridger: The Pioneering of the Emigrant Trails across Utah, 1846–1850*. His early books, written for the Federal Writers' Projects of the Works Progress Administration for the state of Utah, include *A History of Ogden* (Ogden, Utah: Ogden City Commission, 1940), and (with others) *Provo: Pioneer Mormon City* (Portland, Oregon: Binfords & Mort, 1942). *The Humboldt: Highroad of the West* (New York: Farrar & Rinehart, 1943), was the first work to make use of the Blackburn narrative; it is painful to speculate upon what Morgan could have done if he had been permitted to edit the memoirs. *The Great Salt Lake* (Indianapolis: Bobbs-Merrill, 1947) is an excellent regional history. Morgan's overland and gold rush works include *The Overland Journal of James A. Pritchard from Kentucky to California in 1849* (Denver: The Old West Publishing Company, 1959); *Overland in 1846*, 2 vols. (Georgetown, California: The Talisman Press, 1963); *In Pursuit of the Golden Dream: Reminiscences of San Francisco and the Northern and Southern Mines, 1849–1857 by Howard Gardner* (Stoughton, Massachusetts: Western Hemisphere 1970); George P. Hammond and Dale L. Morgan, eds., *Captain Charles M. Weber:*

Pioneer of the San Joaquin and Founder of Stockton, California (Berkeley: Friends of the Bancroft Library, 1966); and Dale L. Morgan and James R. Scobie, eds., *Three Years in California: William Perkins' Journal of Life at Sonora, 1849–1852* (Berkeley: University of California Press, 1964). His articles on the Mormon emigration include "Mormon Ferry on the North Platte," *The Annals of Wyoming* 21, Nos. 2–3 (July–October 1949); "The Reminiscences of James Holt: A Narrative of the Emmett Company," *Utah Historical Quarterly* 23 (January and April 1955); and "Miles Goodyear and the Founding of Ogden," *Utah Historical Quarterly* 21 (October 1953). The article "Literature in the History of the Church: The Importance of Involvement," *Dialogue: A Journal of Mormon Thought* 4 (September 1969), specifically comments on the Blackburn narrative. The bulk of Morgan's papers, a gold mine for any researcher on the American West, are at the Bancroft Library and are available on microfilm at Special Collections, Marriott Library, University of Utah. Morgan's journal collection is in the Madeline McQuown papers at the Marriott Library, while the Utah State Historical Society has a substantial Morgan manuscript collection. Richard L. Saunders, *Eloquence from a Silent World: A Descriptive Bibliography of the Published Writings of Dale L. Morgan* (Salt Lake City: The Caramon Press, 1990), catalogues the work of this unparalleled historian.

Index